CINDERELLA: A CASEBOOK

Edited by ALAN DUNDES

WILDMAN PRESS
NEW YORK 1983

Library of Congress Catalog Card Number 83-70454
ISBN 0-939544-15-6

Contents

Contents

INTRODUCTION

The tale of Cinderella is one of the best-known stories in the Western world, and its popularity has continued unabated into the twentieth century. Insofar as it concerns the relationships between a girl and her sisters or stepsisters, as well as a girl and her mother or stepmother, it has had special appeal for women. It is not surprising, therefore, that the two major comparative studies of Cinderella were both written by female folklorists. The first of these was the astonishing research effort of Marian Roalfe Cox. Entitled *Cinderella: Three Hundred and Forty-Five Variants of Cinderella, Catskin, and Cap o' Rushes, Abstracted and Tabulated, with a Discussion of Medieval Analogues and Notes*, this impressive gathering of versions of the tale, further graced by an introduction by Andrew Lang, was published by the English Folklore Society in 1893. It was no small task to locate so many texts of Cinderella in the days before the creation of such modern folkloristic aids as tale type indices and motif-indices, which facilitate the finding of hundreds of versions found in print and in folklore archives throughout the Western world in a matter of moments. Even today, serious students of Cinderella still have to consult this 535-page pioneering compendium.

More than half a century later, the Swedish folklorist Anna Birgitta Rooth wrote her doctoral dissertation on the tale under the direction of Carl Wilhelm von Sydow, one of the founders of the discipline of folkloristics. Rooth's *Cinderella Cycle*, published in 1951, was based upon some seven hundred versions, about twice the total assembled by her predecessor, Miss Cox. Both Miss Cox and

Professor Rooth were especially interested in distinguishing the separate but seemingly related forms of the story of Cinderella. This is demonstrated by the subtitle of the first work and the title of the second. The *Cinderella Cycle* refers to several distinct subtypes of the basic tale, that is, a veritable complex of different tales which apparently belong under one single rubric.

The tradition of considering distinct forms of the Cinderella plot together was followed by Stith Thompson in his revision of Antti Aarne's tale type index, which was first published in 1910. In Thompson's second revision of *The Types of the Folktale,* which appeared in 1961, he entitles tale type 510 "Cinderella and Cap o' Rushes" and proceeds to delineate both tale type 510A, "Cinderella," and tale type 510B, "The Dress of Gold, of Silver, and of Stars" ("Cap o' Rushes"). Tale type 511, in the Aarne-Thompson typological system, is "One-Eye, Two-Eyes, Three-Eyes." Tale type 511A, "The Little Red Ox," involves a male rather than a female protagonist who is cruelly treated by his stepmother and stepsisters. It may be useful to chart the equivalent distinctions made by Cox, Rooth, and Thompson, although the reader is advised to consult the original discussions if he or she wishes to understand more of the details of the different *Cinderella Cycle* subtypes.

Cox	Rooth	Aarne-Thompson
Type A. Cinderella	Type B	AT 510A. Cinderella
Type B. Cat-skin Type C. Cap o'Rushes }	Type B I	AT 510B. The Dress of Gold, of Silver, and of Stars
Type D. Indeterminate	Type A	AT 511. One-Eye, Two-Eyes, Three-Eyes
Type E. Hero Tales	Type C	AT 511A. The Little Red Ox
- - - - - - - - -	Type AB	AT 511 + AT 510A

From this chart, we can see that two of Cox's subtypes, that is, "Cat-skin" and "Cap o' Rushes," were considered to be one type by Rooth (B I) and also by Thompson (AT 510B). We may also note that Rooth proposed a combined form, Type AB, which consists of two Aarne-Thompson tale types (AT 511 and AT 510A). All of these typological distinctions will very likely become a bit more clear as the reader proceeds through the Casebook.

Introduction

The early scholarly interest in the tale of Cinderella, as in folktales generally, was in trying to discover the oldest form of the story and to trace the development through time of the different types of the tale. Rooth, for example, believed that Type A, which she claimed had originated in the East, gave rise to her Type AB, which she thought had developed in the Near East, which in turn led Type B, which we know as Cinderella, to develop in southeastern Europe, eventually spreading throughout all of Europe. But not all of the many individuals who have thought about Cinderella have been so concerned with form and typology. All along there have been attempts to explain the meaning and significance of the story. Some writers saw reflections of possible historical customs, others saw remnants of ritual, while a few perceived the story as a manifestation of the human soul or psyche. In this Casebook, we shall sample some of these alternative readings of the tale. Indeed, one of the goals of the Casebook approach is to bring together different interpretations of the same item of folklore so that students may see for themselves the various modes of analysis.

A wide selection of different ways of analyzing Cinderella has been made. Some of the important essays devoted to Cinderella were unfortunately too long to be included in this volume. For example, one of the classic ritual interpretations of the tale was made by French folklorist Émile Nourry, writing under the pseudonym P. Saintyves, in his *Les Contes de Perrault et Les Récits Parallèles* (Paris, 1923), pp. 105–164, while one of the most extensive psychoanalytic readings of the tale was made by Bruno Bettelheim in his book *The Uses of Enchantment* (New York, 1977), pp. 236–277. Individuals especially interested in such approaches to Cinderella should definitely read these essays as well as the other suggested sources listed in the selected bibliography found at the end of this volume.

The essays contained in this Cinderella Casebook are intended to be representative. They cover a time period of more than one hundred years, and so it is to be expected that there will be considerable variety in the degree of sophistication encountered from one essay to another. On the other hand, some of the earlier essays demonstrate a better knowledge of the range of comparative materials available than later, more specialized analyses, which often tend to center on single versions of the tale, typically the versions of the Grimm brothers or Perrault. One difficulty in bringing together diverse treatments of Cinderella is the unavoidable repetition of material. Still, when a student of folklore explores the scholarship devoted to a particular folktale of myth or legend, he is likely to discover the same sort of repetition. Besides, two writers may interpret the very same data in quite different fashion, and that is precisely the point. Any analysis of an item of folklore should begin where previous analyses have ended. This is why it is unfortunate that so many of those who have written about Cinderella have failed to make use of the abundant comparative materials assembled so laboriously by Marian Roalfe Cox and later by Anna Birgitta Rooth. One need not accept or agree with previous conclusions, but it is the height of parochial arrogance to assume that no one before has ever considered the problem under investigation. It is to encourage eclectic and improved scholarship in folkloristics that this and other Casebooks have been devised.

The Casebook begins with three famous versions of Cinderella: the version from Basile's *Pentamerone* (1634–1636), Perrault's "Cendrillon" of 1697, and the Grimms' "Aschenputtel" of 1812. Then follow a series of essays by W.R.S. Ralston (1879), E. Sidney Hartland (1893), R.D. Jameson (1932), Photeine B. Bouboulis (1953), and Paul Delarue (1951), experts in Russian, English, Chinese, Greek, and French folklore respectively, who treat various aspects and early theories of the story. An unpublished paper by the late Archer Taylor, "The Study of the Cinderella Cycle" (1970); an essay by Cinderella authority Anna Birgitta Rooth, "Tradition Areas in Eurasia" (1956); and William Bascom's "Cinderella in Africa (1972) complete the comparative approach to the folktale.

The next essays are concerned with meaning. James Danandjaja's "A Javanese Cinderella" (1976) and Margaret A. Mill's discussion of a Muslim women's ritual version of Cinderella from eastern Iran (1980) show how individual cultures reshape a folktale to fit local value systems. Irish philosopher Aarland Ussher's "The Slipper on the Stair" (1951), Marie-Louise von Franz's "The Beautiful Wassilissa" (1972), and Ben Rubenstein's "The Meaning of the Cinderella Story in the Development of a Little Girl" (1955) offer spiritual, Jungian, and Freudian interpretations of the story respectively.

My discussion of Shakespeare's retelling of a form of Cinderella in *King Lear* (1976), David Pace's structural analysis of the tale

(1977), A.K. Ramanujan's sensitive reading of an Indic version of the story (1980), Alessandro Falassi's unique recording and analysis of a Tuscan taletelling session (1980), and Jane Yolen's critique of the popularization of Cinderella in America (1977) bring this generous sampling of approaches to Cinderella to a close. Three of the papers (Taylor, Mills, Ramanujan) are appearing in print for the first time in this volume. Not all of the scholarly considerations of the tale could be included, but most are at least mentioned in the headnotes to each essay or in the concluding selected bibliography of Cinderella studies.

Fairytales, like all forms of human creative expression, are surely worthy of thoughtful reflection. Cinderella in particular is especially endearing and enduring. No other single tale is more beloved in the Western world, and it is likely that its special place in the hearts and minds of both women and men will continue for generations to come. This volume is dedicated to all those who find in the story of Cinderella one of the time-tested facets of the human spirit.

Acknowledgments

I am indebted to Jeanne Harrah for undertaking a preliminary bibliographical search for Cinderella references, and to Simone Klugman of the reference department of the University of California, Berkeley, library for carrying out a computer search for recent Cinderella scholarship. My thanks to Andrée Sursock for assisting me with the translation of Paul Delarue's essay into English. In addition, I am grateful to my daughters, Alison and Lauren, for locating fugitive sources in the Harvard and Stanford University libraries, sources not available at Berkeley. Finally, I thank all the authors and publishers who were kind enough to allow me to print or reprint their essays in this casebook.

CINDERELLA

The Cat Cinderella

Giambattista Basile

One of the first major collections of European folktales taken from oral sources was Giambattista Basile's Il Pentamerone, *published posthumously during the years 1634–1636. Originally entitled* Lo Cunto de li Cunte, *the tale of tales, the work consisted of five sets of ten diversions, or stories. Supposedly each set of narratives represented one day's worth of tale-telling. The sixth diversion of the first day was "The Cat Cinderella."*

Basile (1575–1632) had apparently heard in Naples many of the stories he reported in the Pentamerone. *In any case, the book was published in Neapolitan dialect, which unfortunately made it relatively inaccessible even to readers of other Italian dialects. Not until 1742 was it translated into Bolognese dialect and in 1747 into Italian. It was not translated into German until 1846, when Felix Liebrecht undertook the task. This volume contained an introduction by Jacob Grimm. The Grimm brothers had known of Basile's collection earlier and were quite astonished to find that so many of "their" German "Kinder und Hausmärchen" had been reported in Naples nearly two centuries before. The interesting publishing history of the* Pentamerone *has been carefully traced by N.M. Penzer, and curious readers should refer to this essay for further details.*

The somewhat florid style of the Pentamerone's *prose may not be familiar to some readers. Basile evidently loved the local idioms*

Reprinted from *The Pentamerone of Giambattista Basile,* ed. N.M. Penzer (London: John Lane, 1932), pp. 56–63.

3

in Naples, and he probably took much pleasure in embellishing his version of Cinderella with an ample sprinkling of earthy metaphors and clever conceits. The force of such puns and *patois cannot always survive translation, but even in English one can sense some of the extraordinary energy of Basile's retelling of Cinderella.*

It should be remarked that Basile's Cinderella was not the first reporting of the tale in Europe. Tale number 129, *"Of a Young Girl Nicknamed Ass Hide and how she got married with the help of little ants," added to the original ninety stories contained in Bonaventure des Périers,* Les Nouvelles Recreations et Joyeux Devis *of 1558, is one example of an earlier text. Before that, a sermon delivered in Strasburg in 1501 made extended reference to the tale. However, Basile's version, from a historical and esthetic perspective, is probably the earliest full telling of the tale in Europe.*

For a detailed account of the numerous editions of the Pentamerone, *see N.M. Penzer, "Appendix A: The Bibliography of the Book," in* The Pentamerone of Giambattista Basile, *Vol. 2 (London: John Lane, 1932), pp. 165–271. For the Des Périers text, see Bonaventure des Périers,* Novel Pastimes and Merry Tales, *trans. Raymond C. La Charité and Virginia A. La Charité, Studies in Romance Languages 6 (Lexington: University Press of Kentucky, 1972), pp. 250–252. For an account of the various editions of Des Périers, see James Woodrow Hassell, Jr., "The French Editions of Des Périers' Tales: A Bibliographical Study,"* Kentucky Romance Quarterly, *21 (Supplement No. 2) (1974), 185–210. (I am indebted to Professor Hassell of the University of Georgia for informing me that the version of Cinderella commonly attributed to Des Périers did not appear in the first edition of 1558 and seems not to have appeared until the early 1570s.) For a valuable discussion of the 1501 Strasburg extended allusion to Cinderella, see S. Singer,* Schweizer Märchen, Untersuchungen zur neueren Sprach- und Literaturgeschichte, *10 (1906), 1–31.*

Zezolla, incited by her governess to kill her step-mother, believes that she will be cherished by the former if she helps her to become her father's wife; instead she is kept in the kitchen. After many adventures and by help of the fairies, she wins a king for her husband.

At this tale of the flea all the listeners seemed like statues, and passed a verdict of imbecility on the foolish King who for a silly trifle had exposed the happiness of his own flesh and blood and the succession of the State to such risk. When all had stopped their mouths, Antonella unstopped hers in the following way:

In the sea of malice, envy always exchanges ruptures for bladders, and when she hopes to see others drowned, finds herself under water or dashed to pieces against a rock. This happened to certain envious girls whose story I intend to tell you.

There was once, therefore, a Prince who was a widower, and he had a daughter so dear to him that he saw with no other eyes but hers. He gave her an excellent teacher of sewing, who taught her chain-work, openwork,[1] fringes and hems and showed her more love than was possible to describe. The father, however, shortly remarried, and his wife was an evil, malicious, bad-tempered woman who began at once to hate her step-daughter and threw sour looks, wry faces and scowling glances on her enough to make her jump with fright.

The poor child was always complaining to her governess of her step-mother's ill-treatment, finishing up with "O would to God that you could be my little mother, who are so kind and loving to me," and she so often repeated this song to her that she put a wasp in her ear and, at last, tempted by the devil, her teacher ended by saying, "If you must follow this madcap idea, I will be a mother to you and you shall be the apple of my eye." She was going on with the prologue, when Zezolla (as the girl was called) interrupted her by saying, "Forgive my taking the words out of your mouth. I know you love me well, mum's the word, and *sufficit;* teach me the way, for I am new;[2] you write and I will sign." "Well, then," answered her governess, "listen carefully; keep your ears open and you shall always enjoy the whitest bread from the finest flour.[3] When your father leaves the house, tell your step-mother that you would like one of those old dresses that are kept in the big chest in the closet, to save the one you now have on. As she always wants to see you in rags and tatters, she will open the chest and say, 'Hold the lid.' You must hold it while she is rummaging inside and then suddenly let it fall so that it breaks her neck. After that, you know well that your father would even coin false money to please you, so when he fondles you, beg him to take me for his wife, and then you shall be happy and the mistress even of my life."

When Zezolla had heard the plan, every hour seemed a thousand years until she had carried out her governess's advice in every particular. When the period of mourning for her step-mother was over, she began to sound her father about marrying her governess. At first the Prince took it as a joke, but Zezolla so often struck with the flat that at last she thrust with the point, and he gave way to the persuasive words of his daughter. He therefore married Carmosina, the governess with great celebrations.

Now, while this couple were enjoying themselves, Zezolla was standing at a balcony[4] of her house, when a dove flew on to the wall and said to her, "If ever you desire anything, send to ask for it from the dove of the fairies of the Island of Sardinia, and you will at once have it."

For five or six days the new step-mother lavished every sort of caress on Zezolla, making her take the best seat at table, giving her the best tidbits, and dressing her in the finest clothes. But after a little time the service that Zezolla had done her was forgotten, and banished from her memory (how sorry is the mind that has an evil mistress!) and she began to push forward six daughters of her own that she had kept in hiding till then, and so worked on her husband that they won his good graces and he let his own daughter slip out of his heart. So that, a loser to-day and a pauper to-morrow, Zezolla was finally brought to such a pass that she fell from the *salon* to the kitchen, from the canopy to the grate, from splendid silks and gold to dish-clouts, from sceptres to spits; not only did she change her state, but also her name, and was no longer called Zezolla, but "Cat Cinderella."

Now it happened that the Prince was forced to go to Sardinia on important affairs of State, and before he left he asked one by one of his six step-daughters, Imperia, Colomba, Fiorella, Diamante, Colombina, and Pascarella, what they wanted him to bring back for them on his return. One asked for a splendid gown, another for a head-dress, one for cosmetics for the face, and another games to pass the time; one one thing and one another. At last, and almost to make fun of her, he asked his daughter, "And you! what would you like?" and she answered, "Nothing, except to commend me to the dove of the fairies and beg them to send me something; and if you forget, may it be impossible for you to go forward or back. Bear in mind what I say: thy intent, thy reward."[5]

The Prince went away, transacted his affairs in Sardinia, and bought the things his step-daughters had asked for, but Zezolla went quite out of his mind. But when they were embarked with the sails ready unfurled, it was found impossible to make the vessel leave the harbour: it seemed as if it were detained by a sea-lamprey.[6] The captain of the ship, who was almost in despair, dropped off to sleep with weariness and in his dreams a fairy appeared to him who said, "Do you know why you cannot leave the harbour? Because the Prince who is with you has broken his promise to his daughter, remembering all the others except his own flesh and blood." As soon as he woke up the captain told his dream to the Prince, who was overcome with confusion at his omission. He went to the grotto of the fairies, and commending his daughter to them, begged that they should send her some gift.

Behold, out of the grotto there came a young girl, beautiful as a gonfalon, who bade him thank his daughter for her kind remembrances and tell her to be of good cheer for love of her. With these words, she gave him a date tree, a spade and a golden can with a silken napkin; the date tree for planting and the other articles to keep and cultivate it.

The Prince, surprised at this present, took leave of the fairy and turned towards his own land. When he arrived, he gave his step-daughters the things they had asked for, and lastly he handed the fairy's present to his own daughter. Zezolla nearly jumped out of her skin with joy and planted the date tree in a fine pot, watering it every day and then drying it with the silken napkin.

As a result of these attentions, within four days the date tree grew to the size of a woman, and a fairy came out who said to the girl, "What do you want?" Zezolla answered that she would like sometimes to leave the house without the sisters knowing it. The fairy replied, "Whenever you want this, come to the plant and say:

> O my golden date tree,
> With golden spade, I've dug thee,
> With golden can I've watered thee,
> With golden napkin dried thee,
> Strip thyself and robe thou me,

Then when you want to undress, change the last line and say: Strip thou me and robe thou thee."

One day it happened to be a feast-day, and the governess's daughters went out of the house in a procession all fluttering,[7] bedaubed and painted, all ribbons, bells and gewgaws, all flowers and perfumes, roses and posies. Zezolla then ran to the plant and uttered the words the fairy had taught her, and at once she was decked out like a queen, seated on a white horse with twelve smartly attired pages. She too went where the sisters had gone, and though they did not recognize her, they felt their mouths water at the beauty of this lovely dove.

As luck would have it, the King came to this same place and was quite bewitched by the extraordinary loveliness of Zezolla. He ordered his most trusty attendant to find out about this fair creature, who she was and where she lived. The servant at once began to dog her footsteps, but she, noticing the trap, threw down a handful of crowns[8] that she had obtained for that purpose from the date tree. The servant, fired by the desire for these glittering pieces, forgot to follow the palfrey and stopped to pick up the money, whilst she, at a bound, reached the house and quickly undressed in the way the fairy had told her. Those six harpies, her sisters, soon returned, and to vex and mortify her, described at length all the fine things that they had seen at the feast.

The servant in the meantime had returned to the King and had told him about the crowns, whereupon the King was furious, and angrily told him that he had sold his pleasure for a few paltry coins and that at the next feast he was at all costs to discover who this lovely girl was and where nested so fair a bird.

When the next feast-day came, the sisters went out, all bedecked and bedizened, leaving the despised Zezolla by the hearth. But she at once ran to the date tree and uttered the same words as before, and behold a band of maidens came out, one with the mirror and one with the flask of pumpkin water,[9] one with the curling-tongs and another with the rouge, one with the comb and another with the pins, one with the dresses and one with the necklace and earrings. They all placed themselves round her and made her as beautiful as a sun and then mounted her in a coach with six horses accompanied by footmen and pages in livery. She drove to the same place as before and kindled envy in the hearts of the sisters and flames in the breast of the King.

This time too, when she went away, the servant followed her, but so that he should not catch her up, she threw down a handful of pearls and jewels, which this trusty fellow was unable to resist pecking at, since they were not things to let slip. In this way Zezolla had time to reach home and undress herself as usual. The servant, quite stunned, went back to the King, who said, "By the soul of your departed, if you don't find that girl again, I'll give you a most thorough beating and as many kicks on your seat as you have hairs in your beard."

On the next feast day, when the sisters had already started off, Zezolla went up to the date tree. She repeated the magic spell and was again magnificently dressed and placed in a golden coach with so many attendants around it that it looked as if she were a courtesan arrested in the public promenade and surrounded by police agents.[10] After having excited the envy and wonder of her sisters, she left, followed by the King's servant, who this time fastened himself to the carriage by double thread. Zezolla, seeing that he was always at her side, cried, "Drive on," and the coach set off at such a gallop that in her agitation she let slip from her foot the richest and prettiest patten[11] you could imagine.

The servant, not being able to catch up the carriage, which was now flying along, picked up the patten and carried it to the King, telling him what had happened. The King took it in his hands and broke out into these words: "If the foundation is so fair, what must be the mansion? Oh, lovely candlestick which holds the candle that consumes me! Oh, tripod of the lovely cauldron in which my life is boiling! Oh, beauteous corks[12] attached to the fishing-line of Love with which he has caught his soul! Behold, I embrace and enfold you, and if I cannot reach the plant, I worship the roots; if I cannot possess the capitals, I kiss the base: you first imprisoned a white foot, now you have ensnared a stricken heart. Through you, she who sways my life was taller by a span and a half;[13] through you, my life grows by that much in sweetness so long as I keep you in my possession."

The King having said this called a secretary and ordered out the trumpeters and tantarara, and had it proclaimed that all the women in the land were to come to a festival and banquet which he had determined to give. On the appointed day, my goodness, what an eating and feasting there was! Where did all the tarts and cakes[14] come from? Where all the stews[15] and rissoles? all the macaroni[16] and graviuoli[17] which were enough to stuff an entire army? The women were all there, of every kind and quality, of high degree and low degree, the rich and the poor, old and young, the well-favoured and the ill-favoured. When they had all thoroughly worked their jaws, the King spoke the proficiat[18] and started to try the patten on his guests, one by one, to see whom it fitted to a hair, so that he could find by the shape of the slipper the one whom he was seeking. But he could find no foot to fit it, so that he was on the point of despair.

Nevertheless, he ordered a general silence and said, "Come back to-morrow to fast with me, but as you love me well, do not leave behind a single woman, whoever she may be!" The Prince then said, "I have a daughter, but she always stays to mind the hearth, for she is a sorry, worthless creature, not fit to take her place at the table where you eat." The King answered, "Let her be at the top of the list, for such is my wish."

So they all went away, and came back the next day, and Zezolla came with Carmosina's daughters. As soon as the King saw her, he thought she was the one he wanted, but he hid his thoughts. After the banquet came the trial of the patten. The moment it came near Zezolla's foot, it darted forward of itself to shoe that painted Lover's egg, as the iron flies to the magnet. The King then took Zezolla in his arms and led her to the canopy, where he put a crown on her head and ordered every one to make obeisance to her as to their queen. The sisters, livid with envy and unable to bear the torment of their breaking hearts, crept quietly home to their mother, confessing in spite of themselves that:

He is mad who would oppose the stars.

NOTES

[1] *Punto in aria=Punto a giorno,* open-work or hem-stitch. The needle-stitch lace very highly prized in the seventeenth century, commonly called *punto di Venezia.*
[2] Literally, "for I come from outside": that is, "I come from the country to town."

[3]"Bread white as the flowers": where one may trace an indecent pun.

[4]*Gaifo*, the name given in Naples to a kind of small hanging terrace which projected from the first stories of the house. Cf. Capasso, in *Arch. stor. nap.* XV. 428.

[5]Proverbial way of saying, "If you don't keep your promise, it will be the worse for you."

[6]For the fabulous sea-lamprey, see Pliny, *Hist. Nat.,* IX. 25.

[7]*Spampanate*, like a flower that has opened out its petals.

[8]Text: *Scudi ricci,* which were golden coins struck in 1582 with the effigy of Philip II, and the arms of the Spanish crown on the reverse.

[9]Medicinal and cosmetic oil, which was extracted from certain kinds of pumpkins.

[10]Courtesans were forbidden to ride in carriages along the public walks, or in gondolas along the beach at Posilipo, which were the daily promenade of the Viceroy and nobility. If any infringed this law (which was not infrequent) they were surprised and surrounded by the police and carried off to prison. See the various laws of 1578, 1607, 1610, 1638, 1646, etc. in Guistiniani's collection, Vol. VII. heading CLXXI, *De meretricibus.*

[11]The *pianelle* were worn over the shoes. Celano, speaking at the end of the seventeenth century of the "vico dei Pianellari," which was near Santa Caterina a Spinacarona al Pendino, says that formerly there was no "Neapolitan lady who would have walked without these," but that in his day, "with the exception of some reformed and cloistered nuns," these *pianelle* were out of use "with all women," who instead wore "slippers" (*scarpette*). *Notizie,* cit. IV. 127. We also read ". . . now that the French custom which is all the fashion has ousted the patten formerly in use and banished all womanly decorum from the country" (Busetto, *Carlo de' Dottori,* Città di Castello, 1902, p. 11n.).

[12]The corks of the pattens.

[13]The pattens were made with very high heels, almost stilts.

[14]Neap. text: *pastiere:* Easter tarts made with ground wheat, curdled milk, sugar and other ingredients; *casatielli,* little cakes surrounded with hard-boiled eggs in their shells, also in use at Easter.

[15]*Stufati* or *sottostati,* as Del Tufo calls them (in the previously quoted *Ritratto di Napoli,* f. 21): "*sottestati* of a good piece of tender meat, with plums, garlic and pine-seeds, raisins, sugar, almonds and cinnamon."

[16]It does not appear that macaroni (*maccheroni*) then held, as later, the first place in Neapolitan cooking; for Neapolitans were not called "macroni-eaters" but "vegetable-eaters." Macaroni is often mentioned as coming from Sicily, or Sardinia, and more particularly from Cagliari. On this subject one may read Fasano, in his notes to the translation of the *Gerusalemme,* III. 20, Galiani's *Voc. Nap.,* ad verb., and Pitrè's *Bibl.* VII. 392. See also Cortese's *Viaggio di Parnaso,* V. 7; Sgruttendio's *Tiorba a taccone,* corda IX, "Le grolie del Carnevale," and a passage in Lando quoted by Imbriani in *XII conti pomiglianesi* (Napoli, 1876), pp. 234–5. [See *Notes and Queries,* Jan. 30th, 1932, p. 88; Feb. 20th, 1932, pp. 139, 140.]

[17]*I.e. raviuola,* not to be confused with *gravioli,* which Bruno mentions (*Candelaio,* I. 6) as a kind of sweet prepared in the monasteries.

[18]Text: *profizio* as the "proficiat" or "prosit" was popularly called.

ADDITIONAL NOTES

Day I. *Tale* 6.—Here we have the earliest version of Cinderella in Europe. Perrault's "Cendrillon" did not appear until 1697, sixty years after Basile's "La Gatta Cennerentola" had been published. It will be unnecessary to discuss the origins of the different *motifs* in "Cinderella," as the subject has already been fully treated by several eminent folk-lorists. The works or articles on the subject by authors of the nineteenth century (such as de Gubernatis, Husson, Ralston, Deulin, Lang, Cox, and Jacobs) have been succeeded by those of Cosquin (reprinted in his posthumous work *Les Contes Indiens et L'Occident*, 1922, p. 30–57, 503–16, 525); Bolte and Polívka, *op. cit.*, I. pp. 165–88, containing hundreds of variants; G. Huet, *Les Contes Populaires*, 1923, pp. 85–89 and 105–110; and P. Saintyves, *Les Contes de Perrault*, 1923, pp. 103–64.

The work of Cox, *Cinderella: Three Hundred and Forty-five Variants*, Folk-Lore Society, London, 1893, still remains the standard work, although the versions of Eastern Europe have been greatly extended by Bolte and Polívka. Modern controversies have largely been waged over the original home of the tale, preference being now given to India as its starting-place. There are, however, two minor *motifs* worthy of our attention.

Cennerentola Kills Her Mother-in-Law

The unusual incident of Cennerentola murdering her mother-in-law by letting the lid of a chest fall on her neck reminds us of Grimm, No. 47, where the wicked step-mother shuts the lid of the apple-chest on the little boy as he stoops to get an apple. See Bolte and Polívka, I. p. 422. They omit, however, an interesting variant found in Masuccio, No. XXII., where the wronged husband stabs his wife's Moorish lover, and seeing her stooping over an open chest (*cassone*) lets the lid fall on her neck, "crushing and forcing it down upon her in such wise that he killed her then and there without even letting her cry out 'Alas!'" (Waters, trans., London, 1895, p. 33.)

The most interesting reference, however, is historical and refers to Queen Fredegund (d. 597), who was a living example of the vilest step-mother ever imagined in the pages of a fairy-book. The number of murders and tortures caused by her orders will never be known. She was jealous of her own daughter, Rigunth, who continually declared that she should be mistress (probably, as Dalton says, because Fredegund began life as a palace maid, while she was of royal blood, being a king's daughter) in her place. Fredegund waited her opportunity and under the pretence of magnanimity took her to the treasure-room and showed her the King's jewels in a large chest. Feigning fatigue, she exclaimed, "I am weary; put thou in thy hand, and take out what thou mayest find." The mother thereupon forced down the lid on her neck and would have killed her had not the servants finally rushed to her aid.

See *History of the Franks*, Gregory of Tours, Book IX. Ch. 34, trans. by O.M. Dalton, Vol. II. pp. 405–6. For notes on the amazing life of Fredegund see Vol. I. pp. 73–80. The standard Latin text is in *Scriptores Rerum Merovingicarum, Monumenta*

Germaniae Historica, Vol. I. p. 389. Another reference occurs in the *Völundarkvida* (see verse 24). [This is Motif S121, Murder by slamming down chest-lid, in Stith Thompson, *Motif-Index of Folk Literature,* 6 vols., Bloomington: Indiana University Press, 1955-1958. The motif also occurs in other tale types, e.g., Aarne-Thompson tale type 480, The Kind and the Unkind Girls, which is often combined with Cinderella (AT 510A). For further discussion, see Warren E. Roberts, *The Tale of the Kind and the Unkind Girls* (Berlin: Walter de Gruyter, 1958), pp. 104, 112. Ed. Note.]

> They came to the chest,   and they craved the keys,
> The evil was open   when in they looked.
> He smote off their heads,   and their feet he hid
> Under the sooty   straps of the bellows.
> (Bellows' trans. *The Poetic Edda,* New York, 1923.)

The Stopping of the Ship

This same *motif* occurs again in *Pent.* II. 8, where the forgetful Baron is unable to pass a river until he procures the desired present. An exact parallel occurs in No. XXV. of Stokes' *Indian Fairy Tales,* p. 195, where the boat stops until the present for the youngest daughter has been obtained. Here also there are six other daughters as in our tale. In the notes by Miss Mary Stokes (p. 292) we are referred to an unpublished story from near Leghorn mentioned by de Gubernatis (*Zoological Mythology,* Vol. II. p. 382), where the ship refuses to move for the same reason. Croce (*Cunto de li Cunti,* 1891, p. 286) gives Imbriani, *Novellaja Fiorentina,* 2nd edit., 1877, pp. 333 *et seq.,* as an analogue. See also Cosquin, *Contes Populaires de Lorraine,* II., 221-23, where several other references are given; and Bolte and Polívka, II. 265 n[1], IV. 196 n[1]; though the reference in the latter vol. to Stokes, *op. cit.,* p. 241 (referring to people that shine brilliantly), seems quite irrelevant. [Cf. Motif D1654.6, Ship refuses to move, and Motif D2072.0.3, Ship held back by magic. Ed. Note.]

Cinderella, or the Little Glass Slipper

Charles Perrault

If one were to select the single most popular version out of all the hundreds of texts of Cinderella that have been reported, that version would almost certainly be the tale told by Charles Perrault (1628–1703). Perrault was a man of letters who had studied law and practiced architecture. But it was a work of his final years which has given him a special place in the history of folkloristics.

In 1694, Perrault began publishing several folktales in versified form. However, these tales were not particularly well received. By 1696, Perrault had decided to leave the tales in prose, and he anonymously published "Sleeping Beauty." The following year he published seven other tales, including such favorites as "Little Red Riding Hood," "Puss in Boots," and "Cinderella." In 1697, these tales were gathered together and published under the title Histoires ou Contes du Temps Passé, *with the alternate title "Contes de Ma Mère l'Oye" [Tales of My Mother Goose]. Perrault's name did not appear on the book. Instead, his little boy's name did. It has been suggested that Perrault may have felt that it was beneath his dignity to publish something like fairytales, and that is why he put his son's name on the volume. On the other hand, it is possible that his son may actually have had a hand in a recording of the tales. However the tales may have been learned, there is no question but that they have been enjoyed by countless readers since that time.*

Reprinted from *The Blue Fairy Book*, ed. Andrew Lang (New York: Random House, 1959), pp. 96–104.

The English translation of Perrault's version of Cinderella selected for this Casebook comes from Andrew Lang's Blue Fairy Book, *one of a celebrated series of colored fairytale anthologies. This is appropriate inasmuch as folklorist Andrew Lang had a special appreciation of Perrault as well a longstanding interest in Cinderella. Like Perrault, Lang was a man of some literary talent who enjoyed folktales. In 1888, he edited a fine English translation of Perrault's tales which included a detailed biographical account of Perrault's life. Although Lang tended to be a library scholar rather than a fieldworker, he actually collected several versions of Cinderella himself.*

In the third volume of the Revue Celtique, *Lang published "Rashin Coatie: A Scotch Tale," which he had collected from a Miss Margaret Craig of Darliston, Elgin, in the dialect of Morayshire. The tale was accompanied by comparative notes written by Reinhold Köhler, who for many years served as the librarian of the Ducal Library at Weimar and who possessed an unmatched knowledge of folktales. (Köhler was famous for his elaborate annotations on published tales in the latter portion of the nineteenth century.) In 1880, Lang published in* The Academy *a version of Cinderella he found in Mentone. Finally, in 1893, Lang's introduction to Marian Roalfe Cox's* Cinderella *appeared, as well as an essay in* Folk-Lore *entitled "Cinderella and the Diffusion of Tales." Much of Lang's concern was with whether apparently parallel versions of tales in different parts of the world could be explained by independent invention or by diffusion from a common source. His compromise position was essentially that details of stories may have been independently invented but that story plots as a whole spread through diffusion.*

For a consideration of Perrault's tales, see Marc Soriano, Les Contes de Perrault *(Paris: Gallimard, 1968). For Andrew Lang's view of Perrault, see* Perrault's Popular Tales *(Oxford: Clarendon Press, 1888). For Lang's field texts of Cinderella, see "Rashin Coatie: A Scotch Tale,"* Revue Celtique, *3 (1876–1878), 365–378; and "'Cendreusette,' The Mentonese Variant of Cendrillon, or Cinderella,"* The Academy, *17 (1880), 474. For his discussions of Cinderella, see "Introduction," Marian Roalfe Cox,* Cinderella *(London: David Nutt, 1893), pp. vii–xxiii; and "Cinderella and the Diffusion of Tales,"* Folk-Lore, *4 (1893), 413–433.*

Once there was a gentleman who married, for his second wife, the proudest and most haughty woman that was ever seen. She had, by a former husband, two daughters of her own humor, who were, indeed, exactly like her in all things. He had likewise, by another wife, a young daughter, but of unparalleled goodness and sweetness of temper, which she took from her mother, who had been the best creature in the world.

No sooner were the ceremonies of the wedding over than the stepmother began to show herself in her true colors. She could not bear the good qualities of this pretty girl, and the less because they made her own daughters appear the more odious. She employed her in the meanest work of the house: she scoured the dishes, tables, etc., and scrubbed madam's chamber, and those of misses, her daughters. She lay up in a sorry garret, upon a wretched straw bed, while her sisters lay in fine rooms, with floors all inlaid, upon beds of the very newest fashion, and where they had looking glasses so large that they might see themselves at their full length from head to foot.

The poor girl bore all patiently, and dared not tell her father, who would have rattled her off; for his wife governed him entirely. When she had done her work, she used to go into the chimney corner, and sit down among cinders and ashes, which made her commonly be called *Cinderwench;* but the youngest, who was not so rude and uncivil as the eldest, called her Cinderella. However, Cinderella, notwithstanding her mean apparel, was a hundred times handsomer than her sisters, though they were always dressed very richly.

It happened that the King's son gave a ball, and invited all persons of fashion to it. Our young misses were also invited, for they cut a very grand figure among the quality. They were mightily delighted at this invitation, and wonderfully busy in choosing out such gowns, petticoats, and headclothes as might become them. This was a new trouble to Cinderella; for it was she who ironed her sisters' linen, and plaited their ruffles; they talked all day long of nothing but how they should be dressed.

"For my part," said the eldest, "I will wear my red velvet suit with French trimming."

"And I," said the youngest, "shall have my usual petticoat; but then, to make amends for that, I will put on my gold-flowered manteau, and my diamond stomacher, which is far from being the most ordinary one in the world."

They sent for the best tirewoman they could get to make up their headdresses and adjust their double pinners, and they had their red brushes and patches from Mademoiselle de la Poche.

Cinderella was likewise called up to them to be consulted in all these matters, for she had excellent notions, and advised them always for the best, nay, and offered her services to dress their heads, which they were very willing she should do. As she was doing this, they said to her:

"Cinderella, would you not be glad to go to the ball?"

"Alas!" said she, "you only jeer me; it is not for such as I am to go thither."

"Thou art in the right of it," replied they. "It would make the people laugh to see a cinderwench at a ball."

Anyone but Cinderella would have dressed their heads awry, but she was very good, and dressed them perfectly well. They were almost two days without eating, so much were they transported with joy. They broke more than a dozen laces in trying to be laced up close, that they might have a fine slender shape, and they were continually at their looking glass. At last the happy day came; they went to court, and Cinderella followed them with her eyes as long as she could, and when she had lost sight of them, she fell a-crying.

Her godmother, who saw her all in tears, asked her what was the matter.

"I wish I could—I wish I could——"; she was not able to speak the rest, being interrupted by her tears and sobbing.

This godmother of hers, who was a fairy, said to her, "Thou wishest thou couldst go to the ball; is it not so?"

"Y-es," cried Cinderella, with a great sigh.

"Well," said her godmother, "be but a good girl, and I will contrive that thou shalt go." Then she took her into her chamber, and said to her, "Run into the garden, and bring me a pumpkin."

Cinderella went immediately to gather the finest she could get, and brought it to her godmother, not being able to imagine how this pumpkin could make her go to the ball. Her godmother scooped out all the inside of it, having left nothing but the rind; which done, she struck it with her wand, and the pumpkin was instantly turned into a fine coach, gilded all over with gold.

She then went to look into her mousetrap, where she found six mice, all alive, and ordered Cinderella to lift up a little the trap door, when, giving each mouse, as it went out, a little tap with her wand, the mouse was that moment turned into a fine horse, which altogether made a very fine set of six horses of a beautiful mouse-colored dapple gray. Being at a loss for a coachman:

"I will go and see," says Cinderella, "if there is not a rat in the rattrap—we may make a coachman of him."

"Thou art in the right," replied her godmother. "Go and look."

Cinderella brought the trap to her, and in it there were three huge rats. The fairy made choice of one of the three which had the largest beard, and, having been touched with her wand, he was turned into a fat, jolly coachman, who had the smartest whiskers eyes ever beheld. After that, she said to her:

"Go again into the garden, and you will find six lizards behind the watering pot. Bring them to me."

She had no sooner done so but her godmother turned them into six footmen, who skipped immediately behind the coach, with their liveries all bedaubed with gold and silver, and clung as close behind each other as if they had done nothing else their whole lives. The fairy then said to Cinderella:

"Well, you see here and equipage fit to go to the ball with; are you not pleased with it?"

"Oh, yes!" cried she. "But must I go thither as I am, in these nasty rags?"

Her godmother only just touched her with her wand, and, at the same instant, her clothes were turned into cloth of gold and silver, all beset with jewels. This done, she gave her a pair of glass slippers, the prettiest in the whole world. Being thus decked out, she got up into her coach; but her godmother, above all things, commanded her not to stay till after midnight, telling her, at the same time, that if she stayed one moment longer, the coach would be a pumpkin again, her horses mice, her coachman a rat, her footmen lizards, and her clothes become just as they were before.

She promised her godmother she would not fail to leave the ball before midnight; and then away she drives, scarce able to contain herself for joy. The King's son, who was told that a great princess, whom nobody knew, was come, ran out to receive her; he gave her his hand as she alighted from the coach, and led her into the hall, among all the company. There was immediately a profound silence. The people stopped dancing, and the violins ceased to play, so attentive was everyone to contemplate the singular beauties of the unknown newcomer. Nothing was then heard but a confused noise of:

"Ha! how handsome she is! Ha! how handsome she is!"

The King himself, old as he was, could not help watching her, and telling the Queen softly that it was a long time since he had seen so beautiful and lovely a creature.

All the ladies were busied in considering her clothes and head-dress, that they might have some made next day after the same pattern, provided they could meet with such fine material and as able hands to make them.

The King's son conducted her to the most honorable seat, and afterward took her out to dance with him; she danced so very gracefully that they all more and more admired her. A fine collation was served up, whereof the younger prince ate not a morsel, so intently was he busied in gazing on her.

She went and sat down by her sisters, showing them a thousand civilities, giving them part of the oranges and citrons which the Prince had presented her with, which very much surprised them, for they did not know her. While Cinderella was thus amusing her sisters, she heard the clock strike eleven and three quarters, where-upon she immediately made a courtesy to the company and hasted away as fast as she could.

When she got home she ran to seek out her godmother, and, after having thanked her, she said she could not but heartily wish she might go next day to the ball, because the King's son had desired her.

As she was eagerly telling her godmother whatever had passed at the ball, her two sisters knocked at the door, which Cinderella ran and opened.

"How long you have stayed!" cried she, gaping, rubbing her eyes and stretching herself as if she had been just waked out of her sleep; she had not, however, any manner of inclination to sleep since they went from home.

"If thou hadst been at the ball," said one of her sisters, "thou

wouldst not have been tired with it. There came thither the finest
princess, the most beautiful ever was seen with mortal eyes; she
showed us a thousand civilities, and gave us oranges and citrons."

Cinderella seemed very indifferent in the matter; indeed, she
asked them the name of that princess. But they told her they did not
know it, and that the King's son was very uneasy on her account and
would give all the world to know who she was. At this Cinderella,
smiling, replied:

"She must, then, be very beautiful indeed; how happy you have
been! Could not I see her? Ah! dear Miss Charlotte, do lend me your
yellow suit of clothes which you wear every day."

"Ay, to be sure!" cried Miss Charlotte. "Lend my clothes to such
a dirty cinderwench as thou art! I should be a fool."

Cinderella, indeed, expected well such answer, and was very glad
of the refusal; for she would have been sadly put to it if her sister
had lent her what she asked for jestingly.

The next day the two sisters were at the ball, and so was
Cinderella, but dressed more magnificently than before. The King's
son was always by her, and never ceased his compliments and kind
speeches to her; to whom all this was so far from being tiresome that
she quite forgot what her godmother had recommended to her; so
that she, at last, counted the clock striking twelve when she took it
to be no more than eleven; she then rose up and fled, as nimble as a
deer. The Prince followed, but could not overtake her. She left
behind one of her glass slippers, which the Prince took up most
carefully. She got home, but quite out of breath, and in her nasty
old clothes, having nothing left her of all her finery but one of the
little slippers, fellow to that she dropped. The guards at the palace
gate were asked if they had not seen a princess go out.

Who said: They had seen nobody go out but a young girl, very
meanly dressed, and who had more the air of a poor country wench
than a gentlewoman.

When the two sisters returned from the ball Cinderella asked
them if they had been well diverted, and if the fine lady had been
there.

They told her: Yes, but that she hurried away immediately when
it struck twelve, and with so much haste that she dropped one of her
little glass slippers, the prettiest in the world, which the King's son
had taken up; that he had done nothing but look at her all the time

at the ball, and that most certainly he was very much in love with the beautiful person who owned the glass slipper.

What they said was very true; for a few days after, the King's son caused it to be proclaimed, by sound of trumpet, that he would marry her whose foot the slipper would just fit. They whom he employed began to try it upon the princesses, then the duchesses and all the court, but in vain; it was brought to the two sisters, who did all they possibly could to thrust their foot into the slipper, but they could not effect it. Cinderella, who saw all this, and knew her slipper, said to them, laughing:

"Let me see if it will not fit me."

Her sisters burst out a-laughing, and began to banter her. The gentleman who was sent to try the slipper looked earnestly at Cinderella, and, finding her very handsome, said it was but just that she should try, and that he had orders to let everyone make trial.

He obliged Cinderella to sit down, and, putting the slipper to her foot, he found it went on very easily, and fitted her as if it had been made of wax. The astonishment her two sisters were in was excessively great, but still abundantly greater when Cinderella pulled out of her pocket the other slipper, and put it on her foot. Thereupon, in came her godmother, who, having touched with her wand Cinderella's clothes, made them richer and more magnificent than any of those she had before.

And now her sisters found her to be that fine, beautiful lady whom they had seen at the ball. They threw themselves at her feet to beg pardon for all the ill-treatment they had made her undergo. Cinderella took them up, and, as she embraced them, cried that she forgave them with all her heart, and desired them always to love her.

She was conducted to the young Prince, dressed as she was; he thought her more charming than ever, and, a few days after, married her. Cinderella, who was no less good than beautiful, gave her two sisters lodgings in the palace, and that very same day matched them with two great lords of the court.

Ash Girl (Aschenputtel)

Jacob and Wilhelm Grimm

No two individuals did more to stimulate the study of folklore than did Jacob Grimm (1785-1863) and Wilhelm Grimm (1786-1859). As linguists and folklorists, the Grimm brothers undertook an enormous number of major research projects. Jacob, the more academic of the two, was especially interested in philology and grammar, while Wilhelm, who had more literary talents took the larger part of rewriting and polishing the folktales collected by both brothers from oral sources in Hesse and Hanau.

The publication of the first volume of the Grimm brothers' Kinder und Hausmärchen in 1812 and the second in 1814 burst like a literary bombshell on the European scene. Appealing as the tales did to sentiments of romanticism and nationalism, they soon inspired individuals in other countries to collect their own folktale traditions.

The Grimm brothers initially argued in favor of presenting tales straight from the folk—in their 1812 preface we find such praise-worthy claims as: ". . . we have endeavored to present these fairy-tales as purely as possible. . . . No circumstance has been added, embellished or changed. . . ." Nevertheless, the fact is that the Grimms did not always practice what they preached. They frequently combined different versions of the same tale, thereby producing what modern folklorists call a composite text. Such conglomerates typically

Reprinted from Francis P. Magoun, Jr., and Alexander H. Krappe, trans., *The Grimms' German Folk Tales* (Carbondale: Southern Illinois University Press, 1960), pp. 86–92.

*did not correspond in all details to any one single orally elicited
version of a folktale. So the version of Grimm tale number 21,
Aschenputtel, which appeared in 1812, was by the edition of 1819
already expanded and reworked in the light of three versions from
Hesse. In their preface to the 1856 edition, the brothers admitted the
stylistic changes they had made from edition to edition, saying that
they had only filled out what was incomplete and retold the stories
much more "simply and purely" than in the originals.*

*Contemporary folklorists rightfully deplore the literary "im-
proving" of authentic field-collected texts, but one must not judge the
Grimms too harshly in retrospect. Rewriting folktales was certainly
the accepted practice in the nineteenth century and before. The point
is that twentieth century readers should be aware that the Grimm
versions of traditional folktales do represent more departures from
the original oral sources of the tales. In sum, the published versions of
Cinderella reported by Perrault and the Grimm brothers may well be
the most popular and well known, but they are not necessarily the
most authentic in terms of orally circulating versions of the tale.*

*In the Grimms' corpus, one can find different forms of the
Cinderella story. Besides Grimm number 21, Aschenputtel (which is
an example of Aarne-Thompson tale type 510A, Cinderella), there is
Grimm number 65, Allerleirauh (which is Aarne-Thompson tale type
510B, The Dress of Gold, of Silver, and of Stars (Cap o' Rushes), and
Grimm number 130, Einäuglein, Zweiäuglein, and Dreiäuglein (which
is Aarne-Thompson tale type 511, One-Eye, Two-Eyes, Three-Eyes).
In this Casebook, however, we shall reprint only Aschenputtel.*

*For some idea of the wealth of scholarship devoted to the
Grimms, see Ludwig Denecke,* Jacob Grimm und sein Bruder
Wilhelm *(Stuttgart: Metzler, 1971). For discussions of each of the
tales collected by the Grimms, see Johannes Bolte and Georg
Polívka,* Anmerkungen zu den Kinder- Und Hausmärchen der
Brüder Grimm, *5 vols. (Leipzig: Dieterich'sche Verlagsbuchhandlung,
1913–1932).*

A rich man's wife fell ill and, feeling that her end was approaching, called her only daughter to her bedside and said, "Dear child,
remain devout and good; then dear God will ever be with you, and
I'll look down on you from Heaven and be near you." Then she

closed her eyes and passed away. Every day the girl used to go out to her mother's grave and weep and remained devout and good. When winter came, the snow laid a white blanket on the grave, and when in the spring the sun had taken it off again, the man married a second wife.

The wife brought two daughters of her own into the home; they were pretty and fair of face but ugly and black in their hearts. Then evil days began for the poor stepchild. "Is the stupid goose to sit with us in the living room?" they'd say. "Whoever wants to eat bread must earn it—out with the scullery maid!" They took away her fine clothes, dressed her in an old gray smock and wooden shoes. "Just look at the proud princess! See how dressed up she is!" they'd cry and, laughing, lead her into the kitchen. There she had to do heavy work from morning till night, get up before dawn, carry water, light the fire, cook, and wash. On top of it all her sisters played all sorts of mean tricks on her, mocked her, and used to pour peas and lentils into the ashes so that she'd have to sit and pick them out again. In the evening when she was tired from work, there was no bed for her; she just had to lie down in the ashes beside the hearth. And since for this reason she always looked dusty and dirty, they called her Ash Girl.

Now it so happened that her father was once going to a fair and asked his two stepdaughters what to bring them. "Fine clothes," said one. "Pearls and jewels," said the other. "And you, Ash Girl," he said, "what do you want?" "Father, bring me the first twig that brushes against your hat on the way home. Break it off for me." So he bought fine clothes, pearls and jewels for the two stepsisters. As he was riding home through a green thicket, a hazel twig brushed against him and knocked off his hat; then he broke off the twig and brought it along. When he got home, he gave his stepdaughters what they'd asked for and gave Ash Girl the hazel twig. She thanked him, went to her mother's grave, planted the twig, and wept so bitterly that her tears fell on it and watered it. It grew and became a fine tree. Three times a day Ash Girl would go down there, weep and pray, and every time a little white bird would light on the tree, and every time she uttered a wish, the bird would throw down to her what she had wished.

Now, in order that his son might choose a bride, the king proclaimed a festival which was to last three days and to which all the pretty girls in the land were invited. When the two stepdaughters heard that they, too, were to appear, they were in high spirits and,

calling Ash Girl, said, "Comb our hair! brush our shoes! and fasten
our buckles! We're going to the festival at the king's palace." Ash
Girl obeyed them, but she wept, for she would have liked to go
along to the ball, and begged her stepmother to let her. "You, Ash
Girl!" she said, "you're covered with dust and dirt, and you want to
go to the festival? You've got no clothes and no shoes and you want
to dance?" But when she kept on begging, the stepmother finally
said, "I emptied a dish of lentils in the ashes; if you pick out the lentils
within two hours, you may come along." The girl went out the back
door into the garden and cried out, "You tame pigeons, you turtledoves, and all you birds under heaven, come and help me pick them
out,

> the good lentils into the pot,
> the bad lentils into your crop."

Then two pigeons came in through the kitchen window and after
them the turtledoves, and finally all the birds under heaven whirred
and flocked in and settled down around the ashes. And the pigeons
bobbed their heads and began "peck, peck" and then the others
began "peck, peck" and they pecked all the good lentils into the
dish. It was hardly an hour before they were finished and all flew out
again. Then the girl joyfully brought the dish to her stepmother and
thought that she might now be allowed to go to the festival, but the
stepmother said, "No, Ash Girl, you've got no clothes and don't
know how to dance; you'll only be laughed at." When she wept, her
stepmother said, "If you can pick two dishes of lentils from the ashes
in one hour, you may come along," thinking, "she'll never be able to
do this." When she'd emptied the two dishes of lentils into the ashes,
the girl went out the back door into the garden and cried, "You tame
pigeons, you turtledoves, all you birds under heaven, come and help
me pick them out,

> the good lentils into the pot,
> the bad into your crop."

Then two white pigeons came in through the kitchen window and
after them the turtledoves, and finally all the birds under heaven
whirred and flocked in and settled down around the ashes. And the
pigeons bobbed their heads and began "peck, peck—peck, peck"
and then the others began "peck, peck—peck, peck" and they pecked

all the good lentils into the dishes. And it was hardly half an hour before they finished and all flew out again. Then the girl brought the dishes to her stepmother and was glad, because she thought that she might now go along to the festival. But the latter said, "It'll do you no good. You're not coming along, for you've got no clothes and don't know how to dance. We'd only be ashamed of you." Then she turned her back on her and hurried off with her two haughty daughters.

When everyone had gone, Ash Girl went to her mother's grave under the hazel bush and cried,

> "Little tree, jiggle yourself and shake yourself;
> Scatter gold and silver over me."

Then the bird threw her down a gold and silver dress and silk slippers embroidered with silver. She put the dress on in a hurry and went to the festival. Her sisters, however, and her stepmother didn't recognize her and thought she must be some foreign princess, so beautiful did she look in her gold dress. They didn't so much as think of Ash Girl, who they thought was sitting at home in the dirt, picking lentils out of the ashes. The king's son went up to her, took her by the hand, danced with her, and wouldn't dance with anyone else. He never let go her hand, and when anyone else came to ask her to dance, he'd say, "She's my partner."

She danced till evening and then wanted to go home, but the king's son said, "I'll go with you and escort you," for he wanted to see whose daughter the beautiful girl was. She slipped away from him, however, and jumped into the dovecote. The king's son waited till her father came and told him that the foreign girl had jumped into the dovecote. The old man thought, "Can it be Ash Girl?" They had to fetch him an ax and a pick to break down the dovecote, but there was no one inside. And when they got home, there was Ash Girl in her dirty clothes lying in the ashes, and a dim oil lamp was burning in the fireplace. For Ash Girl had jumped down quickly out the back of the dovecote and had run to the hazel bush. There she'd taken off her fine clothes and laid them on the grave, and the bird had taken them away again, and then she'd sat down in her gray smock in the ashes in the kitchen.

Next day when the festival was resumed, and her parents and stepsisters had gone, Ash Girl again went to the hazel bush and said,

"Little tree, jiggle yourself and shake yourself;
Scatter gold and silver over me."

Then the bird threw down an even finer dress than the day before,
and when she appeared at the festival in this dress, everyone was
amazed at her beauty. The king's son had, however, waited for her
coming, at once took her by the hand, and danced only with her.
When others came and asked her for a dance, he'd say, "She's my
partner." When evening came, she wanted to go, and the king's son
followed her to see into which house she went, but she ran away
from him and into the garden behind the house. A fine big tree stood
there, full of the most magnificent pears. She climbed among the
branches like a squirrel, and the king's son didn't know where she'd
got to. But he waited till her father came and said to him, "The
stranger slipped away from me, and I think she climbed the pear
tree." The father thought, "Can it be Ash Girl?" He had an ax
fetched and cut down the tree, but there was no one in it. And when
they got to the kitchen, there was Ash Girl lying in the ashes as
usual, for she'd jumped down on the other side of the tree, had
returned her fine clothes to the bird in the hazel bush, and put on
her gray smock.

On the third day, when her parents and sisters had gone, Ash
Girl again went to her mother's grave and said to the tree,

"Little tree, jiggle yourself and shake yourself;
Scatter gold and silver over me."

Then the bird threw down a dress more magnificent and more
splendid than anybody had ever had, and the slippers were of solid
gold. When she arrived at the festival in this dress, no one from
amazement knew what to say. The king's son danced only with her,
and when anybody else asked her for a dance, he'd say, "She's my
partner."

When it was evening, Ash Girl wanted to leave, and the king's
son wanted to escort her, but she got away from him so fast that he
couldn't follow her. He had, however, resorted to a trick and had
coated the stairs with pitch, so when she ran down stairs, the girl's
left slipper stuck there. The king's son picked it up, and it was tiny
and dainty and of solid gold. The next morning he went with it to
the man and said to him, "Nobody else shall be my wife but the girl

whose foot this shoe fits." Then the two sisters rejoiced, for they had pretty feet. The eldest took the shoe to her room and was going to try it on, and her mother was standing beside her, but she couldn't get her big toe in, for the shoe was too small for her. Then her mother handed her a knife, saying, "Cut the toe off; once you're queen, you won't have to walk any more." The girl cut off her toe, forced her foot into the shoe, and, suppressing her pain, went out to the king's son. He took her on his horse as his bride and rode off with her. But they had to pass the grave, and there the two pigeons were sitting on the hazel bush and cried out,

> "Look, look!
> There's blood in the shoe!
> The shoe's too small.
> The right bride's still at home."

Then he looked at her foot and saw the blood oozing out. He turned his horse about and brought the false bride home again. He said she wasn't the right bride and that the other sister should try on the shoe. So the latter went into her room and managed to get her toes in, but her heel was too large. Then her mother handed her a knife, saying, "Cut a piece off your heel; once you're queen, you won't have to walk any more." The girl cut off a piece of her heel, forced her foot into the shoe, and, suppressing her pain, went out to the king's son. He took her on his horse as his bride and rode off with her. As they were passing the hazel bush, the two pigeons were sitting there and cried out,

> "Look, look!
> There's blood in the shoe!
> The shoe's too small.
> The right bride's still back home."

He looked down at her foot and saw the blood oozing out of the shoe, dyeing her white stockings red. Then he turned his horse about and brought the false bride back home. "She isn't the right bride either," he said. "Haven't you any other daughter?" "No," said the man, "there's only a little misshapen Ash Girl, daughter by my late wife, but she can't possibly be the bride." The king's son told him to send her up, but her mother replied, "Oh no, she's much too dirty and mustn't be seen." But he insisted on it, and Ash Girl had to be called. She first washed her face and hands and then went and made a deep curtsy before the king's son, who handed her the gold shoe. Then she sat down on a stool, drew her foot out of the heavy wooden shoe and put it in the slipper, which fitted her perfectly. When she stood up and the king looked into her face, he recognized her as the beautiful girl with whom he'd danced and cried, "That's the right bride!" The stepmother and the two sisters were frightened and turned pale with vexation, but he took Ash Girl on his horse and rode off with her. As they passed the hazel bush, the two white pigeons cried,

> "Look, look!
> No blood in the shoe!
> The shoe's not too small.
> He's bringing the right bride home."

And when they'd called out thus, they both came flying down and perched on Ash Girl's shoulders, one on the right, the other on the left, and stayed there.

When her wedding with the king's son was to be celebrated, the two false sisters came and wanted to ingratiate themselves and have a share in her good fortune. As the bridal couple was going to church, the elder sister walked on the right, the younger on the left. Then the pigeons pecked out one of each of their eyes. Later, when they came out of the church, the elder was on the left and the younger on the right. Then the pigeons pecked out the other of their two eyes. Thus for their malice and treachery they were punished with blindness for the rest of their lives.

Cinderella

W. R. S. Ralston

Perhaps the first serious comparative study of Cinderella was written by William R.S. Ralston (1828–1889) in an essay published in The Nineteenth Century *in November, 1879. While this consideration of variants of the folktale was hardly of the scope of Miss Marian Roalfe Cox's compilation of 345 versions published more than a decade later in 1893, it did review some of the theories then in vogue about the possible meaning of Cinderella.*

Ralston, who worked as an assistant in the printed book department of the British Museum, was primarily a specialist in Russian folklore. In 1872, relying heavily upon his translations from Russian collections, he published The Songs of the Russian People, *and in 1873, he published* Russian Folk-Tales. *In his introduction to the latter volume, Ralston suggested that the tale of Cinderella provided a useful analogy for the fate of the popular tale. Speaking of the folktale, he observed; "Long did it dwell beside the hearths of the common people, utterly ignored by their superiors in social rank. Then came a period during which the cultured world recognized its existence, but accorded to it no higher rank than that allotted to 'nursery stories' and 'old wives tales'—except, indeed, on those rare occasions when the charity of a condescending scholar had invested it with such a garb as was supposed to enable it to make a respectable appearance in polite society. At length there arrived the*

Reprinted from *The Nineteenth Century*, 6 (1879), 832–853.

season of its final change, when, transferred from the dusk of the peasant's hut into the full light of the outer day, and freed from the unbecoming garments by which it had been disfigured, it was recognized as the scion of a family so truly royal that some of its members deduce their origin from the olden gods themselves."

The above comment indicates Ralston's own bias. His recapitulation of the history of folkloristics up to his own day includes the original ignoring of folktales, followed by the dressing up of peasant tales for "civilized" consumption, e.g., as did Perrault, and ending with the notion that folktales might be related to older, religious forms such as sacred myths. In this view, Ralston was advocating theories earlier propounded by the Grimms, who maintained that folktales were but the "detritus of myths." In the light of this perspective, the goal of the folklorist was to reconstruct the original mythic form of European folktales, which represented only mangled remnants of these myths.

In reading Ralston's essay on Cinderella, one must keep in mind that the nineteenth-century scholar was very much concerned with historical reconstruction of the past. Most folklore theories reflected this concern. Solar mythologists believed that myths were primitive man's metaphorical description of the rising and setting of the sun; lunar mythologists defended a comparable theory involving the moon. Ralston, though, not a solar mythologist himself, was certainly familiar with that line of argument. Similarly, the English anthropological approach to folktales tended to see them as survivals from a period of savagery. Thus apparently strange events reported in folktales were not so strange when it was realized that they represented actual historical customs practiced in much earlier, prehistoric, savage times. Both solar mythology and the English anthropological evolutionary approach agreed that one had to work backwards from folktales to the far distant past. In one case, one ended up with an event in nature, e.g., a sunrise; in the other case, one ended up with an ancient custom or practice.

Ralston does attempt to present a rational overview of different interpretations. As a result, from his judicious discussion one can obtain an idea of the diversity of Cinderella versions as well as some notion of the folktale theories in vogue in the late nineteenth century.

For more details of Ralston's life, see Richard M. Dorson, The British Folklorists: A History (*Chicago: University of Chicago Press,*

*1968), pp. 387-391. For a more general account of Ralston's views
on folktales, see his "Notes on Folk-Tales," Folk-Lore Record,
1 (1878), 71-98.*

The year 1697 A.D. was rendered memorable, not only by the
Peace of Ryswick which saved so great a part of Europe from the
horrors of war, but also by the earliest appearance in print of
Charles Perrault's 'Cendrillon, ou la petite pantoufle de verre.' It
was in the fourth part of the fifth volume of the *Recueil de pièces
curieuses et nouvelles,* published at the Hague by Adrian Moëtgens,
that the narrative of Cinderella's fortunes, in the form under which
it has become familiar to the whole civilised world, first saw the
light. In the same eventful year it was a second time introduced to
the public, figuring as one of the eight histories contained in the
Histoires ou contes du temps passé, which professed to be written
by the 'Sieur P. Darmancour;' this 'Sieur' being the author's son,
Perrault d'Armancour, a boy then ten years old, who may possibly
have acted as an intermediate relater between the nurse who told,
and the parent who wrote, the tales which were destined to render
that parent's name immortal. Their success was one of the unexpected triumphs which fate has now and then accorded to literature.
As little, in all probability, did the elder Perrault, grave member of
the French Academy and erudite defender of modern writers against
the claim of the ancients to supremacy, dream of the fame which
Cinderella and her companions were to bring to him, as did Charles
the Twelfth, who in the same eventful year succeeded to the throne
of Sweden, foresee the ruinous nature of the conflict in which he was
doomed to engage with his young brother monarch Peter the Great,
just then, on shipbuilding intent, making his way towards the peace-
ful dockyards of Holland.

Cinderella's story had doubtless been familiar for centuries to
the common people of Europe. In the opinion of many critics it had,
indeed, figured for ages among the heirlooms of humanity. But
Perrault's rendering of the tale naturalised it in the polite world,
gave it for cultured circles an attraction which it is never likely to
lose. The supernatural element plays in it but a subordinate part,
for, even without the aid of a fairy godmother, the neglected heroine

might have been enabled to go to a ball in disguise, and to win the heart of the hero by the beauty of her features and the smallness of her foot. It is with human more than with mythological interest that the story is replete, and therefore it appeals to human hearts with a force which no lapse of time can diminish. Such supernatural machinery as is introduced, moreover, has a charm for children which older versions of the tale do not possess. The pumpkin carriage, the rat coachman, the lizard lacqueys, and all the other properties of the transformation scene, appeal at once to the imagination and the sense of humour of every beholder. In the more archaic forms of the narrative there is no intentional grotesqueness. It is probably because so many of the incidents in the life of 'Cucendron' (as she was generally styled at home, 'though the younger of her stepsisters, who was not so uncivil as the elder, called her "Cendrillon"') were so natural, that some mythologists have attached such importance to the final trial by slipper. 'The central interest in the popular story of Cinderella,' says Professor de Gubernatis in his valuable work on 'Zoological Mythology,' is 'the legend of the lost slipper, and of the prince who tries to find the foot predestined to wear it.' But if the tale be sought for in lands less cultured than the France which produced Perrault's 'Cendrillon' and the Countess d'Aulnoy's 'Finette Cendron,' we shall see that 'the legend of the lost slipper' is no longer of 'central interest,' being merely used to supply the means of ultimate recognition so valuable in ancient days not only to the story-teller but to the dramatist. Let us take, by way of example, a Servian version of the story.[1]

As a number of girls were spinning one day a-field, sitting in a ring around a cleft in the ground, there came to them an old man, who said, 'Maidens, beware! for if one of you were to let her spindle fall into this cleft, her mother would be immediately turned into a cow.' Thereupon the girls at once drew nearer to the cleft and inquisitively peeped into it. And the spindle of Mara, the fairest of their number, slipped out of her hand and fell into the cleft. When she reached home in the evening, there was her mother turned into a cow, standing in front of the house and mooing. Thenceforth Mara tended and fed that cow with filial affection. But her father married again, taking as his second wife a widow with one plain daughter. And the new mistress of the house grievously ill-treated her step-daughter, forbidding her to wash her face, or brush her hair, or change her dress. And as she became grimy with ashes, *pepel,* Mara received the nickname of Pepelluga, that is, Cinderella, or Ashypet. Her stepmother also set her tasks which she could never have done, had not 'the cow, which had once been her mother,' helped her to perform them. When the stepmother found this out, she gave her husband no rest till he promised to put the cow to death. The girl wept bitterly when she heard the sad news, but the cow consoled her, telling her what she must do. She must not eat of its flesh, and she must carefully collect and bury its bones under a certain stone, and to this burial-place she must afterwards come, should she find herself in need of help. The cow was killed and eaten, but Mara said she had no appetite and ate none of its flesh. And she buried its bones as she had been directed. Some days afterwards, her step-mother went to church with her own daughter, leaving Mara at home to cook the dinner, and to pick up a quantity of corn which had been purposely strewed about the house, threatening to kill her if she had not performed both tasks by the time they came back from church. Mara was greatly troubled at the sight of the grain, and fled for help to the cow's grave. There she found an open coffer full of fine raiment, and on the lid sat two white doves, which said, 'Mara, choose a dress and go in it to church, and we birds will gather up the grain.' So she took the robes which came first, all of the finest silk, and went in them to church, where the beauty of her face and her dress won all hearts, especially that of the emperor's son. Just before the service was over, she glided out of church, ran home, and placed her robes in the coffer, which immediately shut and disappeared. When her relatives returned, they found the grain collected, the dinner cooked, and Ashypet as grimy as usual. Next Sunday just the same happened; only Mara's robes were this time of silver. On the third Sunday she went to church in raiment of pure gold with slippers to match. And when she left, the emperor's son left too, and hastened after her. But all he got for his pains was her right slipper, which she dropped in her haste. By means of it he at length found her out. In vain did her stepmother, when he walked in with the golden test in his hand, hide her under a trough, endeavour to force her own daughter's foot into the too small slipper, and, when this attempt failed, deny that there was any other girl in the house. For the cock crowed out 'Kikerike! the maiden is under the trough!' There the prince in truth found her, clothed from head to foot in golden attire, but wanting her right slipper. After which all went well.

In a Modern Greek variant of the story (Hahn, No. 2), there is a similar but a still stranger opening. According to it, an old woman and her three daughters sat spinning one day. And they made an agreement that if one of them broke her thread or dropped her spindle, she should be killed and eaten by the others. The mother's spindle was the first to fall, and her two elder daughters killed, cooked, and ate her. But their younger sister did all she could to save her mother's life, and when her attempts proved fruitless, utterly refused to have anything to do with eating her. And after the unfilial repast was over, she collected her mother's bones, and buried them in the ash-hole. After forty days had passed, she wished to dig them up and bury them elsewhere. But when she opened the hole in which she had deposited them, there streamed forth from it a blaze of light which almost blinded her. And then she found that no bones were there, but three costly suits of raiment. On one gleamed 'the sky with its stars,' on another 'the spring with its flowers,' on the third 'the sea with its waves.' By means of these resplendent robes she created a great sensation in church on three successive Sundays, and won the heart of the usual prince, who was enabled to recognise her by means of the customary slipper. The German variant of the story given by Grimm (No. 21) represents the grimy Aschenputtel—a form of Cinderella's name very like the Scotch Ashypet—as being assisted to bear up against the unkindness of her stepsisters by a white bird, which haunted the tree she had planted above her mother's grave. From this bird she received all that she asked for, including the dazzling robe and golden shoes in which she, for the third time, won the prince's heart at a ball in the palace. One of these shoes stuck in the pitch with which the prince had ordered the staircase to be smeared in the hope of thereby capturing her when she fled from the ball; and by it he after a time recognised her. The story is of an unusually savage tone. For not only does one of the stepsisters cut off her toes, and the other her heel, in order to fit their feet to the golden slipper—acting in accordance with the suggestion of their mother, who says, 'When you are a queen you need not go afoot'—but they ultimately have their eyes pecked out by the two doves which have previously called attention to the fact that blood is streaming from their mutilated feet. The surgical adaptation of the false foot to the slipper, and its exposure by a bird, occur in so many variants that they probably formed an important part of the original tale. Thus in a Lowland Scotch variant of the story quoted by Chambers, when the glass shoe was brought by the prince's messenger to the house wherein lived two sisters, 'the auld sister that was sae proud gaed awa' by hersel', and came back in a while hirpling wi' the shoe on.' But when she rode away in triumph as the prince's bride, 'a wee bird sung out o' a bush:—

> "Nippit fit and clippit fit ahint the king rides;
> But pretty fit and little fit ahint the caldron hides."

The blinding of the pretenders, however, is a rare incident. But in one of the Russian stories (Afanasief, vi. 30) the stepsisters of Chornushka—so called from her being always dirty and *chorna*, or black—lose their eyes exactly as in the German tale.

The industry of many collectors has supplied scores of variants of this most popular narrative. But those which have been mentioned will be sufficient to throw a considerable light upon one of its most significant features. Its earlier scenes appear to have been inspired by the idea that a loving mother may be able, even after her death, to bless and assist a dutiful child. In the Servian and the Greek variants, this belief is brought prominently forward, though in a somewhat grotesque form. In the German it is indicated, but less clearly. In one of the Sicilian variants (Pitré, No. 41), the step-daughter is assisted by a cow, as in the Servian story. Out of the hole in which its bones are buried come 'twelve damsels' who array her 'all in gold' and take her to the royal palace. Here the link between the girl and her dead mother has been lost, and the supernatural machinery is worked by fairy hands. In another (No. 43) the heroine receives everything she asks for, exactly as in the German story, from a magic date-tree. But nothing is said about its being planted above her mother's grave, and its mysterious powers are accounted for only by the fact that out of it issue 'a great number of *fati*' or fairies. In the romantic story of 'La Gatta Cennerentola,' told by Basile in his *Pentamerone* (published at Naples about the year 1637), she is similarly assisted by a fairy who issues from a date-tree. This suggests the fairy godmother of Perrault's tale, from which our version appears to have been borrowed. For among us Cinderella's slipper is almost always of glass, a material never mentioned except in the French form of the story and its imitations. On this part of Cinderella's costume it may be as well to dwell for a time, before passing on to the further consideration of her fortunes. As yet we have dealt only with what may be called the 'dead mother' or 'stepmother' opening of the tale. We shall have to consider presently a kindred form of the narrative, the opening of which may be named after the 'hateful marriage' from which the heroine flies, her adventures after her flight being similar to those of the ill-used stepdaughter. That is to say, she is reduced to a state of degradation and squalor, and is forced to occupy a servile position, frequently connected in some way with the hearth and its ashes. From this, however, she emerges on certain festive occasions as a temporarily brilliant being, always returning to her obscure position, until at last she is recognised; after which she remains permanently brilliant, her apparently destined period of eclipse having been brought to a close by her recognition, which is accomplished by the aid of her lost shoe or slipper.

As to the material of the slipper there has been much dispute. In the greater part of what are apparently the older forms of the story, it is made of gold. This may perhaps be merely a figure of speech, but there are instances on record of shoes, or at least sandals, being made of precious metals. Even in our own times, as well as in the days of the Caesars, a horse is said to have been shod with gold. And an Arab geographer, quoted by Mr. Lane, vouches for the fact that the islands of Wák-Wák are ruled by a queen who 'has shoes of gold.' Moreover 'no one walks in all these islands with any other kind of shoe; if he wear any other kind, his feet are cut.' It is true that his authority is a little weakened by his subsequent statement that these isles have trees which bear 'fruits like women.' These strange beings have beautiful faces, and are suspended by their hair. 'They come forth from integuments like large leathern bags. And when they feel the air and the sun, they cry "Wák! WáK!" until their hair is cut; and when it is cut they die.' Glass is an all but unknown material for shoemaking in the genuine folk-tales of any country except France. The heroine of one of Mr. J.F. Campbell's Gaelic tales[2] wore 'glass shoes,' but this exception to the rule may be due to a French influence, transmitted through an English or Lowland Scotch channel. Even in France itself the slipper is not always of glass. Madame d'Aulnoy's Finette Cendron, for instance, wore one 'of red velvet embroidered with pearls.' The use of the word *verre* by Perrault has been accounted for in two ways. Some critics think that the material in question was a *tissu en verre*, fashionable in Perrault's time. But the more generally received idea is that the substance was originally a kind of fur called *vair*—a word now obsolete in France, except in heraldry, but locally preserved in England as the name of the weasel[3]—and that some reciter or transcriber to whom the meaning of *vair* was unknown, substituted the more familiar but less probable *verre*, thereby dooming Cinderella to wear a glass slipper long before the discovery was made that glass may be rendered tough. In favour of the correctness of this supposition we have the great authority of M. Littré, whose dictionary affirms positively that in the description of Cinderella's slipper, *verre* is a mistake for *vair*. In this decision some scholars, especially those who detect in every feature of a fairy tale a 'solar myth,' refuse to acquiesce. Thus M. André Lefèvre, the accomplished editor of a recent edition of Perrault's *Contes*, absolutely refuses to give up the *verre* which 'convient parfaitement à un mythe lumineux.'[4] But the fact that Cinderella is not shod with glass in the vast majority of the lands she inhabits outweighs any amount of mythological probabilities. Besides, a golden shoe is admirably adapted to a luminous myth. It was a golden sandal which Rhodōpis lost while bathing, and which —according to the evidently Oriental tale preserved for us by Strabo and Aelian—was borne by an eagle to the Egyptian King, who immediately resolved to make the sandal's owner his royal spouse. In the venerable Egyptian tale of the 'Two Brothers,' another monarch is equally affected by the sight of a lock of the heroine's golden hair, that is borne to him by the river into which it had fallen, and he makes a similar resolve. In the Lesghian story from the Caucasus,[5] a supernatural female being drops a golden shoe, and the hero is sent in search of its fellow, becoming thereby exposed to many dangers. We may fairly be allowed, without any slur being cast upon mythological interpretation, to give up the glassiness of Cinderella's slipper. If the substitution of *verre* for *vair* be admitted, it supplies us with one of the few verbal tests which exist whereby to track a story's wanderings. For in that case we may always trace home to France, or at least detect a French element in, any form of the Cinderella story in which the heroine wears a glass slipper. A somewhat similar mistake to that which vitrefied Cinderella's slipper caused a celebrated picture by Rubens to be long known by an inappropriate title. Many a visitor to the National Gallery must have wondered why a portrait of a lady in a hat manifestly made, not of straw, but of beaver or a kind of felt, should be designated the *chapeau de paille*, before it was pointed out by Mr. Wornum, in the catalogue, that *paille* was probably a mistake for *poil*, a word meaning among other things wool and the nap of a hat, and akin to the Latin *pileus*, a felt cap or hat, and indeed to the word *felt* itself.

As regards the identification of the heroine by means of the lost slipper, that seems to be, as has already been remarked, merely one of the methods of recognition by which the stories of brilliant beings, temporarily obscured, are commonly brought to a close. In ancient comedy a recognition was one of the most hackneyed contrivances for winding up the plot, a convenient dramatic makeshift akin to that which proves the brotherhood of the heroes of *Box and Cox*. Thus in the numerous tales which tell how a hero who is really brilliant and majestic, but apparently squalid or insignificant, saves a fair princess from a many-headed dragon, but is robbed of his reward and reputation by an impostor, he usually proves his identity with her rescuer by producing, in the final scene, the tongues of the dead monster. Thus also the troubles of the golden-haired hero who, like Cinderella, emerges at times from his obscurity and performs wonders, come to a close when he is recognised by some token, such as the king's handkerchief in the Norse tale of 'The Widow's Son.' All this finale business appears to be of very inferior importance to the opening of the drama, that which refers to the dead mother's guardianship of her distressed child. The idea that such a protection might be exercised is of great antiquity and of wide circulation. According to it, the dying parent's benediction was not merely a prayer left to be fulfilled by a higher power, but was an actual force, either working of its own accord, or exerted by the parent's spirit after death. In the Russian story of Vasilissa the Fair, a dying mother bequeaths to her little daughter her parental blessing and a doll, and tells her to feed it well, and it will help her whenever she is in trouble. And therefore it was that Vasilissa would never eat all her share of a meal, but always kept the most delicate morsel for her doll; and at night, when all were at rest, she would shut herself up in the narrow chamber in which she slept, and feast her doll, saying the while: 'There, dolly, feed: help me in my need!' And the doll would eat until 'its eyes began to glow just like a couple of candles,' and then do everything that Vasilissa wanted. In another Russian tale, known also to Teutonic lands, a dead mother comes every night to visit her pining babe. The little creature cries all day, but during the dark it is quiet. Anxious to know the reason of this, the relatives conceal a light in a pitcher, and suddenly produce it in the middle of the night.

> They looked and saw the dead mother, in the very same clothes in which she had been buried, on her knees beside the cradle, over which she bent as she suckled the babe at her dead breast. The moment the light shone in the cottage she stood up, gazed sadly on her little one, and then went out of the room without a sound, not saying a word to any one. All those who saw her stood for a time terror-struck. And then they found the babe was dead.

In the Indian story of 'Punchkin,'[6] the seven ill-used little princesses 'used to go out every day and sit by their dead mother's tomb,' and cry, saying: 'Oh mother, mother, cannot you see your poor children, how unhappy we are, and how we are starved by our cruel step-mother?' And while they were thus crying one day, a tree, covered with ripe fruit, 'grew up out of the grave,' and provided them with food. And when the tree was cut down, a tank near the grave became filled with 'a rich cream-like substance, which quickly hardened into a thick white cake,' of which the hungry princesses partook freely. A similar appeal to a dead mother is made by a daughter in a Russian story (Afanasief, vi. 28). When in great distress, 'she went out to the cemetery, to her mother's grave, and began to weep bitterly.' And her mother spoke to her from the grave, and told her what to do in order to escape from her troubles.

The last of these tales belongs to the previously mentioned second division of Cinderella stories, that which comprises the majority of the tales in which an ill-used maiden temporarily occupies a degraded position, appears resplendent on certain brief occasions, but always returns to her state of degradation, until at length she is recognised, frequently by the help of her lost slipper. But instead of her troubles being caused by a stepmother or stepsisters, they are brought upon her, in the stories now referred to, by some member of her own family who wishes to drive her into a hated marriage. From it she seeks refuge in flight, donning a disguise which is almost invariably the hide of some animal. In some countries the 'step-mother' form of Cinderella appears to be rare, whereas the 'hateful marriage' form is common. In Pitrè's collection of Sicilian tales, for instance, for one Cinderella tale of the stepmother class, there are four which begin with the heroine's escape from an unlawful marriage. In the Gonzenbach collection there is but one good variant of the Cinderella tale, and it belongs to the second class. The specimen of this second group with which English readers are likely to be best acquainted is the German 'Allerleirauh' (Grimm, No. 65), though it is very probable that to the same division belonged also the story of Catskin which Mr. Burchell presented, with other tales, to the younger members of the family of the Vicar of Wakefield. Perrault's *Peau d'Ane* is a version of the same story, but as it is told in verse it has never achieved anything at all approaching the success gained by its prose companions. Besides, the theme is not adapted for nurseries. It forms the subject of the Lowland Scotch tale of Rashie-Coat, in which we are told that the heroine fled because 'her father wanted her to be married, but she didna like the man.' But the Gaelic story of 'The King who wished to marry his Daughter' (Campbell, No. 14), states the case more precisely. The heroine almost always demands from her unwelcome suitor three magnificent dresses, and with these she takes to flight, usually disguising herself by means of a hide or other species of rough covering. In these dresses she goes to the usual ball or other festival, and captivates the conventional prince. The close of the story is generally the same as that which terminates the ordinary Cinderella tales which we have already considered. Its special points of interest are the reasons given for her flight from home, and the disguise in which she effects her escape.

Cinderella's troubles are brought to an end by the discovery that a slipper fits her foot; those of Allerleirauh, Catskin, Rashie-Coat, and the rest of her widely-scattered but always kindred companions in adventure, are generally brought about by the discovery that a certain ring or dress fits her finger or form. Cinderella's promotion is due to her dead mother's watchful care. Rashie-Coat's degradation is consequent upon her dying mother's unfortunate imprudence.

Thus in the Sicilian tale of 'Betta Pilusa,'[7] the hateful marriage from which the heroine flies, wrapped up in a grey cloak made of catskin, would never have been suggested to her had not her mother obtained a promise from her husband on her death-bed that he would marry again whenever any maiden was found whom her ring would fit. Some years later her own daughter finds the ring and tries it on. It fits exactly, so she is condemned to the marriage in question. By the advice of her confessor, she asks for three dresses, so wonderful that no mortal man can supply them. But her suitor is assisted by the devil, who enables him to produce the desired robes, the first sky-coloured, representing the sun, the moon, and the stars; the second sea-coloured, depicting 'all the plants and animals of the sea;' and the third 'a raiment of the colour of the earth, whereon all the beasts and the flowers of the field were to be seen.' Hidden in her catskin cloak, also procured from the same source, she leaves home, carrying her wonderful dresses with her in a bundle, and thus escapes from her abhorred suitor. To prevent him from noticing her absence, she leaves two doves in her room together with a basin of water. As he listens at the door he hears a splashing which is really due to the birds, but which he supposes is caused by her ablutions. Great is his rage when he at length breaks open the door and finds that he has been tricked. We learn from another variant that he was induced to knock his head against the wall until he died, and so the dressmaking devil got his due. In one of the Russian forms of the same tale, the fugitive maiden has recourse to a still more singular means of concealing her absence. The story is valuable because it supplies a reason for the introduction of the fatal ring. That is said to be due to the malice of a malignant witch, who, out of mere spite, induced a dying mother to give the ring to her son, and to charge him to marry that damsel whose finger it would fit. The ring is evidently of a supernatural nature, for when the heroine tries it on, not only does it cling to her finger 'just as if it had been made on purpose for it,' but it begins to shine with a new brilliance. When Katerina hears to what a marriage it destines her, she 'melts into bitter tears' and sits down in despair on the threshold of the house. Up come some old women bent on a holy pilgrimage, and to them she confides the story of her woes. Acting on their advice, when the fatal marriage-day arrives, she takes four *kukolki*, dolls or puppets of some kind, and places one in each of the corners of her room. When her suitor repeatedly calls upon her to come forth, she replies that she is coming directly, but each time she speaks the dolls begin to cry 'kuku,' and as they cry the floor opens gently and she sinks slowly in. At last only her head remains visible. 'Kuku' cry the dolls again: she disappears from sight, and the floor closes above her. Irritated at the delay, her suitor breaks open the door. He looks round on every side. No Katerina is there, only in each corner sits a doll, all four singing 'Kuku! open earth, disappear sister!' He snatches up an axe, chops off their heads, and flings them into the fire. In a Little-Russian variant of the same story, the despairing maiden flies for solace to her mother's grave. And her dead mother 'comes out from her grave,' and tells her daughter what to do. The girl accordingly provides herself with the usual splendid robes, and with the likewise necessary pig's hide or fell. Then she takes three puppets and arranges them around her on the ground. The puppets exclaim, one after another 'Open, moist earth, that the maiden fair may enter within thee.' And when the third has spoken, the earth opens, and the maiden and the puppets descend 'into the lower world.' Some vague remembrance of this descent of the heroine into the lower regions appears to have given rise to the strange opening of one of the Sicilian variants cited by Pitré (No. 42). The heroine goes down into a well in order to find her elder sister's ring. At the bottom she perceives an opening, and passes through it into a garden, where she is seen by 'the Prince of Portugal,' to whom, after the usual adventures, she is wedded.

As a general rule the heroine makes her escape, disguised in a coarse mantle or dress made of the skin of some animal. In another of the Sicilian variants (Pitré, No. 43) it is a horse's hide in which she is wrapped, and the people who meet her when she leaves home are surprised to see what they take to be a horse walking along on its hind legs. But sometimes this disguise assumes a different aspect, being represented as something made of a less pliant material, a disguise akin to the 'wooden cloak, all made of strips of lath,' which was 'so black and ugly,' and which 'made such a clatter' when the heroine, who was called after it 'Katie Woodencloak,' went upstairs. The Norse story in which she figures commences with the stepmother opening, and it does not close with a slipper-test, but still it belongs properly to the second division of the Cinderella group. In some of the other variants this wooden cloak becomes intensified into an utterly rigid covering or receptacle of wood. Thus in the Sicilian tale

of 'Fidi e Cridi' (Pitré, i. 388), the two daughters of the Emperor of
Austria, one of whom, Fidi, has been destined by a fatal ring to a
hated marriage, make their escape from home in a coffer of gilded
wood. They have previously stored it with provisions and made
arrangements for its being thrown into the sea. The waves waft them
to Portugal, where Fidi becomes the wife of the king. Her wedded
happiness is for a time interrupted by the arrival of the Emperor of
Austria, who inflicts upon his fugitive daughter a parental curse so
powerful that it turns her into a lizard for a year, a month, and a
day. But eventually all goes well. As early as 1550, Straparola
printed in his 'Tredici Piacevoli Notti' (i. 4) a romantic version of
this story, telling how Doralice, the daughter of Tebaldo, Prince of
Salerno, in order to elude her unnatural parent, hid herself in a large
coffer of beautiful workmanship. This coffer Tebaldo, under the
influence of depression produced by his daughter's disappearance,
sold to a merchant, from whose hands it passed into those of
Genese, King of Britain. Doralice used sometimes to issue from her
wooden covering, and one day the King saw her, fell in love with her
at once, and made her his queen.

In almost all the tales belonging to the second or 'hated marriage'
branch of the Cinderella story, the heroine accepts a very humble
post in the palace of the prince whom she eventually weds. Just as
her counterpart, the golden-locked prince of so many tales, becomes
a scullion at court, so she acts in the capacity of scullery-maid or
other despised domestic. But from time to time she quits the scullery
and appears in all the splendour of her mysterious dresses among the
noble guests assembled in the princely banqueting or ball room. In
order to show the close connection between the stories of Goldenlocks and Rashie-Coat, a few specimens of their popular histories
may be given. In the already quoted Russian story (Afanasief, vi. 28)
of the princess who is advised by her dead mother to deceive her
detested suitor by disguising herself in a swine's bristly hide, her
subsequent fortunes are narrated as follows:—After she had fled
from home she made her way on foot into a foreign land, always
wearing her swinish covering. As she wandered through a forest one
day, a terrible storm arose. To shelter herself from the torrents of
rain which were falling, she climbed a huge oak, and took refuge
amidst its dense foliage. Presently a prince came that way, and his
dogs began to bark at the strange animal they saw among the leaves.

The prince gazed with surprise at the singular being thus revealed to him, evidently 'no wild beast, but a wondrous wonder, a marvellous marvel.' 'What sort of oddity are you?' said he; 'can you speak or not?' 'I am Swine's Hide,' said she. Then he took her down from the tree, and set her up on a cart. 'Take this wondrous wonder, this marvellous marvel, to my father and to my mother,' said he. And when the king and queen saw her they were greatly astonished, and gave her a room to herself to live in. Some time afterwards there was a ball at the palace. Swine's Hide asked the servants if she might stand at the ball-room door and look on. 'Get along with you, Swine's Hide,' said they. Out she went afield, donned her brilliant dress with the many stars of heaven upon it, whistled till a chariot came, and drove off in it to the ball. All who were there wondered whence this beauteous visitor had come. 'She danced and danced— then disappeared.' Putting on again her swinish covering, she went back to her own room. Again a ball took place. Again did Swine's Hide appear in radiant beauty, dressed in a dazzling robe, 'on the back of which shone the bright moon, on the front the red sun.' Great was the sorrow of the prince when she suddenly left the dance and disappeared. 'Whatever are we to do,' thought he, 'to find out who this beauty is?' He thought and thought. 'At last he went and smeared the first step of the staircase with pitch, that her shoe might stick in it.' And so, as she fled from the ball on the third occasion, she left her shoe behind her. Vainly did all the fair maidens in the kingdom attempt to get it on. At last the unsightly Swine's Hide was told to try her chance. And when the prince saw that it fitted her exactly, 'he ripped up the swinish hide, and tore it off the princess. Then he took her by her white hand, led her to his father and mother, and sought and gained their permission to marry her.'

In this story, as in the Norse tale of 'Katie Woodencloak,' the recognition is due to a Cinderella's slipper. But more often the discovery is made in a different way. Thus in a Modern Greek version the despised goose-girl, who was nicknamed 'Hairy' on account of the nature of the hide in which she was always wrapped, though she lost a shoe in flying the third time from a ball at the palace, was not discovered by means of it. But when the maids were about to take a basin of water to the king before dinner one day, she obtained leave to carry it. Before she entered the king's chamber, 'she slit the hide a little at the knee, in order that her golden dress might become visible.' And so it came to pass that 'when she knelt down, the golden robe gleamed through the slit,' and the recognition was soon accomplished. Another method of recognition is employed in the class of variants to which the Sicilian 'Betta Pilusa' belongs. When 'Hairy Betty' for the third time won the king's heart, at a ball in which she appeared in the dress on which all the beasts and the flowers of the earth were to be seen, he presented her with a costly ring. One morning she came into the kitchen while the cook was making the bread for the royal table, and she obtained leave to make a loaf herself. Into it she slipped the ring. When the bread was drawn out of the oven, only her loaf proved eatable, so it was served up to the king himself, who, on cutting it, discovered the ring. The cook was examined, and 'Hairy Betty' was produced in her catskin dress. This she flung aside, and appeared 'young and lovely, as she really was, and in her beautiful gleaming robe.' The recognition by means of a ring is, as every one knows, one of the commonest contrivances for bringing a story of adventure to a close.

Now with this tale of a radiant princess who adopts a degrading disguise, appears at times in her natural glory, but conceals it again without any apparent reason, till her own caprice, or an accident which she had not foreseen, leads to her final recognition, let us compare one of the numerous stories about a radiant prince who disguises himself in a like manner, reveals himself at intervals in his true form, returns to his place of concealment with an equal want of apparent reason, and is at last fortuitously recognised. The well-known German tale of 'The Iron Man,'[8] gives a very interesting version of the story, as also does the Norse tale of 'The Widow's Son.' As these are accessible to every English reader, it may be as well to quote here one of the less generally available variants of this widely-spread narrative. The Russian tale of 'Neznaiko,' in Afanasief's collection (vii. No. 10), relates how the young Ivan was persecuted by his stepmother, who tried several methods of killing him, but was always foiled by the wise advice given to him by a mysterious colt to which he was tenderly attached. At length she persuaded her husband to promise that the colt should be killed. Hearing of this, Ivan ran to the stable, mounted the colt in haste, and fled with it from his father's house. After a time they came to a place where cattle were grazing. There the colt left Ivan, promising to return when summoned by the burning of one of the hairs from its tail which it left with him for that purpose. But before parting with its master it told him to kill one of the oxen, flay it, and don its hide; also to conceal his fair locks under a covering of bladder, and never to make any other reply to whatsoever questions might be asked him than 'I don't know.' Ivan did as he was told, and presently, to the surprise of all who met him, there was seen walking along 'ever such a wonder; a beast not a beast, a man not a man, hide bound, head bladder-covered,' answering all questions with an 'I don't know.' 'Well then,' said they, 'as you can only say *Ne Znayu*, let your name be "Neznaiko," or "Don't know."' Even the king to whom he was brought as an acceptable monster could get nothing but his usual answer. So orders were given that he should be stationed in the garden, to act as a scarecrow in order to keep the birds away from the fruit, but he was to get his meals in the royal kitchen. Now it happened about this time that an Arab prince proposed for the hand of the king's daughter, and, when his suit was rejected, raised an immense army and invaded the king's realm. Ruin stared that monarch in the face. But Neznaiko doffed his bladder cap, flung off his ox-hide, went out into the open field, and burnt one of the magic horsehairs. Immediately there appeared by his side a wondrous steed. On to its back vaulted Neznaiko, and rode against the infidel foe. To tear from a slain enemy his golden armour, and to don it himself, was the work of a moment. Then he dashed, irresistible, among the Arab ranks. 'Whichever way he turned, there heads flew before him. It was exactly like mowing hay.' With rapture did the king and his fair daughter view his exploits from the walls of the beleaguered city. But when they came down to greet the victor, there was no such hero to be found. In quite unheroic garb Ivan had returned to his task of scaring the crows from the palace garden. A second time did the Arab prince renew his suit and his invasion, and again did Ivan, as a warrior in golden armour, slaughter his troops and put him to flight. On this occasion he was slightly wounded in the arm, and was also brought before the king. But he would not stay at the palace: he must needs ride away for a time into the open field. Before he rode off, however, the king's daughter took a scarf from her fair neck and with it bound up his wounded arm.

Soon after this a great feast was given at the palace. As the guests strolled through the garden they saw Ivan, and wondered at

his strange aspect. 'What sort of monster is this?' they asked. 'That is
Neznaiko,' replied the king: 'acts for me in place of a scarecrow,
keeps the birds away from the appletrees.' But his daughter saw that
Neznaiko's arm was bound up, and recognised the scarf she had
given to the heroic winner of the fight. 'She blushed, but said
nothing at the time.' Only thenceforth 'she took to walking in the
garden and gazing at Neznaiko, and she quite forgot even so much
as to think about feasts and other amusements.' At length she asked
her father to let her marry his scarecrow. Naturally surprised, he
expostulated. But when she cried, 'If you don't make him my
husband I'll never marry any one, I'll live and die an old maid,' he
reluctantly gave his consent. The marriage had just taken place
when the Arab prince for the third time demanded the hand of the
princess. 'My daughter is married,' replied the king. 'If you like,
come and see for yourself.' The Arab came, saw that the fair
princess was married to 'ever such a monster,' and challenged him to
mortal combat. Then Ivan flung off his bladder cap and his garb of
hide, mounted his good steed, and rode away to the fight, manifesting
himself to all eyes under his heroic aspect. The Arab suitor was soon
knocked on the head. And when Ivan rode back triumphant, the
king perceived that his son-in-law was 'no monster, but a hero
strong and fair.'

In this variant of the story, nothing definite is said as to the
golden nature of the hero's hair. But in many others, as in the
German and Norse tales already referred to, as well as in numerous
variants found in many lands, not only is great stress laid upon the
fact that his locks are of gold, but an account and explanation of the
gilding process is given. Into this, however, it is at present unnecessary to enter. It is sufficient for our purposes to show how closely
the story of the radiant hero—who is persecuted by a stepmother
and aided by a supernatural horse, and whose brightness is temporarily concealed under a covering of skin or hide, but who finally
emerges from it to remain permanently resplendent—corresponds
with the story of the radiant heroine who is ill used by a stepmother
and assisted by a supernatural cow, and whose radiance is likewise
concealed, but only for a time, under some sort of unseemly exterior,
frequently formed out of some beast's hard or furry skin. The tales
of 'Goldenlocks' and of 'Cinderella—Catskin' are evidently twin
forms of the same narrative, brother and sister developments of the

same historical or mythological germ. In one instance the two forms have been combined into one narrative, ending with a double recognition. The Lithuanian story of 'The King's Fair Daughter' (Schleicher, No. 7) tells how a princess was urged to accept a hateful suitor after the death of her mother, who had been a remarkable beauty, having 'around her head the stars, on its front the sun, and on its back the moon.' An old woman's friendly counsels enabled her to obtain 'a silver robe, a diamond ring, and gold shoes,' as well as a disguising cloak lined with skins of an unattractive kind. With these she fled from court. After a time she came to a piece of water, and was obliged to go on board a vessel. The *sziporius* or skipper wanted her to marry him, and when she would not consent, he threw her overboard. But 'she jumped ashore,' and pursued her journey. Coming one day to a place where stood great stones, she prayed that a dwelling might be opened for her. And her prayer was at once granted. In her dwelling within the rock, which always opened to let her in or out, she left her fine raiment, and went forth to live in a grand house, performing the duties of a *pelendruse* or cinder-wench. In that house she found her brother, who had also fled from home, and was acting.as a clerk. But he did not recognise in the grimy servant-maid his princely sister. From time to time she used to go to her stone dwelling, don her fair raiment, and drive to a church in a carriage which always appeared for the purpose, her beautiful visage and costume making a great impression on the mind of the astonished clerk. One day she left the church rather later than usual, so she had not time enough to change her dress, and merely 'put her everyday clothes over those fine ones.' That day she was summoned by the clerk to 'dress his hair.' And while she dressed his hair, his head resting on her knees, 'he took to scratching her dress, and scratched through it down to the mantle' which it covered. 'So when he had lifted his head from her knees, he tore off her headdress from her head, and immediately perceived that she was his sister. Then they two went forth from that house, but no one knew whither they went.'

All commentators will doubtless agree that the stories of Cinderella and Goldenlocks spring from the same root. But they will differ widely when the question arises as to whether that root was or was not of a mythological nature, and also as to what was, in either case, its original form and significance. The majority of the critics who

have lately handled the subject have not the slightest doubt about
the whole matter. 'It is the story of the Sun and the Dawn,' says Mr.
J. Thackray Bunce, in the latest work on the subject, a pretty little
book on 'Fairy Tales: their Origin and Meaning;' 'Cinderella, grey
and dark and dull, is all neglected when she is away from the Sun,
obscured by the envious Clouds, her sisters, and by her stepmother,
the Night. So she is Aurora, the Dawn, and the fairy Prince is the
Morning Sun, ever pursuing her to claim her for his bride.' According to Professor de Gubernatis, in his 'Zoological Mythology'
(ii. 281), 'Ahalyâ (the evening Aurora) in the ashes is the germ of the
story of Cinderella, and of the daughter of the King of Dacia,
persecuted by her lover, her father himself.' It seems unfortunate
that so many 'storiologists' have committed themselves to the support of the cause of the Dawn and the Afterglow, the 'Morning and
Evening Auroras,' before the claims to consideration of other natural phenomena or forces were fully considered and disposed of in a
manner satisfactory to at least the great majority of judges. Too few
of the writers on the meaning of popular tales seem to have remembered Professor Max Müller's warning that 'this is a subject which
requires the most delicate handling and the most careful analysis.'
Instead of warily feeling their way over an obscure and unfamiliar
field, they race across it towards their conclusions, bent upon taking
every obstacle in their stride. The consequence is that they now and
then meet, or to the eyes of unenthusiastic spectators appear to
meet, with mishaps of a somewhat ludicrous nature. Thus, when we
are told that the justly saddened mother of Beanstalk Jack, by
throwing her apron over her head and weeping, figures 'the night
and the rain,' we are apt to be led by our perception of the ridiculous
towards an inclination to laugh at the whole system according to
which so many stories are resolved into nature-myths. But that
system, if used discreetly, appears to lead to results not otherwise
attainable. In the case of certain, but by no means all, popular tales,
it offers an apparently reasonable solution of many problems. Just
as it seems really true that at least many of the stories of fair maidens
released from the captivity in which they were kept by demoniacal
beings 'can be traced back to mythological traditions about the
Spring being released from the bonds of Winter, the Sun being
rescued from the darkness of the Night, the Dawn being brought
back from the far West, the Waters being set free from the prison of

the Clouds,'[9] so it appears not unreasonable to suppose that the large group of tales of the Cinderella class may be referred for their origin to similar mythological traditions. In all the numerous narratives about brave princes and beautiful princesses who, apparently without sufficient reason, conceal under a foul disguise their fair nature, emerge at times from their seclusion and obscurity, but capriciously return to their degraded positions, until they are finally revealed in their splendour by accident or destiny—in all these stories about a Rashie-Coat, a Katie Woodencloak, a Goldenlocks, or any other of Cinderella's brothers and sisters, there appears to be a mythological element capable of being not unreasonably attributed to the feelings with which, at an early myth-making period, prescientific man regarded the effect of the forces, the splendour of the phenomena, of nature. But there is a vast difference between regarding as a nature-myth in general the germ of the legends from which have sprung the stories of the Cinderella cycle, and identifying with precision the particular atmospheric phenomenon which all its heroes and heroines are supposed to symbolise. And there is an equally wide difference between the reasonableness of seeking for a mythological explanation of a legend when traced back to its oldest known form, and the utter absurdity of attempting to squeeze a mythical meaning out of every incident in a modern nursery-tale, which has perhaps been either considerably enlarged or cruelly 'clippit and nippit' by successive generations of rustic repeaters, and has most certainly been greatly modified and dressed by its literary introducers into polite society. No one can fail to perceive how great a gulf divides the system of interpretation which Professor Max Müller has applied to Vedic myths from that adopted in the case of such manifest modernisations as 'Little Red Ridinghood' by critics who forget that (to use his words) 'before any comparison can be instituted between nursery tales of Germany, England, and India, each tale must be traced back to a legend or myth from whence it arose, and in which it had a natural meaning; otherwise we cannot hope to arrive at any satisfactory results' (*Chips,* ii. 249).

Let us turn now to other systems of interpretation. One school of critics utterly refuses to accept any mythological solution of fairy-tale riddles, another is at least inclined to reduce the mythological element in popular tales to a minimum, a third admits mythology into the field but objects to its assuming what is popularly known as the 'solar' form, to which a fourth school is devoted with intense zeal. At least four different explanations of the Cinderella—Rashie-Coat story may therefore be offered to the consideration of an earnest inquirer into its significance. It may be a nature-myth symbolising the renewed brightness of the earth after its nocturnal or wintry eclipse. The rough skin or hide which 'Hairy Betty' wears, not to speak of Katie Woodencloak's still tougher covering, greatly resembles the 'husk' which hides the brilliance of the beast to whom the Beauty of so many tales is married, and is therefore suggestive of an origin connected with Indian mythology.[10] The 'stepmother' opening of the story is too simple to require an explanation, and the appearance in fine clothes, at church or palace, of a usually ill-dressed damsel may be considered not incredible. As to the 'slipper' termination, the opinion has already been expressed that it is merely a convenient recognition makeshift.

The 'unlawful marriage' opening of the Rashie-Coat story offers a difficulty, but it is accounted for to their own satisfaction by critics both of the mythological and of the historical school. Mythologists say that all stories about such marriages mean nothing more than does the dialogue in the Veda between Yama and his twin-sister Yamí, in which 'she (the night) implores her brother (the day) to make her his wife, and he declines her offer because, as he says, "they have thought it sin that a brother should marry his sister."'[11] But by many eyes these narratives are regarded as ancient traditions which preserve the memory of customs long obsolete and all but forgotten. It is because such stories refer to savage times that they are so valuable, it is said, and therefore it is well to compare them with such tales and traditions as are now current among existing savages. This opinion is one that is well worthy of discussion, but at present little more can be done than to point out that the popular tales which are best known to us possess but few counterparts in genuine savage folk-lore. Some of their incidents, it is true, find their parallels in tales which are told by wild races unable to boast of a drop of Aryan blood. But the dramatic narratives known to us as the stories of Cinderella, 'Puss in Boots,' and the like, in which a regular sequence of acts or scenes is maintained unaltered in various climes and centuries, seem unknown to savage countries, unless they have been introduced from more cultured lands. A few of the incidents related in the stories cited in the present article closely resemble parts of savage tales. We may take as an example the Russian account of the sister who, when pursued by her brother, sinks into the earth and so escapes. In a Zulu tale,[12] a sister whose brother is pursuing her with murderous intent, exclaims, 'Open, earth, that I may enter, for I am about to die this day,' whereupon 'the earth opened and Untombi-yapansi entered.' In vain did her brother Usilwane seek for her when he arrived. Her subsequent adventures, also, are akin to those of Cinderella. Originally 'her body glistened, for she was like brass,' but 'she took some black earth and smeared her body with it,' and so eclipsed her natural radiance. Eventually, however, she was watched by 'the chief,' who saw her, 'dirty and very black,' enter a pool, and emerge from it, 'with her body glistening like brass,' put on garments and ornaments which arose out of the ground, and behave altogether like the brilliant heroine she really was. There seems to be good reason for looking upon Untombi-yapansi as a Zulu Cinderella. But how far a foreign influence has been exercised upon the Zulu tale, it would be difficult to decide.

How far, also, the story of Rashie-Coat's proposed marriage refers to ancient ideas about the lawfulness of unions now disallowed, is a question not easily to be answered. There is no doubt that the memory of obsolete customs may be long preserved in folk-lore. We may take as an instance the Russian story of the Lubok or Birch Bark, in which it would seem unreasonable to look for a mythological kernel. There exist in many countries a number of stories showing how a man's unfilial conduct towards his father was brought to a close by a chance remark made by his infant son. In the forms it assumes there is considerable variety, but the moral is always the same. In a well-known German tale in the Grimm collection, an old man is obliged by his son and his son's wife to eat apart, out of a wooden bowl, on account of the slobbering habits due to his great age. His son's little boy is observed one day to be fashioning a small wooden bowl. When asked for what it is intended, he says: 'It's for father to eat out of when he's as old as grandfather.' Whereupon the father's conscience smites him, and the grandfather is allowed a plate at the table as before. In an Italian form of the story borrowed from one of the French *fabliaux,* a man follows the custom of the country and packs off his old father to die in what may be called the workhouse, sending him a couple of shirts by the

hands of his young son, the old man's grandson. The boy brings
back one of them, and explains that it will do for his father to wear
when his turn comes to go to the workhouse. Whereupon the man's
heart is touched, and he fetches his aged parent home. The Russian
story is more valuable, because it refers to a custom which undoubtedly once existed in many lands—that of killing off old people.
Among nomads, who would find it difficult to carry about with
them their aged relations, such a custom might naturally arise. At all
events, it is on such a custom that the tale is founded. It runs as
follows. In former days it was customary, when old folks reached a
certain age, for their sons, if they had any, to take them out into the
forest, and there to leave them to die. Once upon a time a son thus
escorted from home, on what was meant to be his last journey, his
aged father. Wishing to make that journey as comfortable as possible
for the time-stricken traveller, he stretched a large piece of birch-tree
bark in his cart, seated the intended victim upon it, and drove off to
the forest. Along with him went his own young son, a boy of tender
years. Having reached the appointed spot, he thereon deposited the
aged man, having first, with filial attention, stretched on the possibly
damp ground the sheet of bark for him to sit upon. Just as he was
about to drive away home with his boy, that innocent child asked
him if it would not be better to take back the bark. 'Why so?' he
replied. 'Because,' said the boy, 'it will do for you to sit upon when
the time comes for me to leave you in the forest.' Touched by his
child's simple words, the father hastened to where the grandfather
was sitting, put him back into the cart, and drove him quickly home.
From that time he carefully tended the old man till he died. And his
example produced such an effect that all the other people in that
land gave up the practice of exposing their parents to death when
they grew old.[13]

Now, it would be quite beside the mark to suggest a mythological
explanation of this pathetic tale. It evidently refers to an actual
custom once observed by real men, not to some supposed action
attributed to imaginary gods. The evidence for the former existence
of the custom is copious and undeniable. Even the familiar expression 'a sardonic grin' has been supposed by some philologists to
contain a reference to it. For the ancient Sardones were in the habit,
when they grew old, of being killed and eaten by their friends and
relatives. Before their death they used to invite their kith and kin to

come and eat them on a certain day. And they were expected to smile while uttering the words of invitation. But their smiles, on such occasions, were apt to be somewhat constrained and even at times ghastly. Wherefore, the particular kind of contraction of the risible muscles acquired the name of the 'Sardonic grin.' On so clear a point it is unnecessary to dwell longer. But it will be as well to point out that there is sometimes risk in attributing legends and traditions to an historical rather than a mythical origin. Many customs are mentioned in popular tales which can scarcely have prevailed among mankind at even the most prehistoric period. There are a number of stories, for instance, about girls who are so fond of their relatives that they eat them up. In the Russian 'Witch and Sun's Sister,' and in the Avar 'Brother and Sister,' a maiden of this kind is described as first devouring the whole of her family, and then attempting to eat the hero of the tale, her last surviving brother. Now, a belief in such hungry damsels, perpetually seeking what they may devour, is prevalent at the present day in Ceylon, the existence of such 'poison girls,' as they are called, being generally accounted for by demoniacal possession. From such a wild belief tales of the kind just mentioned might naturally spring without their being founded upon any real custom. It is improbable that at any period of the world's history it was customary for sisters to eat their brothers. Nor is it likely that human fathers were ever in the habit of eating their children, as might be supposed, if we thought it necessary to see in the tale of how Kronos devoured his offspring an allusion to a custom or even an isolated fact.[14] What seems to be really demanded from every interpreter of old tradition, every explorer of the dark field of popular fiction, is a wariness that will not allow itself to be hoodwinked by any prejudice in favour of this or that particular theory. Every piece of evidence ought to be carefully tested and fairly weighed, whether it confirms the examiner's own opinion or not. If this be done, he will probably find that different classes of legends must be explained in divers manners. The more he becomes acquainted with popular tales, the less he will be inclined to seek for any single method of solving all their manifold problems. Not over often will he be able to satisfy himself that he has arrived at even a fairy-tale's ultimate reason for existence. The greater pleasure will he have when he is enabled to trace the growth of a narrative, to watch its increase from its original germ to its final development.

NOTES

[1]Vuk Karajich, No. 32.

[2]*West Highland Tales,* i. 225.

[3]*Spectator,* January 4, 1879.

[4]An amusing article on this question appeared in the *Daily Telegraph,* December 27, 1878, in reply to the support given by 'X' in the *Times* to the cause of *vair.*

[5]Schiefner's *Anarische Texte,* p. 68.

[6]Miss Frere's *Old Deccan Days,* No. 1.

[7]Gonzenbach, No. 38. *Pilusa* in the Sicilian form of *pilosa,* hairy.

[8]*Der Eisenhans,* Grimm, No. 136.

[9]Max Müller, *Chips,* ii. 237.

[10]For the mythological meaning of 'Beauty and the Beast,' see the *Nineteenth Century,* December 1878.

[11]Max Müller, *Lectures on the Science of Language,* sixth edition, ii. 557.

[12]Bishop Callaway's *Nursery Tales, &c., of the Zulus,* i. 300, n.

[13]Afanasief, *Skazki,* vol. vii., No. 51.

[14]Since this article was written, an excellent work on savage life has been published by Mr. J.A. Farrer, entitled *Primitive Manners and Customs.* It contains two chapters on 'The Fairy-lore of Savages' and 'Comparative Folk-lore,' to which the reader may be referred for the arguments in favour of preferring an ethnographical to a mythological solution of popular tales. And some interesting articles have appeared in *Notes and Queries* on the subject of *vair.* In No. 286, 'D. P.,' referring to the letters signed 'X.' and 'E. de B.' in the *Times* for December 23 and 24, 1878, quotes from La Colombière's *Science Héroïque* (Paris, 1699) a description of how *vair* was composed of patches 'faites en forme de petits pots de verre.' No. 299 contains three contributions to the *vair* controversy, especially as regards the old English word 'miniver.' As it is often supposed that the idea is a very new one that Cinderella's slipper was really of *vair,* not of *verre,* it may be as well to quote what Balzac said on the subject more than forty years ago. In his *Etudes philosophiques sur Catherine de Médicis,* published in 1836, he wrote as follows:—'On distinguait le grand et le menu vair. Ce mot, depuis cent ans, est si bien tombé en désuétude que, dans un nombre infini d'éditions des contes de Perrault, la célèbre pantoufle de Cendrillon, sans doute de *menu vair* [or miniver], est présentée comme étant de *verre.*'

Notes on Cinderella

E. Sidney Hartland

The beginning of modern folklore scholarship on Cinderella may be said to have been the publication in 1893 of Marian Roalfe Cox's Cinderella. *Fellow members of the English Folklore Society (founded in 1878) were quick to praise the impressive assemblage of Cinderella texts. The journal* Folklore, *organ of the Society, published in the same year a series of articles by Alfred Nutt, Joseph Jacobs, and Andrew Lang, who responded to the mass of data so assiduously gathered by Miss Cox. E. Sidney Hartland (1848–1927), another important folklorist of the period, who had in fact assisted Miss Cox in locating sources for her monograph, wrote his own reaction to the book and presented it at the International Folklore Congress of the World's Columbian Exposition held in Chicago in July, 1893. Apparently, as so often happens with papers given at international congresses, Hartland's essay, though eventually published in the Congress proceedings in 1898, was effectively lost. At least it seems not to have been cited by any of the many scholars who have written on Cinderella since that time.*

Hartland reviews the Cinderella typology established by Miss Cox and then goes on to consider the possible origin of individual incidents as well as the tale itself. Hartland, like most of his British colleagues of that era, was greatly influenced by the Darwinian

Reprinted from Helen Wheeler Bassett and Frederick Starr, eds., *The International Folk-Lore Congress of the World's Columbian Exposition*, Chicago, July, 1893 (Chicago: Charles H. Sergel Company, 1898), pp. 125–136.

theory of evolution. For one thing, he believed in unilinear evolution, according to which all peoples on the face of the earth progressed through identical stages, moving from an early period of savagery through an intermediate period of barbarism before finally arriving at the third period of civilization. For another, Hartland was convinced that folk narratives had also evolved, and he even went so far as to suggest that "a process analogous with that of natural selection, which we may call traditional selection," was largely responsible for determining which version was transmitted from one generation to another. It was traditional selection, Hartland avowed, that tended to "eliminate the ruder and coarser, preserving and refining, not necessarily the more credible, but the more artistic." The notion of evolution as progress made such a view entirely plausible. The reader will see reflections of Hartland's evolutionary bias in his remarks on Cinderella.

Another nineteenth-century theory which enjoyed considerable popularity contended that many European tales derived from Indic origins. The rise of Indo-European studies generally, especially in regard to the demonstrated relationships between languages (Sanskrit and Greek, for example) made this a reasonable enough hypothesis in folktale scholarship. If a proto-Indo-European language could be historically reconstructed, why not a proto-Indo-European mythology? From Theodor Benfey's introduction to his 1859 translation of the classic Indian folktale collection The Panchatantra *to the writings of Max Müller, Joseph Jacobs and the erudite Emmanuel Cosquin, the Indianist origin of European fairytales was forcefully argued. For this reason Hartland felt obliged to take up the question of the possible Indian origin of Cinderella.*

For Cosquin's discussion of the issue, see "La Pantoufle de Cendrillon dans l'Inde," Revue des traditions populaires, *28 (1913), 241-269. Hartland had actually written on Cinderella earlier, in his paper "The Outcast Child,"* Folk-Lore Journal, *4 (1886), 308-349. For more of Hartland's views on folktale, see his major works,* The Science of Fairy Tales *(London: Methuen, 1890), and* The Legend of Perseus, *3 vols. (London: D. Nutt, 1894-1896). For a review of Hartland's accomplishments, see Richard M. Dorson,* The British Folklorists: A History *(Chicago: University of Chicago Press, 1968), pp. 239-248.*

For some of the other responses inspired by Miss Cox's Cinder-
ella, *See Alfred Nutt, "Cinderella and Britain," Folk-Lore, 4 (1893),
133-141; Joseph Jacobs, "Cinderella in Britain," Folk-Lore, 4 (1893),
269-284; and Andrew Lang, "Cinderella and the Diffusion of Tales,"
Folk-Lore, 4 (1893), 413-433. For a more recent appreciation of
Miss Cox's monograph, see Katharine M. Briggs, "Two Great
English Monographs," in Linda Dégh, Henry Glassie, and Felix
Oinas, eds., Folklore Today: A Festschrift for Richard M. Dorson
(Bloomington: Indiana University Research Center for Language
and Semiotic Studies, 1976), pp. 57-63.*

The volume of six hundred pages, recently issued by the Folk-
Lore Society and entitled *Cinderella*, is the largest and most important contribution ever made to the study of a single folk-tale. It
consists entirely of abstracts of variants, with a few useful notes on
special points. Miss Marian Roalfe Cox, to whom we owe it, has
been unwearied in her industry; and her judgment, skill and wide
knowledge of folk-tales have enabled her to produce a collection
simply indispensable to every student. We may differ, perhaps, on
certain points of arrangement—for instance, on twofold tabulation;
but we are quite sure that neither this nor any other detail of
method has been adopted without due consideration, and at least it
has been followed logically to the end.

I feel, however, that, to those students who know the volume,
praise is superfluous. The book has become as much a part of the
apparatus of their study as the blowpipe is of an analytical chemist's.
The following notes, therefore, aim at stating (rather than fully
discussing) a few of the many questions raised by the variants
brought together.

In view of recent controversies the most important of the problems connected with a folk-tale relates to the possibility of tracing its
origin to any definite locality or race of men. Of such a problem a
collection of three hundred and forty-five variants ought to offer
some hopes of solution. Miss Cox finds in the stories three well-
marked types, which she has named after the stories best known to
English-speaking students: Cinderella, Catskin, and Cap o' Rushes.
Beside these three, there is a number of variants sometimes approximating to one, sometimes to another, of the types, but not properly

to be comprised under either of them, and consequently classed together as indeterminate. The stories occur in the following proportions:

Cinderella	137
Catskin	79
Cap o' Rushes	26
Indeterminate	80
	322

To these must be added twenty-three hero-tales, that is, tales wherein the hero is a masculine Cinderella.

Discarding the last class, we may take the smallest of the other classes for the sake of convenience, and inquire whether it reveals anything as to its place of origin. All the stories of the Cap o' Rushes type open with an incident familiar to us as the starting point of King Lear's misfortunes. A king asks his daughters how much they love him. The elder ones give answers which are satisfactory. The youngest merely says she loves him like salt. At this he is so indignant, that he either casts her off, or, in some cases, goes the length of ordering her to be put to death and her blood or some of her organs brought to him in proof of compliance. We may, I think, safely assume that this order is the most archaic form of the incident; for with the softening of manners which accompanies progress in civilization, such an order would become more and more repulsive and more and more useless for the purposes of the story; and it would be, therefore, dropped out. Here we have accordingly taken one step in our search. The next is to examine the form and consequences of the order to kill. The order appears in two forms: first, a simple order to kill; and second, an order accompanied by the requirement of proof, and followed by the king's deception with the blood, etc., of some brute slain for the purpose. Here, again, the simpler form is undoubtedly the less archaic; and we may, therefore, discard it. This is a second step in our search. We have left nine stories containing the deception of the king with a possible tenth, No. 317, only given by Dr. Pitré, who reports it in outline. They are as follows:

No.	Locality or People	Proof of Death
313	Avellins, Southern Italy	Sheep's blood and heroine's finger.
208	Parma	Sheep's heart.
209	Venice	Dog's eyes and heart.
312	Abruzzi	Heroine's clothes soaked in dog's blood.
315	Sicily	Dog's tongue and heroine's garment, rent.
316	″	Dog's blood.
211	Gascony	Dog's tongue.
226	Basque	Horse's heart.
210	Ovideo, Spain	Bitch's eyes.

But the order to kill, and the subsequent deception, occur in some other stories recorded in the volume.

CINDERELLA TYPE

58	Poland	Dog's heart and finger of corpse with heroine's ring on it.

CATSKIN TYPE

204	Poland	Hare's heart. (A dog is the messenger.)

INDETERMINATE (QUERY, CATSKIN?) TYPE

304	Basque	Ass's heart.

INDETERMINATE (LITTLE SNOWWHITE?) TYPE

286	Tuscany	Lamb's heart and eyes, and blood-stained dress.

MASCULINE TYPE

330	Poland	Some portion of dog.

Let us note, before proceeding, the geographical distribution of these proofs of obedience. They occur in Italy, France, Spain, and Poland. In Italy, on the western side of the Apennines, a sheep's

blood or heart and a lamb's heart and eyes are found. On the other
side of Italy (Venice and Abruzzi), and in Sicily, we get a dog's eyes
and heart, clothes soaked in dog's blood, a dog's tongue and a dog's
blood. In Gascony, France, we find a dog's tongue; in the province
of Oviedo, Spain, a bitch's eyes; and in Poland a dog's heart, and
some portion of a dog. Elsewhere in Poland, we come upon a hare's
heart, but a dog is sent by the heroine's father to kill her. Among the
Basques, the trophy is either a horse's or an ass's heart. Further, in
Italy, a part of the heroine's dress is brought, in stories from the
Abruzzi, from Tuscany, and from Sicily; in a story from Southern
Italy, the heroine's finger, and in a Polish tale, a corpse's finger,
wearing the heroine's ring. There appears at first sight to be some
trace of local or racial influence in the selection of these proofs. The
incident, however, occurs in other tales not belonging to the Cinderella Cycle, and, therefore, not included in Miss Cox's selection. We
will examine some of these.

Group to which the Story belongs.	Locality or People.	Proof of Death	Authority
Persecuted wife	Tuscany	Heroine's eyes	De Gubernatis, Sante Stephano, p. 35.
Outcast child (language of beasts).	Monfratto	Dog's heart	Comparetti, vol. i., p. 242.
Persecuted wife	Pistoja	Dog's tongue	Nerucci, p. 421.
Outcast child (language of beasts).	Mantua	Dog's heart	Visentini, p. 121.
Persecuted wife	Sicily	Two kid's hearts and tongues. (Two children)	Gonzenbach, vol. i., p. 15.
Outcast child— Joseph.	Abruzzi	Sheep's eyes	De Nino, vol. iii., p. 172.
Persecuted wife	Italy	Shift dipped in wild beast's blood.	D'Ancona, Sacré Rappresentazioni, vol. iii.; p. 200 citing M.S. Italian poem of the 16th century.
" "	Italian Tyrol	Dog's heart	Schneller, p. 137.

Group to which the Story belongs.	Locality or People.	Proof of Death	Authority
" "	German Tyrol.	Dog's tongue	Zingerle, vol. ii., p. 124.
Outcast child (language of beasts).	Upper Valais, Switzerland.	Deer's eyes and tongue.	Grimm's tales, transl. by Wm. Hurst, vol. i., p. 136.
Persecuted wife	Hesse	Hind's eyes and tongue.	do. p. 127.
Outcast child (language of beasts).	Alsace	Roebuck's heart and heroine's hands and feet.	Stoeber, vol. i., p. 73.
" "	Normandy	Bitch's heart	Fleury, p. 123.
" "	Brittany	Dog's heart	Mélusine, vol. i., col. 300.
Little Snowwhite?	Lorraine	"	Cosquin, vol. ii., p. 323.
Persecuted wife	France	Heroine's clothes.	Chaucer Analogues, p. 397, citing poem in Latin of the 12th century.
Little Snowwhite	Iceland	Dog's tongue, blood, and lock of heroine's hair.	Powell and Magnussen, vol. ii., p. 402., from Arnason.
Outcast child (value of salt).	Catalonia, Spain.	Cup of blood and heroine's big toe.	Maspons y Labros, vol. i., p. 55.
Persecuted wife	Spain	Eyes and heart of another person	D'Ancona, vol. iii., p. 203, citing poem by Juan Miguel del Fuego of 18th century.
Little Snowwhite	Portugal	Bitch's tongue	Pedroso, p. 3.
Outcast child (Joseph type).	Brazil	Heroine's finger.	Romero, p. 12.
" "	Basque	Dog's heart	Webster, p. 137.
" "	Transylvanian gypsy	Dog's blood	Von Wilslocki, Volksdichtungen, p. 289.
" "	"	He-goat's blood.	do p. 294
" (?) "	"	Dog's heart	do p. 269.
" "	Astypalala, Greece.	Blood stained shirt and finger	Geldart, p. 154.

This list contains stories from countries as far apart as Iceland and Japan; and an inspection and comparison with the previous list will dissipate any hopes of being able to trace either local or racial influence in the form assumed by the incident.

If there be direct connection between stories containing the same form of the incident, it must be by oral transmission over vast spaces, and independently of race; a difficult matter to prove or disprove without a much larger collection of examples, and which would lead us far outside the subject of Cinderella. At present, all we can say is that the dog appears to be the favorite animal, whose blood or organs supply the place of the hero's. This is but natural, seeing how universally he is the companion of man.

There is another point to which we may turn for information. In a small number of variants the heroine in disguise becomes a menial having charge of the poultry; and the creatures under her care, seeing her when she dons the gorgeous dresses, betray her by their admiration expressed in human language. Now it need hardly be said that talking birds, like other talking animals, are found all the world over. But the special incident here referred to is found in a very small area, namely, only in Italy (Nos. 139, 140, 141, 183, 217 and 285), and in Brittany (No. 251). In two Spanish tales (Nos. 178 and 210), the geese forget to feed in their admiration, and die, and in a Wallachian story (No. 298), the heroine is seen by reapers when she secretly changes her dress, and they tell of her. These three stories may perhaps be considered as modernized variants. The incident also occurs in a Spanish tale (Masponse y Labros, vol. i., page 55), mentioned in the list given on a preceding page. It could, of course, only be related in places where poultry (hens, geese, or turkeys) were an important part of the domestic *ménage*. It seems, in fact, to be a form of the animal witness, an important personage in a large number of Cinderella variants. But there is nothing to show whence this particular form was derived, unless we may conclude from the greater number of instances which have been collected in Italy, that it is Italian in origin. This, at best, would be a doubtful inference.

Passing for a while from the consideration of single incidents, can we gather by any examination of the story as a whole, whence it has come? It would be impossible to make any such examination exhaustively in a short paper. The most we could do is to test the claims of one country as an example of the method which may be adopted with all. And as India has had more advocates for her copyright of fairy tales than any other land, we may as well deal with her claims to the invention of Cinderella. Miss Cox gives three Indian variants: one (No. 25), originally published in the Bombay Gazette, in 1864; one (No. 235), told to Miss Frere by an ayah who had heard it from her grandmother, a Christian convert with much heathenism still lingering about her; and the third (No. 307), from Salsette, near Bombay.

We may dispose of the second of these tales at once. It is often difficult to decide whether a tale comes within the definition of a given group, so infinitely do the plots shade off into one another. The story of Sodewa Bai has no connection with the Cinderella group, save the lost slipper. The rajah, who is the heroine's father, causes the lost slipper to be cried and reward offered for its restoration. A prince, finding it, by his mother's advice, asks for her lady's hand in recompense and obtains it. The heroine, however, was born with a golden necklace, which contains her soul, and the greater part of the tale is concerned with the necklace and the consequences of its loss. It is obvious that if this tale was rightly included in the tabulation, the Egyptian fable of Rhodopis had still better claim.

In the third tale, the heroine is born of a blister on a beggar's thumb. She and her six sisters (born in the ordinary way) are abandoned by their father and find a palace, where they live. The heroine's room is the best, though her sisters do not know it. The six elder sisters go to church; the heroine follows them in gorgeous array, including golden slippers. At church the king's son falls in love with her. She loses a slipper in hurrying home, and is ultimately identified by it and married to the prince. The tale then falls into the persecuted wife type. Her sisters accuse her of giving birth to a stone and brooms, but the three babes who are really born are providentially preserved from death, and at length the heroine, through them, triumphs over her accusers. Here the heroine's birth and her sisters' envy contain many details which appear to be native. On the other hand, all the Cinderella incidents bear decidedly the impress of Europe. The people who tell the tale are Roman Catholics, and the tale, whatever its primitive form, has become so inextricably mingled with European elements, that no argument can be drawn from it in favor of an Indian source.

There remains the first story. Unfortunately we have it only at second or third hand, and only in an abstract. It is said to run as follows:—"Heroine is ill-treated by step-mother, who, finding that cow nourishes her with its milk, resolves to kill it. Cow bids heroine be comforted, and to take care to collect its bones, horns, skin and every part that is thrown away; above all, to avoid eating its flesh. Cow is killed, and heroine does as bidden. Prince is making choice of bride; heroine is left at home to cook supper whilst step-sister goes to palace. Cow returns to life, gives dresses and gold clogs to heroine. She drops one of these when prince is pursuing her, and when he comes to seek her she is hidden in granary. Cock betrays her presence. Prince marries her. Step-mother and step-sister are punished." This is a very important story for the advocates of the Indian origin of fairy tales; but we have so little information about it that it is not easy to build any structure of argument upon it. The cow certainly does not seem Hindoo. In a variant, we learn it is a fish that befriends the heroine. In Annam, there is a tale of which Mr. Landes has collected two variants (No. 68 and 69). In both of these the helpful animal is a fish beloved of the heroine; when the fish is killed and cooked, its bones collected by her pious hands turn into shoes, and (in the one case) to dresses. A crow carries off one of the shoes to the prince's palace. A proclamation is issued by him, offering marriage to the owner. The heroine, of course, is successful, in spite of the difficulties thrown in her way by her step-mother. Then follows the step-mother's scheme for substituting her own daughter. The heroine is put to death, and undergoes a series of transformations which end in her reappearance out of a fruit more beautiful than ever. She persuades her rival to jump into boiling water, in order to become equally lovely, and pickling her flesh, sends it to her mother as a delicacy. Notwithstanding Buddhism prevails in Annam, there is little evidence of it in this tale. The chief incidents disclose ideas as savage as can well be desired, though many of the externals have been adapted to the comparatively advanced style of civilization enjoyed by the Annamites and Tjannes. We may assume, therefore, that if the story entered Annam from Hindostan, as to which there is at present no evidence, it was not by a Buddhist channel.

Still more archaic are the Santal variants not given by Miss Cox, but found in Mr. Campbell's collection of *Santal Folk Tales*, recently issued from the Mission Press at Pokhuria, India. The Santals are non-Aryan aborigines of Bengal, interesting to students of folk-lore from their curious rites as well as their oral traditions.

They have a masculine, as well as feminine, Cinderella. The former undergoes the following adventures: He has charge of a cow that gives him food when his step-mother starves him. The step-mother feigns illness, in order to have the cow killed, but the cow and boy escape. From the cow descends a whole herd, which the boy tends in the jungle. Bathing one day he drops a hair in the river. A princess lower down the stream finds it and determines to marry the owner. A tame parrot helps her father's servants to find the boy, by stealing his flute and drawing him after it in pursuit. In one variant he is unfortunate, and the princess refuses to marry him after all. In the other, he has three flutes, with magical properties, uttering articulate sounds which twice balk the messenger's efforts to capture him, and ultimately, after his marriage, obtain for him a herd, from whence are descended all the tame buffaloes in India.

The feminine Cinderella is first drowned by her seven brothers' wives. She then reappears as a bamboo, out of which a fiddle is made. The fiddle is acquired by a village chief. The maiden comes out of it, in the absence of the household, and prepares the family meal. The chief's son watches, discovers and marries her. In a variant, she is first eaten by a monkey. The monkey dies. From his dead body a gourd grows, out of which a banjo is made, wherein the heroine hides. She is at length found and married to the rajah, who is already her sister's husband. Another variant relates that she was given by her brothers to a water spirit, in return for water. She reappears as a flower, and is married to the bridegroom, to whom she had been previously betrothed. Her brothers having become poor, come to her village offering firewood for sale; she recognizes and *fêtes* them, treating her youngest brother as Benjamin was treated by Joseph. The brothers, at her reproaches, cleave open the earth and plunge in. She catches the youngest—who had been no party to her ill-treatment—by the hair to save him, but in vain. The hair comes off in her hand. She plants it in the earth, and it becomes the blackthorn grass that now grows in the jungles.

The conclusion suggested by these tales is that the European tales were derived from at least two primitive forms, one approximating to the Cinderella type, the other to the Catskin type, and growing out of incidents of which our oldest example is, in the one case, in the Egyptian tale of the Two Brothers, where the lady's perfumed hair falls into the river and is found by the king, and in the other case in Ragnar Lodbrok's saga, where Aslang, Sigurd's daughter, is

concealed in Heime's harp. But, if so, there is probably no direct
connection between the Indian and European stories. This is confirmed, as to stories of the Cinderella type, by a Gaelic tale from
Inverness-shire, which, amid much of a more modern cast, has
preserved two very antique traits. A king, we are told, has a wife and
children, and also a daughter by a sheep. The wife causes the sheep
to be put to death. Its bones are preserved by its daughter; and the
sheep, after a time, revives as a beautiful princess. On the return of
the king's son there is to be a three days' feast, but the other children
only beat the sheep's daughter when she asks about it. Her mother,
however, clothes her in finery, and sends her to the feast, where the
king's son falls in love with her. She disappears each day, but on the
third day leaves one of her golden slippers behind. A proclamation
is issued offering marriage to its owner. A woman, in order to wear
it, cuts her big toe off, but the heroine is pointed out by a bird and
married to the king's son.[1] In other tales of this type, where the
heroine's mother and the helpful animal are identified, the mother
has originally had human form and has suffered a magical transformation. In many cases, as in the Indian tale reported from the
Calcutta Review, the identity has been completely forgotten. We
cannot doubt that the Gaelic tale, just cited, comes nearer to the
original, in this particular, than when the mother is afterwards
transformed, or where her identity with the helpful animal has been
forgotten. It is obvious, at least, that the tale could only have arisen
among a people so low in civilization that they had not yet attained
to the repugnance against sexual union in stories between man and
beast, and in actual fact between children of one sire but different
mothers. The Santals have passed beyond this stage. Still more
certainly have the Aryan Hindus, to whom the invention and dispersion of fairy tales is attributed by Mr. Cosquin and others; and
they had passed beyond it ages before the Buddhist propaganda,
from which the dispersion is usually dated.

With regard to the Indian origin of stories of the Catskin type,
another test may be applied. They usually open with an attempt by a
widowed father to marry his daughter, the heroine. All these stories
are European, with one exception (No. 189), which comes from
Kurdistan. The incident, needlessly repulsive to the feelings of every
European nation, could hardly have been imagined at a period when
the marriage of father and daughter was a thing quite unheard of.

More likely it was transferred from real life, at a stage in civilization when the sentiment of the community was against such a marriage, though it may not have been, or may only recently have become contrary to the tribal customs. Certain obscure references in the classics may, perhaps, imply that such marriages were not unknown to some of the barbarians with whom the Romans were brought into contact; but, with this possible exception, they have never been known during the historic period. They are reported, however, as practised in modern times among the Wanyoro, of Central Africa,[2] and among the Caribs;[3] while we are assured that it is the rule of the Piojes, of Ecuador, that "a widow shall take her son, a widower his daughter, to replace the deceased consort."[4] The ancient Persians are also asserted to have followed the same custom, though this is contested by the Parsees of the present day,[5] the kings of Siam, who are compelled to marry only into their own family, are said to be sometimes reduced to wedding their own sisters or daughters.[6] The practice is foreign to the universal sentiment of India, nor has the incident yet been discovered, so far as I am aware, in any Indian tale. The existing state of our knowledge, therefore, seems to preclude our attributing either the Cinderella or the Catskin type to an Indian origin.

I regret that the limits of human endurance, even at a Folk-Lore congress, do not permit of carrying these inquiries further, and the more so because I have felt hitherto compelled to draw wholly negative inferences. The subject opens so many vistas that it seems inexhaustible. I have merely attempted to put one or two tests to examine the bearing of a small portion of the material gathered in Miss Cox's learned volume on the question of origin. That the attempt has hardly penetrated beneath the surface of the problem, I should be the first to acknowledge. But it may serve to lead a valuable discussion by some who have studied the question more profoundly.

NOTES

[1]Cinderella, p. 534.
[2]Featherman, *Society History of the Races of Mankind.* Nigritians, p. 110.
[3]Ibid. *Chiopa and Guarawo.* Maranonians, p. 268.

[4]Brinton, *The American Race*, p. 274. Arthur Simpson, *Travels in the Wilds of Ecuador*. (London, 1886), p. 196.

[5]See *Next of Kin Marriages in Old Iran*, by Darab Dasher Reshotan Aunjana, B. A. (London, 1888), where the question is fully discussed by a Zoroastrian priest, anxious to remove the stigma fastened upon his religion.

[6]Col. James Low, in *Journal of the Indian Archipelago*, vol. i., p. 350, citing De Lombre.

Cinderella in China

R. D. Jameson

*Searches for the oldest version of Cinderella reflected a typical Euro-
pean bias insofar as for a long time the search area was pretty much
confined to Europe. Vestiges of such ethnocentrism remain, in the
sense that the two most familiar texts of the tale to this day continue
to be those of Perrault (French) and the Grimm brothers (German).
Yet the most ancient version of Cinderella unearthed thus far comes
from ninth-century China.*

*Evidently, Japanese folklorist Minakata did call attention to this
Chinese version in 1911, but it was not really known in the Western
world until 1932, when R.D. Jameson, then professor in the Department of Western Languages and Literature at the National Tsing
Hua University, devoted one of his series of three lectures on
Chinese folklore to the subject. Since that time, several additional
translations of the tale have been published, one by the distinguished
sinologist Arthur Waley. In 1974, folklorist Nai-Tung Ting of
Western Illinois University published an entire monograph on
Cinderella in China and Indo-China. Professor Ting discusses no
fewer than twenty-one Chinese versions of the folktale. From such
data, it is clear that Chinese materials are considerably underrepre-
sented in previous comparative studies. Miss Cox included no
Chinese texts in her 1893 study, while Professor Rooth discussed
only two, one of them from the Jameson lecture. This emphasizes*

Reprinted from R.D. Jameson, *Three Lectures on Chinese Folklore* (Peking:
North China Union Language School, 1932), pp. 47–85.

the comparative folklorist's great need for versions from every single part of the world where a particular item of folklore exists.

For further discussion of Chinese Cinderella tales, see Arthur Waley, *"The Chinese Cinderella Story,"* Folk-Lore 58 (1947), 226–238; and Nai-Tung Ting, The Cinderella Cycle in China and Indo-China, FF Communications No. 213 (*Helsinki: Academia Scientiarum Fennica, 1974*).

Meaning—The theme—The Chinese version—"T'o Huan"—Is this the original Cinderella?—Annamite versions—Families of the story —Cinderella and myth—The slipper—Friendly animals—The dead parent—Fishes—Conclusions.

Problems connected with the meanings of words have gained such interest among philologers that they have been elevated to a separate cult or discipline, referred to as semantics, and honored by the production of lengthy and sometimes contentious monographs. Popular narrative presents a particular linguistic situation in which problems of meaning become greatly complicated. The folklorists of the great tradition have directed their efforts toward the solution of only two of these. First they have attempted to determine the original meaning of the narrative. The Grimm brothers thought that popular tales were the detritus of Aryan myth[1] and this theory was developed by others, typically by J.G. von Hahn, who suggested that stories were originally the myths of the undivided Aryan people in their central Asiatic home.[2] These originists have been led into discussions of anthropology, ethnology, etymology, only to conclude that, if the original meaning of story is not entirely lost, it can be recovered only in uncertain forms. The second problem connected with the meaning of märchen has been called, light-heartedly, the central meaning of the tale. But this, if we admit that märchen, like the people who tell them and listen to them, occur in a time-space continuum, involves the further questions of central-meaning-for-whom, living-where-and-under-what-conditions, and this leads into psychology and thence back again into the other sciences.

It may be well, before we become completely lost in the mists of controversy, to examine a particular series of stories, drawn in this instance from China, and see what light the various discussions throw on the story and how the story may modify the theories generally accepted. Perhaps, when a more complete analysis is made than is possible with the materials available in Peiping, the suggestions which are here adumbrated will be helpful in furthering our apprehension of origin, distribution and folk psychology. Forty years ago an English anthropologist, Andrew Lang, could make no stronger assertion than a declaration of faith. He could *believe*, he said, in the independent invention of many incidents in popular tales and that some similar sequences may have been evolved independently.[3] Today the student of Chinese popular tales will be able to offer evidence which may change belief to certainty. The problem of origins will be clarified by being made more complex; but a working method will appear from it, for we shall see that some narrative complexes were originated independently in China and that others were importations and that no certainty about diffusion and origination can be arrived at until all the data is assembled independently for each narrative complex. Limitations of time, space and leisure make the collection of all the variants of any one story out of the question for the moment. My attempt here has been to select from the several thousand variants, written and oral, many of which friends have given me, a few which will throw light upon the meaning of story.

Once upon a time there was a little girl who suffered. Her sufferings were various and terrible. Sometimes the person who pretended to be her mother, but was really a witch and not her dear mother at all, forced her to do all the menial work in the household. Her dear mother was dead and her dear father was being deceived by this wicked woman who had taken her mother's place. Her elder sisters, who were really not her sisters at all but the daughters of the witch-mother by another man, could wear lovely clothes and sit in the drawing room with their friends while she, Cinderella, was banished to the kitchen.

Sometimes her sufferings are even more terrible. Her father, whom she loves dearly, fails to appreciate the depth of her affection, and when she, who is honest, upright and disdainful of low flattery, and in English is sometimes known as Cordelia, is disgusted by the exaggerations of her sisters, tells him that she loves him as she loves salt—for salt, as everyone knows, is necessary to happiness and life—he fails to understand the depth of her affection and banishes her or attempts to have her killed.

Her worst suffering of all, however, occurs when her father loves her and wishes to marry her in place of her dear dead mother. The little girl who, when she suffers this way in English is called "Catskin," tests this love by demanding that he give her three of the most beautiful dresses (color of the moon, color of the sun, color of the morning sky) and then a common, ugly dress made of all kinds of rough things (Allerleirau). Disguised in this she runs away from home—but she takes her pretty new dresses with her, lest she be forced to take the place of her dead mother.

In exile, her sufferings continue. She is forced to do the most difficult and impossible tasks, sort the grain from the chaff, untangle a tangled skein and the like. But she is not without friends. A tree on her mother's grave or the animals of the sky, land and water give her advice and help her to get pretty clothes which she can wear to church or to a ball at the palace. The prince sees her and is struck by her beauty. But our little friend is no brazen hussy, nor have her sufferings made her bold and grasping. She is modest, sweet and shrewd, for at midnight her lovely golden dress will be changed back to the rags of every day. She flees. He finds her slipper. He writes a proclamation. He is undeterred by the schemes of her wicked sisters. She is discovered. They are married.

Story tellers in all parts of the world have elaborated on the sufferings of this little girl, nor has her sad case been overlooked by learned and passionate scholars.[4] The oldest written European version which has come to my attention is in Des Periers' *Nouvelles Récréations et Ioyeux Devis*, published at Lyon in 1558.[5] Pernette, the daughter of a merchant who has retired to a farm, is desired by a neighboring squire. She is mistreated by her mother and sisters. She is forced to pick up with her tongue grain by grain a bushel of scattered barley. The merchant, seeing that Pernette's proposed marriage displeases his wife, forces Pernette to wear an ass's skin in the hope that her lover will be disgusted with her. The lover is faithful. The mother consents to the marriage if Pernette will perform her difficult task. The ants help her. She is married.[6]

The oldest Chinese version I have seen was written by a certain Tuan Ch'eng Shih (段成式) in the middle of the ninth century, thus antedating the oldest printed European version by some seven hundred years. Tuan Ch'eng Shih was from Shantung and, as a reward for his father's services to the state, was given the position of Chiao Shu Lang. It is said of him that "he had a very good memory and read extensively, possessing a very large collection of strange and rare books. He died in the position of junior minister in the ministry of rites (太常少卿)." He wrote a book called *Yu Yang Tsa Tsu* which contains the story of Sheh Hsien, a Chinese Cinderella.[7] I shall present it in full as rendered by Mr. Yü.

Tuan Ch'eng Shih says: "Such a story was handed down among the people of the south. Before the T'sin and Han dynasties there was a chief of a mountain cave whose name was Wu. The natives called him Cave Chief Wu (吳洞主). He married two wives one of whom died leaving to him a daughter named Sheh Hsein (葉限). She was a very intelligent girl and very clever in (sifting gold?). Her father loved her (fondly?). Afterwards her father died and she was mistreated by her step-mother. Her step-mother often asked her to cut wood at dangerous places and draw water from deep wells. Once she caught a fish more than two inches long with red fins and golden eyes, so she kept it in a basin in which she poured water. It grew bigger and bigger daily. She changed the vessel several times but at last it became so big that no vessel could hold it. Then she threw it into the pond behind their house. The girl fed it with food scraps which she got. If the girl came to the pond the fish would show its head using the bank as a pillow. It would not show itself when others came. This was known to her mother, so several times she waited on the bank but the fish never appeared. So she tried to defraud her daughter, saying, 'Are you not tired? Let me wash (literally, make new) your coat.' Then she changed into her rough clothes and told the girl to draw water from another spring which was several hundred *li* away[8] and not the spring from which she drew water every day. By and by the mother put on her daughter's clothes and put a sharp sword in her sleeve and went to the pond and called the fish. The fish then put its head out of the water so she killed it. By this time this fish had become more than five feet in length. She cooked and ate its meat which was doubly more delicious than ordinary fish. She concealed its bones under a dung hill.

"The next day the daughter came to the pond but the fish was no more so she wept in the wilderness (fields?). Suddenly a man in dishevelled hair and dressed in rough clothes came down from heaven and consoled her saying: 'Do not weep. Your mother has killed your fish. Its bones are (hidden) under the dung hill. Go back. Take the fish's bones and hide them in your room. If you want anything only pray to it. Your wish will be fulfilled.' The girl followed his advice and got gold, pearls, dresses and food as soon as she wished.

"When the cave festival came to pass the mother went to the feast and told the girl to watch the fruit in the courtyard. The girl noticed that her mother had gone far. She also went there having dressed herself in bluish finery, and put on a pair of golden shoes. (Then) the daughter of her stepmother stared at her and told her mother, saying, 'This lady looks very much like my elder sister.' Her mother also suspected in that way. The girl noticed this so she hurried back and thereby left one of her shoes which fell into the hands of the cave people.

"When her mother came back she found that her daughter was sleeping with her arms embracing the tree. So she put aside her thoughts (about the identity of the finely dressed lady with her step-daughter).

"The cave was near to an island and on that island there was a kingdom named T'o Huan whose military power was the strongest among more than thirty islands. The coastline of that island was several thousand *li* in length. The cave people then sold that shoe to the T'o Huan kingdom (government?) and [it] was got by the king. He asked his subjects to put it on their feet but the shoe was an inch shorter. So he asked all the women in the kingdom to try it but it was suited to nobody. It was as light as a hair and (if a foot were shod with this shoe it would) make no noise when walking on stone. Then the king thought that the cave man got it by improper means, so he imprisoned and tortured him; but he could not tell from where did it come. Then he put it at the roadside and sent people to search every house. At last another shoe of the same pattern was found at Sheh Hsien's house.

"The king of T'o Huan became inquisitive at this so he searched that house and found Sheh Hsien. He asked her to put it on her foot. Then Sheh Hsien dressed herself in bluish finery, put on those shoes and came to the king. She looked as beautiful as a goddess. Then she married with that king, took the fish's bones (with her) and went (with him) to his kingdom. The stepmother and her daughter were then killed by flying stones. The cave people pitied them so they buried them in a stone pit and named it 'The Tomb of Regretful Women.' The cave people took them as goddesses of match-makers. When they prayed to them anything concerning marriage their wish would be fulfilled.

"After the king got back to his kingdom he made Sheh Hsien his first wife. In the first year the king asked greedily infinite numbers of jewels and jades, so the next year it ceased to answer to prayers. Then the king buried the fish's bones on the sea-coast together with one hundred bushels (hu) of pearls and enclosed it with a gold parapet. Afterwards when the recruited soldiers rebelled and (the king?) was going to unearth them and distribute them among the soldiers . . . but one night it was washed away by the tide."

The author concludes, "This story was told by Li Shih Yuan, one of my former servants. He was originally a cave man of Yung Chow and he remembered very much about the strange stories of the south."

*   *   *

The fact that this complete version of Cinderella got recorded in China seven hundred years before the earliest record was made of it in the West raises questions of considerable interest. The servant Li's attribution of the events to periods before the Han and Ts'in dynasties may be significant; but is, perhaps, only the narrator's desire to get his events fixed in time and space.

Information available about the kingdom of T'o Huan is slight and unsatisfactory. In the *Record of the Early T'ang*[9] is the following notice:

"The country of T'o Huan is in the middle of the great sea southwest of Linyi[10] and is near Toholo[11] and in a northwesterly direction from it. It is over three months travel from the Chiao Chih country (French Indo-China—tr.). T'o Huan is on terms of amity with Toholo. The surname of the Prince of T'o Huan is Chashili and his given name is P'omop'ona. T'o Huan has no silkworms and no mulberries and the inhabitants use white felt and chaohsia cloth for clothing. They live in houses of more than one story which are called "kanlan." In the 18th year of Chien Kuan of the T'ang dynasty (645) T'o Huan sent an envoy to the T'ang court. In the twenty-first year of Chien Kuan (648) another envoy was sent with white parrots and p'o-lü (some kind of grease) to present to the court. The Prince of T'o Huan begged that he might be given horses and copper bells. The T'ang Emperor at once issued a mandate granting the request."[12]

These embassies seem to have occurred in the years 645 and 648, some three hundred years before the Cinderella was recorded. Except that T'o Huan is in the south seas and three months from Indo-China, this notice gives us little information. One friend has suggested that the unguent "p'o-lü" is from a tree native in Java. Mr. Chapman thinks that the "chaohsia" cloth was red in color. If the cave people of the south had silk at that time, Sheh Hsien probably wore blue silk finery which must have contrasted pleasantly with the white felt and red cloth of the people of T'o Huan.[13]

*   *   *

Tuan Cheng Shih's statement, based upon information he received from his servant that "such a story was handed down among the people of the South" raises, at least in passing, the question of whether this is the very first story about Cinderella that had ever been told and whether the stories about her which delight age and youth in all other countries are derived from this version. Internal evidence gives reason to conclude, at least tentatively, that this is not the case, that the people from whom Li Shih Yuan got the story were not the authors of it and that the version before us shows signs of some wear and of considerable age.

"When her (Sheh Hsien's) mother came back she found her daughter sleeping with her arms embracing the tree." This seems to be a strange position for sleep and not, unless I am mistaken, the position usually assumed by girls left alone in the house when their parents go to festivals. Moreover, this is the first reference we have yet had to a tree. However, those of us who have engaged extensively in the Cinderella phantasy are not surprised to find a tree here, or to learn that the girl should have embraced it while she slept. In several hundred of our own versions, Cinderella is supported by a tree which *grows from her dead mother's grave.* Here she comes to pray and weep and here she frequently falls asleep. In many of our versions it is the tree which gives her clothes and advice.

Popular tales have their own logic and their own standards of consistency. Popular tales may contain passages that mystify us, indeed they should contain such passages, for if they are true accounts of events and conditions very different from those in which we live, these events and conditions should be strange to us. It is a general rule that if we understand all the references in a story, the story must be suspected of having been modernised; but it is also clear that the story must not contain references which will mystify the people for whom it was told. When this occurs, when an irrelevant tree or sleeping posture is introduced, we may not be wrong in suggesting that the story teller made a mistake, that he was, perhaps, being influenced by some other version which he had heard, and this probability is increased if we ourselves have heard this other version and know that in that version a tree is a logical and necessary part of the story.

Two further items indicate that this version has become somewhat abraded by the ninth century. Sheh Hsien's visit to the cave festival is recounted with much less precision than her other adventures. All that we learn of it is that she sat near her sister, learned of her sister's suspicion and ran away leaving her shoe. She did not marry a man she met at the cave festival, as many of our English and French Cinderellas do, but rather another person whom she had never seen. The vagueness of the phantasy at this point is noteworthy. There seems to be no particular need to introduce the cave festival at all, for as will be shown presently, there are other simpler, and to the story teller, more exciting ways of getting the shoe into the hands of the king of T'o Huan. Again the suggestion intrudes itself that the compiler of this variant was not entirely independent of the other versions we also know in which a festival, a flight, and the loss of a shoe are essential episodes.

Finally the death of the step-mother and the sister, who, by the way, is mentioned comparatively late in the story, in the cave festival incident, and their canonization as the protectors of matchmakers is apparently an intrusion of a legendary nature and is irrelevant to the story. In this version these women had nothing to do with match-making and in the Annamite versions to be mentioned presently we shall see that they stoutly opposed the match.

If the considerations here adduced are sound they indicate that this story is a popular version taken from oral tradition, and that it is influenced by other versions and other stories which were in the consciousness of the narrators. Popular tales are literary creations.

Cinderella, *Hamlet* and the *Aeneid* are words put together by human beings, symbols of human thought and feeling controlled by tradition and communicated to other human beings. But popular art is more transparent than sophisticated art, and by a comparison of many treatments of the same popular theme we can frequently get a glimpse of the strange processes of literary creation. They mark the critical point at which imagination, hallucination and literature, three phases of human experience, meet and remain still distinguishable.

*   *   *

The two Annamite versions of Cinderella to which I have access are similar to the T'ang version here under discussion, whereas the oral versions I have found in the north show points of such divergence as to suggest that they are of recent importation.

In the first Annamite version we learn that on a fishing expedition to decide the superiority of the heroine Cam over her step-sister Tam, Tam steals Cam's fish. A spirit tells Cam to put the remaining fish in a well and feed it. A step-mother slays the fish. A cook asks Cam for three grains of rice, gives her the fishbones, tells her to put them in her bed. The bones of the fish give her clothes and shoes. A slipper is stolen by a crow and carried to the prince's palace. The prince seeks the owner and marries her. She is required to sort spilled grain. Pigeons help her. The step-sister plunges into boiling water to become as beautiful as Cam. Cam salts the sister's flesh and gives it to the step-mother to eat. The crow on a tree reveals the step-mother's cannibalism.[14]

The second Annamite version is similar to the first. There is a fishing competition and the nourishing of one fish. The heroine tends goats and the villain kills and eats the goat. A fish tells the heroine to bury the bones at the crossroads. They turn into gold shoes.[15] The crow here, as in the other version, carries the shoe to the prince and the heroine is discovered. Here too she is forced to perform difficult tasks and is helped by insects and animals. After marriage the phantasy becomes involved. The heroine is permitted to return home and is given opportunity for more suffering. Her mother and step-sister mistreat her. She is transformed in various ways and finally restored to her husband. The punishment of her enemies and the cannibalistic episode are here the same as in the other version.[16]

*　　*　　*

The material available in China is insufficient to enable me to report on the distribution of this story in other parts of the world and the relation between the Chinese variants and the others. Although I have been able to find somewhat inadequate accounts of only 300 versions, an analysis of these may enable us to grasp the broad lines of development and the configuration of incidents.[17] When these variants are put together the story is seen to fall into five parts. (A) A young girl is ill treated. (B) She is forced to do menial service at home or abroad. (C) She meets a prince or a prince becomes aware of her beauty. (D) She is identified by her shoe. (E) She marries the prince. Each of these parts states a situation which, if the auditor and narrator identify themselves with the heroine, generates an appropriate emotion which symbolises itself in the elaboration of each part. At times the suffering is greatly elaborated and the phantasy makes this the larger part of the story, at times the compensatory emotions about the prince, his loyalty, her shyness and dignity are elaborated.[18] In this elaboration, the following episodes are most frequently met:

A. A young girl is ill-treated
    A1 By her step-mother and step-sisters who are unkind to to her; or
    A2 By her father who wishes to marry her. She flees after receiving gifts of clothes; or
    A3 By her father whom she tells she loves as she loves salt and is driven from home; or
    A4 By her entire family who wish to kill her.
B. During a time of menial service at home or abroad
    B1 She is advised, supported (fed) and given clothes by her dead mother, a tree on her mother's grave or a supernatural creature.
    B2 She is helped by birds,
    B3 Goat, sheep or cow,
    B4 When the animal has been killed, a gift-bearing tree grows from its entrails, a box with clothes is found inside it or its ossuaries are otherwise useful in providing clothes.

C. She meets the prince
>   C1 Disguised in her pretty clothes she goes to a ball and
>   dances several times with the prince, who tries in vain
>   to find out who she is, or he sees her as she goes to
>   church.
>   C2 Sometimes she hints to him about sufferings and thus
>   both mystifies and interests him.
>   C3 Sometimes the prince peeps through a keyhole and sees
>   her dressed in her finery.

D. She is identified by
>   D1 The shoe test,
>   D2 The ring she leaves in his soup or bakes in his bread.
>   D3 Her ability to perform some difficult task, such as
>   picking the golden apples.

E. She marries the Prince

F. If her suffering is due to the fact that she told her father she
loves him as she loves salt, she now serves him unsalted
food to prove how necessary salt is to human happiness.

Unfortunately these episodes are too highly generalised to enable
us to form any adequate conclusions as to geographical variations.
If scrutinised carefully, however, we shall see that about a third of
the variants belong to two separate families and that the rest are
intermediate.

The first type of Cinderella story appears to be most popular in
the west of Europe, though it is also found elsewhere and ranges
through the west and north from Czechoslovakia to Iceland. This
version, first published by Perrault in 1697, has become very popular
in England. It makes use of the following arrangement:

>   (A1) A young girl is ill-treated and forced to do menial work
>   by her step-mother and step-sisters. (B1) She is advised sup-
>   ported, (fed) given clothes by her dead mother, a tree on her
>   mother's grave or a supernatural creature. (C1) When dressed
>   in her pretty clothes she goes to a ball and dances several times
>   with a prince who tries to find out who she is. (D1) When she
>   runs away he acquires her shoe and attempts to identify her by
>   it. (E1) He finds and marries her.

The second type of Cinderella story appears to be most popular
in Slavonic language areas:

(A1) This little girl is also ill-treated by step-mother and step-sisters (B3) But is supported, advised, etc. by a helpful animal (B4) From whose viscera she acquires her pretty clothes. (D3) Identification is through her ability to perform a difficult task.

In the Slavonic type there is no ball but there is a great interest in the helpful animal; in the Germanic type there is a ball, comparatively slight interest in the helpful animal and comparatively more interest in the supernatural creature (godmother, bird from tree on mother's grave and the like). In the T'ang version there is a ball—absent in the Annamite versions and apparently irrelevant to the story—and the supernatural creature, "the rough man from heaven" who, in the phantasy engendered by the story, may be a father or a father surrogate. These factors would connect the T'ang Cinderella with the Germanic type. However, in the T'ang version there is considerable interest in the helpful animal, and Cinderella does not marry the man she meets at the ball but another, which would connect this variant with the Slavonic family. I have suggested above that the comparatively slight interest in the cave festival and the reference to the irrelevant tree may have been due to the fact that the people who passed this version on to the servant Li—or, indeed the servant Li himself—were familiar with these variants which seem to have been most popular in northwestern Europe; but who followed, in the main, the story which seems to be best represented in the Slavonic language area. These facts seem to justify the tentative conclusion that the T'ang Cinderella (which came from the far south of China and, through T'o Huan, has connections with Annam) is similar to the Annamite versions in following a type of Cinderella most frequently found in Slavonic territories. An Arabic version from Egypt presents the first parts of this Slavonic type in that a pet animal is killed and from its bones grows a tree which supports an ill-treated child.[19] In one of the Annamite versions, the heroine is assisted by the "Lord Alwah or Aw Law," which in Miss Cox's note is explained as possibly a corruption of Allah. Miss Cox explains that the "story comes from the heathen Tjames who claim that their Musselman congeners adore Allah."[20]

No man can guess what wealth of material still lies hidden in old Chinese texts or in Chinese, Mongol and Tibetan oral tradition.

Whether the Chinese Cinderella was brought into the south of China or Annam by maritime Arabs, or whether it was taken from China by these same Arabs are questions to which a somewhat detailed scrutiny of the facts has returned no answer.

One group of scholars has attempted to see in Cinderella the detritus of a myth by which our primitive ancestors described the rising sun. According to these scholars, primitive man loved nature and was impressed by it in much the same way as the romantic poets who created primitive man in their own image. The spectacle of the rising sun and the ideas of the mythologists filled our savage ancestors with the most charming fancies. Cinderella is the dawn, hidden in the obscurity of the hearth, appearing for a brief time in brilliant clothes but obscured again by the clouds, pursued ever by the ardent prince, the sun, until she is discovered.[21]

A. de Gubernatis reminds us that in the *Rig Veda*[22] the dawn is represented as having fled with such a light step that she seems to have been unshod and that the sun, Prince Mitra, in following the charming young girl, found a slipper which gave him the measure of her foot, a foot so small that no other woman had its mate, a foot almost imperceptible.[23]

Hyacinthe Husson, according to Saintyves, does not definitely suggest that the story derives from a myth; but he thinks it rests on a mythic symbolism. "La chaussure perdue et retrouvée amène en définitive un dénouement heureuse. Il me parrait donc qu'elle correspond à l'idée de *bonne fortune*. Cette conjecture trouve une confirmation dans le nom même de la princesse indienne qui correspond à notre Cendrillon, elle s'appelle *Sodewa-Bai*, c'est-à-dire la dame de bonne fortune."[24]

Loys Brueyere thinks that Cinderella is not connected with a dawn myth but rather with a seasonal myth describing the sleep of nature during winter and the awakening of nature in the spring. The sun, symbolised by a young prince, is required to return to the princess the symbolic attribute which symbolises the union between the spring sun and nature, a fecund marriage from which will come the flowers and the fruits. Cinderella is the debris of an ancient religion[25] or, as Andrew Lang says, the "diamond dust of a myth."

The very learned P. Saintyves[26] maintains the thesis which follows: After the seasonal liturgies which were celebrated at the renewal of the seasons and particularly at the beginning of the year

(winter solstice or spring equinox) popular ceremonies were performed in which the new season or the new year, in this case
Cinderella, was followed by the young sun, and married after the
proof had been given that she was the spouse designated by destiny.[27]
Cinderella, he thinks, is a commentary on these very early rituals,
designed to facilitate the passage of winter into spring. He points
out that the spring festivals have survived in only a fragmentary
fashion in Europe, Christianity has destroyed some of them and
partially assimilated others. Today, popular songs and stories which
were the commentaries on these rituals have been so completely
dissociated that a long and careful preparation is necessary before
the connection can be discovered. But, he exclaims, with what
satisfaction we discover that the personages in our homely popular
tales have connections with our immemorial liturgies and our ancient
European customs. Professor Saintyves would not dare to affirm
with Collin de Plancy that Cinderella originated in Brittany, but he
does think it is a very ancient story in our old Occidental world.[28]

If these speculations be kept in mind and we turn back to the
story which the servant Li Shih Yuan told his master Tuan Ch'eng
Shih in the middle òf the ninth century, we cannot but be struck by
three passages. First, Sheh Hsien's shoe, we are told, was found to
be as light as a hair, and a foot shod with this shoe would make no
noise when walking on stone. Second, when she went to the cave
festival she "dressed herself in bluish finery and put on golden
shoes." Third, when she met the king, "Sheh Hsien dressed herself in
bluish finery, put on those (golden) shoes. . . . She looked as
beautiful as a goddess." The shoe which was light as a hair and
would make no noise when walking on stone is a curious parallel to
the foot of the dawn Goddess referred to by Gubernatis, and the
blue and gold of her clothes, the color of the spring dawn, are colors
which are dwelt upon by the narrator. I have too little information
about the cave people of the south and the kingdom of T'o Huan to
know whether the bluish finery would have any particular significance for them, and discussions of the history of Chinese "superstitions" are too inaccurate to enable me to determine which Goddess
Sheh Hsien resembled when "she looked as beautiful as a Goddess."
Ch'un-t'i the dawn Goddess of Chinese Buddhism is the Brahmanic
Marichi.[29] Her attribute is not, so far as I have able to learn, a blue
robe, and her feet are not in the picture. However, the fact that

under Taoism Ch'un-t'i became an immortal with eighteen arms, in the fourth of which *was carried the viscera of a fish*, may not be without significance when we remember the importance of the fish viscera in the adventures of Sheh Hsien.[30]

In view of these coincidences the possibility may not be rejected that Sheh Hsien, with her bluish finery and her gold slippers so light that they make no noise, is connected in some way with the myth of dawn or spring which is light-footed, blue and gold. Yet we must also remember that it is by no means to be accepted as a fact. The similarities which exist between this T'ang version as well as other versions of Cinderella and the Vedic mythology or Egyptian and early Christian legend are facts of capital importance. Nor can there by any doubt that in Europe, both past and present, there were festivals at carnival time in honor of the spring, or that in historical times a figure representing Cinderella, sometimes, as in some variants, assisted by twelve attendants representing the twelve months, appears and even plays an important part. We must remember however that the authors of the *Rig Veda* were curious and learned scholars. They were quite capable of taking a popular tale and making a myth out of it, and whereas the popular tale would not have been preserved except through oral tradition, the myth, having the sanction of the cult, would be repeated and put into writing. Nor is the use of Cinderella in spring festivals evidence that Cinderella is derived from a very early ritual. The priority of myth over popular tale is an hypothesis so daring in formulation and so irrelevant to what appear to be the present facts that it could be passed over entirely had it not received the support of many learned men and were there not frequently the kind of coincidence—blue clothes, golden shoes, light step, fish viscera—which I have mentioned.

The fact that the subtle scholars of the *Rig Veda* should have used incidents similar to those in Cinderella in their somewhat pedantic elaborations of myth warn us that for them, as also for modern scholars of the mythological school, Cinderella serves as a symbol for cosmic processes. Nor, since meanings are manifold and the processes of human intelligence are obscure, is it entirely impossible that simple folk have also felt that kind of emotion in seeing the sun rise that learned gentlemen now feel in reading Cinderella, and it may be that that is one of the meanings of the tale.[31]

*   *   *

The discovery of Cinderella by means of her slipper is one of the most famous of the episodes[32] in the entire cycle and has led a considerable amount of discussion. Em. Cosquin refers to a story from the southern part of India. A princess marries the prince who saves her from a giant. She loses her slipper in a pond. It is found by a fisherman who sells it to a shopkeeper who gives it to a neighboring king. The king falls in love with the owner of the shoe, hires an old woman to destroy the talisman which protected the life of the heroine's husband and thus succeeds in abducting the heroine.[33] From this point the story is fused with another, frequent in China, and best preserved in an oral version from Tibet which will be discussed elsewhere under the title, "The Tall Man of China."[34]

A similar combination is known in the west. The historian Strabo, who lived in the first century before Christ, recounts the "fable" of Rhodopis[35] an Egyptian courtesan. While she was bathing in the Nile an eagle took her shoe from the hand of a servant, carried it to Memphis, where the king was holding court in the open air, and dropped it in the king's lap. After some search, Rhodopis was identified as the owner and married the king.[36]

In these five variants similar patterns appear: A king becomes enamored of a princess by means of a shoe which he acquires accidentally, by gift in the T'ang and Southern Indian version, by a bird in the Annamite and Graeco-Egyptian versions. In each, the phantasy about the shoe is closely connected with the phantasy about water. In the T'ang and one Annamite version the bones of a fish in a pond supply the shoes. In the other Annamite version the fish tells the heroine how to procure the shoes. In the southern Indian and the Graeco-Egyptian versions the shoe is lost while bathing. Because of these similarities, Em. Cosquin suggests that the story must have come from India,[37] a suggestion which must be rejected if the story is found to be about a small girl who suffers rather than about a girl who married a prince because he saw her pretty shoe. Again it is necessary to insist that the question of origins must be postponed until more variants are available to us for analysis.

Shoes themselves are complex symbols in the folklore of all peoples. In some parts of China, women who wish children take a shoe from the temple of the Goddess who in that district has the power of bringing children. Incense is burned before the shoe and when the child arrives another pair of shoes must be returned to the Goddess.[38] Doré reports that one pair of shoes is deposited before the Goddess Kuan Yin,[39] incense is burned and one shoe is taken away to force the Goddess to perform properly. After the child is born the shoe is returned to the temple, sometimes with a new pair.[40] At times, a second pair of shoes is presented together with the pair or shoe originally taken away if and when the Goddess has performed her duty and produced a child. At times the restoration of the shoes may be accompanied by a banquet for the Goddess. In Shantung the Goddess who is thus honored is the Tai Shan Niang Niang (   ), daughter of the God of Tai Shan. She is also the patroness of the fox fairies.[41]

When a couple has been betrothed, if the bride dies before marriage, the groom asks for the shoes she wore last before death and incense is burned before them for a space of two years.[42] In the south of China a bride sends a pair of shoes to her affianced husband "by way of signifying that for the future she places herself under his control."[43] A similar custom is recorded in the *Book of Ruth* (IV, 7–10), where Ruth's kinsman indicates his renunciation of intention to marry by plucking off his shoe.[44] Professor Shirokogoroff has called my attention to the fact that among the Manchus a bride is expected to give gifts of shoes to her husband's brothers, and that group marriage is practiced in that all of the younger brothers have the right of physical access to the wives of the elder brothers. Moreover, the slippers are ornamented with "lien hau" (   ), which in common speech is the vulgar term for female genitalia.[45]

Professor Saintyves has brought together an imposing array of evidence to show the spread of divination by means of shoes, and in all cases the divinations have to do with the attempt to discover the identity of the future groom, the direction from which he will come or when he will come. The use of the shoe in wedding ceremonies, the sanctification of the shoe in parts of China when it is brought to the temple in a ceremony to obtain children, the worship of a shoe as the characteristic symbol of a dead bride by a mourning groom, the gift of shoes by a bride to her husband in signification of her subordination to him and the gift of shoes among Manchus by a bride to her husband's brothers who share her with the husband all lead to the suggestion that we are here dealing with a very intimate and potent symbol. Dr. Ernest Jones in an article "Psycho-Analysis and Folklore"[46] suggests that although the symbol may have different meanings in different layers of the mind, one meaning would suggest that the shoe is here the symbol of the fruitful female organ itself, "an interpretation," he continues, "that may be supported by the decidedly broad saying that used to accompany (the thrown shoe), 'May you fit her as well as my foot fits this old shoe.' "[47]

Unfortunately we know too little about the ideas associated with shoes in the T'ang dynasty or among the cave people of the south, who told the story, to make definite statement possible; but unless the facts adduced in other parts of the world are modified by some peculiar local condition, we may conclude tentatively that the association between shoes and ideas of marriage were the same there as elsewhere and that when the king of T'o Huan acquired Sheh Hsien's shoe he acquired, at least psychologically, rights over her.

* * *

The functions of the friendly animals in Cinderella stories have been examined by various scholars with some care and they have come to various conclusions about them. In the T'ang version quoted above, Sheh Hsien caught a fish, and nourished it. Her mother killed and ate it, finding its flesh doubly delicious and buried its bones under a dung hill. A man from heaven told Sheh Hsien where the bones were, instructed her to collect them and hide them in her room and told her that they would grant her wishes. The fish is also present in the two Annamite versions. In the first it is caught in a fishing contest. A spirit tells the heroine to feed it. A cock tells her to collect its bones and hide them in her bed. In the second, a goat is killed and a fish gives friendly advice to bury the goat's bones at the cross roads.

Professor Saintyves has analyzed 132 variants and has noted that in fifty-five of them some animal plays the part of protector without counting "les autres versions où les animaux remplissent ce même rôle mais en second plan."[48] In ten of these versions the animal is a fish. He suggests that the animal may be an individual totem or a guardian spirit.

Totem and totemism are terms used frequently by scholars who believe that fairy tales contain "survivals" from very ancient times and types of social organization which are no longer in force. In

totemistic complexes some animal or plant is held sacred and wor-
shipped, sometimes is considered the ancestor of the organization
and is supposed to exercise powers, frequently protective, over the
organization. It is not killed or eaten or if it is the killing and eating
proceed according to ritual. Whenever we meet a friendly animal in
a popular tale, particularly an animal which exercises so powerful
an influence over the characters as these fishes do in the tales here
under discussion, the cry of totemistic survival is certain to be raised
sooner or later. Hartland has cited instances of fish totems from the
gold coast through Babylonia to India,[49] and his list is certainly not
exhaustive. In the T'ang version it will be remembered that the
heroine takes the fish to her husband's kingdom where for a year it
satisfies his greedy demands and then fails and this reminds us of the
instances when wives take their tutelary deities with them into their
husbands' houses. Supporters of the theory that the fish is here a
"survival" from a totemistic society would suggest that as society
changes from totemism to some other form of organization, the
memory of the totemistic animal is retained in stories about animals
that were helpful and useful.

It may appear, however, that totemistic survival is a very large
phrase to describe the phantasy of a small girl who is suffering, is
forced to do menial tasks and has only one pet. Whatever may be
the history of the story in time and space, whatever there may be in
it of primitivism, one kind of primitivism which appears is psychological primitivism. The dream that the pet fish, which lay its head
on the bank as on a pillow when she talked to it, would remain
friendly even after her cruel mother had killed and eaten it, is a
dream which requires no words as large as "primitive totemistic
survival" for its explanation.[50]

The phantasy about the helpful animal is closely connected with
the phantasy about Cinderella's dead mother. The evidence has been
brought together elsewhere.[51] I shall here confine myself to the
excellent summary offered by Professor Saintyves.[52]

In a version from Jutland (Cox, 38) the girl weeps at the mother's
grave and is told to strike a tree three times to obtain pretty clothes.
In a Norwegian tale, the girl weeps at the grave and is consoled by
an angel (Cox, 87). In a German variant, she has planted a tree at
her mother's grave from which a white bird comes to give advice. In
Lithuania the girl weeps at the grave: "And deep down in the earth

the mother said: "It is not the rain. It is not the snow. It is the dew which falls from the trees." "No," said the young girl, "It is not the rain It is not the snow. It is not the dew which falls from the trees. It is I who weep at thy grave'" and receives advice. In a Russian version,[53] the dying mother gave her daughter a helpful cow, in Scotland she gave a calf and the calf continues to be helpful even after it has been killed and its bones are collected under a stone. In a version from Olonetz (Cox, 102) the mother has been transformed into a sheep, gives the daughter advice, is killed, resuscitated, killed again and so on. In our own T'ang version, "a man with dishevelled hair and dressed in rough clothes came down from heaven" and, if analogy were sufficient, one might think that this man was the spirit of Sheh Hsien's father, Cave Chief Wu. But again, there seems to be no further connection between this rough man and the dead father who "loved her fondly" or between this dead parent and the helpful fish except the kind of connection which we find in dreams, the staring simplicity of an animated universe in which all creatures are either friends or enemies.

Ideas connected with fishes may add further kinds of meaning to the story of Cinderella. Unfortunately I have come across little material in China. Doré reports that the dragon assumes the shape of the carp, Li vü, and that countless stories are told of people who are rewarded for freeing a carp which is really the dragon king, Lung Wang. He cites from the *Records of Western Travel* stories which resemble our western story of the King of the Fishes.[54] In a later passage, he suggests that the fish is the symbol of wealth, but suggests that this is due to a confusion between two characters which have the same sound, yü, which means both "wealth" and "fish."

Another series of stories associates fishes with ideas about fertility. In Brazil a supernatural creature is said to have fertilised a virgin by the gift of a fish[55] and a similar incident is said to occur in Samoa.[56] Tavernier reported that in India, about 1642, a woman became pregnant after swallowing a fish and the child when bathed smelled of fish.[57] The Brahmans of Kanara take a newly married pair to a pond and make them throw rice on the water and catch a few minnows. "They let all go except one with whose scales they mark their brows."[58]

Some time ago a Chinese resident of Java, which is near the

kingdom of T'o Huan where Sheh Hsien went to be queen, is said to
have procured for the Ethnographical Museum at Leyden a Flute
Fish from the "Children's Sea" on the south coast of the island. If
eaten by the husband of a childless woman this fish, he said, would
ensure offspring.

*   *   *

This fragmentary discussion has been directed to an exposition
of the varied methods of interpretation which are being used in
analyses of the meanings of items of folklore. The point about which
I have attempted to center this exposition is a story about Sheh
Hsien which the learned junior minister, Tuan Ch'eng Shih, who
read extensively and possessed a collection of strange books heard
from his servant Li, a cave man from the south, and wrote down in
the middle of the ninth century for his entertainment and our
edification. The heroine, Sheh Hsien is certainly the southern
Chinese sister of our own Cinderella, but whether Sheh Hsien came
to Europe or our Cinderella came to China in the ninth century or
whether they both lived in Egypt or India in much earlier times and
one went east and the other went west are questions which cannot
yet be decided. The evidence indicates, however, that the story of
Sheh Hsien was not a new story when it was told to the servant Li
and that the story he told has strange and inexplicable similarities
with a version still popular in Slavonic countries as well as with
versions popular in the west and northwest of Europe.

The color of Sheh Hsien's clothes, her gold shoes and the fact
that she was beautiful as a goddess brought us immediately to the
theories that Cinderella was originally the detritus of a myth of
dawn or of spring, formulated before the Aryans had left their
central home and worn down to a "diamond dust" by processes of
vulgarization. Her clothes, her divine beauty and the fact that one
representation of Marichi the dawn goddess has fish viscera as an
attribute may be conclusive evidence of this hypothesis or they may
be irrelevant coincidences. But even if they be relevant, even if they
are evidences of how decayed myths maintain their sanctions over the
human spirit or how dogmas degenerate into the chatter of old
women about the fireside on a dull night, they tell us nothing of the
priority of myth over märchen and the question of whether myths
were divine revelations or whether they were popular tales. Human

phantasy, emanating from human minds as the result of the strain of living in a harsh, unfriendly and difficult world, still needs an examination which by the nature of the evidence with which we have to deal it may never receive.

An examination of two Annamite versions and a comparison of these and the T'ang version with some three hundred other versions led to the tentative conclusion that the story has two families, but again to the conclusion that until more material is available the question of origins must be postponed. The fact that in the Chinese versions and in stories from India, Egypt and Western Europe the heroine marries a prince who becomes aware of her existence by means of a shoe dropped in the water or procured on the banks of a stream indicates some connection between these stories, but in this case the incidents are so slight that the connection may be due to chance. Certainly the relations between shoe and betrothal and marriage customs in Europe and China, whatever its origins may be, are established fact; and the discovery of the heroine by means of her shoe—whether the shoe is, as Dr. Jones suggests, the symbol of the female genitalia or whether it is concerned with marriage and betrothal in other ways—is properly a part of the phantasy about the small girl who was mistreated but ended by getting prettier clothes and making a better marriage than her sisters.

The meanings of Cinderella are as elusive as her origins. Whatever the symbolism of the various parts of the story may be found to be, whatever emotions and significations may be attached to slippers and fishes, helpful animals and dead parents among the cave people in south China in the ninth century, the spinning of the yarn, the daydream which we call fairy story is organised by the central situation presented near the beginning, the emotions growing out of the fact that here is a small girl who was loved fondly by a father that died and is now being mistreated by her stepmother. The märchen may be a myth, and that possibility brings before us the startling, and it would seem incontrovertible fact, that the myth is also a märchen, that the sanctions it has over human feelings, the appetites it satisfies are derived from the fact that—whatever else it may be—it is a good story. Its episodes are concretions of desires, at times obscure and only partly understood, which grow out of situations which are frequent in the experience of all times and places. The fact that subtle scholars of today and subtle priests of yesterday have raised popular tales to the dignity of myth and connected them with the breaking of dawn and the burgeoning of spring may be their testimony, unconsciously offered, to the power of story.

The immediate set of meanings in Cinderella, and, I think, the set which keeps it alive on the lips of mothers and grandmothers and in the hearts of their daughters, is in Cinderella's appeal to the imagination of the sub-adolescent girl. Cinderella is the story of her phantasy. Her father fixation, her helpful friends the birds and fishes, her desire for pretty clothes, her triumph over her enemies have here been symbolised. The repressed emotions which result from the strain of family life, particularly the feeling that she is mistreated, unloved and unappreciated, are here given release.

The story is a good story because it is good medicine. It is psychic and social medicine. After the daydream has run its course, she is happily married and her persecutors are fittingly punished— although sometimes she is kind even to them—she can return to her tasks and take her part in the family circle. The delusions of persecution may still remain, but the emotional pressure on these delusions will have been relieved. These thousands of Cinderella phantasies which we find in all parts of the world are redolent with the sweet dreams of shy girlhood. When we enter into their meanings, we enter the budding grove, "l'ombre des jeunes filles en fleurs."

NOTES

[1] J. and W. Grimm, *Deutsche Sagen*, Berlin, 1816–1818; *Kinder und Hausmaerchen* (3 vols., completed 1856).

[2] J.G. von Hahn, *Griechische und Albanesische Maerchen*, 2 vols., 1864; Max Müller, *Chips from a German Workshop* (2 vols., 1859), II, 226. E. Cosquin (*Contes populaires de Lorraine* [2 vols., Paris, 1886], I, i, xv) thinks with Benfey (*Pantschatantra* (2 parts, Leipzig, 1859; see "Einleitung") that they are derived from historic India. This suggestion is countered by G. Maspéro in his *Contes populaires de L'Egypte ancienne*, (Paris, 1882) by the suggestion that the stories came from ancient Eygpt. The controversy is summarised in several of the publications of A. Lang. See particularly *Myth, Ritual and Religion* (2 vols., 5th ed., 1913), Vol. II, pp. 300ff., and his *Magic and Religion* (London, 1901), pp. 295ff.

[3] Marian Rolfe Cox, *Cinderella, Three Hundred and Forty-five Variants* (London, Folk-Lore Society, 1893), xxii.

[4]See bibliography in Cox, *op. cit.*; Bolte-Polivka, *Anmerkungen zu den Kinder- und Hausmaerchen der Brüder Grimm* (3 vols., 1913–1918), I. 165ff.; P. Saintyves, *Les Contes de Perrault* (Paris, 1923), pp. 113–209, 609–635.

[5]It is Nouvelle CXXIX.

[6]Based on summary in Cox., *op., cit.*, p. 90.

[7]This material was sent me by Mr. D.C. Yü with a reference to the *Cyclopedia of Chinese Biographical Names*, p. 667a.

[8]One edition says several *li* away. D.C. Yü.

[9]197th Book and 147 Lieh Chuan.

[10]Annam?

[11]Or perhaps Turcaro (?)

[12]I am indebted for the discovery of this passage to Dr. W.B. Pettus and his assistants in the library of the North China Language School; for translation largely to Mr. F.J. Chapman of the American Legation.

[13]Mr. Owen Lattimore has suggested that "Toholo" or "Turkaro" might refer to the Turkari of Central Asia. These peoples probably wore white felt and reddish clothes and were without silk—but not without horses. But if T'o Huan is southwest of Annam it could not be northwest of "Toholo." References in T'ang geography are extremely vague.

[14]Landes, *Contes et légendes annamites* (1886), XXII, quoted in Cox, *op. cit.*, p. 28.

[15]Professor Saintyves suggests that the burial of the bones at the crossroads, or the taking of the bones to her room and the precise directions which are given her in this matter, are evidences of ritualism. "Toutes ces précisions ne sont-elles pas d'ordre liturgique? . . . Nous avons déjà longuement parlé à propos des Fées du respect des primitifs pour les os des animaux auxquels ils rendent un culte." *Op. cit.*, 145. The burial of the bones of a pet animal that has been killed by an enemy and eaten, whether at the crossroads or at the four corners of the bed or merely in the room, or the feeling that one ought to preserve the remains of a pet (i.e., that it is fitting and proper) and the consequent phantasy that some good may come of it, do not appear to be of a liturgical "order" or of necessity connected with any primitive or spring ritual. Nor can this kind of procedure be taken as evidence either that the liturgy preceded the story or that the story preceded the liturgy, unless we assume that small girls who suffered in ninth-century China because their pets were killed and eaten were different from the small girls who suffer for the same reason today, different, that is, in their emotional attachments and responses.

[16]Landes, *Contes tjames* (1887), X; abstracted in Cox, *op. cit.*, p. 28. See also "*Dô Than,* une version annamite du conte de Cendrillon" *in Bull. de l'Ecole française d'Extrême Orient* (1907), VII, 103; and Em. Durand's version in the same publication (1912), XII, pp. 1–35, mentioned in Saintyves but not available in Peiping.

[17]The material is taken from Bolte-Polivka's *Anmerkungen* and Cox except when otherwise stated.

[18]At times the phantasy of suffering recurs after the marriage (as in the second Annamite version), she cannot rid herself of the idea that her mother and sisters are malevolent. After her marriage she may take mother and sisters into the palace where they ill-treat her again, steal her children, accuse her of cannibalism and a paranoia sets in.

[19]Dulac, *Journal asiatique,* 1885, 11; Bolte-Polivka, I. 181.

[20]Cox, *op. cit.,* p. 300.

[21]Ch. Ploix, *Le Surnatural dans les contes populaires* (1891), 102–104.

[22]*Rig Veda,* I, 152–153.

[23]A. de Gubernatis, *Mythologie zoologique,* I, 33–35; *Saintyves, op. cit.,* 120.

[24]H. Husson, *La Chaine traditionnelle,* 14, 15; Saintyves, 121.

[25]Loys Brueyere, *Les Contes populaires de la Grande Bretagne* (1875) p. 47; Saintyves, *op. cit.,* 122–123.

[26]Chargé des Conférences à l'Ecole d'Anthropologie.

[27]Saintyves, *op. cit.,* 123.

[28]Saintyves, *op. cit.,* p. 164.

[29]Henry Doré, *Researches into Chinese Superstitions* (tr. M. Kennelly, Shanghai, 1922), VII, 303.

[30]Doré, *op. cit.,* VII, 306.

[31]E.B. Tylor, in a passage that should be read frequently, amuses himself by mythologising on "Four and twenty blackbirds." The twenty-four birds symbolise the hours of the day. The lower piecrust is earth, the top crust, the sky. The birds begin to sing when dawn like a knife cuts the sky. The queen is the moon and her honey the lucid moonbeams. *Primitive Culture,* I, 319.

[32]It may be of interest to note in passing that the glass slipper in the English version and in that of Perrault ("pantouffle de verre," 1695) is due to a linguistic confusion with the homonym "vaire."

[33]Em. Cosquin, *Les Contes Indiens et l'Occident,* 30; *Saintyves,* op. cit., p. 115.

[34]"The Tall Man of China" was collected by Mr. D.C. Yü.

[35]XVII, 1, No. 33.

[36]Saintyves, *op. cit.,* 117; Bolte-Polivka, *op. cit.,* I, 187.

[37]Quoted in Saintyves, *op. cit.,* p. 117.

[38]N.B. Dennys, *The Folk-Lore of China* (London, 1876), 11.

[39]"The female counterpart or *Sakti of Avalokitesvara,"* Doré, *Researches,* VI, 201.

[40]Doré, *Researches,* I, 1–2.

[41]Doré, *loc. cit.* The burning of shoes before the newly born child's cradle during the first hundred days of its life would seem to have more to do with the offensive odor than with the symbolization of shoes in folk thought. See Doré, *Researches,* I, 22.

[42]Dennys, *op. cit.,* p. 15.

[43]Dennys, *op. cit.,* p. 18.

[44]Cf. Psalm, N LX, 8.

[45]Professor Shirokogoroff suggests, however, that as the making of shoes is particularly the work of women the connection between shoes and erotic symbolism may be accidental. Cf. his *Social Organization of the Manchus.*

[46]*Jubilee Congress of the Folk-Lore Society* (London, 1930), p. 229.

[47]Dr. Jones refers to Aigremont, *Fuss- und Schuh-Symbolik und Erotik,* 1909, not available in Peiping.

[48]*Op. cit.,* pp. 144–145.

[49]E.S. Hartland, *The Science of Fairy Tales* (London, 1891, pp. 27, 324, 331, 346.

⁵⁰Some stories doubtless do contain memories of very ancient times, and Hartland makes out a good case in the *Science of Fairy Tales*, pp. 255ff.; but we must always make quite clear what we mean by "survival," particularly whether we mean that the trait in the story derives from and is a memorial of an earlier form of social organization or whether we think that both the organization and the story derive from similar mental processes.

⁵¹Miss Cox mentions the following cases of a child "receiving help from a dead parent either at the tomb (as in Nos. 33, 38, 64, 70, 96, 153, 197, 199, 204, 328, 340, 341) or through an apparition in a dream (as in Nos. 9, 10, 202, 277)" and in addition refers to the "Lay of Swipday and Menglade" in *Corp. Poet. Boreale* I, 93. Help is obtained from the grave of a mother in her collection Nos. 17, 19, 37, 43, 47, 50, 87, 124, 265, 266 and from a transformed mother in Nos. 31, 34, 95, 101, 102, 127; from the dead father in Nos. 328, 340, 341. Cox, *op. cit.,* pp. 475–476. Saintyves refers to Cosquin's article in *Rev. des Trad. pop.* XXXIII, 202–216 (not available in Peiping) "avec toutes les références désirables" in *op. cit.,* 146.

⁵²In his *Contes de Perrault,* 145 ff.

⁵³Bolte-Polivka, *sup. cit.,* I, 178.

⁵⁴Doré, *Researches,* V, 693–694.

⁵⁵F. Denis, *Une Fête Brésillienne célébrée à Rouen en 1550* (Paris, 1850); Hartland, *Primitive Paternity* (2 vols., London), pp. 8–9.

⁵⁶von Bülow, *Internationales Archiv für Ethnographie,* XII, 67; Hartland, *loc. cit.*

⁵⁷J. B. Tavernier, *Travels in India* (tr. V. Ball, 2 vols., 1889), I, 75; Hartland, *op. cit.,* I, 49.

⁵⁸W. Crooke, *Things Indian* (London, 1906), 222; Hartland, *op. cit.,* 151.

The Bride-Show Custom and the Fairy-Story of Cinderella

Photeine P. Bourboulis

In the study of Cinderella, or, for that matter, in the study of folklore generally, one may usefully divide the critical approaches into two broad categories: the literal-historical and the symbolic-psychological. Approaches falling in the first category seek to find actual, historical events or customs underlying fairytales and other forms of folklore. In contrast, advocates of symbolic-psychological approaches tend to read tales as metaphors or codes. The usual difficulty with the latter approaches is that each competing analyst claims to have exclusive possession of the "correct" key necessary to unlock the alleged secret message contained in code.

Inspired in part by Professor Jameson's essay, Greek folklorist Photeine P. Bourboulis proposes a novel "historical" origin for the study of Cinderella. Dr. Bourboulis is primarily interested in what she calls the bride-show custom. The phrase refers to a reported practice whereby emperors or kings seeking a bride would supposedly order a number of eligible young girls to be assembled. From the group of candidates the royal bachelor would then select one to be his bride. In the first three essays in her Studies in the History of Modern Greek Story-Motives, *Bourboulis attempts to document the existence of the imperial bride-show in Byzantium, in Russia, and in China. She further argues that the custom later passed*

Reprinted from Photeine P. Bourboulis, *Studies in the History of Modern Greek Story-Motives* (Thessalonike, 1953), pp. 40–52.

from fact into fancy by moving into the folktale domain. This is how she was led to consider the story of Cinderella.

After ascertaining the passing of the bride-show into Greek popular fiction it will now be of interest to try and discover similar phenomena elsewhere, of the custom having left its trace on popular imagination.

In several central and eastern European versions of the fairy-story of Cinderella the prince sees the heroine for the first time at a grand ball at the palace, *"where all beautiful girls of the country were invited, that the prince might choose a bride."*[1]

Here I should like to take advantage of a suggestion made to me by Professor Jenkins as to the possibility of connecting this incident of the royal ball in Cinderella with the historical bride-show. A more thorough scrutiny, therefore, of the tale of Cinderella may possibly throw more light on this suggested connexion.

An important question as to Cinderella was raised by E. Cosquin,[2] who drew attention to a story from Southern India, which he considered as the antecedent of the European Cinderella. In this a princess becomes the wife of a prince who saved her from a giant. She subsequently loses her slipper in a pond. It is found by a fisherman and after changing hands is acquired by a king, who is seized by a passion for its owner. He succeeds in killing the husband of the princess through magic means and abducts the heroine. At this point the brother of the prince appears, warned by a magic object. He restores the prince to life and frees the princess.

Now an attempt to derive the European Cinderella from this Indian story is bound to be erroneous, as these two stories belong to clearly different types. The main points of the European Cinderella are a suffering girl, a meeting with the prince, a flight, a lost shoe, a shoe test and a marriage. In the Indian tale a prince acquires accidentally a pretty female shoe; with his imagination inflamed by the beautiful object he seeks and marries the owner. The salient point in this is that a prince becomes enamoured of an unknown woman, while in Cinderella proper the prince has met the heroine. A variant to be placed in the same group as the Indian story is the legend about the hetaira Rhodopis, as recorded by Strabo.[3] Rhodopis lived in Naucratis and became the wife of the Pharoah Psammiticus[4] in the following extraordinary way: While the Pharaoh was holding an open air council at Memphis, an eagle, which had picked up this lady's shoe while she was bathing, dropped it exactly where the Pharaoh sat. Attracted by the lovely shape of the shoe and moved by the strange occurrence he made enquiries about the owner and married her when found. The oldest known variant that could take its place in this group is an ancient Egyptian narrative published by Maspero.[5] A Pharaoh marries the owner of a perfumed lock found in a river. Thus the two types, Cinderella and the above, must be distinguished. On the whole, as A. Lang has noted, there is no peculiarly Indian idea in Cinderella that might speak for an Indian origin.[6]

In recent years an extremely valuable Chinese document was brought to the notice of Western folk-lorists by an American Sino-logue, Mr. R.D. Jameson. This document was destined to throw new light upon the researches on the fairy-story of Cinderella, about which A. Lang, in his introduction to Miss Cox's book,[7] had de-spaired that it will ever be traced to its origin and home. The document in question is a Chinese version of the Cinderella pub-lished by a certain Tuan Ch'eng Shih in the middle of the 9th century A.D., thus antedating by 700 years the oldest printed European version (this, according to Mr. Jameson, being Des Perrier's *Nou-velles Récréations et joyeux devis*, Nouvelle CXXIX, Lyon, 1558). Tuan Ch'eng Shih, Mr. Jameson informs us, was a scholar from Shantung and died in the position of junior minister in the ministry of rites. His book which contains the Chinese Cinderella, or Sheh Hsien, is entitled *Yu Yang Tsa Tsu;* the text that concerns us, translated into English by a Chinese scholar, Mr. Yü, appeared in Mr. Jameson's book *Three Lectures on Chinese Folk-lore,* Peiping, 1932, p. 47 et seq. The story, which is told at some length, can be summarized as follows[8]:

Before the T'sin and Han dynasties there was a Cave Chief called Wu. His wife died leaving him a daughter whose name was Sheh Hsien. She was very intelligent and he loved her fondly. He, how-ever, married another wife who ill-treated her step-daughter. Once Sheh Hsien caught a fish more than two inches long which she put in a basin of water. She fed it and it grew bigger and bigger. She changed the vessel several times, but at last it was so big that she had to put it in the pond behind the house. If the girl came to the pond the fish would put its face out of the water, but it would not do this if anyone else came. The step-mother wanted to kill Sheh Hsien's pet fish. So one day she asked her to give her her clothes to wash and then she sent her to draw water from a distant well. When she had gone the step-mother put the girl's clothes on and hiding a sword in her sleeve went to the pond and called the fish. The fish appeared and she killed it. She then cooked it and ate it and hid its bones under a dung hill. On the next day Sheh Hsien went to the pond, but the fish was not there. So she wept much. Then a man with dishevelled hair came down from heaven and told her that her step-mother had killed the fish and that its bones were under the dung hill. He advised her to take the fish's bones into her room and hide them and if she would like anything she could pray and her wish would be fulfilled. The girl took his advice and got from the fish's bones food, jewelry and dresses.

When the time came for the Cave Festival the step-mother took her own daughter there leaving Sheh Hsien to look after the fruit in the courtyard. When they had gone the girl dressed herself in bluish finery, put on a pair of golden shoes and went to the festival. There her step-sister kept staring at her and told her mother that that girl looked like her elder sister. As Sheh Hsien realized that her mother was getting suspicious she hurried back home leaving behind one of her shoes, which was picked up by a cave man. On her return the mother found her daughter asleep with her arms round a tree. So she gave up her suspicions. The cave people sold the shoe to a neighbouring island that was the kingdom of T'o Huan, and it was bought by the king of that island. He made his subjects try it on their feet, but it suited nobody. The king thought that the cave man who sold it got it by improper means, so he tortured him, but still he could not tell where from it came. Then the king sent people to search every house and another shoe of the same type was found at Sheh Hsien's house. The king of T'o Huan asked Sheh Hsien to put the shoe on and then she went and dressed herself in her bluish finery, put on those shoes and came to the king looking as beautiful as a goddess. Then she was married to the king and went to his kingdom. The step-mother and daughter were killed by flying stones. Sheh Hsien took the fish's bones with her, but in the first year her husband asked for such amounts of jewels that it ceased to produce any more. Then the king buried the bones on the sea-coast together with a great quantity of gold, but one night everything was washed away by the tide.

At the end of the story there is a note by Tuan Ch'eng Shih informing us that the story-teller is Li Shih Yuan, one of his former servants, who was originally a cave man of Yung Chow and knew many of the strange stories of the South.

Regarding this text Mr. Jameson brought up various points.[9] He thought that the story teller's attribution of the events to periods before the Han and Ts'in dynasties may be significant, but, on the other hand it may just be due to the narrator's desire to get his events fixed in time and space. From the information available about the kingdom of T'o Huan (which, it may be noted, is highly unsatisfactory) he gathered that this is probably situated in the South seas; it seems, however, that no overdue importance must be attributed to this name, as it may just be a designation for a distant land.

As Mr. Jameson rightly notes, we cannot describe this text as the first Cinderella that has ever been told, as it shows considerable signs of wear through oral tradition, especially in the incident of Sheh Hsien's visit to the cave festival, which is told with much less precision than the other incidents. Indeed the heroine goes to a festival dressed in all her finery, but we suddenly hear that she did not marry someone she met at the festival, but another man she had never seen. The vagueness at this point is clearly due, as I think, to a contamination of the Cinderella tale proper with another story of the type represented by the Southern Indian narrative published by Cosquin and referred to previously. We have a ball, a flight, a lost shoe, as in Cinderella proper, but from that part starts the confusion with the other type. Here another point may be added. Sheh Hsien's blue finery and golden shoes are entirely incompatible with a cave festival. *Cave men* is a Chinese designation for *savages*[10] and on the whole a festival of this type would by no means be the right background for the heroine's magnificent dress. There is no doubt that this episode in the Chinese variant has greatly suffered from oral tradition and it seems natural that a royal ball, as we have it elsewhere, and not a cave festival, was the original thing. The association of Sheh Hsien with the cave people in general can be explained by the teller's provenance from the cave men. We have been told by Tuan Ch'eng Shih that his servant Li, the story-teller, was himself a cave man from Yung Chow and as is not strange with popular story-tellers, he fixed the tale in his own social surroundings.

When Sheh Hsien's shoe gets into the hands of the king of T'o Huan the story returns to the track of Cinderella proper. He orders all houses to be searched for the owner of the shoe and when she is discovered he takes her as his bride to his own kingdom. Now this silly feature that a foreign king should search another country's houses in order to find a bride is obviously the consequence of the previous confusion of motives. There is no doubt that in the original version the search took place in the king's own kingdom.

Regarding the detail that when Cinderella's step-mother returned, she found her asleep with her arms round the tree, Mr. Jameson thought that this shows signs of contamination from another variant of the tale, where Cinderella is supported by a tree, that grows from her mother's grave. It may, however, be pointed out that we need not resort to an explanation of this kind. The step-mother on going away commands her to look after the fruit in the courtyard. Therefore, to be found asleep with her arms round the tree was meant to show that she carried out faithfully the orders given to her.

The most important feature in the fairy-story of Cinderella is the shoe-test, and on this A. Lang said that one thing is certain about it, that a tale of this kind could not have originated in a naked and shoeless race.[11] More specifically Professor Jenkins has indicated to me that Cinderella must have originated in a people where women's small feet were held in great estimation, because in most European versions the reason why the shoe would not fit any foot is given as the fact it was too small. This led Cinderella's step-sisters to cut their toes off in order to be able to wear it, but the fraud was soon discovered. Now that the Chinese variant has come to light we may be allowed to proceed a step forward and point out that this extraordinary appreciation of extremely small women's feet is peculiar and exclusive to the better classes of Chinese proper, by no means shared by other populations in China itself or outside it.[12]

Thus arose the very painful fashion of artificially small feet by means of compression or binding, which was general in the 10th century, but which must have started, according to some scholars, much earlier, as early as the fifth or sixth century A.D.[13] The term "golden lilies" denoting small women's feet in China is said to have originated with an Emperor of the 5th century, who, while deeply enjoying the dancing of a concubine on a stage ornamented with lilies, cried out "every foot-step makes a lily grow."[14] "The habit of binding girl's feet at an early age lasted until recent years, the reason for this mutilation being the social idea that small feet are both a mark of *beauty and gentility*.[15]

This idea is best illustrated in the statements of five different Chinese people taken by H.A. Giles[16] at the end of the last century:

1st. "If a girl's feet are not bound, people say she is not like a woman, but like a man; they laugh at her, calling her names, and her parents are ashamed of her."

2nd. "Girls are like flowers, like the willow. It is very important that their feet should be short, so that they can walk beautifully, with mincing steps, swaying gracefully, thus showing they are persons of respectability. People praise them. If not bound short, they say the mother has not trained the daughter carefully. She goes from house to house with noisy steps, and is called names. Therefore careful persons bind short."

3rd. *"One of a good family does not wish to marry a woman with long feet. She is commiserated because her feet are not perfect. If betrothed and the size of her feet not discovered till after marriage her husband and mother-in-law are displeased, her sisters-in-law laugh at her, and she herself is sad."*

4th. "The large-footed has to do rough work, does not sit in a sedan chair when she goes out, walks in the street barefooted, has no red clothes, does not eat the best food. She is wetted by the rain, tanned by the sun, blown upon by the wind. If unwilling do all the rough work of the house she is called 'gourmandizing and lazy.' Perhaps she decides to go out as a servant. She has no fame and honour. To escape all this her parents bind her feet."

5th. "Girls are like gold, like gems. They ought to stay in their own house. If their feet are not bound they go here and they go there with unfitting associates; they have no good name. They are like defective gems that are rejected."

We may also quote here a reported interview between the wife of a Chinese representative in the United States and an American newspaperwoman contained in the book of I.T. Headland, *Home Life in China*.[17] The topic is the artificially small feet. (The broken English is preserved in Madame Wu's answers): "But there are those poor little feet; how can you be graceful when you can't walk?"

"I walk," said Madame who had proved it by entering the room alone, with the aid of chairs and tables, then added quickly: "Anyway, I prefer eat to walk."

Reporter's comment: (Mme Wu's feet are not four inches long. They look as if they ought never to touch the floor, but be assigned to a favourite spot on the mantlepiece. They look like samples of feet in miniature, and remind one of the tiny models of battle-ships).

"There," I said, putting a calf-clad No. 4 beside the speck covered with red silk, "is a real foot meant for service."

"I guess so," said Mme Wu and shuddered.

. . . .

"In China not much use to walk," Mme Wu explained: "only around the gardens at home. Chinese ladies not walk abroad like Americans. In streets they go in sedan chairs, always with chaperone."

The reasoning illustrated by the above interview brings to our memory the argument with which in some European versions Cinderella's step-mother persuades her own daughter to cut her toes off, so that she can pass the shoe marriage test. She tells her that on becoming queen her feet will not be of much use to her, as she will always ride about in a carriage.

The feelings of Chinese men towards this fashion are best interpreted by H.A. Giles in his book *The Civilization of China,* 1911.[18]

". . . any Chinaman will bear witness as to the seductive effect of a gaily dressed girl picking her way on tiny feet some three inches in length, her swaying movements and delightful appearance of instability, conveying a general sense of delicate grace quite beyond expression in words."

That the shape of a woman's foot is probably *just as important as her face* for the estimation of her beauty may, perhaps, be shown from the following passage of a Chinese tale[19]: "Miss A-pao; or perseverance rewarded." (Some young men meet a lady at the spring festival, when it is customary for both men and women to be seen abroad.) "Possessed of peerless beauty the ring of her admirers gradually increased, till at last she rose up to go. The excitement among the young men was intense; they criticized her face and *discussed her feet.* . . ."

If the Cinderella is truly of Chinese origin then the element of the shoe in it is quite compatible with Chinese custom. The next thing we must consider is the royal ball, which we believe to be the antecedent of the cave festival in the version of Tuan Ch'eng Shih. In some European versions the royal ball was superseded by a meeting between the prince and Cinderella at church, repeating itself in the usual threefold manner that is one of the laws of popular story-telling. Probably this type arose from the fact that the church to some story-teller's judgement was a more natural place for Cinderella to be seen by the prince.

Now a royal ball where all young girls attend and where the prince selects his bride is again quite compatible with Chinese custom. We have it in Padre De Medonza's testimony.[20] A prince's bride-show in China took place on the occasion of a great banquet and reception at the palace. The daughters of the greatest lords of the kingdom, arrayed in rich apparel, were all present. Unfortunately I do not know of any Chinese variant of the Cinderella describing the ball she attended as a bride-show at the palace. This, however, is clearly stated in an Indian popular version noted by Cosquin.[21] There the magnificent dress and golden shoes are given to Cinderella *"on the day when the prince, wishing to take a wife, called to the palace all the young girls of the country."* This is the only Asiatic version, containing this detail, that has come to my knowledge. However, we may be allowed to conjecture that, just as the bride-show became a story-motif in Byzantium, the reception at the Chinese Imperial Palace for the purpose of a bride-display may have also turned into a motif that found its way into the Cinderella.

As regards another point, the supernatural help granted to Cinderella, the version of Tuan Ch'eng Shih has a fish, but in another Chinese version, recorded from recent oral tradition,[22] I find that the aid offered to Cinderella is from a yellow cow. It is, moreover, stated in the story that the spirit of Cinderella's dead mother was reincarnated in that animal. This idea, which is also found in European variants, is again quite compatible with Chinese beliefs, where reincarnation is a religious doctrine.[23]

Apart from the importance of the small shoe in the tale as a token, possibly, of the great beauty of Cinderella, there is also the shoe test. Unfortunately I cannot find direct evidence as to a historical occurrence of this kind in China, but we know that this was done in Byzantium in connexion with a bride-show.

We learn from the Vita Philareti that all girls in the Empire had to submit to the royal commissioners' examination for the bride-show of Constantine VI. These officials did not only examine face and stature, but also measured «ισὺ πσᾶὁζ ιὸ πεὸιλσν» (the sandal on the foot). How from an occurrence of this kind a story-motif could spring up, like the Cinderella shoe-test for the discovery of a future queen, one can easily imagine. It may be pointed out that among a shoe-conscious race like the Chinese it is highly unlikely that a foot or shoe examination of the prospective royal brides should have been omitted.

In the Cinderella proper the bride-show precedes the shoe-test, forming a prothysteron as to the order of things contained in the custom. It was thus by the skill of the author that all these elements, taken from his native environment, were put together to make up a delightful story. "The märchen," A. Lang says,[24] "is a kaleidoscope; the incidents are the bits of coloured glass. Shaken, they fall into a variety of attractive forms; some are fitter than others, survive more powerfully, and are more widely spread."

If the story of Cinderella is truly of Chinese origin, as we have grounds to think, it is not possible to say how it reached Europe.[25] Tibetan and Mongol folk-lore is practically entirely unknown, and also, until Chinese folk-lore is searched more for other variants of the Cinderella by Sinologues our hypothesis must remain unexplored further.

To the present day, apart from Cosquin's theory two other theories were expressed about the origin of Cinderella. A summary of the specific views of the supporters of each of these theories can be found in Mr. Jameson's work.[26] A group of older scholars saw in Cinderella the detritus of a myth connected with the rising sun. A more recent researcher, Saintyves, considered Cinderella to be a commentary on an early spring ritual. The first one of these opinions is no longer tenable nowadays, as the theory explaining all fairy tales as corrupt versions of ancient myths has ceased to be believed in the field of folk-lore. The reason is that there is, generally, no proof for the priority of myth over popular tale.

In spite of this Mr. Jameson seems to waver as to the possibility of the story of Sheh Hsien having anything to do with a myth about the dawn. The reasons for his hesitation, as he explains, are firstly that Sheh Hsien is said to have looked "as beautiful as a goddess" and then because the Dawn Goddess of Chinese Buddhism is represented with the viscera of a fish in one of her eighteen arms. As he himself admits, she is not believed to wear a blue robe and her feet are not in the picture.

On such vagueness of data it is hard even to base so much as a hesitation for rejecting this theory. That Sheh Hsien looked as beautiful as a goddess seems to be merely a formula of speaking and it is difficult for one to see what weight can be carried by the coincidence that the eighteen-armed goddess is represented holding the viscera of a fish.

Saintyves' view is, in short, that the Cinderella may have derived from a ritual at Carnival, because we find a Cinderella with twelve attendants; as the twelve months, taking sometimes an important part in the European spring festival. Against this Mr. Jameson has rightly said that the use of Cinderella at spring festivals is no proof that she is derived from an early ritual.

Mr. Jameson himself is very cautious about ascribing to the Cinderella a definite Chinese origin and prefers to postpone all discussions until more evidence is available from Asiatic countries. In spite, however, of the dangers of proposing a solution where the evidence is so scanty, an endeavour has been made in the present paper to base an opinion on the tale's internal evidence. It is hoped that this may later be confirmed by discoveries of new data in the field of Asiatic folk-lore.

NOTES

[1]M. Cox, Cinderella, p. 221. Variant from Grimm, *Household Tales,* transl. M. Hunt, London, 1881, Vol. I, pp. 93–100, No. XXI (from Hesse). "King appoints three days' festival to which all beautiful girls are invited that his son may choose a bride. Step-sisters go and Cinderella dresses them." Cox, p. 165. From L. Bechstein. *Deutsches Märchenbuch,* Leipzig, 1846, pp. 242–44. "King gives festival and all young girls are invited that his son may choose a bride." Cox, p. 317. From E. Meier, *Deutsche Volksmärchen aus Schwaben,* Stuttgart, 1852, Story No. IV, pp. 16–20. "Young King, wishing to choose bride, gives grand ball." E. Meier, *op. cit.,* pp. 165–74, No. XLVIII (from Heubach). "Son of the house thinks of marrying and gives grand ball, to which all lovely girls near are invited." Cox, p. 433. From Zingerle, *Tirols Volksdichtungen und Volksgebräuche,* Band I, *Kinder- und Hausmärchen,* Innsbrück, 1852, Story No. XVI, pp. 86–94 (1st ed.); 72–78 (2nd ed.), Hennenpfösl. "The owner of the castle gives a large ball, to which he invites all the neighbourhood, meaning to choose the loveliest girl for his bride." Cox, p. 436. Zingerle, *op. cit.,* Band II, *Kinder- und Hausmärchen aus Süddeutschland,* Regensburg, 1854, pp. 231–35 (from Zillerthal), Der Gehende Wagen. "After some time the count gives a grand ball

which is to last seven days, for he wants to choose a bride." Cox, p. 150. From Afanasiev, *Russian Folk-tales,* Moscow, 1861, Part VI, pp. 152–54, No. XXX. "One day, the king of that country announced that he wanted a wife and invited all maids to the palace."

[2]*E. Cosquin, Les Contes Indiens et l'Occident,* Paris, 1922, p. 48.

[3]XVII, ch. 1, 33.

[4]*Ael. Var. Hist.* XIII, 33.

[5]*Contes populaires de l'Égypte ancienne,* 4th ed., p. 13 (the two brothers).

[6]M. Cox, *Cinderella,* London, 1893, Introduction by A. Lang, p. VIII.

[7]P. VII.

[8]*Three Lectures on Chinese Folk-lore.* Peking, 1932. p. 51 et seq.

[9]Ibid., p. 55 *et seq.*

[10]H.A. Giles, *Strange Stories from a Chinese Studio,* London, 1880, Vol. I, p. 397.

[11]M. Cox, *Cinderella,* Introduction by A. Lang, p. X.

[12]H.A. Giles, *The Civilization of China,* 1911, p. 105 et seq. It must always be carefully remembered that Manchu women (the women of the dynasty that has ruled since 1644) do not compress their feet. Consequently the Empresses of modern times have feet of natural size; neither is the practice (of compression) in force among the Hakkas, a race said to have migrated from the North of China to the South in the thirteenth century; nor among the hill tribes; nor among the boating population of Canton and elsewhere. . . . Outside China the custom is not known.

[13]E.T.C. Werner, *Myths and Legends of China,* p. 39. Also H.A. Giles, *The Civilization of China,* p. 105.

[14]H.A. Giles, *Strange Stories from a Chinese Studio,* Vol 1, p. 188, note 4.

[15]H.A. Giles, *Strange Stories from a Chinese Studio,* Vol 1, p. 430, note 5: "Slave-girls do not have their feet compressed." Also v. I.T. Headland, *Home Life in China,* London, 1914, p. 63.

[16]H.A. Giles, *Strange Stories from a Chinese Studio,* 1880, Vol. I, p. 79, note 1.

[17]I.T. Headland, *Home Life in China,* London, 1914, p. 288, ff.

[18]P. 106.

[19]H.A. Giles, *Strange Stories from a Chinese Studio,* London, 1880, Vol. 1, p. 188, tale XXIV.

[20]Juan Gonzalez de Medonza, *The History of the Great and Mighty Kingdom of China and the Situation Thereof,* reprinted from the early translation of R. Parke, ed. Sir George T. Staunton, London, 1853, Vol. I, p. 62, ff.

[21]*Les Contes Indiens et l'Occident,* Paris, 1922. p. 53.

[22]Wolfram Eberhard, *Chinese Fairy-tales and Folk-tales,* transl. Desmond Parsons, London, 1937, p. 17 (Cinderella).

[23]Chinese folk-tale with the motif of reincarnation can be found *passim* in L. Wieger and Yuan Mei, *Folk-lore chinois moderne,* 1909.

[24]M. Cox, *Cinderella,* Introduction by A. Lang. p. X.

[25]However, the barbarous feature of the aged mother being put to death by Cinderella's sisters, which we find in certain Near Eastern variants is not, probably, without importance as an indication of the tale's journey through the savage tribes of Central Asia. For representative types v. Cox, *op. cit.,* pp. 8, 21, 22.

[26]*Three Lectures on Chinese Folk-lore,* p. 70.

From Perrault to Walt Disney:
The Slipper of Cinderella

Paul Delarue

Scholars preferring a literal-historical approach to Cinderella have had some difficulty in explaining the presence of a number of seemingly fantastic elements in the tale. One of these elements which has spawned a whole academic debate on its own is the glass slipper. Inasmuch as glass slippers do not appear to occur in common everyday reality, it was necessary to explain them or rather explain them away. One ingenious theory was that the French word verre *(glass) must have been mistakenly substituted for an older French word,* vair, *meaning fur. Fur slippers made sense; glass slippers did not. The only problem with this explanation is that Perrault did use the word* verre, *and furthermore, non-French versions of Cinderella also contain references to glass slippers, indicating that they are clearly traditional. Miss Cox, however, found only six instances of glass slippers among her 345 texts, and she felt that they might all have been influenced by Perrault's version. It seems evident that glass slippers are not to be found in the majority of Cinderella tales. Yet they are found in some, and as French folklorist Paul Delarue points out, they occur in other tales as well.*

One reason why the verre/vair *error has been perpetuated is that it crept into such authoritative sources as the* Encyclopaedia Britannica. *Through successive editions, generations of readers were told:*

Reprinted from *Le Monde*, February 7, 1951, p. 7.

"In the English version, a translation of Perrault's Cendrillon, the glass slipper which she drops on the palace stairs is due to a mistranslation of pantoufle en vair *(a fur slipper), mistaken for* en verre." *Could the* Encyclopaedia Britannica *be wrong? For decades, folklorists have been kept busy refuting the unfounded* verre/vair *hypothesis, but to no avail. No sooner was one ignorant writer corrected than another sprang up to take his place.*

So it was that Paul Delarue, an authority on French folktales, was moved to respond when he read an essay by Albert Dauzat on "Des Fautes d'orthographe á la pantoufle de Cendrillon" in Le Monde *of January 24, 1951, where the all too familiar pseudo-theory was rehearsed once more. Delarue in his response succinctly states the folklorist's position on the issue. One could add only that from a symbolic as opposed to a literal perspective, glass is perfectly appropriate. Glass is a standard symbol of virginity. It is fragile and can be broken only once. In Jewish wedding ritual, the groom crushes a glass under his foot—for good luck. In this light, the very attempt by lexicographers and others to substitute "fur" for "glass" is itself worthy of consideration. Interpretations of folklore, like folklore, may serve as projective outlets for fantasy.*

In a newspaper article, Delarue did not have the luxury of footnotes to document his assertions, but the reader should realize that behind each statement made, Delarue had abundant evidence. For example, at one point he presents a brief synopsis of Aarne-Thompson tale type 301, The Three Stolen Princesses. Two years earlier, Delarue in "Les Contes Populaires de France: Inventaire analytique et methodique," Nouvelle Revue des Traditions Populaires, *1 (1949), 312–341, had discussed eighty-one French versions of this tale.*

For samples of the previous debates, see D.B., "Cinderella's Slipper: Glass or Fur," Notes and Queries, *8th Ser., Vol. 10 (1896), 331–332; Edward Latham, "A propos d'une erreur littéraire,"* Mercure de France, *253 (1934), 176–179 (see also E. Latham, "La Petite Pantoufle de Verre,"* Notes and Queries, *Vol. 191 (1946), 233–234). For further discussion of shoe symbolism with special reference to Cinderella, see Dorothee Kleinmann, "Cendrillon et son pied,"* Cahiers de Litterature Orale, *No. 4 (1978), 56–88. For the folklore of the shoe in general, see Paul Sartori, "Der Schuh im Volksglauben,"* Zeitschrift des Vereins für Volkskunde, *4 (1894), 41–54,*

148–180, 282–305, 412–427; and Jacob Nacht, "The Symbolism of the Shoe with Special Reference to Jewish Sources," Jewish Quarterly Review, *6 (1915), 1–22. See also William A. Rossi,* The Sex Life of the Foot and Shoe *(New York: Ballantine Books, 1976); and Howard S. Levy,* Chinese Foot Binding *(New York: Bell, 1972). For more information about Cinderella in the French tradition, see Paul Delarue and Marie-Louise Tenèze,* Le Conte Populaire Français, *II (Paris: G.P. Maisonneuve et Larose, 1964), pp. 245–280.*

In *Le Monde* of last January 24th [1951], Mr. Dauzat gave the judgment of a man of letters on Cinderella's slipper. Would your newspaper perhaps now accept the view of a folklorist who is a specialist in the study of folktales?

It is a fact that Perrault in the edition of his prose tales published in his lifetime wrote "Cendrillon ou la petite pantoufle de verre" (and not *vair*). It is almost certain that he took his narrative from an oral source. (However, the comparative study of traditional French and foreign versions seems to indicate that just as in other tales, he has changed certain traits in order to adapt them to the taste of the gentlemen of his time.) But when he wrote *verre* and not *vair*, I do not think that he made a mistake, as Mr. Dauzat contends, but I believe rather that he only did this to conform to the data from oral tradition, which one can also find in other countries where there is no homonym which permits the confusion.

Those who believe in the slipper of fur try to apply to folk products their literary logic, but it has no role to play in this domain. Long before Littré and the other lexicographers cited by Dauzat, Balzac in his *Études Philosophiques sur Catherine de Medicis* (1836) suggested the only explanation that seemed logical to him: "They distinguished between thick and thin *vair*. But for a hundred years, this word has fallen so out of use that in an infinite number of editions of Perrault's tales, the celebrated slipper of Cinderella, which without doubt was made out of thin *vair*, is presented as being made out of *verre*." Let us note that if indeed one wanted to be logical, *vair* is too thick a fur to be made into slippers suitable for a splendid costume and that only the thinner *vair* would have been appropriate.

But I would stress that it is not our logic which guides the teller of folktales. The motif of the glass slipper is traditional, and can be found in several foreign tale types for each of which I will cite only one example.

In a Scottish version of Cinderella which contains more archaic and more universal traits than Perrault's version (it is a helpful animal, a little black lamb, and not a fairy, who gives the three dresses to the heroine) there are also glass shoes which provide the means of identifying the young girl.

In another Scottish tale of the "Peau d'Ane" (Ass-skin [Cat-skin]) type, the young maiden whose father wants to marry her asks him successively for three marvelous dresses, and then for glass shoes, and it is one of the shoes lost which makes it possible for her to be recognized.

In an Irish tale of the Psyche type, the heroine, leaving to search for her husband, who is in an inaccessible castle atop a glass mountain, receives from an old man a pair of glass shoes which enable her to climb the slippery slope.

In another Irish tale which is related to our "Beast with Seven Heads," the hero, who rescues a princess from a sea serpent who comes every year to devour one of the king's daughters, wears a pair of shoes made of blue glass. The princess snatches one of the hero's shoes before he departs, which allows her later to identify him.

All those who are familiar with *märchen* know that glass, copper, gold, silver, diamonds are the precious materials of which things in the fairytale realm are made, things which in our real world are made of ordinary materials. There one finds castles, cities, mountains made of copper, gold, silver, or of glass, forests in which the trees have leaves of gold, silver, or glass; the tale of the glass (or crystal) mountain is widely distributed in northern and eastern Europe. In the old Celtic legends, it is in a boat of glass or of bronze that the fairies conduct the hero to the isles of bliss. The most unexpected things can be made of glass in the fantastic world of the folktale, where one encounters not only the giant with a beard of gold and the giant with a beard of copper but also the giant with a beard of glass.

But let us return to the lost shoe which identifies the heroine, or less frequently the hero. In Cinderella the slipper, instead of being made of glass, crystal, or diamonds can also be gold, silver, sometimes cloth. . . .

In the tale of John the Bear, the hero rescues three princesses from the underground world, where they were detained by a monster by having them raised successively by his brothers who remained at the top of a well, and the princesses often each leave behind for him a slipper of increasing value, for example, the first leaves him one of copper; the second, one of silver; the third, one of gold or of diamonds. (In the hundred French versions that we know we have not found the glass slipper once, but several times we found one made of diamonds.)

Let us note that slippers of gold, silver, or diamonds are hardly more true to life than those of glass. Without doubt, worries about logic ought to lead commentators on tales to state that the shoes were actually made out of golden, silver, or glass fabric. But the tellers of folktales and their audiences see above all in these objects the precious and shiny aspects of the material of which they are made without troubling themselves about the objects' resemblance to real life.

And to conclude this account, which might appear frivolous in this day and age, we will repeat the closing formula used by certain female raconteurs when they announce the marriage which ends the majority of fairy tales: "I made myself beautiful for the wedding; I had a dress made out of spider web, a hat of butter and shoes of glass, but when I went through the forest, I tore my dress; when I crossed the plain, the sun melted my hat; when I walked on ice, I broke my shoes which went clic-clac. That's the story I had in my sack."

The Study of the Cinderella Cycle

Archer Taylor

One of the acknowledged masters of the comparative approach to folklore was Archer Taylor (1890–1973). Although perhaps best known for his exceptional studies of proverbs and riddles, Professor Taylor wrote on ballads and folktales as well. In the present context, it is of interest that one of the last papers he penned was concerned with Cinderella.

The paper was not easy to find. Professor Nai-Tung Ting, in the acknowledgements in his 1974 monograph The Cinderella Cycle in China and Indo-China, *expressed his thanks to Professor Taylor for allowing him to read his unpublished paper "The Study of Cinderella." Inquiries directed to the Archer Taylor papers housed in the library of the University of Georgia and to Mrs. Hasseltine Taylor, Professor Taylor's widow, proved of no avail. Professor Ting confirmed that he had indeed seen the paper, but unfortunately he had no copy of it. He thought that it might have been presented at the International Society for Folk Narrative Research congress held in Bucharest in 1969, but since the papers given at that congress had never been published, it was not so simple a task to verify this. Both the preliminary and final programs of that congress listed Professor Taylor as giving a completely different paper: "The Wise Carving of the Fowl (MT 1533) and Allied Tales." The paper, if it ever existed, seemed to be lost forever. As a last resort, a letter was sent to the Institutul de Cercetari Ethnologice si Dialectologice in Bucharest, the host institution of the 1969 congress, asking whether a copy of the paper could be located. Four months later, Professor Taylor's paper arrived with a note apologizing for the delay in responding. Apparently the severe earthquake in Romania in 1977 had put the congress records in disarray, and it took some searching to find the paper.*

The paper was written during late 1969 and early 1970. Frances Hagin Mayer, a longtime student of Japanese folklore, visited Professor Taylor in April, 1969, and told him about Kinichi Mizusawa's 1964 compilation of nearly one hundred Japanese versions of Cinderella, Echigo no Shinderera. Although Professor Taylor read many European languages, he did not know Japanese. Still, he was excited at the prospect of having so many additional versions of Cinderella available for comparative studies. In correspondence with Professor J.W. Hassell, Jr., of the University of Georgia, Professor Taylor wrote in April, 1970: "I began to write last November and have perhaps another day's work. I must not let my grip of this confused subject slip or I shall be another month on this job." He added in a marginal note, "She took two days more but she is now ready for public appearance." In a later letter dated April 30, Professor Taylor commented as follows on his own paper "Cinderella was only 12pp., but I never had the troubles in writing anything that I had with this. And it is, alas, a dull job, when finished. But it does contain much information, and I learned a lot."

It is with the hope that readers can learn one last lesson from one of the master scholars of folklore that "The Study of the Cinderella Cycle" is included in this Casebook. It would have been a pity if all the time and effort Professor Taylor devoted to Cinderella had gone to waste. A few editorial footnotes have been added in brackets to bring bibliographical details up to date.

For a short appreciation of Professor Taylor, see Wayland D. Hand, "Archer Taylor (1890–1973)," Journal of American Folklore, 87 (1974), 3–9.

A brief review of the scholarly history of the Cinderella cycle is interesting and instructive for various reasons that will appear in the course of the following remarks. It will assemble a variety of facts that will reward interpretation and suggest tasks that are still to be undertaken. It will give some notion of the nature and purposes of recent studies in folklore and serve as a background for developments that seem to take account of Cinderella only rarely. I shall not try to discover why this is the case. Some have asserted that Cinderella is the most widely known of all *Märchen,* but I should not venture to make such an assertion. It can be safely said that perhaps no other tale has so many early, independent, and widely scattered versions. A ninth-century Chinese version was published twoscore years ago and duly registered in the appropriate typelists. A Japanese version published before (in 1885) was little noticed at the time, although it was caught and properly listed in 1893 and has been identified as belonging to a sixteenth-century chapbook tradition. Other allusions or versions older than 1700 or even 1600 have been pointed out in England, France, Germany, and Sweden. They belong to independent versions of the cycle.

The first scholarly comments on tales belonging to the Cinderella cycle are perhaps those in the *Household Tales of the Brothers Grimm.* Neither these nor the search for similarities to Biblical story or to the Latin and Greek classics proved to be rewarding. Comparisons with Germanic mythology such as were subjects of lively interest in Germany in the first half of the nineteenth century were also unprofitable. The notion that tales were first told in the Far East and were carried to the Near East and disseminated from there during the Middle Ages to Europe was much discussed around the middle of the century and has continued to be studied. In such studies Cinderella played no large part. Emmanuel Cosquin, who championed such ideas in his *Contes populaires de Lorraine,*[1] made brief references to parallels to incidents in Cinderella but not to the whole tale, and continued his interest in the subject to the end of his life; but few others in England or France shared it as far as Cinderella was concerned.

We may terminate a first period in the study of Cinderella with mention of French publications about the origins of tales that aroused little interest in France and less in other countries[2] and the mention of Emmanuel Cosquin's search for parallels in India that had no great success. We may find another terminus about the same time in Andrew Lang's edition of *Perrault's Popular Tales* (Oxford, 1888) because he dwells on details (the italics are his) that his readers did not choose to investigate, although he urged them to do so: "the process by which the agency of a *Fairy Godmother* has been substituted for a *friendly beast;* usually the blood kindred of the hero or heroine, [and] the favoritism shown, in many versions, to the *youngest child,* and the custom which alludes to the child's place in the cinders."[3] We can regard the years around 1890 as marking the end of such activities as these and the beginning of those of a more modern sort in the study of Cinderella.

Since I have mentioned collections containing versions of Cinderella, I may cite here those of major importance. The tales have been taken down in hundreds of texts and published in scores of collections, but only five collections seem to call for notice as contributions to scholarship. The first is Charles Perrault's collections of versified tales (1694) and prose tales (1697), each of which contained a version belonging to the cycle (I have reckoned them as one). The *Household Tales of the Brothers Grimm* was a collection annotated in such a manner that it became a fundamental reference work for a century. Aurelio M. Espinosa, *Cuentos populares españoles* (3 vols., Madrid, 1946–1947), contains annotations dealing with individual Spanish tales that represent the foundation of modern historical comparisons. A. Millien and Paul Delarue, *Contes du Nivernais et du Morvan* (Paris, [1953]), with annotations (pp. 266–270) that in the case of Cinderella were to be continued in subsequent volumes of the series, but only a few of them appeared because Delarue's death stopped publication. Finally, Kurt Ranke, *Schleswig-Holsteinische Volksmärchen* (3 vols., Kiel, 1955–1962), has notes that bring the lists of German variants of individual tales up to date. Each of these collections makes a characteristic and individual contribution to scholarship. Perrault's collections attracted attention to the cycle. The *Household Tales* containing three tales belonging to the cycle (the Male Cinderella was not included) brought annotations that established a continuing interest in scholarly investigation. A.M. Espinosa made a generous addition to rather little-known Spanish traditions and insisted by his example on a truly international commentary. Paul Delarue in his notes to a regional French collection contributed probably the best introduction to the study of the cycle. Kurt Ranke's brief survey of the cycle and his bibliographies of recently collected German texts gave us accounts of German tradition of remarkable accuracy and completeness.

Perhaps the most noteworthy fact about the scholarship of these tales is the variety of small contributions. These have been appearing for almost a century. I shall characterize them briefly without making any effort to list them completely. In 1898 Adhémar Leclere compared versions of a Cinderella tale in three languages of Indochina, citing where they had been published in the preceding fifteen years.[4] This is an unusual utilization of these specialized contributions. They have ordinarily received very little attention. Miss Marian Roalfe Cox published collectanea dealing with Cinderella some years after publishing a major work dealing with the tale.[5] On three occasions Reidar Th. Christiansen published in the journal *Bealoideas* versions of Cinderella found in the Dublin archives. Another scholar brought together three versions from southern Arabia.[6] His interest was linguistic rather than folkloristic. I conclude with three contributions of remarkable variety: Helwig Lüdeke, "Das Aschenbrödel als griechische Volksballade," *Zeitschrift für Volkskunde*, 8 (1936–1937) [1938], 87–91; Arthur Waley, "The Chinese Cinderella Story," *Folklore*, LVIII (1947), 226–238; and Donn V. Hart and Harriett C. Hart, "Cinderella in the Eastern Bisayas with a Summary of the Philippine Versions," *Journal of American Folklore*, LXXXIX (1966), 307–337.

Although interest in the Cinderella cycle begins at a rather early time in the history of the investigation of *märchen*, suggestions of studies that might be pursued, like Andrew Lang's previously mentioned hints, almost always fell on deaf ears. Important general works on the folktale either did not mention Cinderella or, when they did so, elicited no response. Thus, E. Sidney Hartland, *The Science of Fairy Tales* (London, 1891), mentioned Cinderella only incidentally, and J.A. MacCulloch, *The Childhood of Fiction* (London, 1905), did not mention it at all. In contrast to such excellent English works, Gédéon Huet, *Les Contes populaires* (Paris, [1923]) made generous mention of the tale (pp. 85–91) but awakened no interest in following up the suggestions.

Marian Roalfe Cox's book *Cinderella. Three Hundred and Forty-Five Variants of Cinderella, Catskin, and Cap O' Rushes. Abstracted and Tabulated, with a Discussion of Mediaeval Analogues, and Notes*[7] marks the end of an order and the beginning of a modern period in the study of tales generally and of Cinderella in particular. It is a remarkably complete assembling of information about the various tales in the cycle and about details of all sorts. She defined the cycle in this fashion (p. xxv):

> The incidents characteristic of the story of "Cinderella" are interchangeable with a large proportion of the incidents of the "Catskin" and "Cap o' Rushes" stories. . . . The *essential* incidents of each group may be seen as follows:

A. Cinderella

Ill-treated heroine.
Recognition by means of shoe.

B. Catskin

Unnatural father.
Heroine flight.

C. Cap o' Rushes

King Lear judgment.
Outcast heroine.

She adds a fourth group of tales "approximating to these types but not referable to any distinct type" and a fifth group consisting of "hero-tales containing incidents common to the Cinderella variants."[8]

A brief account of the generally used manner of listing tales will clarify the notions of "type" and cycle" that have been referred to in the course of these remarks. In the late 1880s, after he had made large collections of tales in his native Finland, Kaarle Krohn conceived a very important idea. Like Miss Cox's book of texts and related materials for the study of a tale, Krohn's idea of a classification or list as a means of indexing tales is novel enough to be regarded as marking an epoch in the study of tales. The idea was not entirely new, but no one had presented it in a usable form. Some twenty years after conceiving the idea, he commissioned Antti Aarne to index the tales in the archives of the Finish Literary Society in Helsinki. Aarne published a preliminary draft of the headings he had set up in 1910 (FF Communications 3) and followed it with a catalogue in the next year (FF Communications 4). The next major advance was made a decade later, when Reidar Th. Christiansen published a Norwegian list of tales in the archives in Oslo (*Norske*

Eventyr, Kristiania, 1922, and an English abstract in FF Communications, No. 46, 1922). The adequate summaries of the tales that Christiansen added ensured general understanding and acceptance of the list, and archivists in many countries catalogued their collections in this fashion, with such added types as circumstances called for. Krohn now suggested that an international compilation should take account of additions, and Stith Thompson undertook the task (FF Communications 74, 1928). In this the definition of tales to be included was restricted to *Märchen* taken down from oral tradition. While later makers of lists did not adhere strictly to this definition, they ordinarily excluded legends, whether secular (Sagen) or religious; miracles generally and those of the Virgin Mary in particular; etiological tales or explanations of origins like Why the Bear Has No Tail; and formula tales in general (many had been included in early typelists and were retained). This typelist, a compilation of lists by many workers in many lands, is now available in Thompson's second revision (FF Communications 184, 1961, repr. 1964).

In its present form the international catalogue is a landmark in the study of tales. It does not take account, except incidentally, of cycles of tales, that is to say, of tales related for various special reasons such as association with a famous figure (Till Eulenspiegel, Faust, or Nasreddin Hodja) or other unifying concept. The typelist has been more or less drastically revised every twenty or thirty years, and the time is approaching when a revision can be expected. In a new edition we should add many tales, especially those already pointed out as unclassified and not assigned numbers in the typelist by Reinhold Köhler, Johannes Bolte, Walter Anderson, Paul Delarue, and others with knowledge of many tales. In recent years a very valuable list of unclassified tales has been published annually in *Fabula.* In addition to such additions, Antti Aarne planned an index of all the tales in a few widely known standard collections such as the *Household Tales,* Afanasiev's Russian collection, Hahn's Modern Greek collection, and the like. Such an index would be a valuable enlargement of our means of identifying tales. Aarne published a somewhat hastily made list of tales in a few collections, but it should be supplemented by additional titles and should be completed (see FF Communications 10, 1912). Additions of the sorts that I have suggested must await the completion and publication of

the very valuable lists awaiting publication or completion, such as
the Japanese (complete in proof), Rumanian (complete in manuscript), Hungarian (nearly complete), French (about two-thirds
complete), and so on.[9] We can expect to learn a great deal from the
two forthcoming volumes of Katharine M. Briggs, *A Dictionary of
British Folk-Tales in the English Language.*[10] Until such works as
these are available in print, let us hope that no one undertakes a
revision of the typelist.

The investigation of the Cinderella cycle that followed the publication of Miss Cox's book, the many scholarly books about tales,
and the national and international typelists has been surprisingly
small in quantity and inconclusive in results. As I have already said,
little or nothing survives of the earliest scholarly writings about
Cinderella. Although Miss Cox's book contains a surprising amount
of information about tales in the Cinderella cycle and the incidents
in them, it stimulated no studies, and even those who have written
books about these tales made rather little use of it. A mention of the
book in what is perhaps the only general international bibliography
of folklore of that age[11] comments on the compiler's reply to her
inquiry and thus makes it clear that he saw the book; but he gives no
idea of its nature or value.

The failure of Miss Cox's *Cinderella* to stimulate investigation is
very striking. Scholars did not discuss the tale for a generation, and
when they did so they made no use of her book. For example,
Emmanuel Cosquin continued his investigation of possible Oriental
connections during the first twenty years of this century, and left it
to be completed and published as *Les Contes Indiens et l'Occident*
(Paris, 1922). This deals with incidents belonging to the cycle rather
than with the tales but makes little use of what Miss Cox collected.
Paul Saintyves, *Les Contes de Perrault* (Paris, 1923), naturally gave
a conspicuous place to the two versions of Cinderella that Perrault
printed but made little use of Miss Cox's book. His championing of
theories about pre-Christian rituals found no hearty welcome. In
sum, there is little to chronicle between 1893 and 1930 except the
making of indexes, a variety of brief articles dealing with a few
Cinderella tales from one region or another without much effort to
integrate them with any general notions about the cycle. The two
studies that were published either continued the search for parallels
in India—a search that proved unrewarding in the case of our tale—
or started in directions that few wished to pursue.

The event that awoke a fresh interest in Cinderella was R.D. Jameson's discovery of a ninth-century Chinese version.[12] Jameson's situation as a professor in a university in China did not make it possible for him to see the books needed for an adequate commentary on the text, but his essay was noticed in places that brought the version to general knowledge. World War II interrupted the progress of investigations of this sort, and nothing except the brief specialized articles we have already noted kept an interest in Cinderella alive.

Anna Birgitta Rooth, *The Cinderella Cycle* (Lund, [1951]), lays a foundation for further investigation. While it is primarily a study of one tale of the cycle, it deals briefly with other pertinent tales, but not all of them.[13] This and books dealing with other tales are often difficult to read because the author uses designations for the tales that do not accord with those in the typelist (and it may be said that the designations in the typelist in its various editions, as well as in the many national lists, show considerable variation). Dr. Rooth was able to see a large proportion of the variants cited in previous investigations and to make considerable additions to them. Further study of the tale must start from Rooth's study. She has generously deposited copies of her materials in the archives in Lund and in the library of the Institute for Folk-Literature in Copenhagen.

The problems in the study of the Cinderella cycle can now be more clearly stated than before. We can justly regard *The Cinderella Cycle* as marking a new period in our account of the investigation of the cycle. For example, we can now discuss whether Type 923, "As Dear as Salt [Love Like Salt]" should be regarded as belonging to the cycle.[14] Shortly after Dr. Rooth's treatise appeared, Photeine P. Bourboulis published *Studies in the History of Modern Greek Story-Motifs,*[15] a learned discussion of allusions to Central Asiatic and Byzantine customs concerning a prince's selection of a bride at a public show and her identification by a tiny slipper. This excellent piece of work illustrates well the use of historical and ethnological details in interpreting a tale. It made little stir in the scholarly world and is therefore one more example of the surprising reception or lack of reception likely to be accorded to an investigation dealing with Cinderella.

We come in conclusion to the most recent developments in our knowledge of the Cinderella cycle. There is much to tell about the rapid enlargement of our knowledge of the Japanese parallels. One

such parallel was translated into German in 1885 and duly excerpted
by Miss Cox in 1893. Since she classified it as "indeterminate," and
neither she nor anyone else commented on it adequately, it attracted
little notice. It can now be recognized as what is called an "old
woman's skin tale (*ubakawa*)." Since this Japanese version is found
in a chapbook of 1629, it is almost as old as the oldest European
Cinderella tales. The version collected from modern oral tradition
and cited by Miss Cox is as follows:

> A woman sends her daughter and stepdaughter out to
> gather acorns (or chestnuts) in the forest. The stepdaughter
> loses her way and finally comes to a forest-woman, from whom
> she receives an old woman's skin to use as a protection. She
> puts it on, and when she returns home only her half-sister
> recognizes her. When her father returns, he perceives the step-
> mother's unkind intentions and punishes her.[16]

Keigo Seki cites this tale, which is known as "Komebaku and
Awabaku" from the names of the sisters (the names vary considerably), as the Japanese equivalent of Cinderella (Type 510A). It is
briefly as follows:

> A mother gives a torn bag to her stepdaughter named
> Komebaku and an untorn bag to her daughter named Awa-
> buku, and sends them to the woods to pick chestnuts. The girls
> stop at Yama-uba's (a forest-woman's) house in the woods.
> Komebaku picks lice from Yama-uba's head and Awabuku
> does not. When they leave, Yama-uba gives each of them a
> basket. The stepdaughter's basket contains pretty dresses and
> the daughter's contains frogs or dirty things. The mother takes
> her daughter to play (or festival) and leaves the stepdaughter
> at home to carry water in a basket or to separate millet, rice,
> and other grains. A friend (or a priest) and a sparrow perform
> these tasks. The stepdaughter goes to the play with a friend.
> While they are looking at the play, (a) the stepdaughter is
> discovered by her stepsister, or (b) the stepdaughter throws
> something at her stepmother and stepsister. A young man has
> seen the stepdaughter at the play and offers to marry her. The
> mother tries to get him to marry the daughter, but he insists on
> the stepdaughter. Since the daughter wants to marry, the
> mother goes to seek a suitor, carrying the girl on a mortar.
> They fall into a stream and become mud-snails.[17]

A tale found in two collections of translated tales and in Seki's list may also be mentioned here. It has a general similarity to the Cinderella cycle, has a hero and not a heroine, and is not akin to the tales with a hero cited as versions of "The Little Red Ox" (Type 511A).[18] It is entitled "Ash-boy (Hai-bô)" and is as follows:

> A young man is (a) cast away by his stepmother, or (b) is sent away from his home. He is employed by a rich man as a servant in charge of heating the bath. (a) At a play a rich man's daughter sees a fine young man and discovers him to be a servant who works in her home. (b) She eventually learns that the man to whom she has been engaged is a menial servant in her home. She becomes love-sick. According to a fortune-teller's advice, all the servants are led before her so that she may choose the one she likes. The hero appears as a handsome young man and marries her.[19]

The most important recent event in the study of the Cinderella cycle is the appearance in print of Kenichi Mizusawa, *Echigo no Shinderera* [Cinderella in Echigo], Sanjo-shi, Niigata, 1964, pp. 17, 720.[20] Unfortunately, it is now out of print and is altogether unobtainable. Mizusawa, an active collector of folktales, has limited his interest to half a dozen, of which Cinderella is one. In this book, he has published the seventy five versions of Type 510A and nineteen versions of Type 510B that he found in the prefecture of Echigo (now called Niigata). This is clearly a work comparable in its extent and nature to Miss Cox's *Cinderella,* although more limited in its range. The two chapters of discussion in this book have, however, fortunately been reprinted in a recent volume by him that is still to be bought in the book trade.

Our excursion to Japan has been very successful indeed. We can hope to learn much from an excursion in an entirely different direction that Professor William R. Bascom has undertaken. He tells me that he is seeking traces of Cinderella in Africa. There are such traces, but they have not been collected and studied. Miss Cox, for example, cites a few tales, and bibliographies add a few more. We expect to learn much from Professor Bascom's investigation. He expects to publish it soon.[21]

This acount of the study of the Cinderella cycle has taught me not to be rash in offering suggestions. For many reasons they are likely to fall on deaf ears. Andrew Lang's suggestions, made more than seventy years ago, were rejected because the temper of the age and its interests had changed. Let me be content to recall an old bit of advice to one who seeks information. He should ask Who? What? When? Where? and Why? His endeavors to find answers to such questions will guide him well.

NOTES

[1]2 vols., Paris, n.d. [1887]. The individual tales had been published with annotations during the years 1876–1881 in the journal *Romania*. For Cinderella see *Contes*, I, 246–247, Nos. 23, 24. His notes were scarcely likely to attract much attention to the tale. In his later writings Cosquin said much more about Cinderella, but even this has been somewhat neglected.

[2]See P. Saintyves, *Les Contes de Perrault* (Paris, 1923), p. 113 n.

[3]See especially the editorial preface, pp. lxxxvi–cii.

[4]*Revue des traditions populaires,* XIII (1898), 311–337.

[5]*Folklore,* XVIII (1907), 191–208.

[6]M. Bittner, "Das Märchen von Aschenbrödel, in den drei Mahra-Sprachen (Soqotra, Mehri und Shauri)," *Sitzungsberichte der Akademie in Wien, phil.-hist. Klasse,* CLXXXVI (1918), No. 4.

[7]With an introduction by Andrew Lang: Publications of the Folk-Lore Society, XXXI (London, 1893 or 1892), p. lxxx, 535.

[8]According to a footnote, these tales are not medieval heroic legend nor are they to be identified with Type 511A, "The Little Red Ox," which also has a hero and not a heroine as the chief actor (unless indeed the ox is to be so considered). Miss Cox knows the latter tale (see pp. 455–456 and elsewhere) but does not include it in the cycle. Anna Birgitta Rooth also mentions tales with heroes but does not seem to include them in the cycle (see pp. 135–147). On the other hand, Bolte and Polivka, *Anmerkungen,* III, 65–66, seems to include it, while Kurt Ranke apparently does not, and Paul Delarue does (see A. Millien and P. Delarue, as cited, p. 268, and Gaston Maugard, *Contes des Pyrénées,* Paris, [1955], No. 6, which is the tale cited with a slightly different number in the previous book). We need a better summary of Type 511A than we now have, and a better bibliography of it. Both it and some lacking members of the cycle should be included in "Type" 510 (This is not correctly numbered as a type. The reference here is to *two* tales and should be to *four* or *five*).

[9][Some of these type indices have appeared since Professor Taylor wrote this paper: Hiroko Ikeda, *A Type and Motif Index of Japanese Folk-Literature,* FF Communications 209 (Helsinki: Academia Scientiarum Fennica, 1971). Parts of the French index had already been published: Paul Delarue et Marie-Louise Tenèze, *Le Conte populaire Français,* Vol. I (Paris, 1957); Vol. II (Paris, 1964). Moreover, other indices not mentioned by Taylor have also appeared, and they contain many refer-

ences to Cinderella texts: Stanley L. Robe, *Index of Mexican Folktales*, Folklore Studies 26 (Berkeley: University of California Press, 1973); K. Arājs and A. Medne, *Latviešu Pasaku Tipu Rādītājs* (Riga: Izdevniecība "Zinātne," 1977); In-Hak Choi, *A Type Index of Korean Folktales* (Seoul: Myong Ji University Publishing, 1979). Ed. Note.]

¹⁰[This too has been published. Katharine M. Briggs, *A Dictionary of British Folk-Tales in the English Language; Part A, Folk Narrative*, 2 vols. (Bloomington: Indiana University Press, 1970). Ed. Note.]

¹¹L. Scherman and F.S. Krauss, "Allgemeine Methodik der Volksunde . . . 1890–1907," *Kritischer Jahresbericht über die Fortschritte der romanischen Philologie*, IV, Part 3 (Erlangen, 1899), 65–66. For a more generous but hardly more informative review of this period, see Henri Gaidoz, *Mélusine*, VI (1893), cols. 211–215.

¹²See *Three Lectures on Chinese Folklore* (Peking, 1932), pp. 51–83. The text can be found more conveniently in a French translation in the previously mentioned note in Millien and Delarue. For discussion see Wolfram Eberhard, FF Communications 120 (1937), pp. 52–54, No. 32: and Anna Birgitta Rooth, *The Cinderella Cycle*, pp. 194–196. The modern southern Chinese versions cited by Eberhard have yet to be made fully available in the West and to be discussed adequately. [This lacuna has now been filled to some extent by Nai-Tung Ting's *The Cinderella Cycle in China and Indo-China*, FF Communications 213 (1974). Ed. Note.]

¹³For the identification of the types discussed, see Rooth, p. 15. The identifications are, of course, according to the first revision of the typelist (1928) and do not completely agree with the descriptions in the second revision and elsewhere. Chemistry learned long ago to accommodate itself to such an erroneous term as *oxygen* (it is hydrogen, not oxygen, that is essential to an acid), but folklore is still handicapped by rewriting and renumbering its fundamental terminology.

¹⁴I content myself with citing two references to it in recently published lists: Stith Thompson and Warren E. Roberts, *Types of Indic Oral Tales: India, Pakistan, and Ceylon*, FF Communications 180 (1960), No. 923; Heda Jason, "Types of Jewish-Oriental Oral Tales [in the archive in Jerusalem]," *Fabula*, VII (1965), 184–185, No. 923. In both of these collections of variants of the tale, those pertinent to the Cinderella cycle are very few.

¹⁵Hellenika, 2 (Saloniki, 1953), Part I, "The Custom of the Imperial Bride-Show in Byzantium, Its Origin and Its Creation into a Story-Motif in Folk-Literature," pp. 1–52.

¹⁶See Cox, *Cinderella*, pp. 107–108 and 177, No. 277. See a longer version in Fritz Rumpf, *Japanische Volksmärchen* (Jena, 1938), pp. 76–77 and 322, No. 24. (Rumpf cites the numbers of the tale in the notes and the index but not in the text. This procedure is very inconvenient.) See also Rumpf, pp. 328, No. 59, and 329, No. 63. (I have cited here only the notes since these contain the comments to which I draw attention.)

¹⁷This tale is comparable to the English "Cat-skin," the French "Peau d'Ane," the Geramn "Allerleirauh," and Type 510B. (I do not cite the English title in the typelist. It seems to be an editorial invention without traditional basis.) Keigo Seki classifies the tale in "Types of Japanese Folktales," *Asian Folklore Studies*, XXV

(1966), 115, No. 215. (In an earlier list in Japanese it is No. 210.) The similarity to Indic versions cited in Thompson and Roberts, FF Communications 180, No. 510B (dress of an old woman, dress of scabs) is worthy of note. In some Japanese versions the "old woman's skin" may be a cat-skin. It protects the girl from cannibal demons.

[18]See above, note 8.

[19]Seki, *Asian Folklore Studies,* XXV (1966), 115–116, No. 216. For translated versions of the tale, see Rumpf, pp. 114–119 and 326, No. 42; and Seki and Adams, pp. 70–77, No. 24, "The Fire Boy."

[20]My knowledge of this book is limited to a review by Fanny Hagin Mayer, *Asian Folklore Studies,* XXIV (1965), 151–153, some additional remarks in a letter from her, and comment by Professor Hiroko Ikeda. It is surprising that Seki does not mention it in his list (1966) of Japanese tales. More Japanese versions of the Cinderella cycle are to be found in Professor Ikeda's forthcoming list of Japanese tales. These scholars have given me generous help.

[21][The paper has been published as "Cinderella in Africa," *Journal of the Folklore Institute,* IX (1972), 54–70, and is reprinted in this volume. Ed. Note.]

Tradition Areas in Eurasia

Anna Birgitta Rooth

As Archer Taylor has suggested, the history of the study of Cinderella is in part a microcosm of the history of folklore scholarship generally. When more and more folklorists in different areas of the world began to collect and publish the folklore of their respective regions, the task of locating these materials, found in a truly bewildering variety of professional and amateur books and periodicals, became enormous. In addition, an individual investigator faced with the prospect of handling nearly a thousand or more versions of the folktale under consideration had to wonder whether he or she could keep so many texts in mind at one time.

In European folkloristics, the technique devised to handle, or rather display, large masses of field data consisted of mapping such data. The so-called cartographic method eventually led to ambitious "atlas" projects in which specific customs or folk speech idioms or house types were dutifully plotted on a series of maps. The principal aim of such maps was to display visually the available data so as to indicate at a glance the geographic distribution of a particular trait or cluster of traits. Typically, full-fledged comparative (historic-geographic) studies of folktales are accompanied by maps showing the spread of subtypes and forms of the tale in question. While the cartographic method is not so popular among American folklorists, it has been and continues to be widely employed by European scholars.

Reprinted from *Arv*, 12 (1956), 95–113.

130 Anna Birgitta Rooth

Anna Birgitta Rooth, Professor of Folklore at the University of Uppsala, followed the publication of her Cinderella Cycle *in 1951 with an essay in one of the leading Scandinavian folklore journals in which she mapped a summary of her findings. (See pp. 137-143.) The reader will need to consult the "Key to the Symbols of the Maps" following the maps themselves in order to follow the argument, and may also wish to refer to* The Cinderella Cycle (CC) *itself for a fuller account of the specific motifs discussed.*

For a useful introductory essay on the cartographic method, see Swiss folklorist Robert Wildhaber's "Folk Atlas Mapping," in Richard M. Dorson, ed., Folklore and Folklife: An Introduction *(Chicago: University of Chicago Press, 1972), pp. 479-496. For other discussions, see Wilhelm Pessler, "Die geographische Methode in der Volkskunde,"* Anthropos, *27 (1932), 707-742; and Richard Weiss, "Cultural Boundaries and the Ethnographic Map," in Philip L. Wagner and Marvin W. Mikesell, eds.,* Readings in Cultural Geography *(Chicago: University of Chicago Press, 1962), pp. 62-74. For a geographical survey of the distribution of some fifty-six Sardinian versions of Cinderella, see Chiarella Rapallo, "La Fiaba de Cenerentola in Sardegna,"* BRADS *[Bollettino del Repertorio e dell'Atlante Demologico Sardo] 4 (1972-73), 74-86. For a later statement on Cinderella by Professor Rooth, see her* Askungen i öst och väst *(Uppsala: Etnologiska Institutionen, 1977).*

In an earlier investigation of the Cinderella tales[1] my main intention was to inquire into the relationship between the five different types that could be distinguished within the Cinderella cycle.

In the introduction to CC I gave an example of each type which I marked as A AB B BI and C. According to the Aarne-Thompson system,[2] they would correspond respectively to the following types: Aa 511; Aa 511 + 510; Aa 510A; Aa 510B; Aa 511 (Male Cinderella).

In order to investigate these five types it was necessary to map the different motifs, i.e. the episodes, traits, and details of which the tale consists. It was interesting to note that the *main motifs* were found all over Europe and Asia but the *minor* and the less important motifs, or the *detail-motifs*, were limited to certain areas within Eurasia. For the method the geographical distribution of different motifs was of the greatest importance.

As my main intention was to investigate the relationship between the different types as well as their distribution, I had no possibility of stressing as much as I should have liked the importance of establishing the geographical tradition areas.

The establishing of different geographical tradition areas was in itself of interest for ethnological and anthropological investigations of different culture areas. That is why I wish to supply some maps illustrating the different tradition areas based on the geographical distribution of different motifs in the Cinderella tales.

In the three following parts I want to show (1) the five main tradition areas within the Eurasiatic area of the Cinderella tales of types A, AB, B; (2) a graphical system illustrating with the help of the development of the epic motifs the dismission of the tale; and (3) the minimum age for different tradition areas.

1. The Tradition Areas

In order to show the different tradition areas I have laid up six different series containing in all seventeen maps. In all fifty-one different motifs or different forms of one motif are mapped in order to show their geographical limits. Although the motifs in themselves are of no direct interest here I have made a list explaining which motif in the tale is designated by which mark.

The Eurasiatic Tradition Area, Evident from the Distribution of the Main Motifs of the Cinderella Tale

Series 0.—Series 0 contains two maps, A and B, both showing the most important motifs—those which bear the epic construction of tale and are necessary for the skeleton of the tale. Series 0 shows that the important motifs of the Cinderella tale are found over the whole Eurasiatic area. Series 0 forms the background to all the other maps reminding us that when the detailed motifs cover only a part of the whole area the rest—the vacuum, as it seems to be—has a Cinderella tradition but lacking the actual detail-motifs. This series will remind us of the difference between the important motifs and

the detail-motifs and of the necessity of investigating both categories.
Series 0 shows the existing relationship of the tradition of the
whole Eurasiatic area but it cannot give us any information as to
whether there is any difference in the tradition, or whether there is a
nearer relationship of the tradition in adjacent smaller areas. For
this we have to turn to the detail-motifs which are found in Series
I–V.[3]

The Main Tradition Areas in Eurasia, Evident from the distribution of the Detail-Motifs of the Cinderella Tale

Series I.—This series shows that in the Eurasiatic Cinderella tradition we have one Oriental and one European tradition area. Maps A
and B show motifs found only in the Oriental, not in the European
Cinderella tradition. Maps C and D show also the difference between
Oriental and European traditions. Map C motif 1 shows that
Cinderella visits a feast for women and motif 2 a feast or a church
where she meets the prince. Map D motif 1 shows that we have one
Oriental, and motif 2, one European form of the spying motif. This
series shows that the Cinderella tales of the Orient are more closely
related to each other and form a unity in contrast to the European
tradition which has its own peculiar form of motifs showing the
unity of the tales in Europe. These facts will refute any possibility of
the Cinderella tale having emanated from Europe to different parts
of Asia in modern times. In fact, the maps A B C D of Series I
show that within the Eurasiatic area Europe and Asia each has its
own special form of Cinderella story in respect of some motifs.[4]

Series II.—After having shown the Asian tradition as a unit in
comparison with the European tradition, Series II maps A B C show
that within Asia there are two areas, i.e. the Near East and the Far
East or the Indo-Chinese and Malayan tradition areas. The distribution of the detail motifs of Series II in the Far East only, goes to
show that the tradition of the Far East is a unit in comparison with
the Near East, thus indirectly showing the Near East as a tradition
area of its own.[5]

Series III.—This series, maps ABC, shows the distribution of some
motifs in the Orient as well as in Southern and Eastern Europe, thus

indicating a nearer relationship between Asia and these areas. Further, if we study the distribution of the motifs of this series in Europe only, it is evident that some of them—Series III, map A, and C motif 4 (and 1)—are only (or frequently) found in the South of Europe while the other motifs are common to both Southern and Eastern Europe. That the tradition area of Southern Europe is of a special kind in comparison with Eastern Europe will be shown also by the next series (IV), where the motifs common to Eastern and Northern Europe are not found in the South of Europe, thus stressing the differences between them (cf. Series IV, map A motif 3, map B motif 3, and map C).

Series IV.—This series stresses partly the connection between the Asiatic and Eastern and Southern European tradition (map A motifs 1, 2; B motif 1); partly the independence of the European tradition (map B motif 3, B motifs 2, 3, and C) with particular consideration to the relationship between Eastern and Northern European tradition, thus indirectly stressing the difference between these latter areas and Southern Europe as mentioned above.

Series V.—This series, map A, shows motifs only found in North European tradition thus indicating this part as a special tradition area. Map B is given as contrasting to map A. What in map B is left as a blank space is in map A covered with motifs typical of this area only.

Conclusions from the Distribution

The five main areas which are to be distinguished in Series I-V are thus: Far East, Near East, Eastern Europe, Southern Europe, Northern Europe.[6] Within these five large areas smaller areas can be distinguished, always dependent or in close relation to the common tradition of the area in which they are found.

From this it is evident that there is a uniformity of tradition within each main area and its sub-areas. This uniformity of tradition within each area which is evident from the differences between different areas shows that the tale in oral tradition can be geographically outlined. Through these geographical tradition areas it is possible to follow the continuation of motifs from one area to the next, a fact that shows the relationship and intercommunication between the different areas. It is very interesting to observe that there is a geographical continuation in the distribution of the motifs which shows that the tale of Cinderella must have passed from one area into another. This fact is important because it cannot explain the distribution of the tale through travellers, pilgrims, merchants, etc., which is the easiest and most popular way to explain the diffusion of tales. Instead a long and intimate connection between adjacent areas is the only explanation for the geographical continuation.

It is possible to establish a nearer relationship between Northern and Eastern European tradition than between Northern and Southern Europe. Further it is possible to state the close relationship on the one hand between Eastern European tradition and Near Eastern tradition, and, on the other hand, between Southern Europe and the Near East. The difference in the geographical distribution can only be explained by the Near East being the source from which this tale has come to Europe: the Near Eastern tradition contains all the motifs which in Europe were found either only in Eastern Europe or only in Southern Europe.

2. The Graphical Illustration of the Diffusion of the Tale

In the preceding part we have just seen how it is possible to establish different areas as well as nearer relationship between adjacent areas. However, it is not possible from the mapping alone to decide if the relationship is due to a diffusion from east to west or from west to east.

If we study the epic technique and composition of the tale it is possible to follow the epic development of some motifs and their function in the tale as well as their geographical continuity. The reasons and arguments belonging to the "literary" side of the tale are—however necessary they may be for the problem as a whole—of no interest here. In my thesis most of the studies were concentrated on the epic construction and composition which was of course necessary as the tales are first and foremost traditional fiction and must be studied as such. As these reasons and arguments are given in CC I am not going to mention them here. I will just take some examples to illustrate in a graphical way the epic development of the motifs with their geographical background—a method which goes to show the diffusion of the tale.

I have done it here in this way. A filled sign designates a primary form and the same unfilled sign a newer development of the same motif. A further development of the same motif is designated by a semi-circular sign (see for instance Series IV, map B motifs 1, 2, 3).

In Series I, map B, motif 2 has developed into a new form from motif 1 and the same series, map C, shows that motif 2 developed from motif 1, as it did in map D.

Series III, map A, shows that motif 4 came from motif 3, map C that motif 5 came from motif 4. Series IV, map A, shows that motif 3 came from motif 1 and map B shows that motif 1 developed into motif 2 and then into a still newer form, motif 3. In Series V, map A, motif 2 came from motif 1.

Thus, with the help of this graphical method we can follow the diffusion of the motifs as indicated by their epic development. In this case a diffusion of the Cinderella tale is graphically shown from Asia to Europe (Series I C motif $1 > 2$; I D motif $1 > 2$) as well as from the Near East to Southern and Eastern Europe (Series III A motif $3 > 4$; III C motif $4 > 5$; Series IV A motif $1 > 3$; IV B motif $1 > 2 > 3$) and from Eastern Europe to Northern Europe (Series IV A motif $1 > 3$; IV B motif $1 > 2 > 3$).

This goes to show that the Cinderella tradition spread from the Near East to Southern as well as to Eastern Europe, and from Eastern Europe to Northern Europe. The question at what time this diffusion took place will be answered in the following part.

3. The Minimum Age of the Tradition in Different Areas

Although these five main tradition areas are based mostly on Cinderella tales collected in the 19th century, it is possible to state a minimum age for the tradition of many an area or sub-area. In Indo-China the 19th-century tradition has the same special motifs as a version written down in the 9th century (CC, cf. p. 56; App. II). In Iceland the special Icelandic traits were in existence in the 13th century (CC, p. 131ff.). In the Balkans motifs special for Balkan Cinderella tradition were extant 2000 years ago (CC, cf. pp. 233, 163), etc. This goes to show that each tradition area had its special form of the tale already fixed, often more than 1000 years ago and that the diffusion of the tale must have been prior to this date (CC, cf. p. 233).

The method used in CC was invented in order to study the tales for what they really are—traditional fiction. Through the mapping of the motifs the different geographical tradition areas or, in other words, the speciality of the different areas could be distinguished.

For this purpose—to show the peculiarities of different geographical areas and to fix the minimum age for them in order to show when the diffusion took place—the tales or chimerats are extremely useful because of their often very long and complicated epic construction which makes it possible to follow them over vast areas. In this case the chimerats are better fitted than the short epic constructions as legends (Ger. *Sagen*) or oral tradition of beliefs, superstitions etc. which lack the epic skeleton.

Thus with the help of this method the tales will give us excellent evidence when we approach the problems concerning cultural areas and interhuman relationships from times when historical evidence is very scarce.

Map A

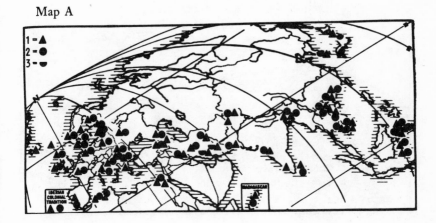

Map B

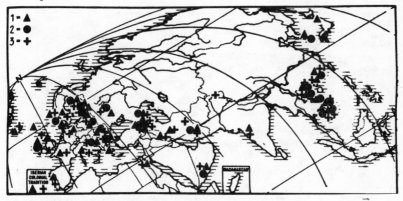

Series 0. The Eurasiatic tradition area
of the Cinderella tale

137

Maps A–D

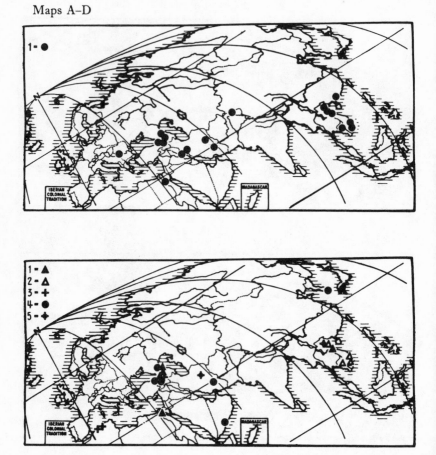

Series I. The Asiatic tradition area
contra the European area

138

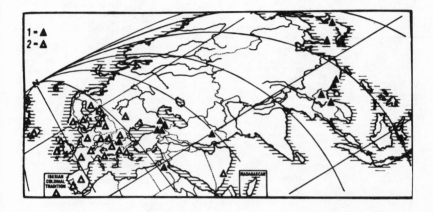

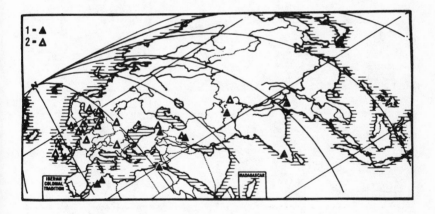

Map A

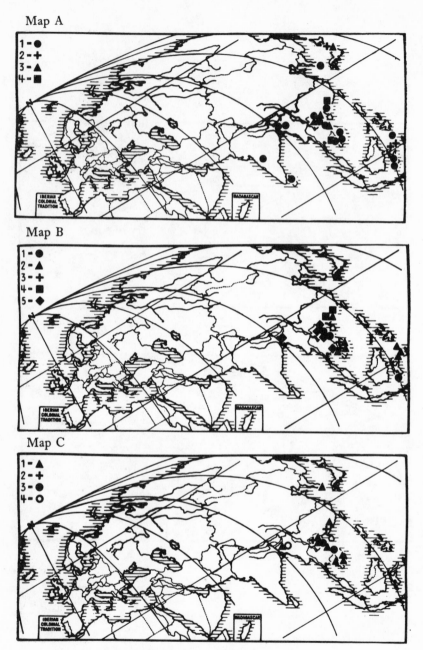

Map B

Map C

Series II. The Far Eastern tradition area
contra the Near Eastern area

140

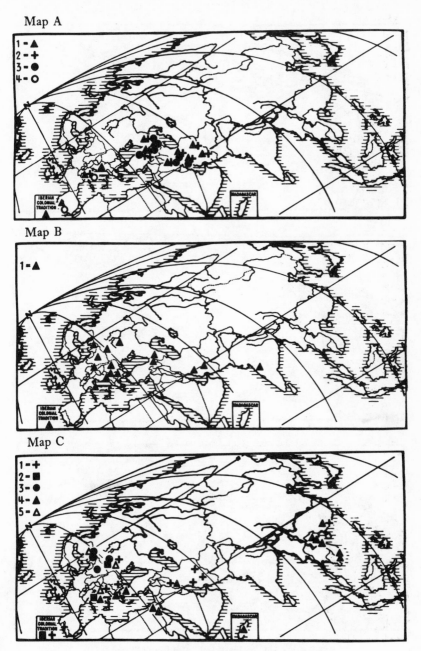

Map A

Map B

Map C

Series III. The connection of the Eastern and Southern
European tradition area with the Near Eastern area

141

Map A

Map B

Map C

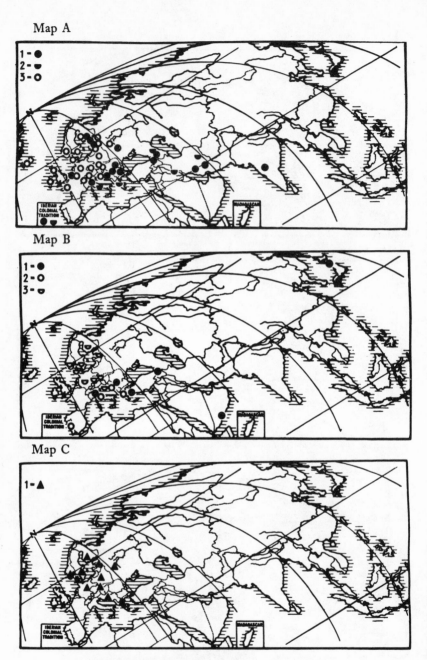

Series IV. The Northern European tradition and its
connection with Eastern European and Near
Eastern tradition areas

142

Map A

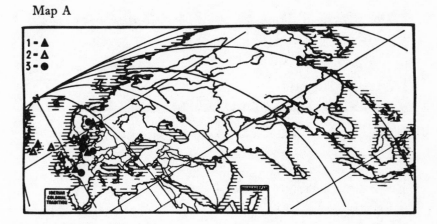

Map B

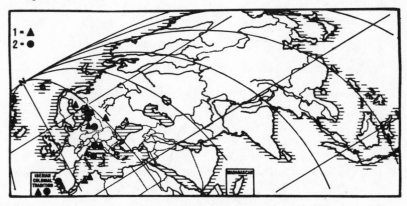

Series V. The Northern European tradition area
contra the Eastern European tradition

143

Key to the Symbols of the Maps in the Series O–V

The Eurasiatic Tradition Area (Distribution of the Main Motifs.)

SERIES O.

Map A:
1. Orphan[7] (step-daughter). CC App. I–XVI.
2. Slaying of the helpful animal. CC App. I–XVI.
3. Helpful animal. CC App. I–XVI; cf. p. 151ff.

Map B:
1. Fine dresses. CC p. 165ff.
2. Grain sorting. CC p. 176ff; cf. p. 192.
3. Lost shoe. CC p. 69ff; 103ff.

The Main Tradition Areas within Eurasia. (Distribution of Detail-Motifs.)

SERIES I.

Map A:
1. Lost object (shoe) found by chance. CC p. 69ff; 75ff.

Map B:
1. Brilliance of the lost slipper (bracelet) frightens prince's horse (elephant). CC p. 72.
2. Bird drops the lost slipper in front of the prince's palace. CC p. 72, 192.
3. The spying sisters receive pus and tar instead of food from the helpful animal. CC p. 203.
4. Filling tubs with water or tears. CC p. 178.
5. Step-mother places crackling bread-crusts in her bed and feigns illness.

Map C:
1. Step-daughter visits a feast for women. CC. p. 75.
2. Feast (or church) meeting-place for the step-daughter and the prince. CC p. 76.

Map D:
1. Oriental form of the spying-motif, i.e. the spying step-brother and step-sister are allowed to taste the food, received by their step-sister and show part of it to their mother. CC p. 160 n. 10.
2. European form of the spying-motif, i.e. 1-2-3-eyed step-sisters spy; the third eye stays open and it is thus revealed that the step-daughter receives food from a helpful animal. CC App. III–XVI.

Series II.

Map A:
1. Fish (turtle) as helper. CC pp. 191, 193; App. I–III.
2. Bird as helper. CC pp. 193, 195; App. I.
3. Names of step-sisters connected with rice or flour.
4. Names of step-sisters connected with their ugliness and beauty.

Map B:
1. Cock or hen reveals hiding-place of the bones of the slayed animal. CC p. 191.
2. Spirit reveals hiding-place of the bones. CC p. 191.
3. The step-daughter buries the bones: at a cross-road, CC App. II.
4. in her room. CC App. II.
5. under her bed. CC App. II.

Map C:
1. Special form of Type Aa 403 added to the Cinderella tale.
2. Cult-place erected.
3. Mother eating daughters fat and raven-formula.
4. "The raven does not eat her own kin."

SERIES III.

Map A:
1. Type Aa 480 incorporated in the Cinderella tale. CC p. 203; cf. p. 82ff.
2. Lousing hair of devs or fairies. CC p. 204.
3. Following fairies' prescription at a certain moment (when many-coloured riders, clouds or water pass). CC p. 204.
4. Following fairies' prescription at certain moment (when cock crows). CC p. 204.

Map B:
1. Cock as witness. CC p. 182 n. 14.

Map C:
1. Cow spins flax by chewing it. CC p. 196, 210, 213.
2. Cow spins with the horns. CC p. 211.
3. Yarn from cow's ear (or by creeping through ear). CC p. 217.
4. Cow's bones are buried in a jar or basket. CC pp. 213 n. 3, 196.
5. Cow's bones are placed in a piece of cloth. CC p. 213 n. 3.

SERIES IV.

Map A:
1. Hiding-place + animal witness. CC. p. 181. n. 11
2. Hiding-place.
3. Mutilated feet + animal witness. CC p. 181 n. 12.

Map B:
1. Distribution of presents at the feast. CC p. 186.
2. Money jewels or sand thrown in order to detain pursuers. CC p. 186 n. 20.
3. Mist produced by formula in order to detain pursuers. CC p. 186 n. 21.

Map C:
1. Pitch trap. CC p. 188.

SERIES V.

Map A:
1. The house in the wood. CC p. 172ff.
2. The house (mound) containing clothing. CC p. 173ff.
2. The tree that plays. CC p. 171.

Map B:
1. Magic object found in the entrails of the helpful animal. CC p. 168 n. 22; cf. p. 165ff.
2. Washing entrails. CC p. 168 n. 21; cf. p. 165ff.

NOTES

[1]Rooth, Anna Birgitta: *The Cinderella Cycle* (Diss.), Lund, 1951, here referred to as CC.

[2]Aarne, A., and Thompson, S., *The Types of the Folk-Tale*, Helsinki, 1928 (FFC 74).

[3]Even if in Europe the actual motifs are more numerous, only one sign can be allotted to designate the number of motifs in each country.

[4]Series I, map A motif 1, and C motif 1, which are Oriental, are found in the Balkans because they belong to a Turkish Cinderella tale which was written down in a Turkish colony living on the Island of Adakaleh in the Danube.

[5]After CC was printed Miss Ikeda kindly sent me two Cinderella versions which are mapped together with the Far Eastern Cinderella tales. One was from Japan, Aomori Prefecture, and the other was from Korea (Y.T. Pyun, *Tales from Korea*, Seoul, 1948, 2nd ed.).

[6]This term covers West and North Europe.

[7]For the naming of the different motifs see CC pp. 15–22.

Cinderella in Africa

William Bascom

Tale type indices, maps, and other technical aids in folkloristics may intimidate the casual student of Cinderella. Admittedly, literary scholars, historians, psychiatrists, and others who have written about this folktale rarely if ever utilize such folkloristic tools of the trade, probably because they are ignorant of their very existence. Yet some kinds of questions cannot easily be answered without recourse to the available tale type and motif indices.

Professor Rooth's maps of Cinderella show not only where Cinderella is found but also where she is not found. Amateur folklore enthusiasts are typically quick to think that a given folktale (or other example of folklore) is universal. Cinderella is one of the world's favorite folktales, they might say. Yet many parts of the world do not know or tell this tale—at least as an indigenous story. (It may have been introduced into some areas by Western missionaries or colonial administrators.) If a particular folktale is not found in Africa, or in native North and South America, or in New Guinea, or in aboriginal Australia, then surely it is wrong to refer to that tale as being "universally" known.

If a story that does bear some resemblance to Cinderella does turn up in the repertoire of an American Indian or African storyteller, is there any way of determining with any accuracy whether the tale is a native parallel, perhaps independently invented, or a definite borrowing from the Euro-Asian tradition of Cinderella? In the

Reprinted from the *Journal of the Folklore Institute,* 9 (1972), 54–70.

following methodological essay by William Bascom, Professor Emeritus of Anthropology at the University of California, Berkeley, one of the leading authorities on African folklore, this question is addressed.

Anthropologists have tended to use the term "Cinderella" as a general one to refer to an unpromising heroine or hero of low status who achieves some kind of success. For this reason, one must be wary when anthropologists speak of a Cinderella theme or plot in native North America. Most of the time they are not talking at all about what folklorists understand by the term, i.e., Aarne-Thompson tale type 510A, Cinderella. See, for example, Betty Uchitelle Randall, "The Cinderella Theme in Northwest Coast Folklore," in Marian W. Smith, ed., Indians of the Urban Northwest *(New York: Columbia University Press, 1949), pp. 243-285. French anthropologist Claude Lévi-Strauss, in his review of Rooth's* Cinderella Cycle, *takes her to task for neglecting what he calls the native American male Cinderella tale, which he suggests is an inversion of the Eurasian Cinderella. See "The Art of Deciphering Symbols,"* Diogenes, *5 (Winter, 1954), 102-108. But Lévi-Strauss's allusions to native American Cinderella stories are again more of a metaphorical reference than to a tale type. To be sure, there are bona fide American Indian borrowings of the European Cinderella. For a fascinating retelling of presumably a Spanish Cinderella, see Frank Hamilton Cushing,* Zuni Folk Tales *(New York: G.P. Putnam, 1901), pp. 54-64, "The Poor Turkey Girl." See also Stith Thompson,* European Tales Among the North American Indians *(Colorado Springs, 1919), pp. 382-385. For further discussion of the occurrence of Cinderella or Cinderella-influenced tales in Africa, see Jourdain-Innocent Noah, "Beti Tales from Southern Cameroon: The Kaiser Cycle,"* Diogenes, *No. 80 (Winter, 1972), 80-101; and Denise Paulme, "Cendrillon en Afrique,"* Critique, *36 (1980), 288-302.*

Three factors may explain the obvious, if not notorious, anthropological neglect of the tale type indexes and motif indexes, so laboriously compiled and so widely used by other folklorists.[1] In the first place, these indexes do not yet adequately cover parts of the world in which anthropologists have been interested. However, this is no intrinsic shortcoming, and the indexes are gradually being extended to new areas. In fact, anthropologists could well contribute to rectifying this situation by indexing the narratives of the areas of their specialty.

The second factor, which is in part a corollary of the first, is simple ignorance. Anthropologists who publish or interpret folktales are often apparently unaware of the tale type and motif indexes, and of their usefulness in locating analogues in other areas. This again can be remedied by extending the area coverage of the indexes, thus making them more relevant to anthropological interests.

The third factor, I believe, involves a certain skepticism about their basic purpose. According to Stith Thompson,[2] these indexes were prepared primarily to furnish a basis for historic investigations of tales, and the historic-geographic method is the most serious attempt to perfect a technique for such studies. Its goal is "nothing less than a complete life history of a particular tale" including, among other things, its original form and its time and place of origin.

I, for one, am still unwilling to abandon my reservations about the possibility of recovering the ultimate origins of particular tales— in time and in place—through the historic-geographic method or the use of tale type and motif indexes. However in this paper, which is primarily an exercise in methodology, I will try to show how tale type indexes and motif indexes can answer questions of a more limited time depth, using the Cinderella tale as an example. I believe that the conclusions which I have reached from a quick examination of the relevant tale type indexes are, indeed, conclusive, and that they are confirmed by only a slightly more time-consuming reference to the relevant motif indexes. I would maintain that the only reasonable doubts about these conclusions would be settled if there were complete tale type and motif indexes for Africa.

The tale with which I am concerned is well known to us all as Cinderella, classified according to the Aarne and Thompson index as tale type 510A. My African example appears to Tale 69 in volume two of Frank Edgar's *Litafi Na Tatsuniyoyi Na Hausa. Litafi Na Farako.* Volume two was published in 1911 in Belfast, but all three volumes of this extensive collection remained closed books to folklorists until Neil Skinner, presently of the University of Wisconsin, undertook their translation. I am happy to say that I have had even a minor role in this undertaking. Through Tom Lanagan, one of my students who was studying Hausa under Neil Skinner at UCLA, I suggested the importance of Edgar's collection. Skinner made the translation while he was in New Zealand, completing volume two in 1965. Volume one of Skinner's translation has recently been published by Frank Cass and Company of London as *Hausa Tales and Traditions*, and two others are to follow.

Another, truncated translation of this tale, omitting the hearth abode motif, has appeared in a selection of Hausa tales drawn from Edgar and others by H.A.S. Johnston.[3] Johnston recognized its relation to the Cinderella tale, but reached a different conclusion from the one presented here:

> Another tale in this section, *The Girl and the Frog and the Chief's Son* (no. 31) is strikingly similar to the story of Cinderella. It can hardly be indigenous in origin and the main question is how it reached Hausaland. It may have come from the east, or filtered down through the Sahara, or perhaps even made its way northward from Guinea or Angola after being transported there by the Portuguese. It is worth remembering that whichever route it took, it probably reached Hausaland generations before the first European explorer.[4]

It is precisely with these historical questions that I am concerned; but the evidence presented here, based on tale type and motif indexes and what additional research I have been able to do, leads me to reject Johnston's conclusions about the time and manner of its introduction.

To return to the tale itself, I give you now Skinner's original (draft) translation, which gave rise to this article.

69. The Maiden, the Frog & the Chief's Son

> There was once a man had two wives, and they each had a daughter. And the one wife, together with her daughter, he couldn't abide; but the other, with her daughter, he dearly loved.
>
> Well, the day came when the wife that he disliked fell ill, and it so happened that her illness proved fatal, and she died. And her daughter was taken over by the other wife, the one he loved; and she moved into that wife's hut. And there she dwelt, having no mother of her own, just her father. And every day the woman

would push her out, to go off to the bush to gather wood. When she returned, she had to pound up the *fura*. Then she had the *tuwo* to pound, and, after that, to stir.[5] And then they wouldn't even let her eat the *tuwo*. All they gave her to eat were the burnt bits at the bottom of the pot. And day after day she continued thus.

Now she had an elder brother, and he invited her to come and eat regularly at his home—to which she agreed. But still when she had been to the bush, and returned home, and wanted a drink of water, they wouldn't let her have one. Nor would they give her proper food—only the coarsest of the grindings and the scrapings from the pot. These she would take, and going with them to a borrow-pit, throw them in. And the frogs would come out and start eating the scrapings. Then, having eaten them up, they would go back into the water; and she too would return home.

And so things went on day after day, until the day of the Festival arrived. And on this day, when she went along with the scrapings and coarse grindings, she found a frog squatting there; and realised that he was waiting for her! She got there and threw in the bits of food. Whereupon the frog said, "Maiden, you've always been very kind to us, and now we—but just you come along tomorrow morning. That's the morning of the Festival. Come along then, and we'll be kind to you, in our turn." "Fine" she said, and went off home.

Next morning was the Festival, and she was going off to the borrow-pit, just as the frog had told her. But as she was going, her half-sister's mother said to her, "Hey—come here, you good-for-nothing girl! You haven't stirred the *tuwo*, or pounded the *fura*, or fetched the wood or the water." So the girl returned. And the frog spent the whole day waiting for her. But she, having returned to the compound, set off to fetch wood. Then she fetched water, and set about pounding the *tuwo*, and stirred it till it was done and then took it off the fire. And presently she was told to take the scrapings. She did so and went off to the borrow-pit, where she found the frog. "Tut tut, girl" said he, "I've been waiting for you here since morning, and you never came." "Old fellow" she said, "You see, I'm a slave." "How come?" he asked. "Simple" she said, "My mother died—died leaving me her only daughter. I have an elder brother, but he is married and has a compound of his own. And my father put me in the care of his other wife. And indeed he had never loved my mother. So I was moved into the hut of his other wife. And, as I told you, slavery is my lot. Every morning I have to go off to the bush to get wood. When I get back from that I have to pound the *fura*, and then I pound the *tuwo*, and then start stirring it. And even when I have finished stirring the *tuwo*, I'm not given it to eat—just the scrapings." Says the frog, "Girl, give us your hand." And she held it out to him, and they both leaped into the water.

Then he went and picked her up and swallowed her. (And he vomited her up.)[6] "Good people" said he, "Look and tell me, is she straight or crooked?" And they looked and answered, "She is bent to the left." So he picked her up and swallowed her again and then brought her up, and again asked them the same question. "She's quite straight now" they said. "Good" said he.

Next he vomited up cloths for her, and bangles, and rings, and a pair of shoes, one of silver, one of gold. "And now" said he, "Off you go to the dancing." So all these things were given to her, and he said to her "When you get there, and when the dancing is nearly over and the dancers dispersing, you're to leave your golden shoe, the right one, there." And the girl replied to the frog, "Very well, old fellow, I understand," and off she went.

Meanwhile the chief's son had caused the young men and girls to dance for his pleasure, and when she reached the space where they were dancing he saw her. "Well!" said the chief's son, "*There*'s a maiden for you, if you like. Don't you let her go and join in the dancing—I don't care whose home she comes from. Bring her here!" So the servants of the chief's son went over and came back with her to where he was. He told her to sit down on the couch, and she took her seat there accordingly.

They chatted together for some time, till the dancers began to disperse. Then she said to the chief's son, "I must be going home." "Oh, are you off?" said he. "Yes" said she and rose to her feet. "I'll accompany you on your way for a little" said the chief's son, and he did so. But she had left her right shoe behind. Presently she said, "Chief's son, you must go back now," and he did so. And afterwards she too turned and made her way back.

And there she found the frog by the edge of the water waiting for her. He took her hand and the two of them jumped into the water. Then he picked her up and swallowed her, and again vomited her up; and there she was, just as she had been before, a sorry sight. And taking her ragged things she went off home.

When she got there, she said, "Fellow-wife of my mother, I'm not feeling very well." And the other said, "Rascally slut! You have been up to no good—refusing to come home, refusing to fetch water or wood, refusing to pound the *fura* or make the *tuwo*. Very well then! No food for you today!" And so the girl set off to her elder brother's compound, and there ate her food, and so returned home again.

But meanwhile the chief's son had picked up the shoe and said to his father, "Dad, I have seen a girl who wears a pair of shoes, one of gold, one of silver. Look, here's the golden one— she forgot it and left it behind. She's the girl I want to marry. So let all the girls of this town, young and old, be gathered together, and let this shoe be given to them to put on." "Very well" said the chief.

And so it was proclaimed, and all the girls, young and old, were collected and gathered together. And the chief's son went and sat there beside the shoe. Each girl came, and each tried on the shoe, but it fitted none of them, none of the girls of the town; until only the girl who had left it was left. Then someone said "Just a minute! There's that girl in so-and-so's compound, whose mother died." "Yes, that's right," said another, "Someone go and fetch her." And someone went and fetched her.

But the minute she arrived to try it on, the shoe itself of its own accord, ran across and made her foot get into it. Then said the chief's son, "Right, here's my wife."

At this, the other woman—the girl's father's other wife— saif, "But the shoe belongs to my daughter; it was she who forgot it at the place of the dancing, not this good-for-nothing slut." But the chief's son insisted that, since he had seen the shoe fit the other girl, as far as he was concerned, she was the one to be taken to his compound in marriage. And so they took her there, and there she spent one night.

Next morning she went out of her hut and round behind it, and there saw the frog. She knelt respectfully and said, "Welcome, old fellow, welcome" and greeted him. Says he, "Tonight we shall be along to bring some things for you." "Thank you" said she, and he departed.

Well, that night, the frog rallied all the other frogs, and all his friends, both great and small came along. And he, their leader, said to them, "See here—my daughter is being married. So I want every one of you to make a contribution." And each of them went and fetched what he could afford, whereupon their leader thanked them all, and then vomited up a silver bed, a brass bed, a copper bed, and an iron bed. And went on vomiting up things for her—such as woollen blankets, and rugs, and satins, and velvets.

"Now" said he to the girl, "If your heart is ever troubled, just lie down on this brass bed" and he went on, "And when the chief's son's other wives come to greet you, give them two calabashes of cola-nuts and ten thousand cowrie shells; then, when his concubines come to greet you, give them one calabash of cola-nuts and five thousand cowries." "Very well" said she. Then he said, "And when the concubines come to receive corn for making *tuwo*, say to them, 'There's a hide-bag full, help yourselves'." "Very well" she said. "And" he went on, "If your father's wife comes along with her daughter and asks you what it is like living in the chief's compound, say 'Living in the chief's compound is a wearisome business—for they measure out corn there with the shell of a Bambara groundnut'."

So there she dwelt, until one day her father's favourite wife brought her daughter along at night, took her into the chief's compound, and brought the other girl out and took her to her own compound. There she said. "Oh! I forgot to get you to tell her all about married life in the chief's compound." "Oh, it's a wearisome business" answered our girl. "How so?" asked the older woman, surprised. "Well, they use the shell of a Bambara groundnut for measuring out corn. Then, if the chief's other wives come to greet you, you answer them with the 'Pf' of contempt. If the concubines come to greet you, you clear your throat, hawk, and spit. And if your husband comes into your hut, you yell at him." "I see" said the other—and her daughter stayed behind the chief's son's compound.

Next morning when it was light, the wives came to greet her—and she said "Pf" to them. The concubines came to greet her, and she spat at them. Then when night fell, the chief's son made his way to her hut, and she yelled at him. And he was amazed and went aside, and for two days pondered the matter.

Then he had his wives and concubines collected and said to them, "Look, now—I've called you to ask you. They haven't brought me the same girl. How did that one treat all of you?" "Hm—how indeed!" they all exclaimed. "Each morning, when we wives went to greet her, she would give us cola-nuts, two calabashes full, and cowries, ten thousand of them to buy tobacco flowers. And when the concubines went to greet her, she would give them a calabash of cola-nuts, and five thousand cowries to buy tobacco flowers with; and in the evening, for corn for *tuwo*, it would be a whole hide-bag full." "You see?" said he, "As for me, whenever I came to enter her hut, I found her respectfully kneeling. And she wouldn't get up from there, until I had entered and sat down on the bed."

"Hey," he called out, "Boys, come over here!" And when they came, he went into her hut and took a sword, and chopped her up into little pieces, and had them collect them and wrap them up in clothing; and then taken back to her home.

And when they got there, they found his true wife lying in the fireplace, and picking her up they took her back to her husband.

And next morning when it was light, she picked up a little gourd water-bottle and going around behind her hut, there saw the frog. "Welcome, welcome, old fellow," said she, and went on. "Old fellow, what I should like is to have a well built; and then you, all of you, can come and live in it and be close to me." "All right" said the frog, "You tell your husband." And she did so.

And he had a well dug for her, close to her hut. And the frogs came and entered the well and there they lived. That's all. *Kungurus kan kusu.*

This tale, first published more than half a century ago, obviously has many elements which are strange to us. Most of them, including *fura, tuwo,* cowrie shells, cola-nuts, Bambara groundnuts, plural wives and concubines, and the Hausa closing formula are clearly derived from Africa, where it was recorded. Nevertheless, I believe that you should be able to recognize it as the Cinderella tale familiar to us from our childhood. In terms of Aarne and Thompson's synopsis of the combined Cinderella/Cap o' Rushes type 510,[7] we can see the following similarities:

I. *The persecuted heroine.* (a) The heroine is abused by her stepmother.

II. *Magic help.* While she is acting as a servant at home, she is fed by her brother and magically provided for by a frog. The identity of the helpful characters differs from those in the tales considered by Aarne and Thompson, where she is fed by (a) her dead mother, (b) a tree on the mother's grave, (c) a supernatural being, (d) birds, or (e) a goat, a sheep, or a cow. Nevertheless we know that characters are easily substituted in folktales, as is obvious from this variant.

III. *Meeting the prince.* She goes to a dance dressed in beautiful clothing, including a slipper of gold, and a slipper of silver. She meets the son of a chief (the prince) and as she goes home, she leaves behind her golden slipper, which the prince finds. (Cf. elements a and c).

IV. *Proof of identity.* (a) She is discovered through the slipper-test.

V. *Marriage with the prince.* She marries the son of the chief.

VI. *Value of salt.* This element is replaced by an episode in which she is displaced by her stepsister, who is eventually discovered and killed. Our heroine is then discovered lying in the fireplace (Cf. I.a'), and is taken back to her husband, the prince.

Certainly not all of the elements mentioned in Aarne and Thompson's synopsis of tale type 510 are present in the Hausa tale, but neither are they all present in each of the tales on which the synopsis is based. Despite its omissions, despite its very different conclusion, and despite its presumably African accretions, such as the vomiting frog, this to me is clearly a Cinderella tale.

What I am concerned with here is the question of (1) whether this tale was introduced into northern Nigeria in the relatively recent period since European contact, or (2) whether it spread southward across the Sahara by diffusion in earlier times. Conversely, (3) is this an indigenous tale which originated in Africa and spread from there to Europe and Asia? Alternatively, (4) does it represent an example of independent invention?

Beyond this, I am interested in finding how useful tale type indexes and motif indexes can be to folklorists in answering such questions, which involve a far more limited time scale than the studies for which they were compiled. All of these questions can be answered quickly.

First, we look at tale types 510, 510A, and 510B in Aarne and Thompson's *The Types of the Folktale.* Here we find references to over a thousand examples from Europe and Asia, eighty-seven from Euro-American sources, thirty-five from the West Indies (Negro), and one from the American Indians. None are cited for Africa.

Next we look at Klipple's "African Folk Tales with Foreign Analogues."[8] If an African Cinderella tale were known thirty years ago it should be here, because Klipple was expressly concerned with African tales which had counterparts in European tradition. We find no entries under tale type numbers 510, 510A, or 510B.

Since a considerable amount of African folklore has been published since 1938, we may look next at the regional tale type indexes for East Africa by E. Ojo Arewa[9] and for Central Africa by Winifred

Lambrecht.[10] Again there are no entries for tale type numbers 510, 510A, or 510B.

On the basis of a quick check of these four tale type indexes alone it seems reasonable to conclude that the Cinderella tale had not diffused across the Sahara from Europe to Nigeria, or from Nigeria to Europe, and that it was not invented independently by the Hausa, because no other African examples are reported. We can conclude then that this tale must have been introduced since European contact, perhaps during the decade between Lugard's entry into Kano and Sokoto in 1903 and the publication of the tale in 1911, or possibly by earlier missionaries or explorers like Clapperton and Barth in the previous century.

Next we may turn to the motif indexes and to the motifs of tale types 510, 510A, and 510B. For this purpose we have, first of all, Stith Thompson's *Motif-Index of Folk-Literature* in six volumes. We also have Kenneth W. Clarke's motif index for West Africa,[11] and the list of East African motifs included in Arewa's study.

Two motifs of the Cinderella tale, cruel stepmother (L55) and stepdaughter heroine (S31) are listed by Arewa; both are found together in the same two Rundi tales. Cruel stepmother is also reported by Clarke and by Thompson for three additional African tales, from Togo, from Cameroun, and from the Ikom of Nigeria. Motif L162, lowly heroine marries prince, appears in one Swahili tale cited by Arewa.

On the other hand, no African examples of the following motifs are cited in any of these three indexes:

Abused youngest daughter (L52)
Cruel stepsister (S34)
Hearth abode of unpromising hero (heroine) (L131)
Supernatural helpers (N810)
Clothes produced by magic (D1050.1)
Golden shoes (F823.1)
Glass shoes (F823.2)
Silver shoes (F823.4)
Carriage from pumpkin (F861.4.3)
Magic animal supplies treasure (B100.2)
Prince sees heroine at ball and is enamored (N711.6)

Tabu: Staying too long at ball. Must leave before certain hour
(C761.3)
Slipper test (H36.1)
False bride's mutilated feet (K1911.3.3.1)
Girl hacks off her heel to get shoe on (J2131.3.1).

Golden slippers are of course common in the European Cinderella tradition, and they appear in the tale from Malagasy to be referred to later. In the Grimms' version silk and silver slippers are worn on the first visit to the festival and golden slippers on the third.

No African examples are reported for animal spitting (vomiting) treasure (B103.4), but helpful frog (B493.1) is cited by Thompson for the Zulu, Ronga, and Suto; by Clarke for Togo; and by Arewa for the Safwa and Gogo, making six instances in all. Moreover, in a Swazi tale a helpful frog saves the heroine by swallowing her and then bringing her up again,[12] and two girls are saved in a similar fashion in a Konde tale.[13] Again in a Lamba tale a helpful frog saves a brother and sister by swallowing them, taking them home, and belching them up.[14] Thompson also reports the helpful frog motif for Jewish folklore and for India, China, and Chile as well; but it is clear that it is widely distributed in Africa, and was probably added to this tale in Nigeria. In another Hausa tale, a mother makes her ugly daughter beautiful by swallowing her and bringing her up again.[15]

The examination of the relevant motif indexes gives us no reason to modify the conclusions which were reached by very quick references to four tale type indexes. In fact, it tends to confirm them.

However, we have a third check, since the Cinderella tale has been subjected to two intensive, comparative studies. Marian Cox's early study of *Cinderella*[16] cites four African tales, but none for the Cinderella tale type (510A). One from Mauritius (Cox no. 145) she classifies as a Catskin tale; because of the heroine's flight from her lecherous father who has promised her dresses like the sun, the moon, and the stars if she will marry him, it belongs to type 510B, Cap o'Rushes, or The Dress of Gold, of Silver, and of Stars.[17] One from Egypt and another from South Africa (Cox nos. 337, 339), she classes as "Hero-Tales" (a hero replaces the heroine). The Hero-Tales have some incidents which are found "in stories of the 'Cinderella' type", and Cox includes them "merely for purposes of comparison, as it seemed inadvisable to pass them over entirely." A Kabyle tale, which belongs somewhere in the type 511 series, is considered only in a footnote to no. 29. None of these four tales involves a dance or a slipper-test, and none of them resembles the Hausa tale with which we are concerned.

For the purpose of making historic-geographical studies of the Cinderella tale it may be necessary to group types 510A and 510B together, since in some narratives they are combined. But in trying to answer the kind of questions I have asked about the Hausa Cinderella tale, types 510B, 511, and the "Hero-Tales" can be disregarded unless they have more in common than a cruel stepmother. Both Cox and Rooth cite tales which are otherwise completely different.[18]

Anna Birgitta Rooth's *The Cinderella Cycle*[19] is an extension and amplification of Cox's study. She reports that only five examples of tale type 510A have been found outside Europe: from Martinique in the New World, from India and Arabia, and from Egypt and Malagasy.

The Malagasy tale consists of two parts, the second of which is clearly the Cinderella tale, complete with cruel stepsisters, a rat that produces fine clothes and golden slippers, three visits to a dance, a prince who dances only with the heroine, her hurried return home at midnight, the slipper left at the dance, the slipper-test, and marriage to the prince. Ferrand,[20] who noted its similarity to the Cinderella tale, reported that the aged Antambahoaka informant who dictated it to him was completely illiterate, that he had known it since childhood, and that his statements were confirmed by other Antambahoaka. This is undoubtedly true of the first part of the tale, since it has been recorded by Renel among the Tanala of Malagasy.[21] However, I would agree with Rooth that the Cinderella portion is obviously of French origin. She believes that the heroine's name, Sandroy, is in imitation of the French Cendron or Cendrillion; and I consider it significant that, in the middle of the narrative, her name is changed to Sandroy from Fara, and that Ifara or Ifaravavy is the heroine's name in the Tanala tale.

The Egyptian tale[22] involves jealous sisters, an enchanted pot which provides food and beautiful clothing, a party at the king's palace, a diamond bracelet dropped as the heroine hastens home, and a bracelet-test. The marriage to the prince follows an episode in which the heroine is transformed into a turtle dove and then released from her spell. This differs considerably from the Hausa tale, but let us accept it as a Cinderella variant.

Among the references to her type B (510A), Rooth[23] cites a Mande tale published by Frobenius.[24] In it a girl is made to sort grain before her cruel stepmother lets her go to a dance; but by the time she gets there the dance is finished, and there is no prince, no slipper-test, and no wedding.

Rooth also cites Chatelain's tale from Angola as involving tale type 510A. Of it Chatelain himself said, "This story is originally that of the 'Cenerentola,' the universality of which has been traced up by Gubernatis in his 'Florilegio delle novelline populari,' p. 5, and by Henry Chasle Coste. In the folklore of Portugal, Madeira, and Brazil it is current under various names and in various versions."[25] The evidence presented here challenges the notion that Cenerentola (Cinderella) is a universal tale; and, if Chatelain's example is really part of the Cinderella tradition, it is highly garbled and probably derived from the Portugese. It involves a cruel sister-in-law, a helpful goat, a helpful old woman who gives Maria magical boxes which produce clothes, a carriage and attendants, a meeting with the Governor in church, and an announcement that the Governor will reward anyone who can take off "only a shoe" from the still unidentified Maria. But shoes or slippers are not mentioned again, and the tale ends with Maria's brother leaving his wife and returning to live with his sister. Klipple must have known of this tale since it was published in the American Folklore Society's Memoir, no. 1; but apparently she did not consider it closely enough related to the Cinderella tale to mention it in her index.

Over half a century ago Tremearne noted that "Cinderella was not the only one who had shoes which would fit no one but her."[26] In view of the tale in the Edgar collection, it would not be surprising to find another Hausa version of the Cinderella tale; and, if there were no others, it would suggest that Edgar's tale was a recent introduction. However, in the Hausa tale to which Tremearne referred, a boot-test identifies a boy hero who has slain a monster by throwing hot stones into its mouth, after he has disposed of his and his sister's slaves, burned all their property, killed the sons of a king, and wounded a bird that has saved him and his sister.[27] In an Egyptian version of this tale, the boy's sister is identified by a dropped sandal, but without having to fit her foot into it; the boy hero in this tale burns all their property, burns the houses of their neighbors, kills the children of a king, tickles a bird that has saved him and his sister, and destroys a monster by throwing burning stones into its mouth.[28] Similarly in the course of a series of adventures in a Fulani tale[29] and in two versions of a Kabyle tale[30] a man is identified by a boot-test as the hero who has killed a crocodile or a snake that kept people from taking water from a river. There is also a Yoruba tale in which a man is identified by a boot-test as the hero who has slain a giant eagle that had been killing people.[31] Motifs suggestive of the slipper-test are incorporated into what are clearly other tale types, distinct from Cinderella.

Because neither the tale type nor its significant motifs, except for the helpful frogs (who are not part of the European Cinderella tale) and the cruel stepmother, have been reported for any of the Hausa's neighbors or for the huge areas which separate Nigeria from Europe, Egypt, and Malagasy, we may safely conclude that this tale did not reach the Hausa by diffusion from these places. And for the very same reasons we may conclude that it did not diffuse to them from Nigeria.

As Daniel Crowley has noted, there are many African tales which have been reported in only one instance, from a single society; but it is most unlikely that the Hausa Cinderella tale represents an instance of independent invention because it contains so many, and such specific, elements that are common to its European counterparts. Again we are left with the first of our four alternatives, that the Hausa Cinderella tale, like the Malagasy one, was introduced in the recent period of European contact.

Negative evidence is not very convincing, and it is of course possible that the conclusions I have reached may have to be modified when a tale type index for all of Africa has been completed; but I consider this relatively unlikely. Even though the available indexes are incomplete, I believe that I have been able to show that tale type and motif indexes can be useful to folklorists by providing quick answers to some questions of restricted time depth.

I imply no criticism of any of the authors of the tale type and motif indexes or of the comparative studies that I have cited for having failed to find the Hausa Cinderella tale or its motifs, such as the slipper-test, in Africa. Many of them deliberately excluded Malagasy and Egypt from their studies and, as I indicated earlier,

Edgar's collection of Hausa tales was a closed book to scholars until Neil Skinner made it available to us in translation. Because he has done folklorists such a great service, I hope that he will not take offense at the final point I wish to make about the Hausa Cinderella tale.

This point is that, however well one may understand a language and however skillful he may be in the very difficult art of translation, he may miss some of the meaning of folktales unless he has a general knowledge of folklore, or at least takes the little time that is required to consult the tale type indexes. When Skinner first sent me a photocopy of his draft translation of Edgar's volume two, there was a marginal notation at the point in the tale where the heroine is found "lying in the fireplace." In this note he asks, "Why? For warmth, as she wasn't allotted a hut?"

The answer, of course, is that this is Motif L131, "Hearth abode of unpromising hero (heroine)" and point Ia[1] in the Aarne-Thompson synopsis of tale type 510, "The heroine . . . stays on the hearth or in the ashes." It is also the source of the heroine's name, Cinder-Ella.

Postscript. After this paper was delivered, Daniel Crowley kindly sent me abstracts of additional tales related to Cinderella made by his students in connection with his work on a tale type index for Africa. Among them were the Equilbecq and Frobenius tales of the hero identified by a boot-test which I have cited above, and a version of the Cinderella tale which is not mentioned in the tale type or motif indexes or in the studies of the Cinderella tale type. I have decided to append it here rather than incorporate it in the earlier discussion, since this is primarily an essay on methodology. The tale comes from Marrakech in Morocco[32] and combines what I would consider to be three tale types: A, A stepdaughter is cared for by a dead cow (her mother); B, Cinderella; and C, The heroine is saved after having been pushed into a well by her stepsister. Both A and C have been recorded elsewhere in Africa, but we are concerned with B.

A. A man has two wives. One is beautiful and has a beautiful daughter; the other is wicked and ugly and has an ugly daughter. The ugly wife transforms the beautiful wife into a cow, makes the beautiful daughter do all the work in the kitchen, throws ashes in the girls hair, and names her "Soiled with Ashes." The cow-mother cleans away the ashes and caresses her child, but the ugly stepmother has the cow sold and butchered. The beautiful daughter gathers the cow's bones, washes them and buries them. The cow-mother returns nightly from the grave to clean and care for her child.

B. The king announces a feast to celebrate his marriage. The ugly stepmother prepares her own daughter and sends her to the feast, leaving the grain. Before the feast ends, the cow-mother cleans her daughter, dresses her in beautiful garments, puts tiny slippers on her feet, and carries her to the feast where she dazzles all with her beauty. Birds sort the grain. Before the feast ends, the cow-mother carries her daughter home, but the girl loses one of her slippers. The king sends his fiancée away, announcing that he will marry only the woman whose foot fits the slipper that has been found. After searching the kingdom, only the girl's house is left. The stepsister's feet are too big for the slipper; a cock tells of "Soiled with Ashes" hiding in the kitchen; the slipper fits on her foot, matching the slipper on the other. The king marries her immediately.

C. The new queen receives her stepmother and stepsister in the palace and gives them presents; but one day her stepsister pushes her into the well. The stepmother magically transforms her daughter so that she looks like the queen, but she repulses the king when he returns from battle. The king sends for water from the well, finds his wife with his new-born child alive in the well, and they are rescued. The stepsister is killed and her body is sent to the stepmother, who eats it, thinking it is a gift from her daughter.

Here, at the opposite end of the Mediterranean littoral from Egypt, we have the motifs of the cruel stepmother, grain sorting, garments magically provided, the feast (dance), the lost slipper and the slipper-test, the heroine soiled with ashes and found hidden in the kitchen, and a marriage to a king. In retrospect, my earlier statements sound rather dogmatic; but on the basis of this one instance I do not feel compelled to change my conclusion about the origin of the Hausa Cinderella tale. The three other African versions of Cinderella are all from the coastal regions of Africa, and Marrakech, like Egypt, is close to Europe.

However, the Marrakech example underscores the importance of completing a tale type index for Africa. Both Cox and Rooth consider African tales of a helpful cow, similar to Part A, but neither cites the one from Marrakech.

I cannot conclude without remarking that only four Cinderella tales for the large area of Africa, generously defined, is a surprisingly small number, considering that the long period of European contact involved both colonial rule and European controlled schools. In his introduction to Cox's *Cinderella*, Andrew Lang observed, "One thing is plain, a naked and a shoeless race could not have invented Cinderella."[33] It is also likely that the absence of shoes in much of the African continent has been a cultural barrier to the adoption of a tale which hinges on a slipper-test. Nevertheless this small total lends little support to the contention that tales of European (or Indian) origin were adopted by Africans, quickly and in large numbers, during the early period of the slave trade. Furthermore, I must agree with what Crowley has said elsewhere: that it is not easy to conceive of the slave traders spending their evenings beguiling their African chattels with folktales.

Admittedly, it is also difficult to imagine Lugard's officers and administrators beguiling their subjects with evenings of telling folktales, especially during the first years of their occupation of northern Nigeria. However, a number of early administrators—including Edgar himself—and missionaries and others did actually record and publish folktales.[34] It is by no means inconceivable that one or more of these individuals told the Cinderella story in order to elicit Hausa folktales from their informants. In fact, Schön says of his fifth tale, "This Story was told to some children in English, and related by Dorugu in Hausa."[35] At this date the evidence is only circumstantial, but both opportunity and motive were present.

NOTES

[1]This paper was delivered at the annual meeting of the American Folklore Society at Indiana University on November 10, 1968.

[2]Stith Thompson, *The Folktale* (New York: The Dryden Press, 1951), 429–430.

[3]H.A.S. Johnston, *A Selection of Hausa Stories* (Oxford Library of African Literature, 1966), 71–74.

[4]*Ibid.*, xlvii.

[5]*Fura* is a kind of gruel and *tuwo* a kind of porridge, both made of millet or other grain; the former is the usual morning meal, the latter the usual evening meal.

[6]Omitted in the Hausa text.

[7]Antti Aarne and Stith Thompson, *The Types of the Folktale* (= FF Communications, No. 184, 1964), 175–176.

[8]May Augusta Klipple, "African Folk Tales with Foreign Analogues" (doctoral dissertation in English, Indiana University, 1938).

[9]E. Ojo Arewa, "A Classification of the Folktales of the Northern East African Cattle Area by Types" (doctoral dissertation in anthropology, University of California, Berkeley, 1966).

[10]Winifred Lambrecht, "A Tale Type Index for Central Africa (doctoral dissertation in anthropology, University of California, Berkeley, 1967).

[11]Kenneth W. Clarke, "A Motif-Index of the Folktales of Culture Area V, West Africa" (doctoral dissertation in folklore, Indiana University, Bloomington, 1957).

[12]E.J. Bourhill and J.B. Drake, *Fairy Tales from South Africa* (London: Macmillan and Company, 1908), 187–197.

[13]Friedrich Fülleborn, *Das Deutsche Njassa- und Ruwuma-gebiet, Land und Leute* (= *Deutsch-Ost-Afrika*, vol. 9) (1906), 334.

[14]Clement M. Doke, *Lamba Folk-Lore* (= *Memoir of the American Folk-Lore Society*, vol. 20) (1927), 247–249.

[15]A.J.N. Tremearne, *Hausa Superstitions and Customs* (London: John Bale, Sons and Danielsson, 1913), 304.

[16]Marian Roalfe Cox, *Cinderella* (= *Publications of the Folk-Lore Society*, vol. 31) (1893).

[17]Anna Birgitta Rooth, *The Cinderella Cycle* (Lund: C.W.K. Gleerup, 1951), 115, concludes that this tale, recorded by Baissac, is derived from Perrault.

[18]For example, E.J. Bourhill and J.B. Drake, *Fairy Tales from South Africa* (London, 1908), 139–150, 198–211.

[19]Op. cit.

[20]Gabriel Ferrand, *Contes populaires Malgaches* (= *Collection de contes et chansons populaires*, vol. 19) (1893), 123–129.

[21]Charles Renel, *Contes de Madagascar*, I (= *Collection de contes et chansons populaires* vol. 37) (1910), 154–1670.

[22]S.E. Yacoub Artin Pacha, *Contes populaires de la Vallée de Nil* (= *Les Littératures populaires de toutes les nations*, vol. 32) (1895), 63–67. I have been unable to locate a second Egyptian tale referred to by Rooth as from Østrup, or a "Yumale" tale from "innerafrika" mentioned by Bolte and Polívka. However all other "Cinderella" tales cited for Africa have been examined.

[23]Rooth, *The Cinderella Cycle*, 251.

[24]Leo Frobenius, *Erzählungen aus dem West Sudan* (= *Atlantis*, vol. 8) (1922), 163–165.

[25]Heli Chatelain, *Folk-Tales of Angola* (= *Memoirs of the American Folk-Lore Society*, vol. 1) (1894), 265.

[26]A.J.N. Tremearne, *Hausa Superstitions and Customs* (London: John Bale, Sons and Danielsson, 1913), 14.

[27]*Ibid.*, 410–412.

[28] Artin Pacha, 149-156.

[29] F.V. Equilbecq, *Essai sur la littérature merveilleuse des noirs, suivi des contes indigènes de l'ouest africain français,* II (= *Collection des contes et chansons populaires,* vol. 42) (1915), 3-42.

[30] Leo Frobenius, *Volksmärchen der Kabylen,* vol. 2 (= *Atlantis,* vol. 2) (1922), 71-90.

[31] Abayomi Fuja, *Fourteen Hundred Cowries* (London: Oxford University Press, 1962), 24-30.

[32] Françoise Légey, *Contes et légendes populaires de Maroc* (= *Publications de l'Institut des Hautes Études Marocaines,* vol. 16) (1926), 19-23.

[33] *Op. cit.,* x.

[34] This includes the following, listed in chronological order:

J.F. Schön, *Grammar of the Hausa Language* (London: Church Missionary House, 1862), xiv, viii, 234.

J.F. Schön, *Dictionary of the Hausa Language* (London: Church Missionary House, 1876), 218, 142, xxxxiv.

J.F. Schön, *Hausa Reading Book, with the Rudiments of Grammar and Vocabularies, and Traveller's Vade Mecum* (London: Church Missionary Society, 1877), viii, 102.

J.F. Schön, *Magána Hausa* (London: Society for Promoting Christian Knowledge. 1885-86), 2 vols., xx, 288; xii, 195.

J.F. Schön, *Appendix to the Dictionary of the Hausa Language* (London: Church Missionary Society, 1888), iv, 206.

A. Dirr, *Manuel pratique de langue haoussa* (Paris: Ernest Leroux, 1895), 140.

C.H. Robinson, *Specimens of Hausa Literature* (Cambridge: University Press, 1896), xix, 112.

C.H. Robinson, *Hausa Grammar, with Exercises, Readings, and Vocabulary* (London: Kegan Paul, 1897). [Second edition: 1905, vii, 210.]

Gottlob Adolf Krause, "Beiträge zum Märchenschatz der Afrikaner," *Globus* 72 (1897): 228-33, 254-58.

E.C. Marré, *Die Sprache der Hausa* (= *Die Kunst der Polyglottie,* vol. 70) (1901), x, 176.

A. Mischlich, *Lehrbuch der hausanische Sprache (Hausa Sprache)* (= *Archiv für das Studium deutscher Kolonialsprachen,* vol. 1) (1902), x, 184.

J. Lippert, "Haussa-Märchen," *Mitteilungen des Seminars für orientalische Sprachen,* Dritte Abteilung: *Afrikanische Studien* 8:3 (1905):223-260.

Rudolf Prietze, "Tiermärchen der Haussa," *Zeitschrift für Ethnologie* 39, (1907): 916-939.

L.E.O. Charlton, *A Hausa Reading Book* (London: Oxford University Press, 1908), 83, 45.

Hermann G. Harris, *Hausa Stories and Riddles* (Weston-super-Mare, England: Mendip Press, 1908), xv, 111.

M. Landeroin and J. Tilho, *Grammaire et contes haoussas* (Paris: Imprimerie Nationale, 1909), xii, 292.

A.J.N. Tremearne, "Some Specimens of Hausa Folklore," *Journal of the Royal Society of Arts* 58 (1909-10): 1061-1068.

A.J.N. Tremearne, "Fifty Hausa Folk-Tales", *Folk-Lore* 21 (1910): 199–215, 351–65, 487–503; 22 (1911):60–73, 218–28, 341–48, 457–73.

A.J.N. Tremearne, "Hausa Folk-Lore," *Man* 11 (1911):20–23, 52–58.

Mary and Newmann Tremearne, *Fables and Fairy Tales for Little Folk, or Uncle Remus in Hausaland* (Cambridge: Heffer and Sons, 1910), 135.

Diedrich Westermann, *Die Sprache der Haussa in Zentralafrika* (= *Deutsche Kolonialsprachen*, vol. 3) (1911), viii, 88.

[35]J.F. Schön, *Grammar of the Hausa Language* (London: Church Missionary House, 1862), 189.

A Javanese Cinderella Tale and
Its Pedagogical Value

James Danandjaja

Regardless of whether a folktale is indigenous or borrowed in a given cultural context, it will—if it is told and retold—reflect the ideology and world view of the raconteurs and their audiences. So a Zuni version of Cinderella becomes a carrier of Zuni values just as a Hausa version of Cinderella encapsulates Hausa ethos. Anthropologically oriented folklorists as opposed to literary folklorists are very much interested in the way folklore functions in culture. Whereas the literary folklorist tends to emphasize the "lore" of folklore, the anthropological folklorist is more concerned with the "folk." Accordingly, literary folklorists often study texts, paying little or no attention to cultural contexts, while anthropological folklorists concentrate most of their energies on questions of function and context, often virtually ignoring the text per se. Of course, the true or complete folklorist is both literary and anthropological. He values the text of a tale, but he also tries to understand its function and context in terms of the people who tell and listen to the tale. "Folk" and "lore" must each be taken into account in the proper study of folklore.

Professor James Danandjaja, who teaches folklore at the University of Indonesia, presents a Javanese version of Cinderella which he collected from an informant and which he himself knew well from

Reprinted from *Majalah Ilmu-Ilmu Sastra Indonesia*, 6, No. 2 (1976), 15–29.

his own childhood. He identifies it in the light of Anna Birgitta Rooth's Cinderella typology, but he goes beyond collection and classification to try to show how this particular version of Cinderella reflects Javanese values and worldview. (The text in Javanese was included as an appendix in the original essay but is not reprinted in this volume.)

This paper is a study of the Javanese folktale called "Andé-Andé Lumut," which I have collected from Mr. Basuki Suhardi, a linguist from the University of Indonesia, and a Javanese from Kêdiri, a small town in East Java. Although I have never done any research on the distribution of this tale, I have the impression that it is rather widespread in Central and East Java. I have come to this conclusion because every Javanese I met from those two places, happened to be familiar with the tale. My informant got this version from his own mother when he was a child in Kêdiri. The tale was told to me last year in November 1970 at Berkeley, California. In fact before this, as someone who has spent his entire childhood in East Java, I was already familiar with this tale. The person who told me this tale, when I was a child, was a man called Pak Mus, who was employed as a gardener by my parents in Malang, a small town in East Java.

In this paper the first thing I would like to do before looking at the function of the tale in the Javanese society is to identify it first by indexing it according to its tale type and motifs, in order to show its universality.

The English translation[1] of the Andé-Andé Lumut tale is as follows:

1. Long time ago, in the village of Dhadhapan, there lived a widow called the Widow of Dhadhapan.
2. The Widow of Dhadhapan had three daughters, who were very beautiful. The eldest was named Klêting Abang (*Klêting:* water jar; *Abang:* red), the second Klêting Ijo (*ijo:* green) and the youngest Klêting Kuning (*kuning:* yellow).
3. We are not sure about the reason why the Widow of Dhadhapan did not like Klêting Kuning. But she loved Klêting Abang and Klêting Ijo very much. Both were showered with beautiful clothes and given the most delicious food. She forced Klêting Kuning to work very hard.

4. But since Klêting Kuning had a good heart and a virtuous character, her patience (to give in) earned her a reward from the gods later on.

5. Every day Klêting Kuning had to do many kinds of manual work, and often she had to go to the river which was located very far from her home to wash clothes and kitchen utensils. If the washing was done badly she would be punished.

6. One day as usual when Klêting Kuning was sent by her mother to wash clothes and kitchen utensils by the river, the load was so enormous that it made her cry and lament her fate: "Oh, Allah and deities, what have I done, that I have to be so wretched. Please show me a way out."

7. At that instant too, a huge stork (*bango Thongthong*) appeared. Klêting Kuning was so scared that she wanted to flee, but the huge bird suddenly spoke to her: "Klêting Kuning, don't be afraid. I am not going to harm you, my coming is in fact to help you."

8. Klêting Kuning was not afraid anymore, and asked: "Hi! who are you? It is very strange for a bird to talk."

9. Bango Thongthong (the stork) replied: "Right; later on I will tell you who I am, but at the moment let me help you first with your chore." The work done by Bango Thongthong was perfect; the washing was very cleanly done. Klêting Kuning was very pleased about it, and she thanked the bird heartily before she went home.

10. The Widow of Dhadhapan, Klêting Abang, and Klêting Ijo were amazed at Klêting Kuning's work.

11. Since then, every day Klêting Kuning was helped by Bango Thongthong.

12. Meanwhile there was a tiding that a prince by the name of Andé-Andé Lumut was looking for a spouse. Many had already made proposals, but were rejected.

13. And accordingly the Widow of Dhadhapan sent Klêting Abang and Klêting Ijo to apply for the position, and before they went they were beautifully dressed and made up.

14. Meanwhile, when Klêting Kuning who was doing her daily chores knew that her two sisters were beautifully dressed, she asked them: "Sisters, where are you going? Why are you dressed and made up so handsomely?"

"We want to go to the castle of Andé-Andé Lumut, to be chosen as his wife," replied one of them.

"Let me go too, sisters. Let me be chosen as his wife," begged Klêting Kuning.

"That can't be, don't you know that you are ugly, while we are beautiful?" replied her sister. On hearing this Klêting Kuning could say nothing and wept.

15. So it was told, when the two girls on their way to the castle had to cross a river, they became very frustrated, because the river was very deep and wide, and there was no boat to cross them to the other bank. So in their desperation they lamented: "Oh god, god, we wish that somebody would like to help us to cross the river."

16. And truly, as if their wish were heard by the gods, suddenly there appeared before them a huge fresh-water crab (*Yuyukangkang*) who could also speak like a man: "Aha, aha, here are two beautiful virgins who are lamenting, what is the matter? Come near and tell me your problems."

"Dear Yuyukangkang if you can speak like us, then you must also be able to help us to cross the river."

"I'll help you if I am being rewarded."

"What are you asking for?"

"A kiss (from each of you)."

"Klêting Abang and Klêting Ijo consented: "We will! we will!" Thus Yuyukangkang helped the girls to cross the river.

17. Meanwhile Klêting Kuning, who was left behind by her sisters, was very sad. Suddenly Bango Thongthong (the stork) came to her saying: "Klêting Kuning, don't be sad. I understand that you are a good girl, and I am sure that the gods know that too."

18. "Bango Thongthong, who are you really? Why are you so nice to me? I am very much impressed by you who are a creature but so wise."

"Yes, yes, now is in fact the time to tell you, but before that I want to ask you whether you will believe me."

"Yes I'll believe you."

"As a matter of fact, I am the messenger of the gods."

"Oh, your holiness, I am very sorry for being improper to you. Please forgive me."

"It's all right, Klêting Kuning. I think my duty is completed. I can't accompany you any longer, but be very careful on your way after I leave you."

"I will, your holiness."

19. "Bless you. Here I have a *sada lanang* (magic cocoanut-palm leaf rib), I hope you could use it for your welfare."

"Thank you, your holiness."

"Yes, yes, good luck, Klêting Kuning."

20. After receiving the *sada lanang,* Klëting Kuning returned home and told her mother: "Mother, mother, please let me offer myself to Andé-Andé Lumut."

"No, no, you can't do that, my dear girl."

21. "Why? why if Klêting Abang and Klêting Ijo did it?"

"You must realize, my girl, that Klêting Abang and Klêting Ijo are beautiful girls, while you are ugly and also sloppy. I am afraid that Andé-Andé Lumut will not want you, so stay to accompany your mother."

"No, I want to follow Klêting Abang and Klêting Ijo."

22. "Well, if you misunderstand my good intention! Go then if you want, but go as you are now, don't wash yourself, nor change your clothes."

23. Klêting Kuning did as her mother wished, because for her the most important thing to do was to catch up with her sisters. She never gave a thought to her dirty and full of patches dress.

24. As she reached the riverbank Klêting Kuning called for the huge crab: "Yuyukangkang, please help me to cross over the river." Yuyukangkang not only did not want to help her, but also mocked her for her sloppiness. Klêting Kuning repeated her request, but the crab refused and continued with his jest.

25. Klêting Kuning was very angry and whipped her *sada lanang* (magic cocoanut-palm leaf rib) strongly toward the water, and the water dried up in a wink of the eye. Klêting Kuning then crossed the river easily. Yuyukangkang asked for forgiveness. The *sada lanang* was whipped once more, and the river was full of water again.

26. At this time Klëting Abang and Klêting Ijo had already reached the home of Andé-Andé Lumut. The mother of Andé-Andé Lumut told her son of their coming.

27. But Andé-Andé Lumut refused to meet them because according to him the girls were already "used" by Yuyukangkang.

28. Klêting Abang and Klêting Ijo were very disappointed and left for home. On their way back they met Klêting Kuning and told her to go home, but she refused, because she intended to try her luck. Klêting Kuning was laughed and mocked at by them, but she did not take any notice, and resumed her journey.

29. (But) when she reached the home of Andé-Andé Lumut, Klêting Kuning was dismissed rudely by his mother because she looked like a beggar.

30. But Andé-Andé Lumut stopped his mother by saying: "Yes, this is the one I have been expecting for days and nights." And he even asked her to be admitted to the castle, had her wash her person, and dressed her up in a beautiful dress. And, really, after being dressed and made up, Klêting Kuning looked as beautiful as a fairy.

31. A wedding party was then held for forty days and nights.

32. The Widow of Dhadhapan, Klêting Abang, and Klêting Ijo were also invited.

33. Klêting Kuning and Andé-Andé Lumut lived in harmony thereafter like *mimi lan mintuna* (female horseshoe and male horseshoe crab).

The tale cited above can surely be classified as a "Cinderella and Cap o' Rushes" No. 510. Ia, Ia²; IId; III, V. i.e., Ia. "The heroine is abused by her stepmother and stepsisters" (see No. 3, No. 5, and No. 6);² Ia². "Is dressed in rough clothing" (see No. 23, and No. 29); IId. "Magic help by birds" (see No. 9, and No. 19, and No. 11)³; III. "Meeting a prince" (see No. 30); IV. "Proof of identity" (unlike her two sisters the heroine is not "dirtied" by the kiss of Yuyukang-kang. (See No. 16, No. 24, and No. 27.) V. "Marriage with the Prince". The motifs are S31. "Cruel stepmother" (see No. 3); L55. "Stepdaughter heroine"; N810. "Helpful bird" (see No. 7); D813.

"Magic object received from fairy (see No. 19"; D1470.1. "Magic wishing object causes to be fulfilled (see No. 19).

What is interesting about this Javanese version of Cinderella is that it fits exactly Anna Birgitta Rooth's classification of a subtype of "Malay tradition," with the following motifs, such as step-daughter, helpful bird, task of washing.[4]

What is unique about this Javanese Cinderella version is "The Proof of Identity," that is, the heroine, unlike her two sisters, is not yet "stained" by the kiss of Yuyukangkang.

There is no doubt that this oral literature is a folktale because it has what Bascom calls a conventional opening and closing formula which introduces and closes a folktale, warning the listener that the narrative which follows is fiction, and that it does not call for belief (Bascom, 1965b:6). The conventional opening of this folktale is *Anuju sawijining dina*, which means "long time ago" (see No. 1), and the closing formula *Klêting Kuning lan Andé-Andé Lumut urip rukun bebarengan kaya mimi lan mintuna*, which means "Klêting Kuning and Andé-Andé Lumut lived in harmony thereafter like the female horseshoe crab, (*mimi*) and male horseshoe crab (*mintuna*)[5] (see No. 33).

After having identified the tale as traditional, let us see what its function is. There are many diverse functions of folklore (Dundes, 1965:277), and according to William Bascom there are four functions, that is: 1) as projective systems; 2) as a means of validating culture, in justifying its rituals and institutions to those who perform and observe them;[6] 3) as a pedagogical device; 4) as a means of applying social pressure and exercising social control; and these four functions can further be grouped together under single function of maintaining the stability of culture. Viewed thus, folklore operating within a society insures conformity to the accepted cultural forms, and continuity from generation to generation through its role in education and the extent to which it mirrors culture. In other words, folklore is an important mechanism in maintaining the stability of culture (Bascom, 1965a:292–298). Since folktale is one of the genres of folklore, its function must be identical with the functions of folklore in general.

As Bascom said, folklore mirrors culture (1965a:297), so in order to understand the function of this Javanese folktale we must relate it to the culture where it comes from, that is the Javanese culture.

After studying this Javanese folktale I come to the conclusion that its function is primarily a pedagogical device, that is, Bascom's folklore function No. 3. I come to this conclusion because the Javanese world view, according to Clifford Geertz, is as follows. The Javanese world view is based on two concepts, *alus* and *kasar*. *Alus* means pure, refined, polished, polite, exquisite, ethereal, subtle, civilized, smooth. A man who speaks flawless Javanese is *alus*, as is high Javanese itself. A piece of cloth with intricate, subtle design painted onto it is *alus*, so is a smooth stone; and one's behaviors and actions are *alus* insofar as they are regulated by the delicate intricacies of the complex court-derived etiquette. Whereas *kasar* is the opposite: impolite, rough, uncivilized, etc. Between these two poles the Javanese arrange everyone from peasant to king (Geertz, 1964:232[7]). And the ideal much preferred is the *alus*. The Javanese thinks that the more refined one's feeling, the more profound one's understanding, one's moral character, and the more elevated one's moral character, the more beautiful one's external aspect. The spiritually enlightened man guards his psychological equilibrium well and makes a constant effort to maintain its placid stability. His proximate aim is emotional quiescence, for passion is a *kasar* feeling fit only for children, animals, peasants, and foreigners (Geertz, 1964: 239–240). According to the Javanese there are three ways of acquiring this calming state, that is, being *trima, sabar,* and *ikhlas*. *Trima* literally means to accept or receive, in value terms it means not to kick against a prick, to accept what comes without protest and without rebellion. *Sabar* is usually translated as indicating an absence of eagerness, of impatience, of headstrong passion. *Ikhlas* means detachment from the contingencies of the external world so as not to be disturbed when things go awry in it or if something unexpected occurs. It is "not caring" on the premise that if one does not care about worldly things they cannot hurt or upset one. The three ideas are obviously very close. *Trima* brings peace through the acceptance of the inevitable with grace: "If you accept unhappiness, it will totally disappear." *Sabar* brings such peace by an inward restraint of emotional drive, an atrophy of the will, an excess of caution. *Ikhlas* brings psychological peace through a lack of attachment to the external world. This kind of attitude is a major Javanese defense mechanism (Geertz, 1964:240–241).

If we return back to our tale, it shows clearly the four functions cited by Bascom, and in this particular version of Andé-Andé Lumut tale it obviously emphasizes the pedagogical device, that is, as an aid in the education of the young. This particular tale is told to Javanese children when they are young, in order to enforce the Javanese world view of being *halus*. This becomes clear if we read the sentence in No. 4: *"Nanging, dasar Klêting Kuning becik budiné tur alus wataké, Klêting Kuning nrima pêlakuan kuwi mau kanti sabar."* (But since Klêting kuning had a good heart and virtuous character, her patience [to give in] earned her a reward from the gods later on.) In this sentence we find words *alus* (or *halus*) and *sabar*, which are two of the basic concepts of the Javanese world view, and two of the three ways of acquiring the emotional placid stability which is considered to be civilized or *alus* by the Javanese value system. The tale as a pedagogical device is further affirmed by my informant, who told me that his mother used to end this tale with a proverb, *"Wani ngalah gêdé wekasan,"* which means, "The person who likes to give in at the end will get a good return."

The function of this tale can further be summed up as what Bascom calls maintaining the stability of culture (1965a:279), in this case the Javanese world view. The Javanese world view is "made in order to maintain the stability of the Javanese society, which is basically up to the present still a feudal society, and a highly stratified one (although now it is already in the process of change toward a more democratic one). According to Koentjaraningrat, the Javanese themselves distinguish two primary social levels: the *wong cilik* ("little people"), comprising the great mass of the peasants and the lower strata of the urban population, and the *priyayi*, including members of the administrative bureaucracy and the academically trained intellectuals. In addition to these they recognize a third level, relatively small in size but prestigious: the *ndara* or nobility (1960:88). The Javanese people are indoctrinated from the time that they are children, by having implanted this kind of story which contains the Javanese world view, into believing that they must be *sabar* (patience), *trima* (to accept what comes without protest), and *ikhlas* (detachment from the contingencies of the external world). If they belong to the lowest level (*wong cilik*) they must be *sabar*, *trima* and *ikhlas*, because this is considered to be *alus* in Javanese world view, and God will reward them, maybe not in this world, but surely in heaven.

As I have said before, this version of Cinderella tale is widespread, and I think it is widespread because it is liked by the Javanese people, who are so hopelessly bound by their world view so that they can do nothing but flee from reality by daydreaming that they too can sometimes become the heroine who is poor, but due to their being *trima, sabar* and *ikhlas* could become noblemen (*ndara*), who are considered to be *alus*.

NOTES

[1] The translation is a rather free translation.

[2] Although in this version it is not stated that Klêting Kuning is a stepdaughter, according to the other version that I got when I was a child in Malang, she is a stepdaughter of the Widow Dhadhapan.

[3] According to the version I got in Malang, a town in East Java, the stork is the reincarnation of the heroine's father (motif:B3131.1 "Helpful animal reincarnation of parent.")

[4] The motifs listed by Rooth as Malay tradition are stepdaughter, sisters, youngest sister, brothers, helpful fish, helpful bird, helpful cow, food, task of washing, helpful animal is borrowed by relative, slaying of animal, burying the bones or remains. From the remains appears a tree, which provides food, or riches; picking fruit; story develops into type Aa510 A (Rooth, 1951: Appendix I).

[5] The male and female horseshoe crabs are believed to love each other because we mostly catch the pair in the position where the male crab is mounting the female crab's back.

[6] Bascom notes that Malinowski emphasized that myth served as "a warrant, a charter, and often even a practical guide (see Bronislaw Malinowski, *Myth in Primitive Psychology*, New York, 1926, p. 29).

[7] According to Geertz, this is the basic concept of the *Priyayi* (gentry) world view (1964:232), but I personally think that this is not the monopoly of the *Priyayi* alone but also the peasants' (*wong cilik*) and the nobles' (*ndara*), because in a stratified society everybody's ideal must be identified with the highest stratum.

REFERENCES CITED

Aarne, Antti, and Stith Thompson. *The Types of the Folktale, a Classification and Bibliography.* 2nd revision. Helsinki: Academia Scientiarum Fennica, 1964.
Bascom, William R. "Four Functions of Folklore." In Alan Dundes (ed.), *The Study of Folklore.* Englewood Cliffs, N.J.: Prentice Hall, pp. 279–298. 1965a. "The

Forms of Folklore: Prose Narrative." In *Journal of American Folklore*, Vol. 78, pp. 3-20, 1965b.

Dundes, Alan (ed.). *The Study of Folklore*. Englewood Cliffs, N.J.: Prentice-Hall, 1965.

Geertz, Clifford. *The Religion of Java*. London: The Free Press of Glencoe Collier-Macmillan, 1964.

Koentjaraningrat, R.M. "The Javanese of South Central Java." In G.P. Murdock (ed.), *Social Structure in Southeast Asia*. Viking Fund Publication in Anthropology, No. 29, Chicago: Quadrangle Books, pp. 88-115, 1960.

Rooth, Anna Birgitta. *The Cinderella Cycle*. Lund: C.W.K. Gleerup, 1951.

Thompson, Stith. *Motif Index of Folk Literature*. Revised and enlarged edition, 6 vols. Bloomington and London: Indiana University Press, 1966.

A Cinderella Variant in the Context of a Muslim Women's Ritual

Margaret A. Mills

One of the older approaches to folklore much in vogue in the late nineteenth and early twentieth centuries was the ritual theory. In "Myth-Ritual" theory, for example, it was believed that myth derived from a ritual origin. And ritual origins were postulated for all the folklore genres: games, children's rhymes, etc. Most of these conjectural arguments were unconvincing because there was rarely any hard data showing the item of folklore actually being used in a ritual context. Invariably, the reader was simply asked to take on faith an author's assertion that a particular myth or game was a vestigial remain of an earlier ritual that had died out or disappeared.

A serious theoretical difficulty with most ritual explanations is that usually no real attempt is made to say where the originating ritual came from. If myth comes from ritual, where does ritual come from? In terms of the endless and mostly futile search for origins, ritual theories offer at best only an intermediate and not an ultimate explanation for an item of folklore's existence. Ritual theories, incidentally, are an obvious instance of the nineteenth century's preoccupation with the historical reconstruction of the past.

In the case of Cinderella, P. Saintyves argues that the story reflected a calendrical ritual, specifically a ritual of renewal intended to encourage the end of winter and to ensure the beginning of spring. Saintyves associates Cinderella with the festival of "Carnaval," mentioning a custom whereby a girl who wishes to divine whom she is destined to marry throws ashes on her clothes. Then she goes to bed, and if she goes to sleep without pronouncing a single word, she will see her future husband in her dream. The association of cinders and marriage explains Cinderella's name, Saintyves insists. The brilliant dresses of Cinderella are calls for light and the sun (to come and begin the new season of spring). The tale of Cinderella thus represents the ritual marriage of the new year with the new sun, the onset of spring after winter. This is one example of a ritual theory of Cinderella.

Even those who are totally sceptical of ritual theories of folklore cannot deny that rituals do exist in the contemporary world and that folklore often plays an important part in such rituals. In the following essay by a young Harvard-trained folklorist who carried out extensive fieldwork in folk narrative in Afghanistan, we find a remarkable account of the Cinderella story as it occupies a central position in a ritual meal. Although Margaret Mills draws heavily on a colleague's fieldnotes, it is her insightful analysis of the ritual and tale that provides a unique view of the way folktales encode the cultural norms concerned with sex roles. We can also see how Cinderella offers a socially sanctioned escape from these same norms. The ritual and the tale in this extraordinary setting provide a fantastic but nonetheless important outlet for the expression of female role anxieties in a society that is famous, or infamous, for its male chauvinism.

The tale is actually a combination of Aarne-Thompson tale type 480, "The Kind and the Unkind Girls," and tale type 510A "Cinderella." This combination is common enough, and the specific set of traits indicates that this version generally conforms to what Warren Roberts has labeled the "Near Eastern Form of the Following the River Subtype" of tale type 480. For further discussion as well as references to numerous analogues to this tale, see Warren E. Roberts, The Tale of the Kind and the Unkind Girls *(Berlin: Walter de Gruyter, 1958), pp. 106–107.*

The tale text presented here is widely known and performed in eastern Iran and western Afghanistan. It combines AT types 510A ("Cinderella") and 480 ("The Kind and the Unkind Girls"). It is examined here for the role it plays in an all-female Ismaili Muslim ceremony, the *Āsh-e Bībī Murād*, in which a food offering and

ritual meal (an *āsh*, or soup, among other items) are prepared by
women as a petition to Bībī Fātimeh (called Bībī Murād, "The
Lady of Wishes"), The Prophet's daughter and 'Alī's wife, who is
the most honored woman of the Prophet's lineage. The woman who
sponsors the ceremony is supported by other women in her petition
for the granting of a wish, and other women may offer their own
petitions along with hers. The narration of the story is the center of
the ritual meal. Unfortunately, I have not attended such a performance. The Ismaili community from which it is reported is a
village south of Mashhad, in eastern Iran. My data were supplied by
Rafique Keshavjee, an anthropologist and himself an Ismaili, who
was conducting research on village organization in the area. Being
male, he was not able to attend the ritual; the description was given
him by an older woman, a principal informant of his who had both
organized and attended such ceremonies. What is given here is
therefore a normative description of the ritual by an insider, not a
description of an actual performance event.

Not being primarily interested in narrative, Dr. Keshavjee was
unaware of this Cinderella variant's wider circulation in the area.
The version he recorded is substantially identical to those I recorded
over one hundred miles east, in the Herat region of western Afghanistan, except that the versions I heard lacked overt phallic imagery
(one version substituting scatology in the punishment of the unkind
sister) and were not, to my knowledge, part of any ritual activity.
None of my informants were Ismailis, so I had no opportunity to
study their popular religious practice in Herat. Nonetheless, the use
of this tale, and particularly the male symbols used in it, in the
context of an all-female ritual point to symbolic dimensions present
if unrealized in the story in its non-ritual circulation. There is some
evidence that the tale told in non-ritual circumstances also belongs
primarily to women. In my own collecting experience, spontaneous
performances of the tale were usually by women and girls, occa-
sionally by adolescent boys. Adult males did not perform the tale
spontaneously. One key adult male informant in particular, an
accomplished storyteller with a huge repertoire of both folktales and
romances, professed not to know the story and refused to perform it
despite repeated requests from me. His claim not to know it is
extremely suspect given its wide currency among women and less
adept, younger male storytellers.

In this particular performance context, admittedly an unusual one, the tale clearly supplies a polar term in the continuum of male and female dimensions of narrative tradition. As part of a ritual organized exclusively by and for women, in which a major theme is female solidarity, it expresses a horror of sexual crossover, perceived as branding.[1] A synopsis of Dr. Keshavjee's field notes on the *Āsh-e Bībī Murād* is provided for readers who would like to pursue detailed or alternative analyses.

Field Notes on the
Āsh-e Bībī Murād,
"Soup for the Lady of Wishes,"
courtesy of Rafique Keshavjee,
Dīzbād, Khorāssān, Iran,
November 10, 1978

The *Āsh* is a food offering and ritual meal conducted entirely by women, in honor of Bībī Fātimeh ("Bībī Murād," the "Lady of Wishes"), the daughter of Mohammed and wife of 'Ali, in supplication for the fulfillment of a wish or wishes. The meal must be made by women members of the *Jamā'at*, the Ismaili Muslim congregation, in the *Jamā'at Xāneh*, the congregational house or mosque, to which a small kitchen is attached. The ingredients for the meal must be begged from three to seven households (an odd number is necessary) which have women in them named Fātimeh, Zahrā, Sekīneh, or Zeināb (the names of the Prophet's daughter and other revered female members of the Prophet's lineage). The ingredients must be begged by a female, "for the sake of Bībī Fātimeh," but the begging itself is silent and conducted after nightfall, the women begging in pairs from houses in their immediate neighborhood, concealing their identities completely by covering their heads with their black *chādors*. The informant told Dr. Keshavjee that Hādī, a fourteen-year-old boy in her household, was so frightened by finding two silent, black shadows at the door that he fainted. Normally, those waiting at the door greet the answerer by saying, "Salām."

or, if they are ordinary beggars, with an appeal to 'Ali or to God. Visiting after dark is unusual in villages, where the narrow streets are pitch-dark and some householders keep mastiffs which are chained by day but let off their chains at night to patrol the compound.

The ingredients which may be given include such things as flour, greens, dried beans, sugar, carrots, meat, oil, chick peas, water, lentils, or *qormeh* (any of a variety of stews of meat and/ or vegetables). The begging must take place after the sunset prayer. A man may give the ingredients, which are placed in a *chādor* the beggars spread on the ground. Women beg in pairs for safety. Whatever is not obtained from begging is supplied by the *sāheb-e nazr*, the "master of the vow," who is the sponsor of the ceremony. While others are begging from surrounding households, the woman who is the *sāheb-e nazr* places bowls of flour in three to seven places in her own house (again, it must be an odd number) for a period of five to ten minutes. Then she "begs" from her own house—with the invocation, "Yā 'Alī— gathering up the bowls of flour she has set out.

All the assembled foodstuffs are taken to the mosque at about 9:00 P.M. A *sofreh* ("table" cloth, off which one eats off the floor) is spread in the middle of the mosque, on which are placed the flour, a *Qor'ān*, a woman's *kohl* (eyeshadow) container, salt in a saucer, powdered lump sugar, a mirror, a set of prayer beads, and a photograph of the Agha Khan, the spiritual leader of the Ismaili community.

All those women who have a petition (not only the sponsor) sit in a circle around this sofreh and recite the Ismaili *do'ā*, the congregational prayer, five to fifteen times. No males can be present. They then leave the materials assembled for the *āsh* in the mosque overnight.

At 8:00 or 8:30 the following morning, the women return to the mosque. If the petition has been accepted, traces of the prayer beads are seen in the flour, and finger-marks in the salt and sugar, and marks of fingers on the *sofreh* itself. If no marks can be seen, the *nīat*, or wish, which is kept secret by the one making it, is no good. The informant told Dr. Keshavjee that "those whose faith is pure" are able to see these traces.

The flour which has been on the *sofreh* (not the entire supply of flour) is now *tabarokī*, "blessed," and it is made into a special bread called *komāj*, which cannot be eaten by men. Other flour is used to make noodles for the *āsh*, which is cooked that morning. It is eaten at noon by ten to fifty women. Little boys can attend, but should not, and can eat the *āsh* and regular bread, but not *komāj*. Adult males can eat neither *āsh* nor *komāj*. The *āsh* must be eaten in the mosque, each woman supplying her own bowl or using bowls from the mosque kitchen.

Before the *āsh* is eaten, a second *sofreh* is spread, with a lamp on it, and everything from the *sofreh* of the night before is moved to the second *sofreh*. Women who have petitions bring sweets, dried fruits, and nuts, which they put on the second *sofreh*. A widow and a motherless virgin sit beside each other at this second *sofreh*. The widow has a bowl full of *āsh*, and the girl has an empty bowl. The widow, as she spoons *āsh* into the girl's bowl, recites the story of Māh Pīshānī ("Moon-Brow"; see below). Every time the girl receives a spoonful of *āsh*, she must answer, "Yes."

The Story

A merchant enrolled his daughter in the *madraseh* (religious school). The teacher, a female *axund* or teaching *mulla*, was a widow, and she asked the girl about her family's financial position, which the girl reported was good. She asked the girl what they had in their house, and the girl replied, "Vinegar." The teacher convinced the girl that she, the teacher, was good and her mother was bad, and she told the girl to tell her mother that she wanted some vinegar, and when she went to get it, to push her in and cover the storage jar. She told her not to tell her father, just to say she fell in.

The mother was dead when the father found her. [Here the informant mentioned spooning *āsh* and the girl answering, "Yes."] Later on, the father found a yellow cow in his stable, "In the place of the murdered mother." The teacher and the father became engaged; then he had both a wife and the cow, and he sent the daughter out to pasture the cow. The new wife gave birth to a daughter, and she began to mistreat the first daughter, giving her one rotten piece of bread to eat when she took the cow out for the day, and sending her with raw cotton to clean and spin while the cow fed, but no tools to work the cotton. Out in the fields, the girl began to cry because she could not spin, and all she could do was hook the cotton fibers on a thorn and back away from them, twisting them with her fingers.

The cow spoke and asked her why she was crying. She complained about the task, and said, "If I don't do it, my stepmother won't let me back in the house." The cow asked to see her bread. [The informant added that the listening girl continues to say "Yes" at intervals.] The girl gave the bread to the cow, and then the cotton to eat, and the cow shat cotton thread until evening. The girl collected all the thread and took it back to her stepmother.

For three days in a row, the stepmother gave the girl bad bread to eat and more cotton to spin. [Listener: "Yes."] On the third day, when the girl gave the cow the cotton, the wind blew a piece away, and it dropped down a well. The girl was about to go down the well after it, and the cow told her, "When you go into the well, you'll see an old woman *bārzangī*.[2] When you see her, say '*Salām!*' and ask for the cotton. The old woman will say, 'Delouse my hair.' You should say, 'Your hair is perfectly all right—it's cleaner than mine.'"

The girl follows directions. When the old woman asks her to delouse her hair, she begins to do it, and the old woman asks, "What does my hair have?" The girl answers, "Nothing, your hair is cleaner than my mother's. Your hair is like a rose, my mother's head is full of dirt." The old woman tells her to take her cotton from a certain room. The daughter goes in and sees that the room is full of jewels, but she takes only her cotton, sweeps the room, and leaves, saying goodbye to the *bārzangī*. She starts to climb the ladder out of the well, but when she is halfway up, the *bārzangī* shakes the ladder to see whether she has stolen anything and hidden it in her clothes. When no jewels fall from her clothes, the old woman prays for her to have a moon in the center of her brow. When she reaches the top of the ladder, the *bārzangī* shakes it again and blesses her again, "May you have a star on your chin!"

The girl returns to the cow, who tells her to cover her forehead and chin so that her stepmother won't see them. She returns home with the cow. That night, while she sleeps, her veil slips and the stepmother sees the moon and star. The next day, she sends her own daughter with the cow instead, giving her raw cotton to work and sweet nut bread to eat. The girl can't spin, but she guesses that the cow did the spinning for her sister, so she gives the sweet bread to the cow, and the cotton, but the cow produces only a little thread.

On the third day, her cotton, too, is blown into the well, and she follows it and sees the old woman. She asks for the cotton without saying "*Salām*," and the old woman asks her to delouse her hair. When the old woman asks about her hair, the girl replies, "Your hair is filthy, my mother's is clean." The old woman tells her to go into the room, sweep it and take her cotton. She takes some jewels, which fall from her clothes when the old woman shakes the ladder. The old woman says, "May a donkey's penis appear from your forehead!"[3] At the top of the ladder the old woman shakes it again, and more jewels fall, and she adds a curse, "And a snake from your chin!"

The girl goes back to the cow, who sees the penis and the snake, but says nothing. She takes the cow home, and her mother cuts off the penis and snake with a knife and covers the wounds with salt, but both objects reappear overnight. The stepmother realizes the cow is behind this and feigns sickness, bribing the doctors to tell her husband that she must eat the meat of the yellow cow and have its skin thrown over her, in order to recover. Meanwhile, the first daughter has realized that the yellow cow is her mother, and she feeds her candied chickpeas and bread. One day the cow cries, and tells her: "They'll kill me today, and if they kill me, your life will become very hard. When they kill me, don't eat the meat. Collect all the bones in a bag, bury them, and hide them." The daughter cries and goes to plead with her father, saying that all their wealth means nothing to her compared with the yellow cow. The father says the cow must be killed, because it is the only medicine for her stepmother.

The girl follows the cow's instructions, gathering up the bones after she is killed. The stepmother "gets well," and a few days later the family is invited to a wedding in another city. The stepmother and her daughter decide to go, so the mother cuts off the penis and snake and applies salt to the wounds, then mixes millet and *toğū* (another tiny seed), places her stepdaughter in front of the empty pool in the garden, and tells her to separate the seeds and to fill the pool with her tears. The two then leave for the wedding. The girl is sitting and crying when she sees a hen with a lot of chickens come into the garden. The hen speaks, telling the girl to put salt and water in the pool, take the horse and good clothes she will find in the stable, and go to the

wedding, while the chicks separate the seeds. The hen adds,
"When you come back, one of your shoes will fall into the water;
don't stop to get it—go quickly so that your stepmother won't
know you."

The girl finds a magically provided horse, fine clothes, and
gold shoes in the stable, and she rides off to the wedding, with
her forehead and chin covered. They place her at the head of the
guests in the women's party when the dancing starts. She dances,
and the stepsister recognizes her and says to her mother, "This is
our Māhpīshānī [Moon-Brow]." The stepmother says, "Impossible!" but they leave to go and see whether she is at home, to see
whether the guest was really she. Māhpīshānī rushes ahead on
the horse to get home before them, but she drops a shoe into
some water. When she gets home, she realizes that the hen had
changed into the horse. She puts on her old clothes and sits
down to separate the few remaining seeds. The stepmother and
stepsister see the seeds and the pool full of "tears," and the
stepmother says, "I told you so!"

Two days later, a prince is riding by the waterside, and his
horse refuses to drink. He looks down, finds the shoe, and takes
it to his father, saying that he wants to wed the owner of the
shoe. The king and his viziers try the shoe on everyone, and
all wish that it would fit, but it does not. Finally they come to
Māhpīshānī's father's house. The stepmother "cleans and cuts"
her daughter's head, but the shoe does not fit. The vizier is
about to leave. The first daughter is locked in the bread oven.
A cock flies up on top of the oven,[4] and begins to crow:

A moon in the oven!	*Māhi dar tannūr,*
A head is in there,	*Sar ar unjeh, qū, qū!*
kū-kū!	
Where is the foot, like	*Pā kū čī bolūr*
glass?[5]	
A head is in there,	*Sar ar unjeh, qū, qū!*
kū-kū!"	

The stepmother and her daughter try to catch the cock,
who escapes them and crows twice more. The vizier gets an-
noyed and insists on looking in the oven, where he finds the
girl. The shoe fits, and she marries the prince.

At the end of the story, the *āsh* which has been cooked is
divided among the women present. No men may eat it, though

the informant added, "They can have other *āsh*, later." Everyone present eats some *āsh*, and the sugar, apricots, and other
sweets are given as alms, which completes the ceremony.

In the performance of *Māh Pīshānī* translated here, we have a
story of, by, and for women. The story, designated variously as
"Moon-Brow" (*Māh Pīshānī*) or "The Yellow Cow" (*Gau-e Zard*),
was performed for me by both male and female narrators, but more
often by females. The forms involving sexual marking of the evil
half-sister or her scatological humiliation were performed by women.
In this form of AT 510A/480, as in most, the dominant relations are
between women: loyalty and disloyalty between mother and daughter; rivalry between the stepmother and her offspring and the first-
born daughter. The telling of the tale in ritual context by a widow to
an orphan girl further emphasizes the themes of female abandon-
ment and solidarity which dominate the tale itself. That the girl first
betrays her own mother is an important element in the equation of
solidarity and redemption, as is the choice of this story as part of a
solidarity ritual for women, in which women join together to call on
a spiritual "mother," deceased but present, in support of the desires
of one or more of their number. The subject of the ritual sponsor's
petition, though it may be known by the participants (and quite
likely is guessed, given the importance of gossip in village life), is
unspoken. Other women support her in her petition, in at least
fictive ignorance of what it is, yet another statement of generalized
female solidarity. (The objects and foodstuffs placed on the ritual
sofreh, the cloth upon which meals are laid, are some of the same
items used in marriage ritual. This connection would bear detailed
analysis, for which I lack the necessary detailed knowledge of Ismaili
popular wedding ceremonies.)

The marking of the wicked daughter with a donkey's penis and a
snake, in contrastive relation to the good daughter's marking with
signs of radiant female beauty, the moon and star, constitutes a
strong rejection of male symbols, here equated with grotesque ugliness. This instance of transsexual marking must be understood in
the context of a broader tendency by female folktale tellers not to
develop themes of transsexual role manipulation. Male narrators
more frequently cast characters in roles which entail their acting like
or appearing to be members of the opposite sex.[6] So far, I have been

able to find *no* instances of sex change *per se* in tales told by women. Among male narrators, outright sex changes, which are rare, are portrayed as disastrous for men but fortunate for women. In two tales told by young men (aged 16 and 18), female main characters permanently acquire male characteristics (physical in one case, social in the other) which are construed as fortunate. In the example told by an eighteen-year-old male high school student, the heroine performs various marital exploits in male disguise, in the process winning a royal bride. The heroine has fled her family because of ill treatment and has no spouse or other male ally to whom to turn over the bride (as often happens when women in male disguises win brides). Ultimately, the problem is solved when the heroine is "cursed" by a dragon with a sex change.

In the second instance, told by an illiterate sixteen-year-old tenant farmer, the wise daughter of a vizier is married to a prince who abuses her because she surpassed him in school. She manages to get him interested in a quest for the Princess of China, in order to get rid of him, but ultimately she has to go and rescue him, in the process winning the Princess of China and three other brides. She turns them over to her husband and announces that henceforth she herself will be his vizier, as her father was his father's, rather than his wife.

In these two male-narrated texts, sex change (or permanent sex-role reversal) is part of the heroine's reward. In the absence of any such formulation by women narrators,[7] the marking of the stepdaughter with grotesque male genitalia and an equally phallic snake on her *face* adds a dimension to the contrastive symbolic set of male:female::public:private. When she is marked for scorn by the community of women celebrating this ritual, the unkind sister is marked with emphatically male characteristics in a manner which cannot be hidden, even by that institution of female privacy and respectability, the veil. She is marked with sexual stigmata as a direct result of her and her mother's attempted exploitation of other females, human and supernatural, and as an indirect result of her mother's antisocial competition for a male. The girl's only recourse is to trade the penis and snake temporarily for raw wounds, rubbed with salt (cf. the multiple, public wounding of the evil stepsisters in Grimm's "Aschenputtel" and other variants). In this tale about women told exclusively for women, acquisition of male characteristics by a female is a grotesque punishment for disloyalty to women. The disfigurement is such that the normal female recourse of veiling is not effective to conceal it: the girl is forced both into maleness and into public.

On the whole, *Māh Pīshānī* ignores male characters as such: the father and the prince are almost completely passive prizes of the women's struggle, male brides. In a performance context from which males are excluded, the humiliation of an evil female is accomplished by the invocation of male symbols. This quintessentially female narration of the Cinderella tale reveals that these women see marking (being made conspicuous) as both disastrous and masculine. Combined with the comparative lack of sex-role crossover in women's stories, this suggests that penis envy has a much higher profile in men's stories than in women's stories, and that women do not greatly covet male characteristics or male social roles, though men see them as doing so. In tales my Afghan women informants told for entertainment, one can discern a certain conservatism reflected in their choices of stories and dramatic roles for women characters. In a ritual context which emphasizes the instrumental power of women directing their will for a common cause, masculinization separates a woman from her female companions and disables her.

Memorates about veiling and women's resistance to its abolition, which my Afghan women friends shared with me, seem to me to be rooted in the same complex of attitudes. Many conservative women do not look with favor on "going public" by adopting male social behavior, because in doing so they forfeit the power of anonymity, a power which they have learned to exploit to give themselves mobility and certain mechanisms to manipulate the public, masculine sphere as well. It may be that these women's less intense interest in disguise themes as a whole, also detectable in their storytelling, is due to the fact that under current conditions they have considerable real-world capacity to conceal identity and thereby manipulate people and situations, whereas men, compelled to regard only the public sphere of male-male relations as "significant," and yet (like women) having little privacy in the small world of domestic gossip, fantasize substantially more about the manipulation and concealment of sexual and other identity. The informant who described the Ismaili rite for Dr. Keshavjee, in her humorous aside about the young boy who was frightened by the silent, veiled women, emphasized the power of the veil for manipulative purposes. The boy's fear was fear of the unknown. The food the women beg acquires its special spiritual status (*barakat*) in part from the way in which it is begged, in which women exploit to the fullest the veil's power to conceal identity.

A fuller consideration of themes of disguise in general, both in Afghan and Persian tradition and cross-culturally, including comparison to taletelling communities in which women do not have real options for concealing identity, is needed to test whether the differential use of disguise and sex-role manipulation themes between male and female narrators can be correlated with other particular asymmetries in the social system, or whether it is a more general feature of male and female storytelling.[8]

NOTES

[1]For a fuller discussion of themes of transsexual behavior in Afghan-Persian oral narrative, see M. Mills, "Sex Role Reversals, Sex Changes and Transvestite Disguise in the Oral Tradition of a Conservative Muslim Community," forthcoming in S. Kalcik and R. Jordan, *Women's Folklore, Women's Culture.* The present essay is an excerpt from that paper.

[2]A monstrous, usually malevolent, supernatural, according to one of my informants, "like a *dīv*, only bigger and worse." The name is derived from *Zangbār*, "Zanzibar," and some but not all informants associate *bārzangīs* with Blacks, whom they for the most part have never seen. Color prejudice is widespread in rural Iran and Afghanistan

[3]Dr. Keshavjee said that the informant first said, "A piece of meat," then laughed and corrected herself.

[4]A beehive-shaped clay structure, about waist-high.

[5]These two translations are a bit speculative. *Bolūr* is old-fashioned blown glass, very thin and delicate.

[6]See Mills, "Sex Role Reversals," *op. cit.*, for a fuller development of this issue.

[7]So far, in a sample of about 170 narrative performances collected over two years, against a sample of about 250 male-narrated tales collected concurrently. I do not mean to argue *ex silentio* that women never tell such stories, only that they seem to be quite rare, while they do appear in the men's corpus.

[8]The field work on which this analysis is partly based was supported by a Fulbright-Hays Dissertation Grant and by supplementary grants from the National Science Foundation and Harvard University's Sheldon Fund, whose help is gratefully acknowledged.

The Slipper on the Stair

Aarland Ussher

The vast majority of those who have commented on Cinderella have not been fieldworkers analyzing versions of the story they themselves have collected from informants. Most are armchair critics who from one perspective or another offer a reading of Cinderella—usually based on the Perrault or the Grimm version. These armchair interpretations tend to be somewhat doctrinaire insofar as anthroposophical, Jungian, or Freudian tenets are shown to be illustrated by details in Cinderella. By and large, if the readers share the bias of the critic, they will agree with the interpretation; if they do not have the same bias, they may summarily dismiss the interpretation as being totally arbitrary and wildly speculative.

An example of what might be termed a spiritual approach to Cinderella is provided by Irish philosopher Aarland Ussher's short essay, which appeared in World Review *in 1951 and was later incorporated into a whole book of similar readings of well-known fairy tales,* Enter These Enchanted Woods *(Dublin, 1957). In this essay, Cinderella is perceived as an allegory—with definite Christian overtones—for the life of the "Soul."*

Lest the reader think that reading fairy tales as Christian allegories is altogether a rarity, we might at least mention the many such interpretations offered by followers of Rudolf Steiner (1861–1925), the founder of a so-called spiritual science known as anthroposophy. In 1908 Steiner gave a lecture in Berlin entitled "The

Reprinted from *World Review*, 25 (March, 1951), 50–52.

Interpretation of Fairy Tales" in which he argued that tales and myths derived from an ancient time when "those who had not yet attained to intellectual powers possessed a partially developed clairvoyance which was the remains of a primeval clairvoyance." In such early times, man was supposedly in tune with nature and in close touch with the spiritual world. According to Steiner, fairy tales contain a "picture-language" which can reveal the spiritual "wisdom" of the past. Steiner's theories were expounded in a number of his books, e.g., Ancient Myths: Their Meaning and Connection with Evolution *(1918), and* The Mission of Folk-Souls (in Connection with Germanic Scandinavian Mythology) *(1929). The latter book's title page bears the following disclaimer notice: "Printed for Members of the School of Spiritual Science. . . . No person is held qualified to form a judgment on the contents of this work who has not acquired—through the School itself or in an equivalent manner recognised by the School—the requisite knowledge. Other opinions will be disregarded; the authors decline to take them as a basis for discussion."*

A sample of the many Steiner-inspired books on folktales, usually with the telltale word wisdom *in their titles, includes: Marie Brie,* Das Märchen im Lichte der Geisteswissenschaft *(Breslau: Verlag von Preuss and Jünger, 1922); Rudolf Meyer,* Die Weisheit der Schweizer Märchen *(Schaffhausen: Columban-Verlan, 1944); F. Eymann,* Die Weisheit der Märchen im Spiegel der Geisteswissenschaft Rudolf Steiners *(Bern: Troxler-Verlag, 1952); and Ursula Grahl,* The Wisdom in Fairy Tales *(East Grinstead: New Knowledge Books, 1955).*

In the present context, we might single out Cinderella: Meaning and Exact Rendering of Grimm's Fairy Tale, *a thirty-three-page pamphlet written by Norbert Glas (Gloucester: Education and Science Publications, [1946]). Glas begins by noting that "the composition of Grimm's version is the most perfect ever written. They have not only preserved the deep meaning and spiritual idea of Cinderella, but they have given it living breath for all times." In his commentary on the king's proclamation of a feast to which fair maidens were invited so that the prince might choose a bride, Glas states that it is clear "how the story puts before us, in picture form, a true development of the human soul. The growing child feels desires unfolding within her; she becomes more mature. The true individu-*

ality, the original ego of the human being, which has descended from the divine world, seeks to unite with the purified soul. . . . The prince looks for the pure soul which shall unite with him." The dove in the Grimm version is interpreted as a manifestation of the Holy Spirit, with reminders that the Dove also descended upon Jesus and was sent from the Ark by Noah. At the end of the Grimm version, the doves pecked out the evil stepsisters' eyes. According to Glas: "This is no ordinary punishment devised by men. No, it is a form of atonement ordained for them out of a realm of higher wisdom. The doves, the messengers of the Spirit, rob the sisters of their eyes, and we are led to hope, now that the outer world is taken from them in their blindness, that they will have time to seek in inner perception the way of purification which Cinderella has found before them."

For Steiner's original lecture, see The Interpretation of Fairy Tales *(New York: Anthroposophic Press, 1929). For a critique of symbolic readings of Cinderella, including several of the anthroposophical variety, see German folklorist Hermann Bausinger's "Aschenputtel: Zum Problem der Märchensymbolik,"* Zeitschrift für Volkskunde, *52 (1955), 144–158.*

The story of Cinderella, known to English children in the rather different version of Perrault's seventeenth-century *Contes de Fées*, is a very sensitive allegory for the Soul's discovery of its Image— that Image which lives hidden, like an invisible spark among the ashes, in the humdrum hours and tasks. We find again the familiar pattern of a rich man who had two wives: one in the past—whose grave is piously decked in winter by the snowfall—and another, a malignant one, in the present. Cinderella is a seed of the intuitive consciousness which, like a Creator in myth, has returned to its heaven; and her growth and dignity are crushed by the 'tares' scattered in the field by that Enemy, the mental consciousness. The *two* step-sisters represent the split and fragmented 'abstractions' of the logical faculty, which usurp the childhood-kingdom of the imagination's singleness; they are not even her half-sisters, for they are wholly bad—the second wife has imported them like bloodless concepts, ready-made, into the house of the mind. Cinderella's father, journeying one day to the market—that universal hive or passional heart, where the values of things are made and dealt out— demands of the maidens what presents he shall bring them; the step- sisters ask for the gold and jewels and other vanities of social acclaim, but Cinderella asks for the first hazel-twig that shall knock against his hat on the home journey. The Tree of Life, one feels, knocks with a perpetual reminder against our closed consciousness on its self-satisfied rounds; and the hazel-wand is the traditional symbol of rebirth, the badge of the magician's craft. The father brings the presents as he is requested, and Cinderella plants the twig on the grave of the mother, where it grows into a noble tree; and, as Cinderella waters the growing tree with her tears, a white bird descends on the tree and throws down, as from a Christian tree, whatever may be the wish of her heart. Connection, we feel, has been re-established between earth and the abyss of air, through the consecrating waters of suffering; and the hard flame of conventional values—typified by the gold and jewels which the father brought from the earth's centre, the market—has turned to the living flame of the heart's wishes, which the mother rains down from the periphery of heaven.

But now the king of the country holds a feast, that his son may choose himself a bride from among all the fair maidens of his kingdom. The step-sisters prepare themselves joyfully to attend it, and Cinderella dearly wishes she might go also; the stepmother, however, gives her permission only if the poor girl shall pick a dish of lentils out of the ashes—where they have been derisively thrown —within two hours. The task is an image of Cinderella's destiny, for she is herself a seed of imaginative life amid the cold ash of dead and self-glorifying mental concepts. The step-mother had reckoned she could not do it within the time, but Cinderella goes, significantly, to the *back-door* and calls all the birds of the air to her aid; for, as in the stories of Wise Simpletons, intuition can cross the breach which our mind-language has set between the human and the animal— and, in the labour of selection, we must call upon the primitive instinctive faculties of all life. The stepmother, baffled by Cinderella's success, ordains a new task—she shall pick out *two* dishes of lentils in *one* hour; but Cinderella again triumphs by the aid of the birds. It was in vain for the cruel stepmother to prescribe any length of time, for the inspiration of Choice is a flash—an Annunciation from another dimension—a fertilisation of Time by the Eternal, as in the ornithological allegories of the conceptions of Leda and Mary. But once more the stepmother revokes her promise, and she departs to the ball with her two daughters; and now Cinderella in despair goes to the hazel tree, and begs that she may be thrown down the silk clothes and embroidered shoes that she needs. The inspiration of the heaven-dwellers is insufficient; it must be joined to the weight and materiality of earth before it has a personality to bring to the dance; Cinderella, like the doubting and despairing disciples, must feel the *physicality* of the over-earthly before she can go forth on her heavenly, conquering path. She puts on the festal clothes and makes her way to the ball, where the stepmother and sisters do not recognise her, for—like the disciples at Emmaus—'their eyes are held', and they lack the 'ghostly' power of divination which can penetrate all disguises. The prince dances with her and is reluctant to let go of her hand; he says to all rival gallants 'This is *my* partner.' It is a vivid touch—'he did not want to let go of her hand'—suggesting the painful transitoriness of the moment of vision; we hold the idea, and know it for our very own, but, even as we hold it, we feel it being wrenched from us by the impersonal logic-chains of the dance. Her noble partner wishes to escort her home, to learn, as other young sparks on like occasions have wished to learn, to whom the beautiful *inconnue* belongs; but she slips from him at her door, and takes refuge (hard though the feat may seem to the imagination) in the dove-cot. The father opens the door to the prince, who demands that he brings axes and hammers and break open her odd place of refuge; but Cinderella in the meantime has jumped out on the other side, surrendered her finery to the befriending bird under the hazel tree, and resumed her place among the ashes. They find no one but a leather-aproned kitchen-wench, sleeping by the glimmer of the oil lamp in the chimney corner, as it were the trimmed lamp of one of the discreet virgins in the parable. Is it not thus that we pursue the fleeting inspiration—with the hammer of our will and the cutting tools of reason—into the recesses of the brain, only to find it has lost the gay hues which charmed us, and has retreated into the Subconscious? On the next day, the same history recurs. Cinderella goes to the tree, and repeats her rhyme—

Shiver and quiver little tree,
Rain down silver and gold over me.

Again, as it were, the Veil of consciousness trembles, and again the friendly bird brings its gifts, the dress and shoes bedecked with silver and gold—silver of reflection and gold of proud instinctive life. Again she appears in the ball and dances all night long with the princely wooer; again he attempts to accompany her to her door and she escapes him—this time into the branches of a pear tree. Axes and hatchets are brought; but she has slipped over the garden wall, dropped the bright raiment, and taken her customary place among the cinders. After the dead wood of the dove-cot—which a German proverb compares to the human head, where thoughts bird-footed come and go—we reach the live wood of the pear tree—the human thicket of the body; the prince is nearing the total and vital apprehension.

On the third day—always that *third* day of resurrections—she is again miraculously at the ball, and now the slippers are of pure gold; but this time the prince has been wary, and has ordered the staircase to be smeared with pitch. An inverted Peter, he has affirmed his faith three times, and the staircase—always suggestive, in fairy tales, of the ladder of logic—has become a sympathetic retentive medium. Again Cinderella escapes him, but on this occasion one of her slippers remains sticking in the pitch. One is tempted to see here a suggestion of that dense dark stuff of our subconsciousness which clogs the bright feet of the passions; it is the element in which Cinderella has lived, the element of the toiling earth, but to draw her out of it the prince must introduce some earthliness into the palace of his own thought—reason must set imaginative traps for the image, as the logic of Greece trapped and held the *Event* of Judea. On the next day the prince takes the slipper to the father—like every Crusoe who has discovered a footprint-on-the-shore, questioning high heaven—and claims for his bride that girl whose foot shall be the perfect fit. The step-sisters try it on, each in turn, but the one must cut off her toe, the other slice her heel; and the prince riding off—first with one, then with the second—is warned by Cinderella's friends, the pigeons, that the shoe is a misfit, that there is blood on the foot, that the true bride sits at home. Those empty and conventional images, like the clichés of our popular press, are not *his* image, and cannot take the shape of his golden new idea; but this is only discovered when he tries to 'ride' with them—the poem must be read, the music played, and some little bird (as we say of a flying hint) will tell you if all is not well. Finally he demands, in impatience, if there be not a third daughter, and the stepmother—though protestingly—produces the poor kitchen-wench; recognition follows and, speedily, the wedding. With the usual ruthlessness of the Tales, the step-sisters—attending the ceremony in ambitious hopes—have their eyes picked out by the pigeons; imagination, we are reminded, is nothing but the deeper apprehension of reality—the conventional valuations are blinded because they were already blind.

Cinderella, the sought-for image, is always there, anonymous, wherever man calls his thoughts like partners to the dance; she is found, and again lost amid her rival's blaze and din. But when despair or sleep has sent the baggages where they came from, he will find, in dreams, *one* slipper on the stair.

The Beautiful Wassilissa

Marie-Louise von Franz

The anthroposophical approach to folktales is not well known to folklorists and has had a minimal impact upon folkloristics. Better known is the Jungian way of analyzing folktales and myths, although the overall influence of this approach in folklore is also slight. Since folklorists tend to be literal-historical in outlook, they are rarely willing to take seriously attempts to interpret fairy tales from a symbolic-psychological perspective, no matter what the brand of psychology might be.

C.G. Jung (1885-1961) was very much interested in myth and fairy tale, for reasons somewhat similar to Rudolf Steiner. He too felt that they contained archetypal truth from the distant past. Jung wrote an essay entitled "The Phenomenology of the Spirit in Fairy Tales" and collaborated with C. Kerenyi in Essays on a Science of Mythology *(1941). In one of those essays, "The Psychology of the Child Archetype," Jung distinguished between two types of fantasies. Personal fantasies refer to events experienced by an individual in his or her life, but fantasies of an impersonal character cannot be reduced to experiences in an individual's life. They are not acquired but rather are said by Jung to be innate in the human psyche. "These fantasy-images undoubtedly have their closest analogues in mytho-*

Reprinted from *Problems of the Feminine in Fairytales* (New York: Spring Publications, 1972), pp. 143–157.

*logical types. We must therefore assume that they correspond to
certain collective (and not personal) structural elements of the human
psyche in general, and, like the morphological elements of the
human body, are inherited." (Emphasis is Jung's.)*

*Jung believed that these manifestations of the human psyche, or
as he termed them archetypes are totally autonomous and pre-
cultural. In one of his last pronouncements on the subject, a preface
to Psyche and Symbol, a selection of his essays, written in 1957, he
noted: "Mind is not born as a tabula rasa. Like the body, it has its
pre-established individual definiteness; namely, forms of behaviour."
When modern man tries to depart from these "still-living and ever-
present instinctual roots, the instincts will then protest and engender
peculiarly shaped thoughts and emotion. . . . The psychological
manifestations of instincts I have termed 'archetypes.' The archetypes
are by no means useless archaic survival or relics. They are living
entities, which cause the praeformation of numinous or dominant
representations." Jung then attempts to address the controversial
notion of the inherited nature of these supposedly pan-human archetypes. "It is important to bear in mind that my concept of the
'archetypes' has been frequently misunderstood as denoting inherited
patterns of thought or as a kind of philosophical speculation. In
reality they belong to the realm of the activities of the instincts and
in that sense they represent inherited forms of psychic behavior."
The reader can judge the clarity of that "clarification" for himself.*

*Since archetypes, according to Jung, operate as entities wholly
independent of individual minds and since archetypes occur in
myths and folktales, he claims: "The primitive mentality does not
invent myths, it experiences them. Myths are original revelations of
the pre-conscious psyche, involuntary statements about unconscious
psychic happenings, and anything but allegories of physical processes." (This last remark is an attack on Freudian analyses of myths
and tales, which claim that such narratives are symbolic renderings
of physical [read: sexual] processes.) Jung makes a similar statement
about fairy tales: "Being a spontaneous, naïve, and uncontrived
product of the psyche, the fairy tale cannot very well express anything except what the psyche actually is."*

*There is a mystical, anti-intellectual aspect of Jung's thought. The
fuzziness or lack of precision of Jung's concepts is recognized by
Jung himself. "Contents of an archetypal character are manifesta-*

tions of processes in the collective unconscious. Hence they do not refer to anything that is or has been conscious, but to something essentially unconscious. In the last analysis, therefore, it is impossible to say what they refer to." Other important Jungian concepts besides the archetype include the anima, the feminine component in males, and the animus, the masculine component of females. Another recurring notion is "shadow," which somewhat vaguely refers to the dark, mostly negative side of an individual. It is difficult, if not impossible, to summarize all of Jung's complex thought in a brief paragraph or two. The interested reader should consult the large body of his prolific writings for further discussion.

Anthropologists committed to the notion of cultural relativism and folklorists familiar with the limited distribution of any particular myth and tale have been sceptical, to say the least, of Jung's universalistic theory. If all people share the same collective unconscious and the same archetypes, why don't all these peoples have the same myths and fairy tales? Moreover, any folklorist who has collected folk narratives in the field would resent Jung's implication that the tellers of tales are but mechanical, unthinking transmitters of a priori compositions, experiencing rather than inventing myths. Presumably somewhere, some time, an individual did invent each myth and each folktale.

Among those who have sought to apply Jungian psychology to folktales is Marie-Louise von Franz. Her books include: An Introduction to the Interpretation of Fairy Tales *(New York: Spring Publications, 1970);* Patterns of Creativity Mirrored in Creation Myths *(New York: Spring, 1972); and* Problems of the Feminine in Fairy Tales *(New York: Spring, 1972). The latter consists of a series of lectures presented at the C.G. Jung Institute in Zurich in 1958–1959; one of these lectures, the tenth, analyzed a Russian version of Cinderella. In this lecture the reader will find references to archetypes, anima, and shadow, as well as allusions to Christian symbolism.*

For a helpful summary of Jung's theories as they apply to myth, see Wilson M. Hudson, "Jung on Myth and the Mythic," in Wilson M. Hudson and Allen Maxwell, eds., The Sunny Slopes of Long Ago *(Dallas: Southern Methodist University Press, 1966), pp. 181–197.*

In an empire in a faraway country there once lived a merchant and his wife and their one beautiful daughter called Wassilissa. When the child was eight years old, the wife suddenly became very ill. She called Wassilissa to her deathbed, gave her a doll, and said, "Listen, my dear child, these are my last words and don't forget them. I am dying and leave you my blessing and this doll. Keep it always with you, show it to nobody, and whenever you are in any trouble ask it for advice." Then she kissed her daughter for the last time and died.

The merchant mourned his wife for a long time, but then decided to marry again and chose a widow with two daughters. But for his daughter Wassilissa the marriage was a disappointment, for the new wife was a real stepmother who gave her all the hard work to do, hoping that the sun and wind would spoil her beauty and that she would begin to look like a peasant girl. But Wassilissa bore everything without grumbling and became more beautiful every day, while her stepsisters got thinner and thinner and uglier all the time, because of their envy, although they sat still with their hands in their laps all day. The doll, however, always comforted Wassilissa and did a lot of the work for her.

A year passed in this way, but Wassilissa, though much sought after, was forbidden to marry before her stepsisters, whom nobody looked at. Then the merchant had to go away to another country. In his absence the stepmother moved to a house at the edge of a great forest. In this same forest there was a little house in a clearing in which the Baba Yaga lived. The Baba Yaga permitted nobody to approach, and anyone who did she ate up. The stepmother, for whose plans the new house stood in exactly the right place, always sent Wassilissa into the wood, but she always returned safely, thanks to the doll.

One autumn evening the stepmother gave the three girls work to do. One had to knit and the other to embroider, but Wassilissa had to spin. The stepmother then put out the fire and left a small light burning so that the girls could see to work, and went off to bed. The candle burned down and the stepsister took her knitting needle to clean the wick and in so doing deliberately put it out. But one daughter said she didn't need any light, her knitting needles gave enough, and the other said her embroidery needle gave her enough light too, but Wassilissa must go to the Baba Yaga and fetch fire; and they pushed her out of the room. The latter went to her room and fed her doll as usual and told her about going to the wood. The doll told her not to be afraid, but to take her with her and nothing bad would happen.

Although terrified, Wassilissa put the doll in her pocket, crossed herself, and went into the wood. Suddenly a man in white rode by on a white horse, and day came. Farther on, a man in red rode by on a red horse, and the sun rose. All through the night and the next day Wassilissa walked through the wood and in the evening came to a hut surrounded by a hedge made of human bones with skulls stuck on the posts. The doors were made of bones, the bolt to the door of a human arm, and in place of the lock there was a mouth with grinning teeth. Wassilissa was almost senseless with horror and stood rooted to the spot. Then suddenly another rider came by, this time all in black and sitting on a black horse. He jumped off and opened the door and disappeared as though swallowed up by the ground, and it was black as night. But soon all the eyes in the skulls that made the hedge began to twinkle, and it was as light as day in the clearing. Wassilissa trembled with fear, but didn't know where to go and stood still.

Then the trees began to rustle and the Baba Yaga appeared sitting in a mortar, steering with a pestle, and wiping out her tracks with a broom. When she reached the door she sniffed and cried out that it smelled like Russians and asked who was there.

"I am, Grandmother. My stepsisters sent me to you to fetch the fire."

"Good," said the Baba Yaga, "I know you. Stay with me for a bit and then you shall have the fire."

So they went in together and the Baba Yaga lay down and told Wassilissa to bring her everything that was in the oven to eat. There was enough there for ten, but the Baba Yaga ate everything up and left only a crust of bread and a little soup for Wassilissa. Then she said, "Tomorrow when I go out you must sweep up the yard, sweep out the hut, cook the midday meal, do the washing, then go to the cornshed and sort out all the mildewed corn from the good seed. Everything must be done by the time I get home, for otherwise I shall eat you."

When the Baba Yaga began snoring in bed, Wassilissa gave the doll the food she had and told her of the hard work she had to do. But the doll said she should eat the food herself and not be afraid, yet say her prayers and go to bed, for the morning was cleverer than the evening.

In the morning when Wassilissa woke up the eyes in the skulls were just shutting, the white rider ran by, and the day came. The Baba Yaga whistled and the pestle and mortar and broom appeared; the red rider rode by and the sun came up. When the Baba Yaga had gone, Wassilissa was left quite alone and troubled as to which work she should begin, but it was all done, and the doll was just removing the last seeds of the mildewed corn. Wassilissa called the doll her savior, saying it had saved her from great misfortune, and the doll told her that now she only had to cook the dinner.

When evening came, Wassilissa laid the table and waited, and when the Baba Yaga came she asked if everything was done. "Look yourself, Grandmother," said Wassilissa.

The Baba Yaga looked at everything and was furious not to be able to find any fault, but she only said, "Yes, it's all right," and then called on her faithful servants to grind her corn. Thereupon three pairs of hands appeared and began to grind. The Baba Yaga ate just as much as the evening before and then told Wassilissa she should do the same work the next day, but in addition, she should sort the poppy seeds in the granary and clean the dirt away.

Again Wassilissa asked the doll, who told her to do the same as the evening before, and next day the doll did everything Wassilissa was supposed to do. When the old woman came home she looked everything over and then again called to her faithful servants. The three pairs of hands came and removed the poppy seeds and pressed out the oil.

While the Baba Yaga was eating her meal Wassilissa stood silently beside her. "What are you staring at without speaking a word?" asked the Baba Yaga. "Are you dumb?"

"If you will allow me to do so, I would like to ask some questions," said Wassilissa.

"Ask," said the Baba Yaga, "but remember that not all questions are wise; much knowledge makes one old."

Wassilissa said she would only like to ask about the riders. The

Baba Yaga told her that the first was her day, the red her sun, and the black her night. Then Wassilissa thought of the three pairs of hands, but didn't dare to ask and kept silent.

"Why don't you ask more?" said the Baba Yaga.

"That's enough," said Wassilissa. "You said yourself, Grandmother, that too much knowledge made people old."

The Baba Yaga then said that she was wise only to ask about what she saw outside the hut, but that now she would like to ask *her* questions, and she asked how Wassilissa had managed all the work?

Wassilissa said that her mother's blessing helped her. "Is that so?" said the Baba Yaga, "then get out of here, I don't want any blessing in my house." And she pushed Wassilissa out of the room and out of the door and took a skull from the hedge with the burning eyes in it and put it on a pole and gave it to Wassilissa, saying, "Here is your fire for your stepsisters. Take it home with you."

So Wassilissa hurried away and by the evening of the next day arrived home and thought she would throw the skull away, but a voice came from it saying she should not do so but should take it to her stepmother. And because Wassilissa saw no light in the house, she did just that.

For the first time the stepmother and her stepsisters came to meet her in a friendly way and told her they had had no fire since she left, that they had not been able to light any fire and what they fetched from the neighbor was extinguished as soon as it got to their room. "Perhaps your fire won't go out," said the stepmother. She took the skull into the living room, but the glowing eyes stared unceasingly into hers and her daughters' eyes, right down into their souls. They tried to hide but the eyes followed them everywhere, and by the morning they were burnt to ashes.

When day came, Wassilissa buried the skull, shut up the house, went into the town and asked a lonely woman to let her stay with her until her father came home, and so she waited. But one day she told the old woman that she was bored with nothing to do, and that she should buy her some thread and she would spin. But the thread which Wassilissa spun was so even, and was as thin and fine as silk hair, that there was no machine fine enough to weave it, so Wassilissa asked the doll for advice. In one night the doll got a beautiful machine, and in the spring when the cloth was finished, Wassilissa gave it to the old woman and told her to sell it and keep the money. But the old woman took it to the royal castle where the king noticed it and asked how much she wanted for it. She said nobody could pay for that work and that she had brought it as a present.

The king thanked her, gave her presents, and sent her away. But no tailor could be found to make the stuff into shirts, for it was too fine. So the king called the old woman and said that since she had spun and woven the cloth, she should be able to make the shirts. Then she told him a young and beautiful girl had made it. The king said the girl should make the shirts, so Wassilissa made a dozen of the finest shirts and the old woman brought them to the king. Meanwhile Wassilissa washed herself and combed her hair and put on her best clothes and waited at the window.

Presently a servant came from the court and said that His Majesty wanted to see the artist who had made the shirts, so that he could reward her with his own hands. Wassilissa followed the servant to the palace and appeared before the king. When he saw the beautiful Wassilissa, he fell in love with her, and said he would not be separated from her. She should be his wife.

He took her hands and put her on the throne, and they were married the same day. Soon Wassilissa's father came back from his travels, rejoiced over her good fortune, and from then on stayed with his daughter. Wassilissa also brought the old woman to the palace. And the doll she kept with her to the end of her life.

This story is much richer than the German and other Cinderella versions. I have chosen it particularly for the motif of the doll and because of the plastic description of the mother problem. Here the *dramatis personae* are the merchant, his wife and their only daughter. The wife dies when the daughter is eight years old. In fairy tales the age of fourteen or fifteen is often an important age for a girl since it is a transition stage and the end of early childhood. But here the fatal change takes place when the mother is replaced by a stepmother. In general, as you are aware, ruling persons in fairy tales represent dominants of collective consciousness, and the heroes are often poor peasant people. But this time there is a kind of average bourgeois milieu, so we can take this father figure as a symbol of the average collective attitude. The father does not play a great role; he is neither good nor bad and appears only at the beginning and at the end, where the problem does not seem to be very concentrated. The whole drama takes place in the feminine realm. The merchant's wife dies suddenly. As shown by the fact that she has no name, she would represent the average feminine type in life, the habitual type repeated over and over again in a country. There are always women who live the average life in various forms. But here there is suddenly an accident, and the life which collapses and cannot function any more is replaced by something magical, i.e., the mother's blessing and the helpful doll.

In the German version of Cinderella, the mother dies and is buried. On her grave grows a tree on which there is a bird, or from which there comes a voice which helps the girl, so she gets all she requires from the tree. In the Irish version, she finds a tortoise-shell cat that give her everything. The general motif is that after the death of the positive mother figure, something unnatural and numinous survives, i.e., the ghost of the mother, a fetish in which the mother's positive ghost is incorporated. In primitive countries ancestral ghosts are often incorporated in such fetishes and so carry on with their helpful functions.

What does it mean when a human being is replaced by a cat or a ghost? Archetypal contents sometimes appear in human and sometimes in other shapes. If they approach consciousness, then they come in human form. Human personification of a content of the unconscious shows that it can be integrated on the human level. One has a kind of feeling or vague idea as to what it could be. When an animus figure appears as a human being in a dream, you know that it can be dealt with, more or less, and you can usually make the working hypothesis that the dreamer has a general idea as to what it could be. But if there is a destructive voice coming from a grave, which would also be a personification of the animus, you would say that she could not deal with that, for it is removed and relatively autonomous and is therefore more powerful and not yet within the field of consciousness.

The death of an archetypal figure is its de-personification, for archetypes cannot die. They are eternal, instinctive inherited dispositions. But they can lose one form of symbolic appearance for another. If they lose their human shape, it means they do not function any more in a form which can easily be integrated into human life. Here the positive mother archetype of the little girl dies, but there remains with her the doll, representing the deepest essence of the mother figure, though not the human side. Most daughters have a certain archaic identity if they have a positive relationship with the mother, especially in childhood when the child talks to its doll as the mother talks to her, even repeating the mother's voice and words. Many women with a positive mother complex arrange the linen, cook for the family, and decorate the Christmas tree "as mother did," even educating the children in the same way. That would be continuity of the same form of life, with the idea that everything goes smoothly and life goes on. But it has the disadvantage of preventing the individuation of the daugher who continues the positive feminine figure as a type, not an individual, and cannot realize her specific difference from her mother.

If the mother dies, that means, symbolically, a realization that the daughter can no longer be identical with her, though the essential positive relationship remains. Therefore the mother's death is the beginning of the process of individuation; the daughter feels that she wants to be a positive feminine being, but in her own form, which entails going through all the difficulties of finding that. Here the archaic mother-daughter identity is broken off and the feminine human being realizes its weaknesses. Again and again it is the great problem in feminine psychology. Women, even worse than men, tend to identify with their own sex, and to remain in this archaic identity. In a girls' school, for instance, one girl copies the other's new hair styles or way of talking. They are like a flock of sheep, all of the same type. As far as I know from what I have read, the same thing seems to be true in primitive villages. The archaic *participation mystique* has a great impact on women, who in general are more interested in eros, in relationship, and are identical with each other and swim along together. The fact that they have trouble in dis-identifying accounts a lot, I think, for the habitual "bitchiness" among women. Because they are so apt to identify, they malign each other behind their backs. Being unconscious of their own unique personality, they indulge in all such tricks in order to make a separation.

In the Swiss mountains there exists a relationship between doll and ghost in the spook known as the Doggeli or Toggeli. The lonely man who lives with no woman around is oppressed by the Toggeli, which comes in by the keyhole and sits on his chest and suffocates him, and he wakes up with a nightmare and repressed sexual feelings. The doll here expresses a primitive anima with sexual desires and fantasies. The same Toggeli sometimes comes as the hunting spook; it also comes through the keyhole and makes little rapping noises. There you have the same relationship between doll and ghost as in this Russian material. I think the basic archetypal idea is the same as that of the fetish with which you meet all over the world.

Usually the doll is regarded as the projection of the child's fantasy of having children. If you watch little girls playing, they imitate the whole mother-child relationship. But this seems not to be the only aspect of the doll, for in an earlier stage of childhood it is more the object which contains the divinity. Many little children between two and four cannot sleep without perhaps their washcloth near their pillow, or a little teddy bear, or some kind of fetish, which has to be in a certain place, for otherwise the child cannot sleep and is exposed to the dangers of the night. It is not yet the child's child, like the doll, but is the child's god; it is like the soul stones of the Stone Age. In those days people made so-called *caches*, some of which have been found in Switzerland. A hole was made in the ground and stones of a special shape were collected and a nest was made in which they were kept. The place was kept secret and was a symbol of the person's individual secret power. Australian aborigines have such caches.

Heyerdahl has written about caches in a book called *Aku Aku,* which I recommend. In the Easter Islands, Heyerdahl, after slowly becoming intimate with the population, discovered that some families had a key hidden under a stone that opened a door down into the earth. But only one member of the family knew of this hole in the earth, or cache, in which were stone carvings of the most different types, some of them recent and not particularly artistic, but others of beautiful old imported Indian sculptures, as well as stones of different regions and a number of animal sculptures. Lobster fishers had a beautiful stone lobster, which, if rightly kept, provided the lobsters, a kind of hunting magic. Formerly such stones used to be washed and brushed four times a year. The owners waited until nobody was around, then took the stones out and cleaned them, spread them on the sands to dry, and then hid them away again in the cache. When the man who had the secret died, another member of the family was always initiated, though not necessarily the eldest son, perhaps even a nephew. There you see the original meaning of the magic object which has the divine power and guarantees the survival of the clan. You could say that, on a clan level, this is the whole secret of the process of individuation. These stones are a symbol of the Self; they represent the secret of eternity and uniqueness, and the secret of the essence of the life of the human being.

I think the early relationship of the child with the doll or with the washcloth, carried the earliest projections of the Self. It was the magic object on which the life of the child depended and by which it kept its own essence, and therefore it was an awful tragedy if lost. It is an essential relationship. Later on it turns more into the parent-child play. This I think is at the bottom of a terrible problem which I have lately met with in several cases in my practice and about which I did not know before. I have had to analyze mothers who could not get away from daughters and daughters who could not get away from mothers. They could not detach, and then there were constant quarrels. The daughter's marriage made no difference and that the daughter had left home was no guarantee—the thing could go on to any age.

In the second half of life the mother usually cannot get to her own work and creativity and does not know why; the daughter is out of the house, and she has the time, but somewhere there is sand in the machinery. One of the mothers in such a case had the following dream: She saw a big potato and a smaller one attached to it, just as in oranges there is sometimes a small orange inside, which can happen in any fruit. Out of the potato, at the joint between the two, came a pole with a crucified snake around it. This winged snake had a crown on its head with light coming from it. It was a kind of tree of life symbol and very impressive, but at the bottom were these two potatoes in the earth. The mother was tortured over the problem of her daughter, who seemed to be going the wrong way in life. She tried constantly to have it out with her. The two would talk and cry together, but to no effect. Something is not right; the potatoes are in the earth and not detached, yet the tree of life is growing. The process of individuation is developing in the bad spot, in the places of evil where something is tied and the thing is not clear. There is such a basic archaic identity of mother and daughter that a supernatural effort has to be made for them to get away from each other, and both must become completely conscious of her own personality. The mother must take back all her projections on the daughter and become individual herself, and that is very difficult for all women. You hear of mothers eating their sons but in many cases they are in a worse way tied up with their daughters. It is a natural phenomenon, and a typically feminine problem. In such cases one always finds that the mother has projected a symbol of the Self onto her daughter and, since the daughter represents the Self for her, she cannot get out of the projection. In a woman's psychology the Self is represented by an older or a younger woman, just as for men there is the older man or younger man, the *senex et puer,* the God-Father and God-Son, the father and the boy, i.e., the oldest and the youngest. It is the eternally old or the eternally young woman and probably has to do with the timelessness of the Self. If the Self appears as a young person in a woman's material, it means the newly and consciously discovered Self. Then the Self is my daughter. But in so far as the Self is also always within me, the Self is my mother, and existed long before my ego consciousness. I was born of the Self. My feminine ego consciousness rests on the superstructure of the Self which has always existed in me, and is the eternal mother. In so far as I discover the Self within, it enters completely naturally into my life, and then it is my daughter. That is why the Self is like the father and son in male psychology and mother and daughter in feminine psychology. This woman has projected onto the daughter the divine figure of the Self and cannot get the projection back. In the second half of life, when the daughter is adult, this begins to be a problem.

Usually the process of individuation begins in the second half of life. But if development is disturbed, or in innumerable other cases, it begins much earlier. Therefore, one should not keep to hard and fast rules and say, "That does not belong to you; you should get into life." The ways of God are strange and very young people sometimes have to assimilate certain aspects of the process of individuation in the first half of life. I have seen young people who have had to assimilate a great amount of the process of individuation at nineteen and twenty who could not continue without knowing certain aspects of it. Naturally, it then takes a different form, and is not quite the same thing as with an adult. Symbols must be interpreted honestly, but the way the thing gets assimilated is different with a young person. One must allow for exceptions. The mother having to pull away from the daughter is always a problem of the second half of life, for it arises only when the daughter is that age.

In the moment when Wassilissa receives this magic doll from her dying mother, instead of being archaically identical with the mother she begins to realize a germ of her own personality, the first hunch of the Self which one perhaps does get at about the age of eight. It is the first initial realization of being a personality, though one cannot guess how it will take shape in one's own life.

The merchant then marries the horrible woman with the two daughters, three jealous witches who persecute the girl. This is an archetypal motif: where the pearl is, there is also the dragon, and vice versa. They are never separate. Frequently just after the first intuitive realization of the Self, the powers of desolation and darkness break in. A terrible slaughtering always takes place at the time of the birth of the hero, as for instance the killing of the innocents at Bethlehem when Christ was born. Some persecuting power starts at once to blot out the inner thing. Outwardly, it is often that the innermost kernel of the human being has an actually irritating effect upon outer surroundings. Realization of the Self when in *statu nascendi,* when only a hunch, makes a person unadapted and difficult for those around, for he disturbs the unconscious instinctive order. Jung says it is as if a flock of sheep resented it bitterly that one sheep wanted to walk by itself.

In Germany, group psychology experiments have been made with hens and other birds. Hens and crows, for instance, observe a certain order. There is the rooster, and his first wife, who has first rights. The others have special rank in the order in which they may eat and build their nests. Most animals, and also apes, have an order which one calls the alpha, beta, gamma order. A German psychologist says that in a psychological group, or in a crowd, people also try to peck each other. The alpha hen, he says, is generally the most disgusting and pushing, and the best in I.Q. are the gamma and delta hens. Clearly, wherever people form a group there is this interplay of unconscious balance. But then if any one person gets just an idea of the Self, he falls out of the group, and the balance has to be re-established. Now that one factor is out, the others feel the gap and are naturally angry and try to force the miscreant to the former unconscious level. If you analyze one member of the family, usually the whole family begins to wobble and gets upset. In so far as we are herd animals, we have that essential conflict within ourselves between the inertia which wants to remain in the flock, and the disturbing thing, the idea, or possibility of realization. A woman who gets the first hunch of the Self is immediately attacked, not only by the stepmother outside, but from within, by the inner stepmother, i.e., the inertia of the old collective pattern of femininity, that regressive inertia which always pulls one back to do the thing in the least painful way. As in many other Cinderella stories, the stepsisters are characterized as lazy, and Wassilissa has to do tremendously hard work, such as separating the grains, which entails a superhuman effort. There is the conflict between that which calls upon you to make the superhuman effort, and the desire to follow the old pattern.

As soon as the merchant leaves the country, the stepmother and her family move near to the woods: i.e., she regresses from the human way of functioning to the borders of vegetative unconsciousness. Women, much more than men, especially if they do not have a strong animus, vegetate in an amazing way. They can live ten or twenty years like plants, without either a positive or a negative drama in their lives. They just exist. This is a typical form of feminine unconsciousness and regression and means sinking into inertia, into doing things the easy way and just following the daily plan. That is known as the conservatism of woman; there is no conflict but also no life. The stepmother here has a definite plan to push out Wassilissa, but she just goes to live near the woods and hopes the thing will happen. She has a plot and wants Wassilissa to be eaten by the Baba Yaga, who here is almost completely evil, though when she hears that the girl is a "blessed daughter" she tells her she does not want her in her house. So, in a hidden way, she is not thoroughly evil, and sometimes even helpful; she wonderfully portrays the Great Mother in her double aspect.

There is a Russian story of the Virgin Czarina, in which the Baba Yaga lives in a little round house standing on chicken feet, and you have to say a magic word before you can enter. The Czar's son goes in and finds her scratching among the ashes with her long nose. She combs her hair with her claws and watches the geese with her eyes, and then she says to the hero, "My dear little child, are you on this quest voluntarily, or involuntarily?"

You see, one of the great tricks of the mother-complex in the man is always to implant doubt in his mind, suggesting that it might be better to do the other thing; and then the man is lamed. But the boy in the story says, "Grandmother, you should not ask questions of a hero! Give me something to eat, and if you don't . . .!" Whereupon the Baba Yaga goes and cooks him a marvellous dinner and gives him good advice, and it works! So it depends on the boy's attitude. She tries to make him infantile, but when she sees he is up to her, she helps him.

So the Baba Yaga can be good or bad, just as the male image of the Godhead has usually a dark side, like the devil, so the image of the feminine Godhead, which would be within female psychology the image of the Self, has both a light and dark side. Usually in Catholic countries the light side is projected onto the Virgin Mary. She represents the light side of the Great Mother, of the anima, and of the woman, but lacks the shadow. The Baba Yaga would represent the more archaic similar figure in which the positive and negative are mixed. She is full of the powers of destruction, of desolation, and of chaos, but, at the same time, is a helpful figure. The divine rank of this figure is clearly proved by the fact that she has three riders at her disposition—"My Day," "My Night," and "My Sun." So she is a cosmic Godhead. There are also the three pairs of hands—that unspeakable, horrible secret no one ought to ask about. The principle of consciousness is in the power of this nature goddess who rules over white and black; the red would be the dawn. The three hands are probably the secret of complete destruction or death. She sits in a mortar, steers with a pestle and, as a witch with a broom, blurs or extinguishes all her traces. Human witches like to do the same thing with the famous "Hush, hush" technique—"For God's sake do not mention me!" Mother Nature likes to hide herself, it is said in Greek philosophy. The mortar and pestle are the great things in this story. I have not met them in other stories yet.

The vessel, naturally, is the feminine symbol. The Virgin Mary is called the vessel of grace, and the Holy Grail has also been applied to the Virgin Mary. The Baba Yaga too has a round vessel, but in it substances are ground to powder. She sits in a vessel that serves to pulverize matter. In alchemical literature the basic fantasy of the alchemist was that at bottom there is one ultimate basic material on which all the rest is built up. This is still the working hypothesis for many physicists, i.e., the idea of a basic building stone that would unify the whole thing, and by means of which one could get to the root of the phenomenon. This hunt for the basic material has always haunted the human mind and particularly natural scientists. It is, so to speak, God's own secret. It was the material with which he built up reality, and, therefore, is divine and contains a divine secret. In former times, before the splitting of the atom, the simplest way of getting such a material was to burn everything to ashes, and call that the basic material, or to pulverize it to the finest dust in a mortar, and the projection was that that was the *prima materia,* the most elemental basic element of matter. With these two procedures it was hoped to get to the bottom of the secret. *Tero* is to grind, and from it is derived a very interesting word used in religion, namely *contritio,* contrition. If you realize your sins, you feel remorse and penitent. If you get to the bottom and feel annihilated by your sins, then you are reduced to ashes and pulverized and are in a state of contrition, which would be the deepest kind of remorse, and, therefore, has the highest merit; by contrition you can be healed of all your sins. It is a realization of the shadow, which goes so deep that one can say nothing more about anything. As in all highly disagreeable situations, it has the advantage that you are at the bottom of the hole and cannot fall lower. Therefore, it is the turning point. The ego in its negative aspect has been pulverized, has reached the end of its selfish willfulness, and has to give in to greater powers.

The Baba Yaga has this instrument of contrition, the pestle and mortar; therefore, she symbolizes that life power which, with its ultimate truth, will bring the human being to his own ultimate truth. Hence her archaic connection with the principle of death. Many people keep a little bit above the hole and reach this stage of complete contrition only when they have to face death. We are like corks. When God does not depress us too much, we float on the surface, but when death approaches people suddenly shut up and sink to something more substantial. On the deathbed their expression changes and for the first time you feel that they are quiet and really themselves and that all the fuss of the ego has come to an end. So the Baba Yaga is also the demon of death; she brings this ultimate contrition. But she is also the great alchemist who reduces everything unnecessary to its essence. If you remember, I spoke in the beginning lectures of the revengefulness of nature and of the goddess Themis, nature, as an ultimate spirit of truth and justice, who, in her own way, grinds people to their essences.

The Baba Yaga goes to sleep, leaving the girl to select the good from the bad grain. This is a theme to be found in many Cinderella fairy tales and also comes in *Amor and Psyche*. It is a typical task in mythology for the heroine. Separating the good from the bad grains is a work of patience, which can neither be rushed into nor speeded up. *Krino* means to decide, to make a cut between *A* and *B;* it is a work of careful, detailed discrimination, but not discrimination as done by the male logos. When the latter is confronted with chaos, he says let's make the cross threads as in the telescope, etc. That is the superior birdlike working of the logos principle.

The feminine principle also has its way of seeing clearly, but it acquires it in a different psychological development, more by the selection of innumerable details, showing that this is this and that is that, an activity which compensates the tendency to archaic identity. With women it is important to go into things in detail, to see, for instance, how and where a misunderstanding began, for this is frequently caused by a lack of clarity. By working it out in detail the grains are selected. In a problem of relationship one has to do this all the time. Boring as it is, and gossipy as it seems, a psychological problem cannot be worked out without all these little details. One discovers that women love to be a little unclear, giving rise in that way to those marvellous witch muddles where nobody knows what is what any more. That is the famous way by which women get into their shadow troubles. Jung always said that women love to be unclear even about a rendezvous, and to add something such as, "If I am not there, ring up So and So." They make a vague arrangement, then a big scene if the thing does not work. Men do it also, but women much more. The shadow cannot function in the same way if you are precise.

I can give you an example. A daughter has a pair of ski shoes she cannot wear any more. The grandmother thinks the other daughter should have them. Then the daughter-in-law comes in and tries them on, but says they are too big. Grandmother suggests wearing socks inside, but they are still too big. Grandmother thinks the daughter-in-law has refused them and tells the other daughter to take them, but they cannot be found—the daughter-in-law has taken them with her! Then the son has to defend his wife and there is a general family battle because all these ladies did not take the trouble to be clear as to what they meant! The daughter-in-law *seemed* to refuse them, but goes off with them! At the back of such things there is a *participation mystique* among the women. Women love to do the same thing with money, bringing about all the famous muddles which arise from that; it is always the witch shadow. So the process of becoming conscious for a woman is that, within herself, she has to become clear about her positive and negative reactions and know where they are, instead of making a lot of muddles and half muddles.

Therefore, when the witch gives the girl this task, it is as though she were saying that if the girl could make the selection, she would not fall into the witch's power. One of woman's tasks, every time such things happen, is to ask herself why she has been vague. She will generally discover it is a question of getting the penny and the cake, wanting the ski shoes, but not wanting to owe them to your mother-in-law. You say they are not any good to you, but take them all the same. That is how the shadow works.

The Meaning of the Cinderella Story
in the Development of a Little Girl

Ben Rubenstein

*One should keep in mind that when practitioners of Jungian ana-
lytical psychology or Freudian psychoanalysis turn their attention
to folklore, they are primarily concerned with therapeutic considerations. Their usual goal is the care of mentally ill patients, and
accordingly the analysis of folklore is simply one technique among
many which has proven to be of assistance in a number of clinical
cases. Often one or more of these case histories are cited in support
of an interpretation of a folktale. In the large number of psychoanalytic essays devoted to folklore, one finds about half of them em-
ploying folklore analysis to illuminate a patient's problems and the
other half using a patient's free associations (or the analyst's free
associations) to explicate the alleged unconscious significance of an
item of folklore.*

*Sigmund Freud (1856–1939) was himself very interested in folk-
lore.* His brilliant study of traditional jokes, Wit and Its Relation in
the Unconscious (*1905*), *and his posthumously published co-
authored paper* Dreams in Folklore (*1958*) *attest to this. Many of his
early followers (including Jung) were equally fascinated by folklore.
Otto Rank's* The Myth of the Birth of the Hero (*1909*) *and various
writings of Karl Abraham, Ernest Jones, and especially Géza Róheim
constitute a substantial body of psychoanalytic interpretations of*

Reprinted from *American Imago,* 12 (1955), 197–205.

folklore. Readers desiring to locate such interpretations are advised to consult Alexander Grinstein's multi-volume reference work Index of Psychoanalytic Writings *(1950ff).*

Cinderella has been the subject of essays by a number of psycho-analysts. In most of these essays, one finds virtually no reference whatsoever to the standard folkloristic works of Cox, Rooth, and others. Instead, the analyst relies solely on a single version, plus his clinical experience with patients. In fairness, it should be pointed out that psychoanalytic studies of Cinderella and other folktales have been equally ignored, in turn, by folklorists. One reason is the lack of documentation provided by analysts. Too often, purported symbolic equations are simply asserted ex cathedra *as self-evident truths, e.g., "The association of pumpkin with pregnancy is well known"—well known to whom? and if it is a valid equation or association, why not present at least some minimal evidence of the existence of such an equation?*

In the following essay, psychiatrist Ben Rubenstein analyzes the latent content of Cinderella in the light of his own young daughter's experience. In the paper we find such conventional Freudian con-cepts as "penis envy," that is, the idea that little girls, upon once noticing the anatomical differences between males and females, feel somehow deprived and envious. (Inasmuch as penis envy rarely occurs explicitly in folklore, one wonders whether penis envy isn't simply a form of male projection! We know that in folklore and in fact males are envious of females' ability to procreate, that is, males exhibit pregnancy envy by having goddesses born from their brows [Athena], insisting that Eve was created out of Adam's body, or speaking blithely of their latest "brainchild." But for a long time, rather than admit that men were jealous of women, psychiatrists— mostly male—argued that it was women who were jealous of men.) One may also question in this particular essay whether a father can be perfectly objective in analyzing his own daughter—and her rela-tionship to him—even if he is a trained psychoanalyst. In any event, the combination of case history and fairy tale is representative of the psychoanalytic literature of Cinderella.

Among the other studies of Cinderella from this general perspec-tive are: Helen Huckel, "Cinderella as a Case History," American Imago, *14 (1957), 303-314; Mary Jeffery Collier, "The Psychological Appeal in the Cinderella Theme,"* American Imago, *18 (1961),*

399–406; Donald M. Marcus, "The Cinderella Motif: Fairy Tale and Defense," American Imago, 20 (1963), 81–92; Julius E. Heuscher, "Cinderella, Eros and Psyche," Diseases of the Nervous System, 24 (1963), 286–292; Beryl Sandford, "Cinderella," The Psychoanalytic Forum, 2 (1967), 127–144; Stanley Rosenman, "Cinderella: Family Pathology, Identity-Sculpting and Mate-Selection," American Imago, 35 (1978), 375–398; and, of course, Bruno Bettelheim's extended analysis of Cinderella in The Uses of Enchantment (New York: Vintage Books, 1977), pp. 236–277.

Fairy tales and myths have attracted scientific interest since Freud drew attention to their close relationship to the world of dreams, hysteria, and psychosis. Especially masterful was his analysis of the role of the fairy tale in the neurosis of the "Wolf Man."[1] Many of the early psychoanalytic investigators specifically noted the rich symbolism and the character of wishfulfillment in the fairy tale. We recall that psychoanalysis was under bitter attack at this time and the early defenders turned to fairy tales and myths with the enthusiasms of miners uncovering a rich vein of gold. Their assay of the new raw material through the device of dream analysis uncovered the true nature of the mechanisms of both symbolism and wish in fairy tales.

The universal and perpetual attraction of fairy tales, as with myths and legends, is based upon the ego-syntonic character of the libidinal aspirations. Franz Ricklin,[2] in a classical monograph written in 1915, reviewed large groups of fairy tales from various countries and marked their universal psychosexual themes. He drew attention particularly to the wishful character of these themes with respect to the oedipal strivings of children. Ricklin also noted two additional themes in the tales he examined: (1) the almost inevitable presence of the cruel stepmother, and (2) the sexual pursuit of the daughter by the father.

Karl Abraham[3] subjected various myths to analysis and described his results. He successfully demonstrated that both myths and dreams expressed wishes that had been subjected to identical mechanisms. In the Prometheus Saga, Abraham traced the influence of the censor, the work of condensation, displacement, and secondary elaboration—all recognizable as elements of dream work.

Common to all investigators was agreement upon the major role of sexuality in fairy tales. In essence, sexual symbolism in the tales was found to be identical with dream symbolism.

My own interest in the fairy tale was stimulated by my young daughter's identification with a specific fairy tale heroine. Her intuitive choice of the fairy tale as well as the character selected brought many questions to my mind. Specifically, I was concerned with the appeal of certain fairy tales to children in certain developmental phases, i.e., how children's interest in the stories reflects the relationship to both obvious and disguised wishes and defenses. Through the use of analytic understanding, might not the choice of a fairy tale give some insight into the character of the phallic strivings, sexual rivalry with parents, jealousy of siblings, and sado-masochistic resolution?

One Thanksgiving afternoon, my five-and-a-half-year-old daughter and her three-year-old sister visited a family which included an infant son. The five-year-old entertained the little baby and was quite maternal with him. Upon our return home, she went off into the living room to play. The younger sister, in the meantime, had become quite unreasonable with her mother. As a result, I was forced to take her to her room. It might be normally expected that the older child would derive some pleasure from her sister's predicament. Strangely, the opposite occurred. A sharp scream followed by uncontrollable sobbing was heard. When I entered the room, I found her on the floor. In response to my questions, she would only answer that her knee was hurt. Although it was clear that she was unhurt, she remained inconsolable and, as a result, she, too, joined her younger sister in their room.

By the time dinner was served, they both were again in good spirits. During the meal, the older asked rhetorically if it were fair to send a girl to her room just because she hurt herself. Her mother asked her if she would bring some salt to the table, and as she walked away, she was heard to say as though in continuity, "Why do you treat me like Cinderella?" Almost speechless, her mother managed to ask, "Why do you think I treat you like Cinderella?" She enthusiastically replied, "Because you make me do all the hardest work in the house." After bringing the salt, she gaily threw herself into the spirit of the story. She ran back to the kitchen and bringing with her a toy broom, she began furiously to sweep the rug. The room was swept and she continued a running commentary: "You won't let me go to the ball. You make me iron my sister's dress."

The sister was drawn into the play. Our Cinderella brushed her hair and ironed her dress. The three-year-old was told how pretty and lucky she was. The busy actress returned to the table for a moment to eat her dinner. She told us that her stepmother was forcing her to eat bones and to drink water. She added, "And now I must lay down on ashes on the hearth." My role— that of the good father who did not like what the mean stepmother did to the daughter—was carefully delineated by her.

She ran back to the little sister and greeted her as though the three-year-old had returned from the ball. Questions were fired at the bewildered little one: Had she enjoyed the dance? Had the stepmother looked beautiful, etc.? When she tired of this play, the five-year-old returned to the table, saying to the mother, "And you shouldn't be jealous of me just because I am the most beautiful one in the family."

The timeliness of her use of the Cinderella story led me to re-examine its familiar contents in an effort to determine by analysis of the heroine role why my daughter chose to identify with her. I shall relate the particulars of the Grimm version[4] of the story:

Cinderella is a little girl whose mother dies after telling the child to be devout and good. The father takes another wife who has two daughters of her own. The "drudge of all work" theme develops in which Cinderella becomes a dirty, tired little servant girl. Upon leaving on a journey, the father asks Cinderella what gift he can bring her on his return. She modestly tells him to break off the first twig which brushes his hat. The twig, nurtured by her tears, grows on her mother's grave to become her wishing tree. The Prince announces a three day festival to choose his bride. Cinderella is forced to help her stepsisters prepare for the ball. When she asks permission to go, she is given seemingly impossible tasks to perform by the stepmother. Aided by magic, she performs them and attends the ball without discovery. The Prince is attracted to her but each night she eludes him. Once, she hides in the pigeon house which her father demolishes with an axe, while the second evening, she climbs a tree which the father chops down. But on the third evening, Cinderella loses her slipper.[5] During the Prince's attempts to regain his lost love, the two stepsisters try vainly to fit their feet into the slipper; one amputates her toe to do so, the other her heel, with both amputations taking place at the stepmother's suggestion. Deceit is uncovered as Cinderella's birds discover the bloody trail, and virtue triumphs with the Prince taking Cinderella for his own. In final revenge, our heroine's birds pluck out the eyes of her stepsisters.

Let us now try to see what sense our analytic understanding can bring to the tale. The least disguised wish in the Cinderella story is the method of resolution of the sexual rivalry with the mother. The stepmother theme is a common one in a large group of fairy tales. Ricklin describes the meaning of the mother in the role of the stepmother as an overdetermined one. We recognize that the stepmother (the giantess and the witch in other tales) is the sexual rival. The infantile thinking which permits the good mother to die stems not only from the common wish but, in addition, from the fact that the good mother no longer exists because she is now a bad figure, a rival. The Cinderella motive then is clear. That the mother must die is beautifully symbolized in the story. The wishing tree which will grant her dearest hope grows on the grave of her mother.

The "drudge of all work" theme is common to many tales and is likewise overdetermined. What are its attributes that make it so strangely agreeable and acceptable to children? Its masochistic character is clear. It would seem that, in part, the identification of children with poor, mistreated, dirty Cinderella portrays the reversal of the sadistic punitive feelings they experience in relationship to the mother and to the siblings. We here see a similarity to the paranoid patient who projects his feelings outward and says, "They are mean to me and don't like me." It is the fate of this turning in of aggression upon the self which makes the "drudge of all work" group of fairy tales of particular interest. It is possible further for the heroine and her imitators to assume the above role because teleological and magical thinking are operative. Cinderella accepts her miserable lot because there is no doubt that she will win her prince and that her bad mother and sisters will earn their just due.

In this same connection, one wonders whether, as is true with the compulsion neurotics, the narcissistic gratification arising out of increased feelings of self-esteem from the severe reaction formations does not play an important part? The strong ego-syntonic feelings of righteousness would appear to be a prominent factor in the acceptance of the drudge role.

Another aspect of the Cinderella tale is of interest. It will be recalled that when the father asks her what it is she wishes him to bring her, he is told to break off the first twig which strikes his hat. It is this little twig that grows into a fine tree which grants all of her wishes. Can not the twig be related, at least in part, to the penis envy and phallic aspirations of the little girl? In addition, it is as though the phallic strivings have undergone some transformations since this thought leads directly into another familiar fairy story theme, i.e., the sexual pursuit of the daughter by the father. Although this second theme is admittedly not as clearly depicted as in many other stories, what other possible explanations can be offered for the strange behavior of the father who goes with an axe to smash the pigeon houses in which he believes Cinderella is hiding? A second night he chops down the pear tree believing that she hides there. In both instances, his motive is to prevent her marriage to the prince.[6] With the magical aid of her birds, Cinderella outwits him. We are so well reminded of Freud's thinking[7] in this connection. He felt that phallic masturbation of little girls foundered in their humiliating recognition of the anatomical distinction between the sexes. A new equation of penis equals child develops and the father becomes the love object with this end in view. Therefore, the twig also becomes the child.[8] The attack of the father is, likewise, reminiscent of "A Child Is Being Beaten" where the underlying phantasy was the sexual attack of the father upon the child.

To recapitulate the Cinderella tale establishes our story book heroine developmentally, ego and libido-wise, in somewhat the following position. She remains firmly fixed in her oedipal strivings since the good mother is dead and her bad mother, the rival, is now a stepmother who persecutes her. With the aid of defensive mechanisms of regression, projection, and magical thinking in order to satisfy super-ego demands, she becomes the poor little servant. Magical and teleological thinking permit her to accept this role since all of her wishes will be granted in the future. In this same fashion, her siblings are sadistically punished. Phallic strivings are somewhat transmuted as the magical phallus now becomes the total girl who will be beaten. Certainly, to be beaten in this sense can mean only to be sexually attacked.

We are now ready to return to the five-and-a-half-year-old Cinderella. It is important at this point to offer additional information about her general behavior and adjustment prior to the incident. Her behavior in this period immediately preceding the episode could be described as phallic. Blue jeans were the only apparel she would wear and dresses were definitely excluded. She was unkempt, dirty, and happy. She did not hesitate to sadistically punish her little sister. In a period preceding the one described above, I had observed the reverse. Only dresses were worn and she was meticulous. She appeared unable to compete with her younger sister and was quick to dissolve into tears when the younger one barely touched her. She had, in some ways, clearly regressed. Her behavior became infantile. She would speak with longing of her desire to be an infant. We may assume that she was retreating from massive amounts of jealousy. Freud expressed the thought[9] that, after penis envy had abandoned its true object, it continued in the character trait of jealousy. He suggested a transition from the awareness of her poor sexual equipment to the demonstration of jealousy toward the sibling. It is this sequence which prepares the way for the beating phantasy first in respect to her sister and secondly to herself. However, in the middle of the last phallic period, she constantly launched verbal attacks upon her mother, often accusing her of every conceivable and fancied wrong. Several weeks prior to the Cinderella incident, she had become more comfortable and remained so.

I suggest that her play with and the observation of the infant boy stimulated not only the identification and rivalry with the mother described above, but in addition must have recalled for her her bitter feelings about her sister's birth. We might conjecture that her observation of the male infant's genitals strengthened her feelings of her own phallic insufficiency while also recalling the superiority of the father's genitals. Freud's well-proven thesis[10] in respect to another consequence of penis envy, i.e., the loosening of the girl's relationship with her mother as a love object, is here operative since the mother is held responsible for the child's lack of a penis.

She returned from her visit with these revived feelings and then had opportunity to overhear my firm, i.e., angry handling of her younger sister. It is my belief that her unconscious constructed a beating phantasy arising sharply out of her castrated feelings. Recall her cry: "My knee, my knee!"[11] It was obviously her wish that I would come and beat (attack) her. I had, many times, been quite impressed by the obviousness of this wish. The subsequent uninvolved treatment she received from her parents forced her feelings to find expression in acting out the masochistic Cinderella phantasy. The mind is a fairy poetess in its own right and accordingly we note the similarity between unconscious productions and fairy tales. Marie Bonaparte[12] clearly explains the psychic sequence:

> The active sadistic oedipus must submit to the castration [the knee] with disappointment in the too small clitoris. In this way, the executive organ of sadism becomes depreciated and the big paternal penis [the axe of the story] . . . takes its place as the true representative of sadism. . . . The little girl desires the father's assaults and blows. [The interpolated material is, of course, my own.]

It is of interest to note the similarity here to the attack with the axe by the father upon the pigeon house and the tree in the Cinderella tale. The beating is a step before penetration. Quoting Bonaparte again:

> It is the clitoris, executive organ of the phallic sadistic infantile sexual aggression, that was turned on the mother, which then becomes, through the subject's own sadism turning upon herself, the phantasied object of the sadistic aggression by the father and his large penis. The clitoris re-becomes, in the little girl's masturbation phantasies which the passive oedipus has attached to the father, an organ of passive sensuality.

As mentioned earlier, my daughter's wish to be beaten and the father's attack on Cinderella with the axe appears similar to the feminine phantasy described by Freud in "A Child Is Being Beaten." It is common for us to refer to little girls in the phallic phase as being totally phallic, i.e., the body as phallus. To be beaten is equated in the little girl's unconscious as having her clitoris beaten. Bonaparte suggests this equation may form the connecting link by which the formerly active sadistic clitoridal libido of the girl evolves into full vaginality by passive and masochistic regression.

In conclusion, I feel that the identification with the fairy tale by my little Cinderella was already a portent of the coming latency or the long waiting sleep like that of Sleeping Beauty. Expressed in the identification was the tacit recognition of her minute clitoris with accompanying phantasies of castration and being beaten masochistically by the father.

NOTES

[1]Sigmund Freud, "Case of an Obsessional Neurosis," *Collected Works,* Volume III. Hogarth Press.

[2]Franz Ricklin, "Wishfulfillment and Fairy Tales," *Nervous and Mental Disease Monographs.* New York, 1915.

[3]Karl Abraham, "Dreams and Myths," *Nervous and Mental Disease Monographs.* New York.

[4]My daughter was acquainted also with the Lang version in her school. Lang and Perrault are the most popular versions in America. They are widely known through the publicity of their editions by the Disney cartoons. This version contains the familiar theme of the transformation of the pumpkin and mice into the carriage and horses.

[5]An additional piece of symbolism was lost to speculation in the translation of the tale from French to English. Cinderella's slipper was not made of glass, it was made of fur. The similarities in the French words "vair" meaning fur, and "verre" meaning glass, caused the error in the translation.

[6]In a recent performance, the Sadlers Wells Ballet Company danced John Cranko's "Shadow," which appeared to depict the strange behavior of a father who alternately offered his daughter to a lover and took her back for himself.

[7]Sigmund Freud, *Collected Papers,* Volume V. "Some Psychological Consequences of the Anatomical Distinction Between Sexes," Hogarth Press.

[8]It is of interest to find this same equation supported by the symbols found in the other versions of the Cinderella story. The association of pumpkin with pregnancy is well known. In addition, the siblings are alluded to by the mice, which in turn are transformed into phallic horses.

[9]Sigmund Freud, *ibid.*

[10]*Ibid.*

[11]My attention was drawn to an article, "A Psychoanalytic Notation on the Root GN, KN, CN," by Henry Alden Bunker and Bertram D. Lewin. (*Psychoanalysis and Culture,* edited by George B. Wilbur and Warner Muensterberger, International Universities Press.) The authors trace the universal meaning of the word "knee" and find it related to the male womb and to root words meaning to beget, to procreate, generate, and genital.

[12]Marie Bonaparte, *Female Sexuality,* International Universities Press.

"To Love My Father All": A Psychoanalytic Study of the Folktale Source of *King Lear*

Alan Dundes

Cinderella has become so much a part of Western culture that the very word can be found in most English dictionaries. Not many fairy tale heroes or heroines have been so honored. The word conjures up a whole host of associations. An underdog political candidate or athletic team who wins a victory unexpectedly may be referred to as a Cinderella. The plot of Cinderella has inspired countless short stories, novels, plays, operettas, and films, often using the very name in the title. But surely there is no more famous literary use of a version of Cinderella than Shakespeare's King Lear.

Shakespeare drew upon folklore for many of his plays. For a valuable listing of many of the studies of Shakespeare's use of folklore, see Philip C. Kolin, "A Bibliography of Scholarship on Shakespeare and Folklore," Mississippi Folklore Register, *19 (1976), 210–233. Other studies not cited in that bibliography include: G. Di Niscia, "Per una Fonte Probabile della 'Bismetica Domata' [The Taming of the Shrew]," in Nozze* Percopo-Luciani, 30 luglio 1902 *(Napoli: Stab. Tip. Luigi Pierro e Figlio, 1903), pp. 29–56; Berta Viktoria Wenger, "Shylocks Pfund Fleisch: Eine stoffges-chichtliche Untersuchung,"* Shakespeare Jahrbuch, *65 (1929), 92–*

Reprinted from *Southern Folklore Quarterly,* 40 (1976), 353–366.

174; H.C. Lake, "Some Folk-Lore Incidents in Shakespeare," Folk-Lore 39 (1928), 307-328; Theodor Zachariae, "Indische Parallelen zu König Lears Fragen an seine Töchter," Zeitschrift für Volkskunde, 3 (1931), 141-147; and W. Ruben, "'Ende Gut, Alles Gut' Ein Maerchen bei Indern, Türken, Boccaccio, Shakespeare," Türk Tarih Kurumu Belleten, 7 (1943), 135-155.

The study of folklore in literature entails at least two distinct methodological steps: identification and interpretation.[1] The first step is to identify accurately and fully a possible folkloristic element or form occurring in a given literary (con)text. This is an empirical, objective process which can be verified by any literary scholar sufficiently conversant with the normal critical apparatus employed by folklorists. Once the identification has been successfully completed, the more difficult task of interpretation may be attempted. Interpretation, in contrast to identification, is often subjective and is not necessarily empirically demonstrable. Frequently, interpretations are like beauty insofar as they lie primarily in the eyes of the beholders rather than in the literary text analyzed. This is why interpretations, especially psychoanalytic ones, are commonly criticized as being "read into" rather than being "read out of" the text.

One problem with the twofold methodology of identification and interpretation is that both steps are all too rarely achieved. Folklorists for their part are too often wont to stop after making identifications. Accordingly one finds scholarly contributions consisting of little more than long lists of "proverbs" in the works of so and so. Such lists of proverbs, nursery rhymes, or allusions to children's games typically fail to include any attempt to explain why a particular proverb, rhyme, or children's game was used by a particular poet in a particular literary context.

Literary scholars unfamiliar with folkloristics are guilty of a different error. Such scholars are not averse to plunging headlong into interpretation without benefit of proper identification of folkloristic source material. The vast majority of literary source studies assume literary, not folklore, precursors and the inevitable search is invariably for a missing manuscript rather than an oral tale. Literate scholars falsely believe that the authors they study must have read rather than heard an earlier version of the story line. This is despite the fact that the literate scholars themselves have heard folktales, legends, and jokes all their lives. Without considering folkloristic sources for literature, would-be critics are deprived of an absolutely essential means of seeing how poets transform the common clay of folk imagination into a literary masterpiece.

It is not unduly defensive mindedness or disciplinary chauvinism on the part of folklorists when they decry their literary colleagues' failure to utilize conventional folkloristic identification tools. The sad fact is that far too many professional students of literature are totally ignorant of such aids. Thus it is perfectly possible to write entire books on Homer's use of folktale and have such books published by reputable academic presses without revealing any knowledge whatsoever of the tale type index—an indispensable vade mecum which has been available since 1910. Neither Rhys Carpenter, *Folk Tale, Fiction and Saga in the Homeric Epics*, published by the University of California Press in 1946, nor Denys Page, *Folktales in Homer's Odyssey*, published by Harvard University Press in 1973, refer to the tale type index, or, for example, to the fact that tale type 1137, The Ogre Blinded (Polyphemus) is an identifiable, independent folktale which certainly must have been incorporated by Homer into the *Odyssey*. Similarly, there are surely Chaucerian scholars who are not aware of all of the dozen and a half tale types cognate with various *Canterbury Tales*.[2]

In Shakespearian criticism, one does find some awareness of the relationship of several of his plots to folktales, but typically these relationships are couched in the vague, imprecise language of critics apparently ignorant of folklore scholarship. It is clear, for instance, that *Cymbeline* is related to tale type 882, The Wager on the Wife's Chastity; *The Taming of the Shrew* to tale type 901; Taming of the Shrew; and *Merchant of Venice* to a combination of Motif L 211, Modest choice: three caskets type, and tale type 890, A Pound of Flesh.[3] Not only do most conventional Shakespearian scholars merely allude en passant to possible "old stories rooted in the popular faith" to borrow (and alter slightly) Coleridge's well turned phrase, but they rarely if ever stop to consider the psychological implications of the folktale plot lying at the base of a given work of literature. In short, they do not always properly identify possible folktale sources and without such identification, they are in no position to make a judicious psychological or for that matter any other type of interpretation of literature derived from folklore.

So the study of folklore in literature cannot be expected to advance so long as folklorists identify without interpreting and literary critics interpret without identifying folklore sources. It serves little purpose for folklorists to point accusing fingers at literary critics when they themselves undertake only the first of the two steps. Identifying a folktale source for a Shakespearian play does not per se automatically yield esthetic and psychological insights into the meaning of either the tale or the play. Identification is simply no substitute for interpretation.

In the case of _King Lear_, it has long been recognized that the plot was borrowed in part from folklore. Specifically, the often discussed love-test of the opening scene has been recognized as tale type 923, Love Like Salt. In 1886, Hartland even labelled the first of what he considered to be five distinct types of "The Outcast Child" as the "King Lear type," and not long thereafter in 1892, Marian Roalfe Cox in her _Cinderella_, one of the first major full length comparative studies of a folktale, elected to call the initial elements in Cap o' Rushes (tale type 510B) "King Lear judgment—Loving like salt."[4] Many of the standard studies of the sources of the play acknowledge the folkloristic origins of the love-test. Perett devotes considerable notice in his 1904 monograph while Bullough in 1973 briefly mentions the appearance of the love-test in a Grimm tale.[5] (Here incidentally is another illustration of my contention that literary scholars are unaware of folklore scholarship. Perrett writing in 1904 did not have a tale type index to consult, but there is no excuse for any scholar writing after 1910 not to know of the tale type index.) On the other hand, Muir in his otherwise useful 1957 survey of the principal sources of _King Lear_ makes no mention whatever of the folktale, Love Like Salt.[6] I hope to show that not only is the folktale in question a crucial source for _King Lear_, but that it is not possible to understand much of the inherent dramatic power of the play without knowledge of the underlying folktale and its essential psychological dimensions.

The folktale contains the basic plot consisting of an initial love test in which a king asks his three daughters to declare their love for him. The third, his favorite, answers that her love is like salt and she is forthwith banished by the outraged king. The folktale typically ends with the marriage of the third princess—as most *Märchen* end with marriage, a fact confirmed by Propp's *Morphology of the Folktale*.[7] Normally, the king and his favorite daughter are reconciled at the end of the tale. Different versions of the folktale manifest interesting details. For example, in one version, the father becomes insane and the heroine's care restores him to his senses. In another, the father falls dead upon recognizing the heroine.[8]

One very important point is that in the folktale the central figure is the daughter-heroine. In fairy tales, the protagonists are almost always sons or daughters, not parents. This means that in the underlying source of *King Lear*, the central figure is the analog to Cordelia. It follows that Shakespeare's emphasis upon Lear—one must keep in mind that Cordelia is technically absent for the bulk of the action of the play—is a critical literary change from the folklore source.

We have not yet finished with the task of identification. Not only is the daughter the central figure in the folktale, but the general tale involved is closely related to and perhaps a subtype of Cinderella, one of the most popular tales in the world. This is a feature of the identification of the folktale which has not been sufficiently appreciated by students of the play. Cox in her pioneering study of Cinderalla called the story subtype C, Cap o' Rushes, but in a more recent comprehensive investigation of Cinderella by Swedish folklorist Anna Birgitta Rooth, the tale is considered to belong with Catskin under the same general plot rubric. In Rooth's 1951 study of the Cinderella cycle, this grouping of Cap o' Rushes and Catskin is labelled Type B1 and it corresponds to Aarne-Thompson tale type 510B, The Dress of Gold, of Silver, and of Stars.[9] Tale type 510B is somewhat distinct from tale type 510A, Cinderella, which is probably the best known version of the Cinderella plot. (Nevertheless, Stith Thompson's grouping of 510A, Cinderella, and 510B, The Dress of Gold, of Silver, and of Stars, under the same basic tale type number, reflects the probable cognation of the subtypes.)

The similarity of Catskin, which Cox called type B, and Cap o' Rushes (Cox's type C) was recognized by Cox herself. In fact, the only differentiating incidents were the occurrence of the "King Lear judgment" and the "Outcast Heroine" in Cap o' Rushes. These incidents were not found in Catskin. However, in Catskin were the functionally equivalent incidents of "Unnatural father" and "Heroine flight."[10] This is of enormous significance in seeking to understand *King Lear*. The summary of tale type 510B, The Dress of Gold, of Silver, and of Stars, which includes both Catskin and Cap o' Rushes, begins: "Present of the father who wants to marry his own daughter." The principal constituent motifs in the tale type include M 255, Deathbed promise concerning the second wife; T 411.1, Lecherous father; S 322.1.2, Father casts daughter forth when she will not marry him; T 311.1, Flight of maiden to escape marriage. Usually the queen on her deathbed makes the king promise to marry only someone who can wear her ring.[11] After the queen's death, the king tries in vain to find someone only to discover that the ring fits his own daughter. In another folktale motif, the king decides to marry the woman who most resembles his recently deceased wife and that person turns out to be his daughter. The gist of all this is that the "love like salt" plot appears to be a weakened form of the folktale plot in which a "mad" father tries to marry his own daughter. In making this assertion, it is not just a matter of identifying "love like salt" as a folklore motif, but rather of identifying its typical context as part of tale type 510B, The Dress of Gold, of Silver, and of Stars.

The theme of incest is a powerful one and it would be no surprise to learn that it provides one of the most important undercurrents of *King Lear*. It should be recognized that the theme occurs in somewhat muted form in the play. It is not as overt as in the folktale where the king demands his daughter's hand in marriage. This is how it is expressed in tale type 510B and in tale type 706, The Maiden Without Hands. In *King Lear*, the love test is rather a matter of a daughter's declaring her total love of her father "To love my father all" (I,i,104).

A number of psychoanalytically oriented critics have remarked on the possible incest theme in the play. Bransom in 1934 ever so timidly and hesitatingly suggested at the very end of his book *The Tragedy of King Lear* that a factor which might have influenced Lear's conduct was "an old, repressed, incestuous passion for one of his daughters." Bransom was careful to warn readers in his introduction that they might prefer to omit his final chapter if they found the subject distasteful. Freud in a letter written to Bransom about his book agreed that "the secret meaning of the tragedy" had to do with Lear's "repressed incestuous claims on the daughter's love."[12]

Earlier in 1913, Freud had himself written about *King Lear* in his essay "The Theme of the Three Caskets" in which, interestingly enough, he compared Cordelia with Cinderella, but he made no reference to incest. Rather he suggested that Cordelia symbolized death, an interpretation which has not received much enthusiasm from critics sympathetic to psychoanalysis.[13] More recent psychoanalytic treatments of *King Lear* have also drawn attention to the incest theme. Pauncz went so far as to speak of a "Lear Complex," as a kind of a reverse Oedipus complex, referring to a father's being sexually attracted to his daughter.[14]

None of the critics who see an incest theme in *King Lear* appear to be aware of the existence of the same theme in folktale sources from which the play is definitely derived, but there is sufficient textual evidence in the play itself for them to cite in support of their interpretation. Lear during the storm scene specifically refers to incest (III,ii,55). Later he maintains that he "will die bravely like a smug bridegroom" (IV,vi,194) and in the final meeting with Cordelia, Lear depicts himself and Cordelia as lovebirds "Come, lets away to prison. We two alone will sing like birds i' th' cage." (V,iii,8–9). The incestuous nature of the love-test is also hinted at by France's astonishment upon hearing Lear's surprising denunciation of Cordelia. "This is most strange! That she . . . should . . . Commit a thing so monstruous to dismantle So many folds of favor. Sure, her offence Must be of such unnatural degree . . ." (I,i,216–223). It may or may not be germane that the adjective "monstruous" was in fact used on another occasion by Shakespeare to refer to father-daughter incest. The final lines of *Pericles* begin: "In Antiochus and his daughter you have heard/Of monstruous lust the due and just reward." (V,iii,85–86; cf. the father-daughter incest riddle in *Pericles*, I,i, 64–71.)

All the psychoanalytic readings of the play treating the incest theme and that includes Freud's later one agree that it is a matter of father-daughter incest. This stems in part from their looking at the drama from Lear's point of view rather than Cordelia's. This may be appropriate in view of the centrality of Lear in the play, but insofar as the basic plot structure comes from a daughter-centered fairytale, it is *in*appropriate. In brief, the fairy tale evidence would suggest that it is "daughter-father" incest rather than "father-daughter" incest! Furness once remarked "that of all departments of Shakespearian study none seems . . . more profitless than this search for the sources whence Shakespeare gathered his dramas."[15] The error of this incredible statement is just as serious for psychoanalytic literary criticism as it is for literary criticism in general. I submit that psychoanalysts and several literary critics may have erred in reading *King Lear* as a literal expression of incestuous desires on the part of a father figure. What the folktale behind the play and very likely the play itself does entail is *a projection of incestuous desires on the part of the daughter*. In this sense, the plot revolves around Cordelia, not Lear, and as we shall see, a great many details which have puzzled critics for some time may be explained.

First a word about projection might be in order. Projection is a defense mechanism which translates unacceptable or taboo inner thoughts to an external outer object with the thoughts in question then neatly attributed to the external object. In Freud's terms, "I hate him" becomes "He hates me."[16] Projection obviates any feelings of guilt inasmuch as the original crime is displaced onto the object of the initial guilt-producing wish. The subject (original wisher) has become the object (victim) while the original intended victim has become the doer of the guilty deed. Projection in myth and folktale is common enough. Otto Rank in *The Myth of the Birth of the Hero* showed convincingly how the son's Oedipal wish to remove the father (so as to have sole access to the mother) is a taboo one. So in the resultant folkloristic projection, it is not the son-hero who wishes to get rid of his father but rather the wicked father figure who tries to get rid of the son figure. The son is thereby able to slay the villainous father figure without guilt.[17]

In comparable daughter-centered fairy tales, the girl would like to eliminate her mother and marry her father. Many folktales begin with the queen or original mother already dead—perfect wish fulfillment! So in *King Lear*, there is no Queen Lear—leaving the father available as a sexual object for his daughters. But just as the son's wish to marry his mother is taboo, so the daughter's wish to marry her father is equally so. Consequently, in the fairy tale projection, it is always the father who insists upon marrying his own daughter. The specific details of how the dying queen insists that the new wife must be just like her would appear to reflect the common fantasy of a girl wishing to literally replace her mother—with respect to being her father's mate. The daughter either looks just like her mother or she is the only one who fits into her mother's wedding ring. (Cf. Kent's use of a ring to summon Cordelia, III,i,47.)

If the present interpretation is correct, then it is perfectly true that *King Lear* and its folktale source concerns a girl's inability to express her (sexual) love for her father. The interpretation explains not only why there is no Queen Lear, but also why Cordelia's husband appears so little in the play. The play is about a daughter-father relationship, not a wife-husband relationship. This is why, dramatically speaking, Cordelia's husband "France" cannot appear in the final act. Cordelia's line "O dear father, It is thy business that I go about" (IV,iv,23–24) is perhaps more than an obvious Christian echo of Jesus explaining, after having been found in the temple, "wist ye not that I must be about my Father's business?" (Luke, 2:49). It affirms that Cordelia is primarily concerned with her father, not her husband. Possibly there may even be a double meaning in "It is thy business that I go about" meaning both that it is her father's fault that she is wandering around, and that she is engaged in looking after his interests. In any case, it is the emotional reunion of daughter and father which provides the only logical and psychological denouement for such a plot.

The present interpretation also illuminates the punishment of Cordelia. Many critics have been bothered by Cordelia's death. In many of the literary versions of the story, Cordelia takes her own life. Perrett, for example, observes how common this ending is, but he is troubled by such a "meaningless" suicide since "it is not connected in any way with the events of the story proper."[18] From the psychoanalytic perspective, the story is a daughter's incestuous projection, not a father's. For this reason, Lear is quite right when he claims that he is "a man more sinn'd against than sinning." The original sin is Cordelia's. Once again, the available evidence from folklore is helpful. In tale type 706, The Maiden Without Hands, we have another extremely popular fairy tale which begins with a father's incestuous wish to marry his daughter. The daughter's response is to cut off her hands—perhaps signalling in a rather macabre punning way that she refuses to give her "hand" in marriage to her father. In any case, the point is that the girl punishes herself as a response to a "crime" purportedly about to be committed by her father. (In terms of female masturbatory behavior, it would be appropriate for a girl to cut off her "sinning" hands as a suitable punishment for indulging in incestuous thoughts about her father.) Thus if Cordelia is a sinner, then it is poetic justice to have her guilt lead her to suicide. Of course, Shakespeare elected to depart from the literary sources of his plot and Cordelia does not take her own life. The suicide is shifted to Goneril. In the present context, it is noteworthy that the apparent motivation for Goneril's decision is unrequited lust (for Edmund).[19]

The fairy tale projection also helps explain Cordelia's relationship to her two sisters who are obviously the wicked older sisters (often stepsisters) in Cinderella and other *märchen*. Among sisters, there is commonly sibling rivalry for the affection of the father. Each daughter wants to be her father's very favorite. In theory Cordelia ought to be pleased for Lear admits publicly that he "lov'd her most" (I,i,124). But in the fairy tale, overt sexuality on the part of the girl is denied. The adamant denial of sexuality and unadulterated purity of Cordelia is contrasted throughout the play with the unabashed animality and sexuality of both Goneril and Regan.[20]

The marked contrast between Cordelia and her sisters is also indicated by the sexual symbolism of speech. Speech is sexual; dumbness, not speaking, is asexual. Cordelia is unable or unwilling to speak. Her name which may derive etymologically from heart (cor) may be related to Lear's request for her heart (I,i,106), but she cannot heave her heart into her mouth (I,i,94). Freud interpreted Cordelia's dumbness as a representation of death, an interpretation which is not incompatible with the asexuality suggested here. If dumbness is death, then speaking is life. Among other examples of the sexuality of speech, there is Albany's attempt to communicate that his wife is sexually unavailable to Edmund: "My lady is bespoke" (V,iii,90). Regan refers to Goneril's "most speaking looks" before admitting that Edmund and she "have talk'd" (IV,v,30) which means presumably that they have come to some sexual understanding.[21]

Understanding *King Lear* as a transformation of a folktale fantasy concerned with a daughter's disguised incestuous love of her father also affords insight into the particular verbiage used by Goneril and Regan in the love-test itself. Goneril declares "A love that makes breath poor and speech unable" (I,i,61). Whether there is gasping or panting in the delivery of the lines is irrelevant,[22] for the words themselves hint of passion. Regan's response to the love-test includes mention of the "very deed of love" as well as reference to her "most precious square of sense" (I,i,72,75).[23] Regan, one may recall, is later to speak bluntly of the "forefended place" referring again to the female genital area (V,i,10). Such teasing seductive allusions are in accord with a daughter's sexual fantasies revolving around her father.

The final reunion of Cordelia with Lear provides her triumph over her sibling rivals. In the very first scene of the play, Cordelia has to suffer her father's asking for the love of her two older sisters before he gets around to asking her for her love. In the final scene, however, Cordelia has her father all to herself. She even asks, "Shall we not see these daughters and sisters?" (V,iii,7), but Lear emphatically says no and speaks of himself and Cordelia as "two alone" in the lovebird metaphor. Without either rival mother or rival sisters, Cordelia enjoys the culmination of her Electral complex fantasy for but a brief instant before being led away with her father to prison and death.

One could interpret the struggle between Goneril and Regan for the sexual attentions of Edmund as another reflection of sibling rivalry. Moreover, since a father is a married man, a daughter must commit adultery in order to gain his sexual favors, and this might explain the single curious reference to Lear's wife. Here the sexual rivalry is not between siblings, but between daughter and mother. In Lear's meeting with Regan, he tells her that if she weren't glad to see him, he would divorce himself from her mother's tomb because it would hold an adulteress (II,iv,131). This implies that if Regan weren't glad to see him, she couldn't be his true daughter. But is also evokes a daughter's various fantasies concerning her rivalry with her mother for her father. From the daughter's point of view, if the daughter possesses the father, then the mother is the outsider, the adulteress.

In terms of the initial argument of this essay, we have provided both identification and interpretation. The objective identification was made of the love-test as more than simply "Love like salt". Rather it belongs to a major form of the Cinderella cycle, a folktale whose normal form includes an overt paternal demand for an incestuous relationship with a daughter. If nothing else, this more complete identification of the ultimate source for *King Lear* would tend to support those many critics, including Freud himself, who have claimed that there is an underlying theme of father-daughter incest in the play. The more subjective and speculative interpretive portion of the essay, however, suggests that the fairy tale in question is a remarkable example of projection. Through projection, the basic daughter-father incest wish is transformed into an attempted father-daughter incest act. This does not mean that there are not fathers who are sexually attracted to their own daughters. There most surely are. But the existence of such paternal desires in no way precludes the existence of an Electra complex. To argue that it does would be tantamount to claiming that seductive behavior on the part of mothers towards sons rules out the possibility of the existence of the Oedipus complex. Clearly such parental fantasies add fuel to the fire of children's fantasies. (The confusion of generations is suggested in *King Lear* when Cordelia seems to be both daughter and mother to Lear.) The point is that incestuous desires may be mutual on the part of both daughter and father.

Some may doubt the wisdom of applying a modern concept such as projection to the artistic materials of past centuries. Yet in *King Lear* we find striking evidence for the plausibility of projection as a psychological device or defense mechanism. Lear himself (IV,vi, 156–158) demonstrates considerable insight into the nature of projection: "Thou rascal beadle, hold thy bloody hand! Why does thou lash that whore? Strip thy own back. Thou hotly lusts to use her in that kind For which thou whipp'st her." In the same way, fathers should not punish daughters for indulging in sexual fantasies which fathers themselves hold and consciously or unconsciously encourage. We can see other examples of projection in the play. The daughter's anger because her father doesn't love her best is transformed in the fairy tale into the king's anger because his daughter doesn't love him best (to the exclusion of husbands present or future). Similarly, the daughter's wish to turn her home into a brothel (where she can more easily seduce her father) is transformed into her accusation that it is the father and his retinue which is making the house into a brothel ". . . our court . . . more like a tavern or a brothel Than a grac'd palace" (I,iv,250).

In his book *Psychoanalysis and Shakespeare*, Norman Holland mentions that although Freud planned to attempt a synthesis of folkloristic and psychoanalytic approaches to *King Lear*, he never did so.[24] The present essay is intended to be a first step towards that synthesis. If valid, then the delineation of the projection pattern of the fairy tale underlying *King Lear* may provide a new perspective for students of the play. To be sure, one must be careful to separate the fairy tale source and the Shakespeare play. Even if the psycho-analytic argument broached here were adjudged applicable to the fairy tale, it does not necessarily follow that it must be equally so to the play. The play represents a literary reworking of folk material and more importantly it reflects an older male's reworking of a female-centered fairy tale. Whether Shakespeare's choice of subject matter and treatment stems from autobiographical factors is a moot question. Sharpe suggests that there might be a connection between the writing of *King Lear* in 1606 and Shakespeare's relationship with his own daughters—e.g., Susannah was married in 1607.[25] In this connection, one is tempted to venture the view that one possible reason for Shakespeare's giving vent to such vitriol with respect to the sexuality of women in *King Lear* as opposed to his witty and positive treatment in other plays[26] might be his normal father's repugnance at the thought of his 'innocent" daughter becoming a sexual object for men (himself included).[27]

Regardless of any possible 'play-as-biography' significance of the present interpretation of the play, it is at any rate safe to say that Shakespeare's utilization of a folktale plot involves much more than changing the fairy tale happy ending into a poignant, powerful tragedy.[28] Crucial is the emphasis upon the father-figure in a standard daughter-father fantasy. In other words, *King Lear* is a girl's fairy tale told from the father's point of view. Upon the fairy tale frame have been woven intricate philosophical and religious patterns which reveal the marvelous complexity of man.[29] Yet despite the sophistica-tion of the overlay, the strongly articulated attitudes towards sexu-ality, the unmistakable expression of sibling rivalry, and the playing out of the Electra complex in *King Lear* provide abundant evidence for the view that the fairy tale frame is never really absent. That a "kissing cousin" of Cinderella, one of the world's most beloved and celebrated fairy tales, could have been metamorphosed into one of the great literary dramatic masterpieces of the stage is an eternal tribute to the unequalled creative genius of Shakespeare.

NOTES

[1]Alan Dundes, "The Study of Folklore in Literature and Culture: Identification and Interpretation," *Journal of American Folklore*, LXXVIII (1965), 136–142, re-printed in Dundes, *Analytic Essays in Folklore* (The Hague, 1975), pp. 28–34.

[2]Unfortunately, the best and most comprehensive survey of possible and probable relationships between Chaucer's *Canterbury Tales* and traditional tale types is located in a fairly obscure publication, namely in a report of an international congress which appeared as a volume (XXII) of the Greek folklore journal *Laographia.* See Francis Lee Utley, "Some Implications of Chaucer's Folktales," in *IV International Congress for Folk Narrative Research in Athens,* Georgios A. Megas, ed., (Athens, 1965), pp. 588-599.

[3]The standard reference for tale types is Stith Thompson's second revision of Antti Aarne's *The Types of the Folktale,* FF Communications 184 (Helsinki, 1961). Motif numbers refer to Stith Thompson, *Motif-Index of Folk Literature,* 6 vols. (Bloomington, 1955-58). For a sample of how folklorists approach folktales in Shakespeare, see Max Lüthi, "Shakespeare und das Märchen,"*Zeitschrift für Volks-kunde,* LIII (1956-57), 141-149, reprinted in Lüthi, *Volksmarchen und Volkssage: Zwei Grundformen Erzrahlender Dichtung* (Bern, 1961), pp. 109-117; Katharine M. Briggs, "The Folds of Folklore," *Shakespeare Survey,* XVII (1964), 167-179; and Jan Harold Brunvand, "The Folktale Origin of The Taming of the Shrew," *Shakespeare Quarterly,* XVII (1966), 345-359. For *King Lear* in particular, see Giuseppe Cocchiara, *La Leggenda di Re Lear* (Torino, 1932), which is briefly summarized in F.D. Hoeniger, "The Artist Exploring the Primitive: King Lear," in Rosalie L. Colie and F.T. Flahiff, eds., *Some Facets of King Lear: Essays in Prismatic Criticism* (Toronto, 1974), pp. 98-100. (I am indebted to my colleague Norman Rabkin for the latter reference.)

[4]E. Sidney Hartland, "The Outcast Child," *Folk-Lore Journal,* IV (1886), 308-349; Marian Roalfe Cox, *Cinderella,* Publications of the Folk-Lore Society XXXI (London, 1893), pp. xxv, 80-86.

[5]Wilfrid Perrett, *The Story of King Lear from Geoffrey of Monmouth to Shakespeare,* Palaestra XXXV (Berlin, 1904), pp. 9-15, 27, 283; Geoffrey Bullough, *Narrative and Dramatic Sources of Shakespeare,* Vol. VII (London, 1973), p. 271.

[6]Kenneth Muir, *Shakespeare's Sources,* I, Comedies and Tragedies (London, 1961), pp. 141-166.

[7]Vladimir Propp, *Morphology of the Folktale* (Austin, 1968). The final function of Propp's series of thirty-one which he claims comprises the basic structure of Russian fairy tales is "The Hero Is Married and Ascends the Throne." Since the first function is "One of the Members of a Family Absents Himself from Home," Propp's morphology would appear to suggest that fairy tales depict in the form of fantasy the movement of a young man or woman away from the initial family situation towards the formation of a new family unit through marriage.

[8]Cox, *Cinderella,* pp. 85, 81.

[9]Anna Birgitta Rooth, *The Cinderella Cycle* (Lund, 1951), pp. 14-15, 19-20.

[10]Cox, *Cinderella,* p. xxv.

[11]Rooth, p. 10. Even though Stith Thompson does treat "Love Like Salt" as a distinct tale type (923), he does, in the discussion of its plot, refer explicitly and exclusively to the analysis of tale type 510, Cinderella and Cap o' Rushes, for its content. This implies that the "Love Like Salt" story can be considered as an abridged form of the basic tale type 510.

[12]J.S.H. Bransom, *The Tragedy of King Lear* (Oxford, 1934), pp. 221, 9. For a useful discussion of Freud's interpretations of *King Lear,* see Norman N. Holland, *Psychoanalysis and Shakespeare* (New York, 1964), pp. 64-66.

[13]Sigmund Freud, "The Theme of the Three Caskets," in *Collected Papers*, Vol. IV (New York, 1959), pp. 244–256, reprinted in M.D. Faber, *The Design Within: Psychoanalytic Approaches to Shakespeare* (New York, 1970), pp. 195–206. For an account of the reaction to Freud's early interpretation of *King Lear*, see Kenneth Muir, "Some Freudian Interpretations of Shakespeare," *Proceedings of the Leeds Philosophical and Literary Society*, VII (1952), p. 47. Judging from other surveys of psychoanalytic criticism of *King Lear*, Freud's first interpretation has had little impact. See Holland, *Psychoanalysis and Shakespeare*, pp. 214–219, and M.D. Faber, *The Design Within*, pp. 207–231.

[14]Arpad Pauncz, "Psychopathology of Shakespeare's 'King Lear,'" *American Imago*, IX (1952), 57–78. Other discussions of the father-daughter incest theme in the play include: John Donnelly, "Incest, Ingratitude and Insanity: Aspects of the Psychopathology of King Lear," *Psychoanalytic Review*, XL (1953), 149–153; F.L. Lucas, *Literature and Psychology* (Ann Arbor, 1957), pp. 62–71; Mark Kanzer, "Imagery in King Lear," *American Imago*, XXII (1965), 3–13; Paul A. Jorgensen, *Lear's Self-Discovery* (Berkeley and Los Angeles, 1967), pp. 128–129; S.C.V. Stetner and Oscar B. Goodman, "Lear's Darker Purpose," *Literature and Psychology*, XVIII (1968), 82–90; William H. Chaplin, "Form and Psychology in *King Lear*," *Literature and Psychology*, XIX, no. 3–4 (1969), 31–45, Simon O. Lesser, "Act One, Scene One, of Lear," *College English*, 32 (1970–1971), 155–171, and Leslie Fiedler, *The Stranger in Shakespeare* (New York, 1972), pp. 209–220. Sometimes critics sense the nature of the father-daughter relationship without actually mentioning the word incest. See, for example, Stanley Cavell, "The Avoidance of Love: A Reading of *King Lear*," in *Must We Mean What We Say?* (New York, 1969), pp. 267–353.

[15]Horace Howard Furness, ed., *A New Variorum Edition of Shakespeare: King Lear* (Philadelphia, 1880), p. 383.

[16]Freud articulated this particular transformation in a 1911 paper. See "Psycho-Analytic Notes Upon an Autobiographical Account of a Case of Paranoia (Dementia Paranoides)," *Collected Papers*, Vol. III (New York, 1959), p. 449. In the present fairy tale context, the relevant transformation would be "I love him" becoming "He loves me."

[17]Otto Rank, *The Myth of the Birth of the Hero* (New York, 1959), p. 72.

[18]Perrett, p. 241. Chambers was also troubled by Cordelia's suicide in the majority of literary versions of the plot. See R.W. Chambers, *King Lear* (Glasgow, 1940).

[19]M.D. Faber, "Some Remarks on the Suicide of King Lear's Eldest Daughter," *University Review*, XXXIII (1967), 313–317. With respect to the assessment of guilt, it is tempting to see a shift from Lear's saying "I did her wrong" (I,v,25) about Cordelia to his saying "You do me wrong . . ." (IV,vii,44) to Cordelia.

[20]Robert Bechtold Heilman, *This Great Stage: Image and Structure in King Lear* (Baton Rouge, 1948), pp. 93, 104.

[21]Bransom, p. 160, n. 1.

[22]S.C.V. Stetner and Oscar B. Goodman, "Lear's Darker Purpose," *Literature and Psychology*, XVIII (1968), p. 86.

[23]Paul A. Jorgensen, *Lear's Self-Discovery* (Berkeley and Los Angeles, 1967), p. 128; Stetner and Goodman, p. 86; Marvin Rosenberg, *The Masks of King Lear* (Berkeley, 1972), pp. 53, 134. In considering the content of the answers of the daughters to their father's request for a declaration of love, one is reminded of the

third daughter's response in the folktale: "love like salt." The sexual symbolism of salt (as in salacious) has been extensively investigated by Ernest Jones who even mentions the folktale in question. See "The Symbolic Significance of Salt in Folklore and Superstition," in *Essays in Applied Psycho-analysis*, Vol. II, Essays in Folklore, Anthropology and Religion (London, 1951), pp. 22–109. Shakespeare did not use the "love like salt" phrase so common in the folktale source, but it is interesting that he does have Lear refer to himself as "a man of salt" (IV,vi,191). Presumably the reference is simply to crying (salty tears). Still the line does come following a mention of his "most dear daughter" and immediately before his stated intention to "die bravely like a smug bridegroom."

    [24]Holland, pp. 66, 215.

    [25]Ella Freeman Sharpe, "From *King Lear* to *The Tempest*," in *Collected Papers on Psycho-Analysis* (London, 1950), p. 216. See also William H. Chaplin, "Form and Psychology in *King Lear*," *Literature and Psychology*, XIX, no. 3–4 (1969), p. 45, n. 7. In this connection, Holland, p. 65, reminds us that Freud confessed to Ferenczi that his interest in the play was very probably conditioned by his own close relationship to his daughter Anna.

    [26]Eric Partridge, *Shakespeare's Bawdy* (New York, 1960).

    [27]Cf. Robert H. West, "Sex and Pessimism in *King Lear*," *Shakespeare Quarterly*, XI (1960), p. 58.

    [28]Katharine M. Briggs, "The Folds of Folklore," *Shakespeare Survey*, XVII (1964), p. 172. Of course, the very use of fairy tale as signalled by the love-test scene at the outset probably serves to suggest to the audience that there is likely to be a happy ending. This makes the final outcome of the play even more tragic than it would have been without the explicit fairy tale frame.

    [29]It cannot be stressed too strongly that a psychoanalytic reading of *King Lear* is but one interpretation of a play which has inspired dozens. Too often psychoanalytic critics give the impression that they believe their reading is *the* rather than *a* meaning of a literary text. The folkloristic and psychoanalytic perspectives utilized in this essay do not pretend to explicate all facets of the play.

Beyond Morphology: Lévi-Strauss and the Analysis of Folktales

David Pace

Folklorists may be reluctant to apply psychological theories to folktales, but they have proved at least willing to consider some type of structural analysis in studying tales. The translation of Russian folklorist Vladimir Propp's 1928 Morphology of the Folktale *into English in 1958 and the influential writings of the French anthropologist Claude Lévi-Strauss, from his 1955 essay in the* Journal of American Folklore, *"The Structural Study of Myth," and his tour de force "The Story of Asdiwal" (in Edmund Leach, ed.,* The Structural Study of Myth and Totemism *[London: Tavistock, 1967], pp. 1–47) to his four-volume magnum opus on South American Indian myths,* Introduction to a Science of Mythology *(*Mythologiques*)—The Raw and the Cooked (New York, 1969); From Honey to Ashes (New York, 1973),* The Origin of Table Manners *(New York, 1979) and* The Naked Man *(New York, 1981)—have produced a flood of structuralist readings of myths and tales. For an idea of the range of such studies, see Bengt Holbek, "Formal and Structural Studies of Oral Narrative: A Bibliography,"* Unifol, *1977 [Copenhagen: Institut for Folkemindevidenskab, Københavns, Universitet, 1978], 149–193. For a sample of critical overviews, see Joseph Courtes,* Lévi-Strauss et les contraintes de la pensée mythique *(Tours: Maison Mame, 1973); Alan Dundes, "Structuralism and*

Reprinted from *Folklore Forum*, 10, No. 2 (1977), 1–7.

Folklore," Studia Fennica, *20 (1976), 75-93; L.L. Thomas, J.Z. Kronenfeld, and D.B. Kronenfeld, "Asdiwal Crumbles: A Critique of Lévi-Straussian Myth Analysis,*" American Ethnologist, *3 (1976), 147-173.*
    It was only a matter of time before structuralists turned to Cinderella. One of the first of such attempts was Pierre Maranda's "Cendrillon et la theorie des ensembles. Essai de définition structurale," in *Strutture e Generi delle Letterature Ethniche, Atti del Simposio Internazionale Palermo 5-10 Aprile 1970 (Palermo: S.F. Flaccovio, 1978), pp. 101-114 (also in C. Chabrol, ed.,* Semiotique, narrative et textuelle [Paris: Librairie Larousse, 1973], pp. 122-136). *Other studies in the same tradition include Joseph Courtès, "De la description à la spécificité du conte populaire merveilleux français,*" Ethnologie francaise, *2 (1972), 9-42; the same author's "Une lecture semiotique de 'Cendrillon,'" in Joseph Courtès,* Introduction à la sémiotique narrative et discursive: méthodologie et application *(Paris, 1976), pp. 109-138; and the joint essay by A.J. Greimas and J. Courtès, "Cendrillon va au bal . . . Les rôles et les figures dans la littérature orale française,*" in *Systèmes de Signes (Paris, 1978), pp. 243-257. Another essay more or less in the structuralist mold is Timothy C. Murray, "A Marvelous Guide to Anamorphosis: Cendrillon ou La Petite Pantoufle de Verre,*" Modern Language Notes, *91 (1976), 1276-1295. Structuralist interpretations, like so many anthropological analyses of folk narrative, have a consistent habit of reducing a story plot to a series of binary oppositions involving kinship relations.*
    The essay chosen for inclusion in this volume by David Pace, Professor in the departments of History and West European Studies at Indiana University, is a remarkably lucid albeit brief account of structuralism followed by a demonstration analysis of Cinderella. Except for the insistence on calling the Cinderella story a "myth"— in strict folkloristic parlance, a myth is a sacred narrative telling how the world or man came to be in their present form—the discussion is exemplary.

    There is a kind of residual Hegelianism which still constrains us to seek an underlying unity, a single *Zeitgeist,* behind the bewildering intellectual diversity we find around us. In recent years this tendency has nowhere been more obvious than in the attempt to "discover" (i.e., create) a single Structuralism from a number of quite distinct intellectual positions. One might quote a number of such attempts to define a single "structuralist" field of inquiry, but in the discipline of folklore the most significant early effort to create a broad definition of the methodology was probably that of Alan Dundes, who in his 1964 study of *The Morphology of North American Indian Tales* provided an early overview of structuralism. Characterizing as "structural" the work of Vladimir Propp, Claude Lévi-Strauss, and their followers, he related their work to a wide range of different disciplines:

> The structural approach to folklore in general and to folktales in particular is entirely in keeping with new approaches to a variety of other disciplines. It has affinities with Formalism and New Criticism in literary theory; synchronic structural linguistics, Gestalt psychology, and the pattern approach in anthropology.[1]

While this kind of broad characterization of structuralism was quite common in the 1960s, it seems unwarranted from the perspective of the 1970s. Dundes has cast his net so broadly that it is not at all clear what he has caught. The fact that these diverse methodologies are held together by undefined "affinities"—a word whose alchemical origin points to its mystical significance—suggests the uselessness of such a loose umbrella concept.

But even within Dundes' narrower conception of structuralism, even among those approaches to folklore which he refers to as "structural," there would seem to be a great deal of diversity. By using this term to characterize the work of both Propp and Lévi-Strauss, Dundes creates the impression that these two writers have something basic in common, that they share some assumptions or approaches which are hidden from the superficial reader. This is a claim which must be explored, because if this linguistic conflation of the systems of Propp and Lévi-Strauss is not warranted, the thought of both thinkers may be distorted by faulty categorization. Lévi-Strauss may be unjustly transformed into a Proppian-in-French clothing, or Propp may be seen as a proto-structuralist who had simply restricted the use of the paradigm to a limited number of Russian folktales.

In justice to Dundes, it should be noted that he did draw a certain distinction between the methodology of Propp and that of Lévi-Strauss. The former he characterized as a "syntagmatic" structuralism, which searched for the linear sequential structure contained in the plot of the story. The latter—that of Lévi-Strauss—was "paradigmatic," in which the material was rearranged in search of the structural oppositions which gave a pattern to the story as a whole.[2]

This distinction between syntagmatic and paradigmatic approaches is very important, but it in no way exhausts the differences between a Proppian folktale analysis and a Lévi-Straussian study of myth. The contrasts between the two methodologies is so great, in fact, that a closer analysis suggests that the only reason that they were ever associated under the same rubric was that neither fit into older schools of thought.

The gap between the two thinkers was made quite explicit by Lévi-Strauss himself in a 1960 review of Propp's *Morphology of the Folktale*. He began by drawing a basic distinction between form and structure. "Contrary to formalism," Lévi-Strauss wrote, "structuralism refuses to set the concrete against the abstract and to recognize a privileged value in the latter. *Form* is defined by opposition to material other than itself. But *structure* has no distinct content; it is content itself, apprehended in a logical organization conceived as property of the real."[3]

The distinction may be seen in the manner in which the two scholars approach the analysis of their respective material. Propp begins with a series of tales and divides the elements within the entire group into two categories: variables and constants. On one hand are the concrete names and attributes of the characters which change from tale to tale. On the other hand are the abstract functions of the characters, which remain the same. It is this second category of formal constants which Propp studies. The details introduced by particular storytellers are completely outside his purview.[4]

Propp then develops a complex analysis of the formal patterns of the 101 tales in his sample. He demonstrates that each of the characters in these tales may be seen as fulfilling one or more of thirty-one functions and that all the stories are made up by arranging some subset of these functions in a prescribed order.

The details of Propp's scheme are not of relevance here. What is important is his division of the universe of oral tales into two incommensurate orders: the functions, which are abstract, general, and invariant; and the content, which is specific to a particular tale and is the creation of the storyteller. Given this division, most of the specific details of the story are part of the telling, not of the tale; they are, in the language of Saussure, elements of *parole,* not of *langue.*

Lévi-Strauss' approach is very different. He begins not with a series of tales, but rather with a single myth. He seeks oppositions between specific qualities, such as high and low, wet and dry, raw and cooked, honey and tobacco, and then seeks to reconstruct the grid of oppositions through which the native culture speaks. In a sense he abstracts from the concrete stories before him. But his abstract patterns are always grounded in the relationships between concrete elements in specific myths.

Dundes has attempted to minimize the significance of the distinction between form and content. Most scholars, he argued, use the terms interchangeably. Moreover, Lévi-Strauss himself has on occasion so departed from the concrete that he has used abstract mathematical models to describe particular myths.[5]

But these comments do not address the crucial methodological distinctions drawn by Lévi-Strauss. When Propp approaches a new tale, he does so with Platonic forms in mind. The tale is always generated by the abstract functions and then elaborated with concrete details. But these details are not relevant to understanding the form of the tale.

A Lévi-Straussian analysis, by contrast, is always immanent—one might even say Aristotelian. The structure is discovered by creating a model of the relationship between the elements in a particular myth. The details are of primary importance. If a character is described as the "Butterfly-Woman" or is said to climb up a tree rather than down, these facts are of primary importance. It is through the juxtaposition of these sorts of details that the structure is created.

Thus, Propp can describe his work as a morphology. In his system there is a distinction between form and content which allows him to study the former in isolation. For Lévi-Strauss, morphological studies are impossible. Borrowing from his mentor Marcel Mauss, he views all human structures as embedded in concrete human practices and perceptions.[6] Without the media there is no message.

This methodological distinction has immense practical implications. As a natural corollary to his approach, Propp's tales are automatically isolated from the society in which they are told, whereas Lévi-Strauss' myths are always embedded within a particular culture. Propp's studies remain horizontal and present the formal interrelations between elements within folktales. Lévi-Strauss' analyses are, at least in theory, vertical and bridge the gap between the myth and the concrete elements in the life of a people.

Dundes recognized this distinction and praised Lévi-Strauss for his notion of the myth as a model of social relations. But once again, he minimized the distinction by implying that Propp's analysis is only the first step in a very complex process of reconstructing a complete oral tradition. "Possible correlations of structural models of folklore with other aspects of culture," he wrote, "can come only after such models are accurately identified."[7]

But, once again, Dundes has characterized as trivial and practical a distinction which is actually crucial and theoretical. Propp's morphology—isolated as it is in a realm of pure form—has no direct point of tangency with the everyday world. It can be related to the broader cultural context only by introducing new and alien concepts. In Lévi-Strauss' structural anthropology, by contrast, the concentration upon concrete elements keeps the analyst in constant contact with the culture and its environment. When, for example, Lévi-Strauss studies the symbolic opposition within a myth between boiling and broiling or between marrying in and marrying out, he is not far removed from the study of material conditions or custom. Thus, the transition from myth to social context is a smooth and continuous one.

This distinction should be quite obvious even to the casual reader of the works of these two students of oral tales. Propp's *Morphology* deals strictly with the tale itself, but in Lévi-Strauss' *Mythologiques* there are innumerable references to ethnographic details not specifically contained in the story.

Thus, Propp's Soviet censors were correct: his work is totally antithetical to the Marxist concept of the primacy of material conditions. Lévi-Strauss, by contrast, can argue that he has developed a science of superstructures created by Marx.[8] This claim may be exaggerated, but it is clear that Lévi-Strauss does view each myth as an intersection between preexisting versions of the story and modifications induced by changes in the social or environmental infrastructure.[9]

It should be clear from what has been said that adherence to the methodology of Lévi-Strauss would produce a very different type of folklore than that created by the followers of Propp. But, in fact, the implications of Lévi-Strauss' approach generally have not been recognized. Scholars either have completely ignored his distinction between formal and structural studies, or they have acknowledged the distinction and then openly chosen to ignore it.[10] In either case, the result has most often been morphological studies which deal only with the forms of oral tradition and not with its specific content.

To counter this tendency, I will present in the following pages a brief demonstration of the manner in which Lévi-Strauss' method of myth analysis can be used to relate a story back to its social and ideological context. I have chosen a very immediate and contemporary tale—the story of Cinderella as reproduced by a group of college students. This version undoubtedly owes as much to the technicians of the Disney studios as to the informants of the brothers Grimm. But, as Lévi-Strauss has pointed out, in a structural analysis of a myth all versions share a certain aspect of the same message. Moreover, the use of such a commonly known story avoids the necessity of a lengthy repetition of the tale or a detailed discussion of the social infrastructure of premodern Germany.[11]

The outline of the contemporary Cinderella myth is simple. The death of her father consigns the beautiful Cinderella to the role of scullery maid, while her wicked stepmother and two ugly stepsisters enjoy the riches of the house. When these ungenerous step-relatives leave to attend the royal ball, Cinderella is left behind. Her fairy godmother, however, intervenes, and after a series of magical transformations Cinderella is sent off to the ball with all the trappings of wealth, but with the admonition that she must return before midnight. At the ball, the prince falls in love with Cinderella, but at the stroke of midnight she flees the palace, leaving behind the glass slipper her fairy godmother had created for her. The prince, determined to marry this mysterious beauty, searches the kingdom for the woman who can fit into the tiny slipper. The stepsisters attempt to put it on and fight among themselves, but only Cinderella can wear it. The story ends with the marriage of Cinderella and the humiliation of her stepmother and stepsisters.

A Proppian, faced with this story, would begin by seeking to identify the various segments of the plot with the functions common to that particular type of tale. If the functions in contemporary American children's stories resembled those in Propp's sample, one might, for example, identify Cinderella's desire to go to the ball with function VIIIa ("lack"), or the gift of the coach, footmen, and so on, with function XIV ("provision or receipt of a magic agent"). Then the functions would be arranged according to an invariant order, a diagram of the succession of functions created, and the analysis would be complete. Something would have been learned about the formal patterns which lie behind this genre of stories, but the tale would remain completely isolated.

A Lévi-Straussian analysis would begin at a different place and move towards a very different conclusion. All concern with sequential development in time would be dropped, and instead the analyst would search for oppositions between concrete elements.

In a study of Cinderella, for example, a structuralist might begin not with the individual characters which appear at the beginning of the story, but rather with the configuration of relations among these characters. This pattern may be expressed in a simple diagram:

Diagram #1

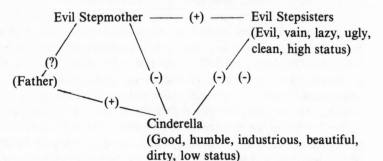

The dramatic tension in this story can be grasped readily from this diagram: the qualities ascribed to Cinderella and to her stepsisters respectively are not homologous. In the world of fairy tales the qualities "good," "humble," "industrious," and "beautiful" should be associated with cleanliness and high status. Conversely, the negative characteristics of the stepsisters should be associated with dirtiness and low social status. In other words, the external, social signs of virtue have not been assigned to the right persons.

This contradiction provides the dramatic core of the story and is resolved at the end of the tale, as may be seen from a second structural diagram:

Diagram #2

Final Situation ("They lived happily ever after")

Prince ——— (+) ——— Cinderella
(Good, humble, beautiful, clean, very high status)

(-)

Stepmother ——— (+) ——— Stepsisters
(Evil, vain, lazy, low status, and, in some versions of the story, dirty)

The initial imbalance in the story has been corrected by a transformation of status relations and justice prevails.[12]

These structural diagrams provide an insight into both the causes of the initial imbalance and the factors which re-established equilibrium. The story may be viewed in terms of an economy of the sexes. The removal of a male at the beginning of the story (through the death of the father) created an initial imbalance which could only be rectified by the introduction of a new male (the prince).

This pattern can also be viewed, on an ideological level, as a restatement of certain conditions which exist in the infrastructure of society. It is clearly implied that only blood or marriage ties can hold a family together. Once Cinderella is isolated within a family unit without the protection of either form of social linkage, she is exploited and treated not as a family member, but rather as a servant.

This situation can be rectified only by removing her from this unstable, uncemented family and by forming a new unit through her marriage to the prince.

Viewed from another perspective, the transition from the initial to the final situations conveys messages about social mobility. As Michel Butor has argued, many fairy tales provide children with the promise that they will be able to gain status and independence as they mature and form their own families.[13] In the Cinderella myth this theme of mobility through maturation is combined with an adult myth that it is possible to move from the scullery to the palace, provided one is patient and undemanding. Behind both notions of social mobility lies the belief that there is an innate justice within the social system and that wrongs will eventually be righted.

It is also interesting that in both the adult and the childhood fantasies, marriage rather than social change is presented as the means of escaping an inferior social position. Moreover, the marriageable females are treated as incomplete and in need of immediate union with a male of high social position. Thus, to reduce a rich story to a cold equation, it might be said that in the Cinderella myth, unmarried-low status and married-high status.

But the story of Cinderella does not consist solely of a beginning and an end. In between there appear two episodes which provide dramatic tension and color and which reinforce the ideological messages of the story. These two episodes involve the intervention of the fairy godmother and of the prince. The first may be summarized in this diagram:

Diagram #3:
　　　　　　Mediation 1 (Supernatural, temporary)
Fairy Godmother
(very high status)

$$\neq$$

(Stepmother)　　　　　　　　　　Footmen, horses, coach, and
　　　　　　　　　　　　　　　　gown (signs of high status)

　　　　　　　　　Cinderella

Mice, rats, pumpkin, and rags
(signs of low status)

In this episode a supernatural being (the fairy godmother) intervenes to redress the imbalance of the initial episode. Her identity is of great interest because she stands in implicit contrast to the stepmother. These two roles (stepmother and godmother) are sociologically the closest to that of the biological mother. But the qualities attributed to these two figures are diametrically opposed. The stepmother is demanding and selfish, favors her natural children, and is defined as the protagonist's father's wife. The fairy godmother, by contrast, is giving and generous, is concerned with Cinderella rather than with her stepsisters, and has no romantic or sexual connection with the father. The Oedipal implications of this division are obvious. It is clear that on a psychological level, the myth simply has divided the real mother—a being for whom the most violently conflicting emotions are experienced—into two different mother surrogates: the stepmother, who may be hated without guilt, and the godmother, who may be loved without reservation.

But this same opposition is also used to express another basic social tension. The stepmother treats Cinderella as a servant. She is only concerned about her charge's immediate economic value. The fairy godmother, who is removed from all economic considerations, prepares Cinderella for marriage. Thus, the opposition between the two surrogate mothers expresses not only an Oedipal ambivalence on the part of children, but also a social ambivalence on the part of mothers. On the one hand, mothers have an economic motive for exploiting their daughters and for keeping them at home. On the other hand, they have a social duty to expend money on them and to prepare them for marriage.

The fairy godmother's method of aiding Cinderella is also interesting. As a supernatural being, she can see the natural virtues of this poor scullery maid. Thus, her task—both as a "good" mother and as a force for justice—is to bring Cinderella's outward, cultural attributes into harmony with her internal, natural qualities.

The fairy godmother achieves this goal by transforming the signs which accompany Cinderella's low status (mice, rats, the pumpkin, and rags) into signs of high status (footmen, horses, a carriage, and a gown). This transformation of cultural signs sets the stage for the general recognition of Cinderella's natural qualities.

The magic of the fairy godmother is, however, temporary, and when this episode is compared with the next this fact takes on a new significance. In this portion of the story, the prince searches for the woman who can fit into the glass slipper left at the ball, and in the process he elevates Cinderella to a position of very high status.

Diagram #4

Mediation 2 (Sociological, permanent)

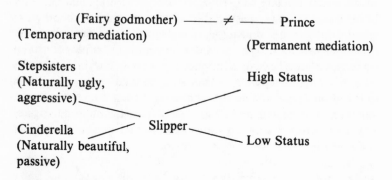

Just as the role of the fairy godmother is defined from the previous episode through its opposition to that of the stepmother, so the role of the prince is defined in opposition to that of the fairy godmother. The fairy godmother, as the "good" mother, can make Cinderella's plight less painful, and she can prepare her for the social recognition of her natural qualities. But this supernatural being is female and as such is incapable of permanently altering Cinderella's position in society. The prince, however, is a man and the social laws dictate that as a male he is able to change the situation permanently. Thus in this episode, the slipper, a gift of the positive mother surrogate, allows the prince to test the natural goodness of Cinderella and to rectify the imbalance between nature and culture which created the dramatic tension of the story.

The ideological messages of the story are furthered by the contrasts between the female characters in this episode. The active attempts of the two stepsisters to win the prince are treated as negative, whereas the passive and shy Cinderella is rewarded. Moreover, the stepsisters are often presented as willing to betray one another to win the favor of the prince, once again suggesting that relationships between women are unstable unless they are mediated by a man.

As this brief and sketchy analysis of the Cinderella tale indicates, the differences between a Proppian and a Lévi-Straussian analysis are overwhelming. On one hand, the result is a better understanding of the abstract form of a specific tale; on the other is an analysis which embeds the story tightly in a particular social context. With Propp we have a study which is relatively closed and hermeneutic, which relates the tale only to other tales of the same genre. With Lévi-Strauss we have an analysis which opens the tale to the outer world, which relates it to sex, age, and class roles and to the power relations of the society in which it is transmitted. With the formalist we have a method which is automatically apolitical (i.e., conservative), while the structuralist offers an approach which can be used to reveal the origin and nature of ideology. Thus, from that slender gap between form and structure a vast division has come into being, a division which forces a vital choice upon all future students of culture.

NOTES

[1]Alan Dundes, *The Morphology of North American Indian Folktales, Folklore Fellows Communications* 195 (1964): 32.

[2]Alan Dundes, "The Making and Breaking of Friendship as a Structural Frame in African Folk Tales," *Structural Analysis of Oral Tradition*, eds., Pierre Maranda and Elli Köngäs Maranda (Philadelphia, 1971), pp. 171–172; Alan Dundes, "Introduction to the Second Edition" in Vladimir Propp, *Morphology of the Folktale* (Austin, 1968), pp. xi–xii.

[3]Claude Lévi-Strauss, "Structure and Form: Reflections on a Work by Vladimir Propp," *Structural Anthropology*, Vol. II (New York, 1976), p. 115.

[4]Propp, *Morphology of the Folktale*, pp. 20, 112–13.

[5]Dundes, *North American Indian Folktales*, p. 57.

[6]Claude Lévi-Strauss, "Introduction à l'Oeuvre de Marcel Mauss," in Marcel Mauss, *Sociologie et Anthropologie* (Paris, 1950), pp. xiv–xxx, xxxiii.

[7]Dundes, "Making and Breaking of Friendship," p. 174. See also Dundes' "Introduction," in Propp, *Morphology of the Folktale*, p. xiii.

[8]Claude Lévi-Strauss, *The Savage Mind* (Chicago, 1966), p. 130.

[9]Claude Lévi-Strauss, *L'Homme Nu* (Paris, 1971), p. 562.

[10]Elli Köngäs Maranda and Pierre Maranda, *Structural Models in Folklore and Transformational Essays* (The Hague, 1971). p. 31.

[11]It is interesting to note that the characteristic "industrious" is no longer relevant to Cinderella when she reaches a very high status in society. While the

audience is apt to assume that she has not lost this trait, it has no form of expression in her new situation. This asymmetry in the transformation points to another distinction implicit in the story—that between those levels of society at which women must concern themselves with work and those at which they are expected to remain idle.

[12]Michel Butor, "On Fairy Tale" in *European Literary Theory and Practice from Existential Phenomenology to Structuralism*, ed., Vernon W. Gras (New York, 1973), pp. 349–362.

[13]As an historian interested in the theoretical concerns of folklorists but untrained in the methodology of collecting folktales, I collected this version of "Cinderella" from a group of students in a seminar on structuralism at Indiana University, Bloomington, Indiana, in the fall of 1976.

Hanchi: A Kannada Cinderella

A.K. Ramanujan

*Different theoretical approaches are not necessarily mutually ex-
clusive, and a truly eclectic scholar may find that it is precisely a
combination of approaches which yields the greatest insight. In this
unusual essay, A.K. Ramanujan, Professor of Dravidian Studies
and Linguistics at the University of Chicago, who is a poet, a
linguist, and a folklorist, draws on a variety of theoretical concepts
to illuminate a tale he collected himself in 1955. The reader should
note that the tale analyzed is technically a version of tale type 510B,
The Dress of Gold, of Silver, and of Stars, rather than type 510A,
Cinderella. Professor Ramanujan's use of Propp and Lévi-Strauss
brings structural criteria to bear on the tale and he also borrows
from Freud (symbolism) and Jung (individuation). This suggests
that both structural and psychological approaches may be produc-
tively employed in the same analysis. Not only does Professor
Ramanujan offer a reading of an Indic tale, but he also elucidates
the Grimm text of Cinderella.*

*It is surprising, in view of French folklorist Emmanuel Cosquin's
suggestion that Cinderella may have originated in India, that there
have previously been so very few studies of Indian Cinderella stories.
For Cosquin's views, see "La Pantoufle de Cendrillon dans l'Inde,"*
Revue des Traditions Populaires, *28 (1913), 241-269. See also his
"'Le Cendrillon' Masculin,"* Revue des Traditions Populaires, *33
(1918), 193-202; "Cendrillon sur la Tombe de sa Mère,"* Revue des
Traditions Populaires, *33 (1918), 202-233; and "Une Variante de
'Cendrillon' et un Épisode de 'Dame Holle,'"* Revue des Traditions

Populaires, *33* (*1918*), *245-253. For a more recent discussion of several versions, see P. Goswami, "The Cinderella Motif in Assamese Folk-Tales,"* Indian Historical Quarterly, *23* (*1947*), *311-319.*

1

In this essay, I attempt a study of individuation in a well-known folktale. Worldwide types, forms, and motifs are reworked by a local (illiterate) teller into a uniquely patterned *story.* Both the pattern and the motifs are seen as signifiers. Though the typical structures are common, the realized tale means different things in different cultures, times, and media. It is regarded here not merely as the variant of a tale-type, a cultural object, a psychological witness (or symptom), etc., but primarily as an *aesthetic* work. I believe that, in such tales, the aesthetic is the first and the experienced dimension, through which ethos and worldview are revealed. The other kinds of meanings (psychological, social, etc.) are created, and carried, by the primary, experiential, aesthetic forms and meanings.

Let me begin by telling you the Kannada story as I heard it in Kittūr, in a North Karnatak village, from a sixty-five-year-old Virasaiva woman named Chennamma, in 1955.

The Story of Hanchi[1]

An old woman had two children—a son and a daughter. The girl had golden hair, but the brother had not noticed it. One day, when both of them were grown up and the girl was a lovely young woman with hair of gold,[2] he happened to notice it and at once fell in love with her.

He went to his mother and begged her to give his sister in marriage to him. The poor old woman was shocked and knew at once that disaster was ahead. But she hid her feelings and sent him to the nearby town to bring all the rice and flour and lentils for the wedding. As soon as he had left the house she went to her daughter and said to her: "Daughter, the time has come for you to leave me.

You're as good as dead to me after this day. You're too beautiful to live here in safety. You have hair of gold; no one can look at it without desire. So I shall get a mask made for you; it will hide your face and save you from future danger." Then she ran to the potter and gave him a gold vessel and bought a clay mask to fit her daughter's face. That very night she sent away her daughter with the parting words, "Never remove the mask from your face, till your situation is better." When her daughter was gone, the poor woman poisoned herself in grief. When the son came home next day he found his sister gone and his mother dead; he went mad and became a wandering madman.

The girl wandered from place to place as long as her mother's bundle of bread and rice lasted. She changed her name to Hanchi.[3] She would stop by wayside brooks, untie her bundle of bread, and eat at noon and by moonlight.

At last she came to a place very far from her home town and struck up acquaintance with an old woman who gave her food and shelter. One day the old woman came home and said that a nearby *Saukar* (rich man) wanted a servant maid, and that she had arranged to send Hanchi to his place. Hanchi agreed and went to the big house as a servant maid. She was an expert cook, and no one could equal her in making dishes of sweet rice. One day, the *Saukar* wished to eat a banquet in his orchard and ordered Hanchi to make her dishes of sweet rice. That day, everyone in the household went to the orchard for a grand meal—everyone, that is, except Hanchi and a younger son of the *Saukar*, who had gone out. Hanchi thought she was alone, so she heated water for an oil bath. She wished to finish her bath before they all returned. She undid her splendid golden hair, took off her mask, and started bathing. Meanwhile, the young man who had gone out came back home and shouted for the maid. Hanchi did not hear him in the bath-house. Impatiently, he came in search of her, heard noises, peeped in the bath-house, and saw her in all her beauty. He was still young. He ran away before she saw him but fell deeply in love with the glory that was her hair and decided at once to make her his wife.

As soon as his mother returned from the orchard he took her aside and told her of his desire. She was quite puzzled by her son's fascination with a black-faced servant maid. She asked him not to make a fool of himself over a dark, unlovely lass and promised to get him a really good-looking bride from a rich family, if he would wait a little. But he would not hear of it. He was stubborn, and they had a heated argument at the end of which he took her to Hanchi, put his hand to her face, snatched off her mask, and dashed it to the ground. There stood Hanchi, in all her natural loveliness, crowned by her splendid tresses of gold. The mother was struck dumb by this extraordinary beauty and found her son's infatuation quite understandable. Moreover, she had always liked the modest, good-natured Hanchi. She took the bashful Hanchi with her to her inner chamber, where she asked her a few questions, listened to her strange story, and liked her all the better for it. At the first auspicious moment, Hanchi was married to the young man.

The newlyweds were happy as doves, but their happiness didn't last long. For there was a holy man named Guruswami in the *Saukar's* house; he was the rich man's chief counselor and had a reputation for secret lore and black arts of many kinds. This man had been casting lecherous glances at Hanchi and wanted her for himself. When Hanchi's mother-in-law told him one day of her eagerness to see a grandson by Hanchi, he had his plan ready. He told her that he could make Hanchi conceive with the help of his magic arts and asked her to send Hanchi to him with some plantains, almonds, betel leaves, and nuts.

On an auspicious day Guruswami summoned Hanchi. He had before him all the fruits and nuts, over which he had chanted his magical formulae. If she had eaten them, the magic would have worked on her, and she would have been irresistibly drawn to him. When she visited him, he was chanting secret spells and praying that Hanchi should become his. Hanchi was a clever girl and knew all about these wicked magicians. When he gave her a plantain, she secretly dropped the enchanted fruit into a trough and ate another which she had brought with her. Guruswami went to his room, trusting that his magic would draw her to him and bring her into his waiting arms. While he lay waiting for her, a she-buffalo ate the enchanted plantain in the trough and fell in love with Guruswami. She was in heat and came running to Guruswami's chamber and pushed at his door. Thinking that Hanchi had come, he hastily opened the door and was badly mauled by the amorous buffalo.

But he did not give up. On several days he asked Hanchi's gullible mother-in-law to send Hanchi to him for certain rites. When she came, he gave her enchanted almonds, betel leaves, and nuts. But clever Hanchi played the same old trick on him and ate harmless almonds, leaves, and nuts which she had carefully brought with her. She palmed away Guruswami's gifts, and put them into measures and bowls. As Guruswami lay waiting for her in his bedroom, the measures and vessels came and knocked on his door; he hastily opened his door for the long-awaited Hanchi, and instead of her caresses received hard blows from inanimate vessels which were irresistibly drawn to him. The third time, she threw the nuts at the broomstick in the corner. When Guruswami opened the door and received a thorny broomstick into his greedy arms, he accepted failure and changed his tactics.

He went to his friend, Hanchi's father-in-law, and suggested that they should have another of his picnics in the garden. The old man agreed. As before, Hanchi prepared her fine dishes of sweet rice, and like a good daughter-in-law, she stayed back to look after the house while everyone was away.

When everyone was at the orchard picnic, Guruswami found an excuse to go back home. He told everyone he had left something behind, and hurried home. On his way, he took pieces of men's clothing like coats and turbans; he entered Hanchi's room secretly, planted all of the men's clothing there, and threw bits of chewed betel and smoked stubs of cheroot on the floor.

After planting all of this false evidence in Hanchi's room, he ran breathlessly to the garden, where the family was enjoying itself, and cried: "Your daughter-in-law is a whore! I surprised her with a lover. She has forgotten the dignity of her family, her womanhood. This is sinful; it will bring misfortune to your door! Oh, how wicked!" At these shocking words from their trusted family friend, all of them ran to the house. With righteous indignation, Guruswami showed them the hidden clothing and the telltale cheroot stubs and betel pieces as unquestionable evidence of Hanchi's adultery. Hanchi was as surprised as the rest of them, but her protests were just not heard. She accused Guruswami herself of being a bad man and told them of his black magic, but they all got so angry that they beat her till she had blue welts. When she found that everyone was against her, she became silent and trusted to her fate. They shut her up in a room and starved her for three days, but they got no confession out of her. Her stubborn silence put her husband and his father into fits of rage.

Then Guruswami, finding that his plot prospered, suggested: "All this will not work with this wretched woman. We must punish her properly for her sin. Put her into a big box and give the box to me; I will have it thrown into the river. You are too good to this sinner. Punish her as she deserves!"

Anger and shame had made them blind. They listened to him. She was dragged out, shut up in a box, and handed over to Guruswami. He had it carried out of the house, happy that his plot had succeeded.

Then he thought of a way of getting rid of the servants. He asked them to carry the box to an old woman's house outside town and leave it there till morning, as the river was still a long way off. The old woman was no other than Hanchi's good friend, who had helped her get a job and settle in the town. Guruswami told the old woman that there were ferocious mad dogs in the box; he was taking them to the riverbank to get them killed next day. He asked her to be very careful with it, not to meddle with it or open it lest the dogs should be let loose. When he left her he had scared her more than he had intended to. He promised that he would soon come back to take the dangerous dogs away.

After he left, the old woman heard peculiar noises coming from the box. At first she thought it was the dogs, but then she heard her own name being called. Hanchi, in the box, had recognized her old friend's voice and was calling for help. The old woman cautiously pried open the lid and to her great astonishment found Hanchi crouching inside the box! She helped the miserable girl out of her prison and gave her food and drink, as she appeared to be ravenously hungry. Hanchi told her all about her misfortunes and the villainous Guruswami's plot to get her. The old woman listened carefully, and her mother-wit soon found a way out. She hid Hanchi in an inner room, went into town, procured a muzzled mad dog, and had it locked up in the box. She had taken care to loosen the muzzle before she locked up the dog.

Guruswami was back very soon. He was eager to taste his new power over Hanchi. He came perfumed and singing. When he examined the locks, the old woman assured him in a frightened voice that she had been too scared to even touch the box. He asked her now to leave him alone in the room for his evening prayers.

He closed the door carefully and bolted it from the inside. And calling Hanchi's name lovingly, he threw open the lid of the box. His heart leaped to his mouth when he saw a hideous dog, foaming at the mouth, who sprang upon him and mangled him horribly with its bites. He cursed his own wickedness and cried that he was served right by all-seeing God, who had transformed a woman into a dog! Full of remorse, he called for mercy as he sank down under the dog's teeth. Neighbors, drawn by the cries of the wretched man, soon gathered, and killed the dog. But they could not save Guruswami; he was fatally infected with the rabid dog's lunacy.

Hanchi's husband and his family were shocked by what had happened to their friend Guruswami. Months later, one day, the scheming old woman invited them to her house. The good woman could not rest till she had seen justice done to Hanchi. When Hanchi's people came, the old woman served them a scrumptious meal, wonderful dishes of sweet rice which no once could prepare but Hanchi. They were all reminded of her and felt sad. They naturally asked who the excellent cook was who had equaled Hanchi. Instead of a reply, the old woman presented Hanchi herself in flesh and blood. They were amazed and could not believe their own eyes. They had believed Hanchi was dead and gone, drowned beyond return in the river; Guruswami had got rid of her for them, and the poor fellow had gone mysteriously mad soon after. The old woman cleared up the mystery of Hanchi's reappearance by telling them the true story about her and the villain of the plot, Guruswami.

They were very sorry for what they had done to Hanchi and were ashamed that they had been taken in by such a viper as Guruswami. They cursed him at length and asked Hanchi to pardon them. Hanchi's good days had begun; her luck had turned and brought her every kind of happiness from that day.

2

The Aarne-Thompson Index (1961:175–78) identifies the general type as 510. Their archetype or composite is reconstructed from variants found all over the world (see also Cox, 1893; Rooth, 1951):

510 *Cinderella and Cap o' Rushes.*

I. *The Persecuted Heroine.* (a) The heroine is abused by her stepmother and stepsisters and (a[1]) stays on the hearth or in the ashes and, (a[2]) is dressed in rough clothing—cap of rushes, wooden cloak, etc., (b) flees in disguise from her father who wants to marry her, or (c) is cast out by him because she has said that she loved him like salt, or (d) is to be killed by a servant.

II. *Magic Help.* While she is acting as servant (at home or among strangers) she is advised, provided for, and fed (a) by her dead mother, (b) by a tree on the mother's grave, or (c) by a supernatural being or (d) by birds, or (e) by a goat, or sheep, or a cow. (f) When the goat (cow) is killed, there springs up from her remains a magic tree.

III. *Meeting the Prince.* (a) She dances in beautiful clothing several times with a prince who seeks in vain to keep her, or she is seen by him in church. (b) She gives hints of the abuse she has endured as servant girl, or (c) she is seen her beautiful clothing in her room or in the church.

IV. *Proof of Identity.* (a) She is discovered through the slipper-test or (b) through a ring which she throws into the prince's drink or bakes in his bread. (c) She alone is able to pluck the gold apple desired by the knight.

V. *Marriage with the Prince.*

VI. *Value of Salt.* Her father is served unsalted food and thus learns the meaning of her earlier answer.—Adapted from BP.

Of these possibilities, our variant realizes the following:

I *The Persecuted Heroine:* I(b) The heroine flees in disguise from her father (here, her brother) who wants to marry her.

II *(Magic) Help:* While she is acting as servant (at home or among strangers) she is advised, provided for, and fed by a kind old mother-figure (a variant of IIa, the dead mother?).

III *Meeting the Prince:* Instead of being seen in beautiful clothing, she is seen without her mask (naked?). N716.

IV *Proof of Identity:* She is discovered through a special dish which identifies her—neither IVa, b, nor c.

V *Marriage with the Prince*

I have one Kannada variant which stops here. But our story goes on to a second move (in Propp's sense; see Propp, 1968) with a second villain-figure who initiates the action again. This is really the tale of the Lecherous Holy Man and Maiden in Box (Type 896), which seems to be a special Indian oikotype; the Type-Index lists fifteen Indian variants and none from any other part of the world.[4]

The Hanchi story is distinguished from the other ten Indian variants (see Thompson and Roberts, 1960:73) by the presence of Type 896, which provides it with a second move.

3

Is the addition of Type 896 to Type 510 arbitrary? Does the addition serve a new structure, make a difference in meaning? I think it does both.

The addition of Type 896 is remarkably apt, for it makes for a perfect symmetry between the two parts of *Hanchi*. One could display them in a chart as follows:

MOVE 1

1. Brother desires Hanchi.
2. She wears a mask, hides her face.
3. Exile; old woman as mother-figure.
4. a. The food episode,
   b. which leads to her discovery and marriage.
5. Brother goes mad.

MOVE 2[5]

1. Lecherous guru desires Hanchi. His efforts to seduce her, repeated thrice.[6] *Type 896.*
2. a. She is put in a box; her body is hidden from her family till the end.
   b. She is hidden in the old woman's house.
3. Exile; the old woman again.
4. a. Another food episode, which leads to rediscovery and reunion.
5. *Guru* goes mad.

Now, we might ask, what is the function of this two-move structure? I'd suggest that structures of this kind, found at whatever "level" of abstraction, are signifiers. Here the two moves enact and signify the two threats (temptations?) of a family woman: incest and adultery. Move 1 shows Hanchi fleeing the first, Move 2 shows her withstanding the second. Till she has successfully faced both tests, her marriage is not secure, and she is not a mature wife. Chastity in the Hindu sense is not celibacy, absence of sex, but sex within marriage; it is synonymous with fidelity, as well as with an endurance of ordeals to prove it. It is a *vrata,* a vow, an observance that requires character. Threats to chastity by near kin like fathers and brothers as well as by non-kin have to be withstood, till one finds a marriageable kin or non-kin. The world is divided into kin/non-kin, and further into marriageable/non-marriageable:

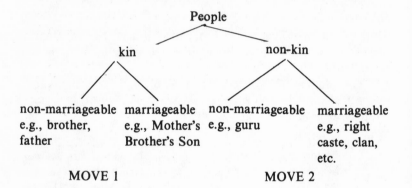

Though the second possibility (marriageable kin) is not explored here, it often is in other tales: a woman (or man) is threatened by marriage to a relative who is crippled or cruel, and has to flee him (or her), toward an eligible, proper groom. The Hanchi tale drama-tizes the ramifications of a joint family, the threats and temptations of incest and adultery it poses. I might add here that both kinds of threats are amply attested in other tales of the area: the popularity of Type 896 speaks for the one, the frequency of motifs and tales of what I've called the Indian Oedipus type—father-figures desiring daughter-figures—are evidence of this preoccupation (see Ramanu-jan 1970). Tradition also warrants our seeing the *guru* as a father-figure outside the family.

As Hanchi moves from Move 1 to Move 2, she is really moving through the "initiatory scenario" of a chaste wife (*pativrata*). If we collapsed the brother and the guru into a single "villain-function," as Propp would probably do, we would lose the above meanings.

4

Can we go one step further and ask, Is there a "deeper" structure? Can we do a summation of the structural ratios, the symmetries of correspondence? In each, the heroine is threatened; goes into exile, obscurity, or hiding; and emerges with a new or renewed relationship. Both the moves have a single pattern. If we were Solar Mythologists (Dorson, 1965), we could see it as Danger/Eclipse/Release. Certainly the following formulae seem to fit the pattern: Disguise/ Discovery, Losing Self/Finding Self, Being Lost/Being Found. However we phrase it, this pattern seems to characterize all Type 510 Cinderella tales. We need ask again of this pattern or "deep structure" or "ratio" (Lévi-Strauss, 1963), What does it signify? For structures are not meanings, but carriers of meanings, signifiers that are rendered into signs by the given culture (in space, time, or society). Even the "deepest" structures have to be *interpreted*[7] culturally or individually, depending on our point of view. Our summary phrases like Losing Self/Finding Self suggest only partially the possible meanings.

What do the two-move structures mean (in North Karnatak), with their twice-repeated Disguise/Discovery pattern? I think that the cultural meanings of this double structure will be illuminated by a comparison with a European Cinderella story. I shall use Grimm's well-known "Aschenputtel" in Manheim's translation (1977:83–89). The Grimm tale also has a structure of two moves, but they are not symmetrical. One could use episode labels similar to those of Hanchi and display them thus:

Aschenputtel

MOVE 1 Loss of mother leads to the dominance of stepmother and stepsisters.

Living among ashes, cinders, etc., which obscure her true beauty.

Discovery at a feast (three times).

Meets the Prince; leaves a slipper behind.

MOVE 2 Exile again among the ashes.

Search for the owner of the slipper.

Stepsisters cut off toes and heels to wear the slipper.
Aschenputtel's foot fits the slipper perfectly.
The Prince marries her.

Despite important differences (the presence of Good and Bad
Mothers, the important theme of sibling rivalry, a dead mother's
magic help), the shared two-move structure is clear: disguise and
discovery, being found by a Prince-figure temporarily in the first
move, eluding him again, being rediscovered through an object
identified with her (slipper in "Cinderella/Aschenputtel,"/food in
"Hanchi"), and re-uniting with the Prince firmly and permanently.

The European tale is not necessarily about a girl; as Bettelheim
(1976:236) points out, and as I have found in classes, it appeals to
both boys and girls. Bettelheim's psychoanalytic essay sees the
following themes in "Aschenputtel": the agony of sibling rivalry,
maturity through suffering (dwelling in ashes), the growth of basic
trust (a sprig is nurtured into a tree), being loved for one's true
character and beauty though dressed in rags. The slipper[8] itself is a
symbol of the vagina (for the complementary symbolism of foot and
slipper, like finger and ring, see Bettelheim, 1976:272).

I see in the European tale another important theme, which is
enacted by the two-move structure: the Dream Coming True. This
theme is best seen in the seventeenth-century, courtly Perrault version. In the first part, the dream of "making it," and marrying a
Prince, is partially realized. As the widely popular Perrault version
emphasizes, it is *conditional.* Cinderella can "have a ball" only till
the witching hour of twelve o'clock. But the dream-experience leaves
behind a remnant in reality, the slipper, which leads the Prince back
to his elusive beauty and identifies her securely; the remnant helps
them reconstruct the entire dream fully, unconditionally, and on firm
ground, triumphing over a life of ashes, cruel mother-figures and
siblings, and the insecure transience of a dream.

5

A classical Indian tale reworked by Kalidāsa (fifth century?) into a
great seven-act play, *Sākuntalā*, has the same kind of Cinderella-

pattern.[9] In it King Dushyanta meets Sakuntala, illegitimate child of a celestial nymph, now dressed in bark garments and living as the foster-daughter of a hermit. They fall in love and marry by a special private rite. His royal duties take him back to his capital, but he leaves a signet ring with his beloved Sakuntala as a love-token and an identification. While she is languishing in the hermitage, an irascible, touchy hermit finds her inhospitable and places a curse on her that she will be forgotten by her husband till he sees the ring. She is pregnant, and her good foster-father sends her to King Dushyanta, who, under the curse, has no memory of her; he accuses her of being a scheming, loose woman. The insulted and rejected Sakuntala is carried off by her celestial mother.

Fishermen find Sakuntala's ring in the maw of a fish and are dragged before the king. His memory returns when he sees the ring, his love-token, here truly a "memento." But Sakuntala is nowhere to be found, and he is grief-stricken.

Years later, returning from a war, Dushyanta visits a hermitage and admires a small boy wrestling with a lion cub; the boy is his own son. The lovers are reunited.

Here too, in an unexpected place, we find a Cinderella. Sakuntala is in exile, her beauty and true divine origin obscured by her bark garments. The King finds her, and their union is temporary. In the second move, she is slandered, forgotten, and exiled (like Hanchi) due to a curse by Durvāsa (a guru, a father-figure). It is the loss and recovery of a ring[10] associated with her that reunites the lovers, permanently. In the Sakuntala play, the ring is displaced by the child (who is already in Sakuntala's womb when she is rejected) in sealing the reunion.

In this play, the two parts enact the growth and trials of love between a man and a woman: the first part shows them in love physically, infatuated, in a state of *kāma* (desire) and *moha* (fascination). The second part, with its separation, rejection, and the chastening years of sufferings, brings the lovers to a mature marriage of the spirit, an experience of *prema* (love). Other elements, like the imagery of flowers in the first parts and the images of fruition in the second, support this view of the play.

Thus we find the same "deep" structure enacting three different possible meanings in three different cultures: the classical Sanskritic, the Kannada, and the German.

6

In this concluding section, I would like to point to elements in the so-called surface structure, the "texture" if you will, that signify culturally contrastive meanings. For one thing, Cinderella tales tend to be similar not only in "deep" structure, but even in particular surface details. For instance, the names of the heroines tend to draw attention to the mode of their disguise: "Cinderella" from *cinders,* "Aschenputtel" from *ashes*; "Katie Woodencoat" and "Allerleirauh" are other examples (Thompson, 1946:128). Even in faraway Kannada tales, the feature is stable: "Hanchi, from *hanchu* (clay tile), and "Maragōpi" (*gopi,* or girl of the tree) from *mara* (tree, or wooden [dress]).

On the other hand, the identifying object is a slipper in the European tale, food in the Kannada, a ring in the classical Sanskrit. Like items of vocabulary in a language, cultural content is clearest in such details—though, as we have seen, even abstract structures must be interpreted for cultural and contextual meanings.[11]

The meanings of the Hanchi tale are subtly carried by a number of culturally significant motifs. For instance, a slipper seems appropriate for a tale of sexually fitting partnership as well as of a dream coming true (rising socially from rags to riches). Food, identified with Hanchi, and identifying her finally, is pervasive in Hindu symbolism. In this tale, it appears at least five times: when Hanchi leaves her mother, when she is first discovered by her husband-to-be, when the guru tries to seduce her with his love-magic, when she is "discovered" again as an adulteress, and finally when she is reunited with her husband and family. The central importance of food in Hindu ritual and worship, and of food-transactions as markers of caste-rank (Marriott, 1968), is well-known. Less well-known is the symbolism of food in the sexual realm. The word for eating and (sexual) enjoyment have often the same root, *bhuj*, in Sanskrit. Sexual intercourse is often spoken about as the mutual feeding of male and female. Furthermore, in a story like "Hanchi," with its theme of attaining proper wifehood, sexuality is inseparable from maternal nurturing. The breast is both wifely and motherly; it is often said that a woman has two breasts, one for her child, another for her husband.

That the love-magic used by the seducer involves phallic food objects like bananas and nuts requires no further comment.

The detail of animals is also significant. The she-buffalo eats the charmed nuts of the lecherous guru and *automatically* desires him, unlike the human Hanchi, and mauls him in a sexual attack. Later, when he lies to the old woman that the box contains a mad dog (and not Hanchi), he finds to his grief that it indeed contains a mad dog. His own animality seems projected onto his partners. In folk-versions of saints' legends (e.g., Allama, the Virasaiva saint), the saint-to-be lusts madly after a woman and works hard to get her, but when he finally embraces her she turns into a savage she-bear.

One is struck often by a design among the variants of a central motif—like the disguise of the heroine. For instance, in "Hanchi" the disguise is by means of a clay mask. If one looks at the Indian variants of this tale-type (for bibliography, see Thompson and Roberts, entry under 510B) one sees the following range: a mask, a wooden coat, an old woman's skin, an animal skin, an actual animal body (tortoise, crab) which is later burned by the beloved or lover to recover the hero(ine)'s human form, and finally a caterpillar.[12] If we do not collapse these variants into an abstract "motifeme," or function, like "disguise," we see that the series points to an interesting transformation: from the clay mask of culture to the use of human and animal skin, to the possibility of inhabiting an animal form (crossing the line between human and animal), and to nature's metamorphosis of caterpillars into butterflies. In an ancient Upanishadic image the soul is a caterpillar that moves from form to form. One may ask whether the clay mask; the box in which she is shut up, with the imminent danger of drowning; and her double emergence do not point to a rebirth theme. The skin-dress motif is an old Hindu motif: the changing of skins, clothes, masks, *personae* and even bodies in self-transformations (Elwin, 1944). Both snakes and Brahmins are called the "twice-born." In Hindu coronation and initiation rituals, the initiate wears an antelope-skin; in Brahmin initiation, a small piece of it is tied to his sacred thread.

Thus, lining up the corresponding details in several variants of the same type, one gains new hypotheses, if not insights. The variants at this "level" of inquiry form a meaningful series that point to a cultural theme.

NOTES

[1]For an earlier, clumsier translation, see Ramanujan, 1956. I have used no transliterations for Indian names in this paper.

[2]Blonde hair is unheard of in Dravidian south India and would be considered grotesque on a Kannada girl. So the hair in this well-known European motif (H71.2) is seen here as actually made of gold, exerting a magical influence on onlookers. In this part of India, a woman's hair is part of her sexual attractiveness, and respectable, old-fashioned women keep it covered by the sari.

[3]*Hanchi* is derived from *hanchu,* a clay tile or mask.

[4]Presently available reports allow us to call this a possible Indian oikotype; of course, absence of data is no conclusive argument.

[5]If we read the table across, we get paradigms *à la* Lévi-Strauss; if we read down we get a syntagm *à la* Propp. The actual story, of course, goes on from Move 1 to Move 2—like two sentences conjoined in a compound one, with parallelism as a rhetorical device. The rather exact repetitions are enriched and artfully disguised from the listener by the various details of Type 896: the three attempts at love-magic, the slander and the rejection of the heroine, the maiden in the box, the substitution of a mad dog for the young woman, etc.

[6]Other Cinderella tales (e.g., Grimm's) repeat other episodes thrice, e.g., the prince's ball.

[7]Both Jung's archetypes and Lévi-Strauss's ratios tend to be self-evidently "meaningful"; often they are the "signified" for other surface "signifiers." This is one of the points where the early Chomskyan model of "deep structures mapped onto surface structures" will not do for cultural or literary analysis.

[8]Hanchi's mask can also be seen as a hymen, broken by the groom—not unlike the shattering of a mirror or glass in Jewish and other wedding rituals.

[9]See Basham, 1954: 435–440, for a short summary.

[10]A well-known motif, Polycrates' ring, H 94.2. Some Cinderella stories do have a ring, instead of a slipper, that identifies the heroine. For an example, see "Cap o'Rushes" in Briggs, 1970.

[11]Like the grammar and lexicon of a language, the type-structure and motific detail inhabit continuous, interacting fields of meaning. Their relations are not merely those of empty (structural) slots which are filled by (lexical) members, or of surface structures that get all their "sense" from participating in Platonic "deep structures." As we have seen, structure at each level of abstraction can signify; meanings are not archetypal, universal, do not inhere in them; they require cultural assignment. Similarly, and more obviously, the motifs so usefully collated by the indexes, need interpretation, both from structure and culture. Motifs, defined as traits with an independent history, would give us a lexicon without a language.

[12]At the end of the series, the Cinderella cycle passes into the Animal Groom cycle.

REFERENCES

Aarne, Antti A., and Stith Thompson, *The Types of the Folktale*. A classification and bibliography translated and enlarged by Stith Thompson. 2nd revision. Helsinki: Suomalainen Tiedeakatemia, 1961.

Basham, A.L. *The Wonder That Was India*. New York: Grove Press, 1954.

Bettelheim, Bruno. *The Uses of Enchantment: The Meaning and Importance of Fairy Tales*. New York: Knopf, 1976.

Briggs, Katharine M. *A Dictionary of British Folk Tales*. 4 vols. Bloomington: Indiana University Press, 1970–1971.

Cox, Marian R. *Cinderella: Three Hundred and Eighty-Five Variants*. London: David Nutt, 1893.

Dorson, Richard M. "The Eclipse of Solar Mythology." In Alan Dundes, ed., *The Study of Folklore*. Englewood Cliffs, N.J.: Prentice-Hall, 1965.

Elwin, Verrier. *The Folktales of Mahakoshal*. New York: Oxford University Press, 1944.

Lévi-Strauss, Claude. *Structural Anthropology*. Trans. from the French by Claire Jacobson and B.G. Schoepf. New York: Basic Books, 1963.

Propp, Vladimir. *Morphology of the Folktale*. Trans. by L. Scott. 2nd ed. Austin: University of Texas Press, 1968.

Manheim, Ralph, trans. *Grimm's Tales for Young and Old: The Complete Stories*. Garden City, N.Y.: Doubleday, 1977.

Marriott, McKim. "Caste Ranking and Food Transactions." In B.S. Cohn and Milton Singer, eds., *Structure and Change in Indian Society*. Chicago: Aldine, 1968.

Rooth, Anna B. *The Cinderella Cycle*. Lund: Gleerup, 1951.

Ramanujan, A.K. "The Story of Hanchi." *Southern Folklore Quarterly*, XX, 3 (Sept. 1956).

———. "The Indian Oedipus." In A. Poddar, ed., *Symposium on Indian Literature*. Simla: Indian Institute of Advanced Study, 1971.

Cinderella in Tuscany

Alessandro Falassi

Folklorists who collect folktales from informants in the field and who are familiar with the various theories and methods of folkloristics would appear to the ideally equipped to interpret such tales. An armchair analyst is forced to rely on field data gathered by others which may or may not be reported accurately. When a folklorist analyzes his own data, at least he can be certain of its authenticity.

Those who have never collected folklore may not realize the vast difference between the tale as it is orally told and the tale as it ordinarily appears in print. False starts, mistakes, interruptions by members of the audience or collector are almost always edited out by either the collector or the editor of the journal or book in which the tale is published. Yet it is only in the actual performance situation that folklore lives. What appears in print is really just a pale echo of what was once a live folklore event. One reason why transcripts of folklore performances are so rarely reported verbatim is that what sounds fine to the ear doesn't look right to the eye, accustomed as it is to works of written, not oral, literature.

In order to convey something of what an oral performance of Cinderella is like, a segment of a remarkable taletelling session in Tuscany will be presented. This fascinating account in which three different versions of Cinderella are recounted, the last by the seven-

Reprinted from Alessandro Falassi, *Folklore by the Fireside: Text and Context of the Tuscan Veglia* (Austin: University of Texas Press, 1980), pp. 55–68.

year-old grandson of the first raconteur, is part of an important longer study by folklorist Alessandro Falassi of the veglia, the traditional evening around a Tuscan hearth. The competitive feelings of the three storytellers, each of whom wishes to tell his or her favorite version, are manifest even through the English translation from the Italian transcript.

Present on the occasion are a grandfather, a grandmother, their grandson, a friend of the grandfather, a six-year-old girl, and the collector. No sooner does the grandmother begin the tale than Gino Anichini, the friend of the grandfather, interrupts her to say that there were three girls, not two. The grandson concurs that there were three. But the grandmother, while politely deferring to the male pressure, eventually tells the tale as she knows it: with two daughters, not three. Such interplay between male and female, between grandmother and grandson, would normally be omitted from the typical collection of folktales found in print. Nevertheless, it is often in the taleteller's offhand remarks or the audience's spontaneous heartfelt responses that one finds clues to the meaning of a folktale to the people among whom it is told.

Dr. Falassi does much more than convey the sense of an actual performance of Cinderella, or rather three performances of the tale. He also deftly shows how these Tuscan versions, collected near his home in Siena, display distinctive features of Tuscan social life. His analysis of plot structural features and of the symbolism are not dogmatic rehearsals of a priori *principles but are meaningfully integrated with such critical concerns as courtship, virginity, and marriage in Italian culture.*

For more details about the significance of folklore in Tuscany, the reader should consult Alessandro Falassi, Folklore by the Fireside: Text and Context of the Tuscan Veglia (*Austin: University of Texas Press, 1980). For further discussion of the importance of performance in the study of folklore, see Dan Ben-Amos and Kenneth S. Goldstein, eds.,* Folklore: Performance and Communication (*The Hague: Mouton, 1975); and Richard Bauman,* Verbal Art as Performance (*Rowley, Mass.: Newbury House, 1977*).

On one of many such occasions three versions of the story were told by three different people, one the kind of old woman that commonly tells such fireside stories, one an old man, and, finally, the grandchild of the woman who in fact was the hostess for the occasion. What was both significant and amusing in this narrative situation was that the child was able, through adept maneuvering, to tell the story more clearly and successfully than his grandmother.

That evening, an animated discussion began on the variations of Cinderella: some called it the story of Lina, some knew it as Cinderella, others as the Cenderacchiola; Gino repeated: "No! No! It's the one about the count!"

GRANDFATHER SESTILIO CIONI: *Gino knows it, too.*

GINO ANICHINI (friend of grandfather): *No, I heard it was being told to my little girl.*

GRANDMOTHER ANNINA: *There was a woman who had two children, no . . .*

GINO: *Three!*

GRANDMOTHER: *Two! Not three!*

GINO: *Three! She had two daughters of her own and another one. Whom they kept as . . . They made her into a cinder girl; she sat near the ashes and tended the ashes . . .*

GRANDMOTHER: *Yes, in short, one of them always remained behind to take care of the ashes and the others went dancing. You're right. So there were three. Well, two or three.*

ALESSANDRO FALASSI: *But two of them were hers?*

GRANDMOTHER: *One was not hers and two were hers. So this poor little Cinderella . . . One of them was called . . .*

FABRIZIO CIONI (the seven-year-old): *No, listen, I'll tell it!*

GRANDMOTHER: *Well, then you tell it.*

FABRIZIO: *There is . . . there was a man and wife. They got married and they already had two little girls. One day his wife died. So he was left all alone. And he had these two little girls.*

GRANDFATHER: *Not so loud!*

FABRIZIO: *One day he went to look for a . . . for a . . . for another woman. And he found one. But this woman . . .*

GRANDFATHER: *Don't yell!*

FABRIZIO: *No . . . yes, yes, yes, she had . . .*

GRANDMOTHER: *Keep quiet, you're getting everything all mixed up.*

FABRIZIO: *I'm all confused.*

GRANDMOTHER: *Shut up now, this is how it goes!*

FABRIZIO: *The man had one daughter and the other woman had two. The stepsisters!*

GRANDMOTHER: *I'll tell it this way, because there are one hundred ways of telling it. I'll tell it as I remember it. And then . . .*

AF: *That's right you tell it as you know it,* [to Fabrizio] *and then we'll hear the way you know it.*

GRANDMOTHER: *Yes. I know it this way. There once was a woman and a man and they had two daughters. One always took care of the ashes and the other always went dancing. So . . .*

GINO: *No, that's a different one!*

GRANDMOTHER: *In the evening she got all dressed up. You can see that it's another one.*

AF: *Let's hear yours!*

GRANDMOTHER: *And she said, "Well, are you going to the dance tonight?" "No, no," she replied. "I'm not going to the dance because I like to tend the ashes . . ." "Oh, come on to the dance, you'll see how much fun it is." "Hmm. No, no, I'm not coming." So one day her mother said to her, "Listen, you have to come to the dance, because if you don't, I'm not going to take your sister either." But she still refused. At this point, let's see, how does it go . . .*

FABRIZIO: *Well, it isn't the one that I was thinking of . . .*

GRANDMOTHER: *Yes, yes, this is how it goes. All right now, all right. So in the evening she had this little bird called Verzicolò, and after the others had gone she said:*

> *Verzicolò, little bird,*
> *Make me more beautiful*
> *Than has ever been heard.*

The little bird turned her into a beautiful woman and then she entered the ballroom to dance. But as suddenly

as she arrived, just as suddenly she disappeared at
midnight. Every evening they saw this beautiful girl enter
the ballroom but at a certain moment she would
disappear. A young man said, "Oh, dammit, you'll see;
some evening I'm going to get her."
     One evening after the dancing and dancing and
dancing, this Cinderella lost a shoe. Oh, dear! The next
morning her sister said to her: "So you didn't come to
the dance! But at midnight a beautiful girl came . . . if
you would only have seen her . . ." "Oh, what do I
care," she said. "I take care of the ashes . . ." "Oh,
come on, always here taking care of the ashes . . ." So
this night then she came home missing a shoe, and she
said, "Oh, what should I do, what shall I do, what shall
I do." Then she said, ". . . ah, this young man had the
shoe in his pocket; you'll see, she'll come back." So that
evening she ran out after the other had gone to the
dance; she started out once more. She started out,
however, this time without one shoe. She didn't have the
shoe and the little bird was unable to provide her with
another one; it did not help her:

> *Verzicolò, little bird,*
> *Make me more beautiful*
> *Than has ever been heard.*

     Well, to make it short . . . this young man put the
shoe by the door saying, "I want to see who you are."
When she entered and . . . turned around and saw the
shoe at the door, she put it on and danced all night
long. He said, 'Now, when you leave, I'll follow you,"
this young man said to her. So then while they were
dancing her mother recognized her. She stopped her,
saying, "Well, look at you, you must be my daughter."
So when it was time to leave she said to the other
sister, call her: "Lina!" She said. "Call her, you'll see that
that is Lina." So when they left they both left together.
     When they arrived home her mother said to her,
"You came to the dance without saying anything! Ah,

*but you'll see," she said. She said to her other daughter:
"I'll show her. You know what we'll make her do
tomorrow morning? Tomorrow morning we'll send her
to where the kittens live. You'll see that the kittens will
scratch her. Tomorrow morning you know what we'll
make? We'll make* polenta [*corn bread*]." *So her mother
said to Cinderella, "You go and get the sieve where the
kittens live." She replied, "No, I won't go." "What do
you mean, you won't go; you will go!" Then she said,
"Well, if she won't go then you go." She told the ugly
daughter: "Listen to me. When you climb the stairs ask
if you might have the sieve to make* polenta. *And go
slowly because the stairs are made of glass." And she
said nothing to the beautiful daughter. But the beautiful
daughter was also intelligent. One day she sent the ugly
daughter to get the sieve. And she carefully explained to
her how to go about getting it.*

GINO: *Cinderella!*

GRANDMOTHER: *No, her sister, the other one. She got to the
door and knocked. She said, "My mother sent me to get
the sieve to make* polenta." "Yes, but be careful, the
stairs are made of glass." And she stomped so hard she
broke every step. And they gave her the sieve.*

   *When she got back home she said, "Mamma, I
brought you the sieve." "Were you careful?" She
answered, "I broke all the steps, and the kittens
scratched me all over." "Poor thing," said her mother.
"Now tomorrow morning I'll send Cinderella." She was
well mannered and said to her, "Go to where the kittens
live and take the sieve back." And so she went slowly,
slowly with much care, and didn't break a single step
asking permission of the kittens and the kittens didn't
touch her. She gave back the sieve and returned home.
Her mother saw that nothing happened to her; how is
that possible? "Tomorrow morning you go back to the
kittens again." "No, I will not go back there." She said
to the ugly daughter: "You've got to go back. And along
the road when the rooster crows turn around, and when
the ass sings don't turn around." So the ugly daughter*

*took her leave. The rooster crowed and she did not turn
around. The ass sung and she turned around, and she
grew a long tail. So the next evening . . . the next
evening she sent Cinderella saying, "When the rooster
crows, don't turn around, when the ass sings, turn
around." But, instead, when the ass sang she did not
turn around. When the rooster crowed she turned
around. And a star appeared in the middle of her
forehead. So one of them ended up with a star and the
other with a tail. But it was beautiful. But this must be
only a part of the story.*

In fact, Annina's tale was a mixture of motifs taken from two
different tale types: Cinderella and The Kind and the Unkind Girls.[1]
Some observations on obedience and the relationship between
the mother and her daughters should be made. The stepmother asks
Cinderella to go to the dance and to go get the sieve. In both cases
Cinderella refuses and disobeys, "she does as she likes." On the
other hand, her stepmother gives Cinderella orders that are destined
to do her harm. By doing just the opposite or not following the
orders at all, Cinderella avoids getting scratched, she marries, and
she receives a star on her forehead. In fact, a folk song still sung
says "Quando ti vedo quella stella in fronte/voglio piu bene a te che
a mamma mia" ["When I see that star in your forehead/I love you
more than my mother"]—further folk evidence of the equation
between mature femininity, enduring light, and the fire on the
hearth. The mother gives good advice instead to the daughter she
prefers, who disobeys and does just the opposite and ends up badly:
she gets scratched, she doesn't marry, and an ass tail grows in the
middle of her forehead.[2]
In this and in numerous other examples of Tuscan folklore, two
aspects of motherhood are presented: the mother who always gives
good advice but only to the daughter she prefers, and the mother
who gives bad advice to the daughter she does not like. A daughter,
then, must obey the orders of her own good mother (lacking the
mother, then she had to obey the fairy) and do the opposite of what
stepmothers or bad mothers say.
The version of the loss of the shoe is interesting, being a loss
which is not made up for even with the help of the magic powers of

the little bird (he "was unable to provide her with another one"). The shoe can be hypothesized as a virginity symbol, a feminine virtue which once lost cannot be replaced but remains in the hands of the man responsible for the loss. In the story the shoe remains with the prince. In everyday conversation, when referring to a girl who seems particularly adapted to a certain young man, one says, "She is just the right shoe for his foot" ["è la scarpa pel su' piede"]. At the same time the proverb warns that "two feet cannot fit into the same shoe" ["due piedi in una scarpa non ci stanno"], that is, a woman cannot have two lovers. Another folk expression is "If you want my shoe you must wear a sock" ["se vuoi la mi' scarpa mettiti il calzino"], demanding the man to use a contraceptive during sexual intercourse. An old woman is often referred to as "an old slipper" or a "worn-out shoe." Also, losing one or both shoes during a dance as well as taking them off voluntarily were acts that a woman did if she got caught up in the rhythm of a dance and the excitement it caused, and the act was considered excessive and improper: "She even took off her shoes!" meant "She has really let herself go." In the story Cinderella loses her shoe during a dance, the erotic meaning of which is common in the symbolism of folklore: one of the famous examples of dishonest womanhood is that of the woman who was made to dance by the devil until she dropped dead. Duff-Gordon relates that, at a country dance at the turn of the century, a girl lost her shoes and her partner kneeled and put her shoes back on, while the audience laughed, having interpreted the incident as a parallel of the Cinderella tale.[3] The future husband putting the shoes on the bride was one of the most widespread customs related to the engagement ritual in Tuscany.[4]

Annina, responding to a question asked by the children, explained that "afterward the young man married her," even if the ending had been omitted in the story. The young man in fact had danced all evening with Lina-Cinderella, committing her and himself in the eyes of everyone present. Just as in stories, so it was in reality at dances in Tuscany: the woman who danced with only one man indicated that she belonged exclusively to him. The young man in the story, after having put her to the test, married her and did his duty as would every other well-intentioned young man in reality, as witnessed by Annina and her stories. The central narrative structure appears to be the following:

The girl has the virtue object that is magic and irreplaceable	She loses it, passing it on to a young man	The young man puts her to the test	She passes the test
He gives the magic object back to her		They marry	

Events in real life, according to traditional custom, as expressed in rite of passage, take place along parallel lines:

The girl is a virgin and respected	She goes with a young man	She loses her respectability, compromising herself	Her respectability is in his hands	He puts her to the test
She passes the test	She is "respected" again as a fiancée	He marries her		

Annina admitted that her story was perhaps "not exact." And Gino replied immediately, "But you had almost begun the one about . . ." Then she asked him, "But how does yours go?" And he replied, "I've always heard my Nunzia tell it this way." And after a pause he cleared his throat and began:

> GINO: *The one about the count goes like this. Once there was a woman who had three daughters. She was fond of two of them and could not stand the other one. The third girl always sat near the cinders. One evening the two daughters decided to go the the ball. They told the third daughter they were going to the ball and that she had to stay home and tend the cinders. "I don't care, I don't care if I stay home," she replied. "I don't care, not at all!" So the others went to the ball, and as soon as they arrived at the ball, the fairy appeared to the third sister and turned her into a beautiful woman with beautiful clothes and everything. As they entered the*

ballroom no one recognized them. Dressed in that way
not one knew who she was.

AF: *Do you mean the fairy?*

GINO: *No, the fairy was with her. The one who was with
her was the fairy.*

FABRIZIO: *The fairy was with her.*

GINO: *So they entered the ballroom and began to dance.
"However," said the fairy, "when you dance with someone
who asks who you are . . . 'I don't know' you have to say,
'I don't know!' At midnight on the dot . . ."*

FABRIZIO: *You have to go home. Leave immediately, eh! Uh,
huh!*

ROSANNA BERNINI (age 6): *Uh, huh.*

GINO: *You leave, eh! Me too. Get into the coach and leave.
Eh. So she arrived at the ball. There was a count who
grabbed this lovely girl and danced with her. "Miss," he
said, "tell me, how old are you?" She replied, "I don't
know." "Well, where are you from?" "I don't know."*
[*The children laugh.*]

GRANDMOTHER: *He wasn't able to get anything out of her.*

GINO: *At midnight she was dancing with the count, with
this young man. All of a sudden she disappeared.* Boh.
They did not see a thing.

FABRIZIO: *Hah, hah.*

GINO: *This is strange. And she left. And returned home. The
other two returned from the dance. They came back
from the ball. Cinderella was already back tending the
ashes. She was at home again. They said to her: "If
only you could have seen the girl who danced with a
young man . . . she was dressed so well . . . she was
beautiful! But really beautiful! I've never seen anything
like this."*

FABRIZIO: *Her sisters! It's that one, it's that one!*

GINO: *Yes, yes! Well! What do I care . . . what do I care. The
next evening the same old thing. The next evening the
same thing all over again. They go again to the ball.
"You come along, too," they said, "so you can see that
girl too, that beautiful girl, she's really something. Oh,*

*come, come, come." "No, no, no. I'll not come. I'll stay
here; I want to stay here." And so she stayed
home . . . And after the sisters had gone, when they'd
already arrived at the ball . . .*

FABRIZIO: *The fairy appeared again! The fairy came
back. She dressed her up!*

ROSANNA: *Good! Good! And she went to the ball!*

GINO: *And . . . she began to dance again with the count.
Virgin Mary! She was, she was, she was an eyeful for
the count. And so during the evening . . . the usual
words. "Miss, where are you from, you didn't want to
tell me." "I don't know!"* [*Laughter.*]

GRANDMOTHER: *God screwed, then!*

GINO: *"I don't know!" And every time he asked her
something she replied, "I don't know."* [*children's
laughter.*] *At midnight the same thing happened again.*

FABRIZIO: *On the road . . .*

ROSANNA: *. . . the road.*

GINO: *Along the road when she was climbing into the
coach, she lost a shoe.*

ROSANNA: *The shoe . . .*

GINO: *And this count ran and found this shoe. No—Yes!
He found this shoe and asked all the women who were
at the ball if any of them had lost a shoe. One replied,
"Not I"; another said, "No"; another said, "No." "Try it
on and see who it fits. It doesn't fit anyone."*

ROSANNA: *No one!*

FABRIZIO: *Yes, yes, it's that one, it's that one!*

GRANDMOTHER: *The one you know, eh!*

ROSANNA: *It's that one* [*story*]*!*

GINO: *Eh . . . and so there . . . So then what did he do.
He went . . . he went down . . . to that family, the
one that knew something about the mystery of who the
shoe would fit and who it wouldn't fit. He went down
there saying, "But you, housewife, housemother,"
however he called her, "you have three daughters." She
said: "Yes! I have three. Two are here but the other is
always tending the ashes; she's there." "Try on this shoe,
he said to the two daughters. "Does it fit?" "No." To*

> *the other daughter he said, "Oh, try it on." "No." "I'd*
> *be pleased if the daughter who takes care of the ashes*
> *would try it on too," said the count.*

FABRIZIO: *Just in case she would fulfill his eye! He put the*
shoe on her, and it fit.

GINO: *It fit her, he said whoever the shoe fit . . .*

FABRIZIO: *Will be my wife!*

ROSANNA: *I'll marry her, I'll marry her!*

GINO: *And in fact he married her, she became the wife of a*
count and . . .

FABRIZIO: *Rich.*

GRANDMOTHER: *And they married and had fun,*
And of this to me they gave none.
They gave me a tiny doughnut.
In that little hole I put it,
And now it's all gone.

[Laughter]

AF: *Listen here, didn't that fairy dance?*

GINO: *No, no, she disappeared.*

GRANDMOTHER: *Eh, the fairy disappeared.*

GINO: *She disappeared. She reappeared at midnight.*

ROSANNA: *Yes.*

FABRIZIO: *To take her back home.*

GINO: *To take her away. The . . . the fairy accompanied her.*

The basic structure characterized in the fragment of the preceding
narrative is present in this story too. In addition, we can observe the
presence of the fairy as the maternal figure (pertinent to Cinderella)
who, besides making her into a beautiful woman, accompanies her
to the dance and waits for her at the exit, but without participating
in the ball, just like Tuscan mothers. Following the fairy's advice—
not speaking to strangers, coming away at the right time—the
heroine ends up marrying a man with a title, "and rich," as Fabrizio
added to ensure the happy ending. "There are also counts without
money," he explained to me later, laughing. The fairy finds a
husband for Cinderella, the evil mother ends up like the mother in
the story of one little eye and three little eyes, and her two old maids
at home. It is interesting to note that the count goes to the family

that "already knew" something and asks formal permission to put
the daughters to the test. The mother suggests he try the shoe on the
two daughters she wants to marry off. The count is allowed to test
Cinderella only after her sisters have failed. In reality a similar order
of preference existed for girls in a patriarchal Tuscan family. So it is
that the characters in the story are obliged by the storyteller to
follow the social rules of real life courtship.

It was at the end of the version proposed by Gino that Fabrizio
—at seven years one of the youngest storytellers I have ever listened
to—got the attention of the audience after having repeated over and
over, "Can I tell it my way, can I tell it my way?" Finally his
grandfather, recognized by his guests as host in charge of the
storytelling session, gave his consent. The boy began from the
beginning and narrated his version of Cinderella, which previously
he had left hanging because he couldn't remember it.

FABRIZIO: *Once upon a time there was a man and a woman who*
got married. The woman . . . they had one daughter.
Cinderella. It's almost the same one as he told. It's
almost the same. They had one daughter, this man and
this woman. The woman died. So he was left alone with
his little girl. What did he do? He took another wife.
And this one had two daughters. Those two stepsisters
that he mentioned.

GINO: *So there were three.*

FABRIZIO: *There were three. They come to three. And*
this . . . his wife was fond of her two girls, and her
husband was fond of his own girl. However, he . . . the
two of them were two and the others were three. What
could he do? He went to work, and the others made his
little girl clean the ashes out of the fireplace because
they didn't like her. The others went out dancing. One
day something happened, like you said. The fairy
appeared. She made Cinderella beautiful. She called for
a coach and sent her to the dance. Yes. And she sent
her to the dance. Then . . . however, the fairy said, "At
midnight on the dot you must come home because if
not next time I won't make you beautiful and I won't
let you go to the dance." When it was midnight "ding,

dong!" The girl, when she heard the clock strike midnight, she ran! Waiting for her . . . waiting for her was the coachman with the carriage. She climbed in and away they went. And she went back among the cinders.

That night when . . . in the morning when she saw her stepsisters, they said to her: "Virgin Mary, there was a beautiful woman at the dance," like Gino said . . . "I would like to know who she was." [His grandmother laughs.] "Well," said Cinderella, "it certainly wasn't me. Because you always leave me here in the midst of all these ashes." And . . . "Well, then, you come this evening," said her stepsisters. "No, no, I want to stay here in the cinders with my little cat; it's fun, I play with it, I pet it, I cry . . ." and so on. The following evening, after they had left, the fairy reappeared; she made Cinderella beautiful once more and away she went. Virgin Mary!

GINO: *It's very similar, eh!*

FABRIZIO: *And she kept on dancing with this . . . no like you said in your story, it wasn't a count. It was a . . . king, the son of a king.*

GRANDMOTHER: *A king!*

AF: *The son of a king?*

FABRIZIO: *The son of a king. And so she said to him . . . and so he says: "Virgin Mary, but that girl there is a real beauty! I must see why it is that she disappears like that at midnight." And so he puts glue on the stairs. So naturally that evening when midnight came she left the dance, and naturally when she got to the last step where he had put the glue her shoe got stuck. And away she went. She didn't even stop to pick it up. She climbed into the coach and away she went. And she did the same as before. In the evening . . . the next evening the prince didn't see anyone. "Virgin Mary! Oh, what has she done?" And he found this shoe, the night she ran home. And he said, "Oh, whose shoe is this?" He tried it on everyone but it fit no one [he hits his fist on the table]. So then he sent . . . what's his name, he sent these . . .*

GRANDMOTHER: *The coachmen?*

FABRIZIO: *Not the coachmen. These . . . what did they call those men who went around with megaphones making public announcements . . .*

AF: *The town crier?*

FABRIZIO: *Town criers! He sent town criers around. And so they also went to this family and said: "There's a shoe . . . last evening it was lost! It was lost while she was dancing—whose is it, whose is it?" Everyone came to the door. And the town crier said to the mother, "It couldn't be yours, could it?" She tried it on; it didn't fit. She said to him: "I have two daughters. I can let them try it on. I have three. However, I'm not very fond of one of them. You can try it on them." "Yes, yes," he said . . . said the king's son. "However, I must marry whoever this shoe fits. Even if she's ugly I have to marry her." And so all three tried the shoe on, but it didn't fit.*

GRANDFATHER: *Eh, eh, eh!*

FABRIZIO: *Said the mother: "I also have this other daughter, another girl who is more pea-brained . . . as we say in Italian, she's always sitting in the cinders . . . she's all . . . she's all covered with ashes . . .*

GRANDMOTHER: *Yes, yes, but . . . all this bungling, wait till you hear what comes next. Go on, go on!*

GRANDFATHER: *Shut up!*

FABRIZIO: *She's all covered with soot. And you keep quiet! She's all covered with soot. She's all dirty. And so . . . [to his grandmother] you get me all mixed up!*

GINO: *Go on, go on!*

FABRIZIO: *And so he said, "Yes, yes, let's try it on her, too." When she tried the shoe on, it fit. "Eh," said the prince, "so then this is the shoe that fits . . . that fits that girl who came. Oh, how did someone who's so dirty . . . someone who's so dirty get so beautiful?" [He hits his fist on the table.] The prince sat with his mouth open and said, "I'll marry her." And so they left in the town crier's coach and . . . and went to the castle. And the king's son said to the king, "Father I have found my*

*bride." Then the king said, "Well, when will the wedding
take place?" "On such and such a day," he said . . . he
said. And on such and such a day they got married.
And the stepsisters all . . . all . . . all . . . not all . . .*
GINO: *Dirty?*
GRANDMOTHER: *Scared!*
FABRIZIO: *They were . . . not scared. They were . . . [he
says excitedly] they wanted to be more beautiful than
she was and so they put on some make-up, but they put
on so much . . . they seemed to be wearing masks!
[Everyone laughs.]*[5]
FABRIZIO: *[He continues in an excited tone.] And so then
they were so ugly. They got married . . . [slowly, in a
lower tone] and . . . they went to the king and lived in
the castle happily every after.*[6]
GRANDMOTHER: *My goodness, that boy! [She smiles, satisfied.]*

That's how Fabrizio got to "tell it his way." As the transcription
shows, his first attempt was interrupted as soon as the occasion
presented itself—at his first mistake—by his grandmother, who was
then his rival for the attention of the audience. The boy had to
resign himself and return to the rank of listener to prepare his
comeback. He immediately changed seats and went to sit near his
grandfather. He then began to make comments when the other
storytellers paused—thereby participating in the narration himself
—repeating that he knew and recognized the story being told. He
subsequently obtained our invitation to tell a story, with the formal
consent of the head of the house. He then told his story, replying
brusquely to his grandmother's interruptions, supported in this by
his grandfather and by Gino, who was happy for having been able
to tell his story and in particular because it had been well received
by us.

The three versions of the story had also brought about a unani-
mous stipulation: Fabrizio had begun by saying that his Cinderella was "the same, almost the same" as Gino's, who commented
halfway through the story ("it's similar"), even though both had
changed it in their own way. Annina's version, instead, was refused:
"That's not it." Therefore, "who knew it straight," "who told it
correctly," "who knew it all" was established for the story as well as

in the other discussions of the *veglia*, while disapproval was expressed by "What story are you telling?" "I never heard it told like this," "You always want to tell stories your way!" The basic narrative order of the stories had to be recognizable and accepted, an order that demanded a certain number of actors to guarantee the right degree of redundancy, and, with it, the appropriate underscoring of the social *message* or *point*. Only by establishing this order firmly could one embellish the stories with individual details presented by the narrative inspiration and ideological baggage of the storyteller. Fabrizio introduced the town criers who called the women with megaphones—perhaps using as models the dry cleaners or the haberdashers or the itinerant salesmen who came to his village every week, in old automobiles, and with croaking megaphones called all the women to their windows, calling them "ladies" like the criers in the story.

The version of Cinderella told by Fabrizio was liked very much by all, including Annina; her pride as grandmother subordinated her being upstaged by one younger than herself.

NOTES

[1]Cinderella is AT 510; The Kind and the Unkind Girls is AT 480. A version of the second part originating in the Florentine region was collected by Temistocle Gradi, with the title "Nina-the-Star and Betta-the-Tail." Nina ("Nina" in Italian also means "sister" and is an affectionate term; that is, it means "good sister") behaves in a well-mannered way, she is helpful, and she chooses the ordinary over the luxurious. The fairies reward her with pearls, dresses, and a star in the middle of her forehead. Betta is rude, and she chooses the luxurious over the ordinary. A donkey's tail grows in the middle of her forehead. See Gradi, *La vigilia di pasqua de ceppo* (Turin: Vaccarino, 1870), pp. 20–25. The Palace of Cats, which scratch the rude sister and reward the helpful one, is in a version cited by Angelo De Gubernatis, "Novelline di Santo Stefano di Calcinaia," *Rivista di Letteratura Popolare* 1 (1878), p. 62, n. 1. for a general discussion, see also Gail A. Kligman, "A Socio-Psychological Interpretation of the Tale of the Kind and the Unkind Girl," M.A. in folklore thesis, University of California at Berkeley, 1973.

[2]From a psychoanalytical point of view, the symbology can be interpreted as follows: Lina saves her own virginity (she doesn't get scratched) while Betta loses it (is scratched). Lina obtains a visible form of virtue (the star in the middle of her forehead) and Betta a *prolaxum*; one becomes desirable, the other repulsive. Among the fairies' gifts—in other versions gifts from the cats or from the king of the cats—is

a symbolic one earned through the test of having to delouse some women and having to choose modest garments; the bad sister only receives bugs and lice, a dress that is ripped, and a monkey on her head (Vittorio Imbriani, *La novellaja fiorentina* (Leghorn: Vigo, 1877), pp. 186–187). Thus one finds a husband, and the other will remain forever the object of mean jokes; see Gradi, *La vigilia di pasqua di ceppo,* p. 25.

³Lina Duff-Gordon, *Home Life in Italy* (New York: Macmillan, 1912), p. 111.

⁴Raffaele Corso, *Patti d'amore e pegni di promessa* (San Maria Capua Vetere: La Fiaccola, 1925), pp. 42, 45, 46.

⁵A typical *exemplum* is "the young girl whose cheeks were all eaten by make-up." In fact, when a woman puts on make-up, she "erased from her face the image and figure of God and in its place she put that of the Devil." See Fra' Filippo da Siena, *Gli assempri* (Siena: Gati, 1864), p. 21. This iconographic stereotype has remained in "edifying" literature up to now. For one such portrait—a stepmother with bleached hair, painted lips, and a painted face who gives indignant orders, who never goes to church, who doesn't ever pray, and who often strikes her stepdaughter—see Remo Manfredi, *Mondo allegro* (Padua: Messaggero di S. Antonio, 1944), pp. 119–127.

⁶The story of Cinderella (AT 510) is among the most common and best known in folklore. For a collection of 345 variants in different areas and cultural surroundings, see Marian Cox, *Cinderella* (London: Nutt, 1893). The symbolism of Cinderella has been analyzed over and over again psychologically and psychoanalytically. See, for example, Ben Rubenstein, "Meaning of the Cinderella Story in the Development of a Little Girl," *American Imago* 12 (1955):197–255; M. Collier, "Psychological Appeal of the Cinderella Theme," *American Imago* 14, no. 4 (1961):399–412; Anna Birgitta Rooth, *The Cinderella Cycle* (Lund: CWC Gleerup, 1955).

For a rigorous analysis, based on mathematics, see Pierre Maranda, "Cendrillon: Theorie des graphes et des ensembles," in *Semiotique narrative et textuelle,* ed. Claude Chabrol, pp. 122–136 (Paris: Larousse, 1973). Maranda discusses the tale at the level of family structures and at the level of the conflictual interaction. The history and a discussion of this well-known tale that has antecedents recorded as early as the ninth century are in Bruno Bettelheim, *The Uses of Enchantment* (New York: Vintage, 1977), pp. 236–277.

America's Cinderella

Jane Yolen

It is a commonplace that folklore changes as it moves from place to place and is transmitted from generation to generation. Each group or individual may alter an item of folklore to make it fit local social or psychological needs. But most changes are unconscious, or at any rate unselfconscious.

As more and more folklore began to appear in print, the shift from oral to written or literary style caused changes. It is one thing to tell or listen to an oral tale; it is another to read a fixed text of that tale in print or to listen to an unchanging phonograph or tape recording of the same tale. Writing allows an author to edit, revise, and "correct" his text. And so it is that some children in Western cultures come to know fairytales only through children's books rather than from traditional storytellers. Insofar as such versions are consciously crafted by writers, they may embody different values and worldview than those held by earlier oral tellers of the tale. What has happened in part is that an unconscious process has become conscious. Generally speaking, it can probably be legitimately argued that raising levels of consciousness is a positive activity which should be encouraged. But the critical issue for folklorists is: What happens to unconscious folklore when it becomes consciously changed for political or other reasons?

Marxists, for example, believe that folklore is the weapon of class conflict and that the folk (by which they mean the oppressed

Reprinted from *Children's Literature in Education*, 8 (1977), 21–29.

peasants or proletariat) uses folklore to express resentment of capitalist society. And, moreover, if the folklore doesn't properly demonstrate the "correct" ideological view, it is perfectly appropriate, according to Marxist doctrine, to change that folklore to bring it into (party) line! So in the East German "revision" of Cinderella, the fairy godmother has been eliminated, the king has been "unmasked as a witless minor despot" whose court members are revealed as "decadent parasites," and the prince is depicted as "a revolutionary who rejects his previous fruitless parasitic existence." Similarly, in a revised version of Cinderella performed in a theater in Cluj, Romania, in 1950, a striking change in the denouement served the same purpose: "When the prince wished to marry Cinderella, a poor girl, the king disclaimed him, saying that he was a working-class child whom he had adopted. The prince, delighted to hear this, said that it explained why he had never felt affection for his "father," and now he could marry Cinderella as an equal."

In capitalist countries, the changes are made by writers and movie-makers not so much for ideological reasons as for financial ones. The idea in the West is to make a product which will sell well. (To be sure, there are ideological factors at work in the West too. Walt Disney's personal philosophy of life definitely affected the way he presented the Disney version of Cinderella.)

In any case, it does no good for purist, academic folklorists to deplore the changes in folklore as departures from the good old oral versions of yesteryear. The point is that folklore changes—with or without the folklorist's blessing. And that is why it is essential that folklorists study the popular versions of Cinderella, including the versions appearing in children's books and animated cartoons. For it is those changes, some subtle, some not, that provide invaluable clues to understanding the world of today.

To illustrate this, Jane Yolen, a noted writer of children's books, analyzes what has happened to Cinderella in the mass-market popularizations of the story. The rise of feminism and the women's rights movements make it clear that students of modern society must examine both folklore and children's literature to see exactly what stereotypes are being perpetuated and encouraged. If Cinderella is a role model for young girls, is she an appropriate one or not?

For an all too brief mention of the Marxist versions of Cinderella, see "Re-writing of Fairy Stories in Eastern Germany," Folklore,

64 (1953), 431, and Folklore, *65 (1954), 54. For an interesting
political poem in which Cinderella stands for Czechoslovakia, see
Miroslav Holub, "Cinderella," East Europe, Vol. 7, No. 1 (January,
1958), p. 14. For the feminist view of fairy tales, see Marcia Leiber-
man, "Some Day My Prince Will Come: Female Acculturation
Through the Fairytale,"* College English, *34 (1972), 383–395; and
Kay Stone, "Things Walt Disney Never Told Us,"* Journal of American Folklore, *88 (1975), 42–50.*

It is part of the American creed, recited subvocally along with
the pledge of allegiance in each classroom, that even a poor boy can
grow up to become president. The unliberated corollary is that even
a poor girl can grow up and become the president's wife. This rags-
to-riches formula was immortalized in American children's fiction
by the Horatio Alger stories of the 1860s and by the Pluck and Luck
nickel novels of the 1920s.

It is little wonder, then, that Cinderella should be a perennial
favorite in the American folktale pantheon.

Yet how ironic that this formula should be the terms on which
"Cinderella" is acceptable to most Americans. "Cinderella" is *not* a
story of rags to riches, but rather riches recovered; *not* poor girl into
princess but rather rich girl (or princess) rescued from improper or
wicked enslavement; *not* suffering Griselda enduring but shrewd
and practical girl persevering and winning a share of the power. It is
really a story that is about "the stripping away of the disguise that
conceals the soul from the eyes of others. . . ."[1]

We Americans have it wrong. "Rumpelstiltskin," in which a
miller tells a whopping lie and his docile daughter acquiesces in it to
become queen, would be more to the point.

But we have been initially seduced by the Perrault cinder-girl,
who was, after all, the transfigured folk creature of a French literary
courtier. Perrault's "Cendrillon" demonstrated the well-bred seventeenth-century female traits of gentility, grace, and selflessness, even
to the point of graciously forgiving her wicked stepsisters and
finding them noble husbands.

The American "Cinderella" is partially Perrault's. The rest is a
spun-sugar caricature of her hardier European and Oriental for-
bears, who made their own way in the world, tricking the stepsisters

with double-talk, artfully disguising themselves, or figuring out a way to win the king's son. The final bit of icing on the American Cinderella was concocted by that master candy-maker, Walt Disney, in the 1950s. Since then, America's Cinderella has been a coy, helpless dreamer, a "nice" girl who awaits her rescue with patience and a song. This Cinderella of the mass market books finds her way into a majority of American homes while the classic heroines sit unread in old volumes on library shelves.

Poor Cinderella. She has been unjustly distorted by storytellers, misunderstood by educators, and wrongly accused by feminists. Even as late as 1975, in the well-received volume *Womenfolk and Fairy Tales,* Rosemary Minard writes that Cinderella "would still be scrubbing floors if it were not for her fairy godmother." And Ms. Minard includes her in a sweeping condemnation of folk heroines as "insipid beauties waiting passively for Prince Charming."[2]

Like many dialecticians, Ms. Minard reads the fairy tales incorrectly. Believing—rightly—that the fairy tales, as all stories for children, acculturate young readers and listeners, she has nevertheless gotten her target wrong. Cinderella is not to blame. Not the real, the true Cinderella. Ms. Minard should focus her sights on the mass-market Cinderella. She does not recognize the old Ash-girl[3] for the tough, resilient heroine. The wrong Cinderella has gone to the American ball.

The story of Cinderella has endured for over a thousand years, surfacing in a literary source first in ninth-century China.[4] It has been found from the Orient to the interior of South America and over five hundred variants have been located by folklorists in Europe alone. This best-beloved tale has been brought to life over and over and no one can say for sure where the oral tradition began. The European story was included by Charles Perrault in his 1697 collection *Histoires ou Contes du temps passé* as "Cendrillon." But even before that, the Italian Straparola had a similar story in a collection. Since there had been twelve editions of the Straparola book printed in French before 1694, the chances are strong that Perrault had read the tale "*Peau d'Ane*" (Donkey Skin).[5]

Joseph Jacobs, the indefatigable Victorian collector, once said of a Cinderella story he printed that it was "an English version of an Italian adaption of a Spanish translation of a Latin version of a Hebrew translation of an Arabic translation of an Indian original."[6]

Perhaps it was not a totally accurate statement of that particular variant, but Jacobs was making a point about the perils of folktale-telling: each teller brings to a tale something of his/her own cultural orientation. Thus in China, where the "lotus foot," or tiny foot was such a sign of a woman's worth that the custom of foot-binding developed, the Cinderella tale lays emphasis on an impossibly small slipper as a clue to the heroine's identity. In seventeenth-century France, Perrault's creation sighs along with her stepsisters over the magnificent "gold flowered mantua" and the "diamond stomacher."[7] In the Walt Disney American version, both movie and book form, Cinderella shares with the little animals a quality of "lovableness,"[8] thus changing the intent of the tale and denying the heroine her birthright of shrewdness, inventiveness, and grace under pressure.

Notice, though, that many innovations—the Chinese slipper, the Perrault godmother with her midnight injunction and her ability to change pumpkin into coach—become incorporated in later versions. Even a slip of the English translator's tongue (*de vair*, fur, into *de verre*, glass) becomes immortalized. Such cross fertilization of folklore is phenomenal. And the staying power, across countries and centuries, of some of these inventions is notable. Yet glass slipper and godmother and pumpkin coach are not the common incidents by which a "Cinderella" tale is recognized even though they have become basic ingredients in the American story. Rather, the common incidents recognized by folklorists are these: an ill-treated though rich and worthy heroine in Cinders-disguise; the aid of a magical gift or advice by a beast/bird/mother substitute; the dance/festival/church scene where the heroine comes in radiant display; recognition through a token. So "Cinderella" and her true sister tales, "Cap o' Rushes" with its King Lear judgement and "Catskin" wherein the father unnaturally desires his daughter, are counted.

Andrew Lang's judgement that "a naked shoeless race could not have invented Cinderella,"[9] then, proves false. Variants have been found among the fur-wearing folk of Alaska and the native tribes in South Africa where shoes were not commonly worn.

"Cinderella" speaks to all of us in whatever skin we inhabit: the child mistreated, a princess or highborn lady in disguise bearing her trials with patience and fortitude. She makes intelligent decisions for she knows that wishing solves nothing without the concomitant action. We have each of us been that child.[10] It is the longing of any youngster sent supperless to bed or given less than a full share at Christmas. It is the adolescent dream.

To make Cinderella less than she is, then, is a heresy of the worst kind. It cheapens our most cherished dreams, and it makes a mockery of the true magic inside us all—the ability to change our own lives, the ability to control our own destinies.

Cinderella first came to America in the nursery tales the settlers remembered from their own homes and told their children. Versions of these tales can still be found. Folklorist Richard Chase, for example, discovered "Rush Cape,"[11] an exact parallel of "Cap o' Rushes" with an Appalachian dialect in Tennessee, Kentucky, and South Carolina among others.

But when the story reached print, developed, was made literary, things began to happen to the hardy Cinderella.[12] She suffered a sea change, a sea change aggravated by social conditions.

In the 1870s, for example, in the prestigious magazine for children *St. Nicholas,* there are a number of retellings or adaptations of "Cinderella." The retellings which merely translate European variants contain the hardy heroine. But when a new version is presented, a helpless Cinderella is born. G.B. Bartlett's "Giant Picture-Book," which was considered "a curious novelty [that] can be produced . . . by children for the amusement of their friends . . ." presents a weepy, prostrate young blonde (the instructions here are quite specific) who must be "aroused from her sad revery" by a godmother.[13] Yet in the truer Cinderella stories, the heroine is not this catatonic. For example, in the Grimm "Cinder-Maid,"[14] though she weeps, she continues to perform the proper rites and rituals at her mother's grave, instructing the birds who roost there to:

> Make me a lady fair to see,
> Dress me as splendid as can be.

And in "The Dirty Shepherdess,"[15] a "Cap o' Rushes" variant from France, ". . . she dried her eyes, and made a bundle of her jewels and her best dresses and hurriedly left the castle where she was born." In the *St. Nicholas* "Giant Picture-Book" she has none of this strength of purpose. Rather, she is manipulated by the godmother until the moment she stands before the prince where she speaks "meekly" and "with downcast eyes and extended hand."

St. Nicholas was not meant for the mass market. It had, in Selma Lanes' words, "a patrician call to a highly literate readership."[16] But nevertheless, Bartlett's play instructions indicate how even in the more literary reaches of children's books a change was taking place.

However, to truly mark this change in the American "Cinderella," one must turn specifically to the mass-market books, merchandised products that masquerade as literature but make as little lasting literary impression as a lollipop. They, after all, serve the majority the way the storytellers of the village used to serve. They find their way into millions of homes.

Mass market books are almost as old as colonial America. The chapbooks of the eighteenth and nineteenth century, crudely printed tiny paperbacks, were the source of most children's reading in the early days of our country.[17] Originally these were books imported from Europe. But slowly American publishing grew. In the latter part of the nineteenth century one firm stood out—McLoughlin Bros. They brought bright colors to the pages of children's books. In a series selling for twenty-five cents per book, *Aunt Kate's Series*, bowdlerized folk tales emerged. "Cinderella" was there, along with "Red Riding Hood," "Puss in Boots," and others. Endings were changed, innards cleaned up, and good triumphed with very loud huzzahs. Cinderella is the weepy, sentimentalized pretty girl incapable of helping herself. In contrast, one only has to look at the girl in "Cap o' Rushes"[18] who comes to a great house and asks "Do you want a maid?" and when refused, goes on to say ". . . I ask no wages and do any sort of work." And she does. In the end, when the master's young son is dying of love for the mysterious lady, she uses her wits to work her way out of the kitchen. Even in Perrault's "Cinderilla,"[19] when the fairy godmother runs out of ideas for enchantment and "was at a loss for a coachman, I'll go and see, says Cinderilla, if there be never a rat in the rat-trap, we'll make a coachman of him. You are in the right, said her godmother, go and see."

Hardy, helpful, inventive, that was the Cinderella of the old tales but not of the mass market in the nineteenth century. Today's mass-market books are worse. These are the books sold in supermarket and candystore, even lining the shelves of many of the best bookstores. There are pop-up Cinderellas, coloring-book Cinderellas, scratch-and-sniff Cinderellas, all inexpensive and available. The point in these books is not the story but the *gimmick*. These are books which must "interest 300,000 children, selling their initial print order in one season and continuing strong for at least two years after that."[20] Compare that with the usual trade publishing house print order of a juvenile book—10,000 copies which an editor hopes to sell out in a lifetime of that title.

All the folk tales have been gutted. But none so changed, I believe, as "Cinderella." For the sake of Happy Ever After, the mass-market books have brought forward a good, malleable, forgiving little girl and put her in Cinderella's slippers. However, in most of the Cinderella tales there is no forgiveness in the heroine's heart. No mercy. Just justice. In "Rushen Coatie"[21] and "The Cinder-Maid,"[22] the elder sisters hack off their toes and heels in order to fit the shoe. Cinderella never stops them, never implies that she has the matching slipper. In fact, her tattletale birds warn the prince in "Rushen Coatie":

> Hacked Heels and Pinched Toes
> Behind the young prince rides,
> But Pretty Feet and Little Feet
> Behind the cauldron bides.

Even more graphically, they call out in "Cinder-Maid"

> Turn and peep, turn and peep,
> There's blood within the shoe;
> A bit is cut from off the heel
> And a bit from off the toe.

Cinderella never says a word of comfort. And in the least bowdlerized of the German and Nordic tales, the two sisters come to the wedding "the elder was at the right side and the younger at the left, and the pigeons pecked out one eye from each of them. Afterwards, as they came back, the elder was on the left, and the younger at the right, and then the pigeons pecked out the other eye from each. And thus, for their wickedness and falsehood, they were punished with blindness all their days."[23] That's a far cry from Perrault's heroine who "gave her sisters lodgings in the palace, and married them the same day to two great lords of the court." And further still from Nola Langner's Scholastic paperback "Cinderella"[24]:

> [The sisters] began to cry.
> They begged Cinderella to forgive them for being so mean to
> her.
> Cinderella told them they were forgiven.
> "I am sure you will never be mean to me again," she said.
>
> "Oh, never," said the older sister.
> "Never, ever," said the younger sister.

Missing, too, from the mass-market books is the shrewd, even witty Cinderella. In a Wonder Book entitled "Bedtime Stories,"[25] a 1940s adaptation from Perrault, we find a Cinderella who talks to her stepsisters "in a shy little voice." Even Perrault's heroine bantered with her stepsisters, asking them leading questions about the ball while secretly and deliciously knowing the answers. In the Wonder Book, however, the true wonder is that Cinderella ever gets to be princess. Even face-to-face with the prince, she is unrecognized until she dons her magic ballgown. Only when her clothes are transformed does the Prince know his true love.

In 1949, Walt Disney's film *Cinderella* burst onto the American scene. The story in the mass market has not been the same since.

The film came out of the studio at a particularly trying time for Disney. He had been deserted by the intellectuals who had been champions of this art for some years.[26] Because of World War II, the public was more interested in war films than cartoons. But when *Cinderella*, lighter than light, was released it brought back to Disney—and his studio—all of his lost fame and fortune. The film was one of the most profitable of all time for the studio, grossing $4.247 million dollars in the first release alone. The success of the movie opened the floodgates of "Disney Cinderella" books.

Golden Press's *Walt Disney's Cinderella*[27] set the new pattern for America's Cinderella. This book's text is coy and condescending. (Sample: "And her best friends of all were—guess who—the mice!") The illustrations are poor cartoons. And Cinderella herself is a disaster. She cowers as her sisters rip her homemade ball gown to shreds. (Not even homemade by Cinderella, but by the mice and birds.) She answers her stepmother with whines and pleadings. She is a sorry excuse for a heroine, pitiable and useless. She cannot perform even a simple action to save herself, though she is warned by her friends, the mice. She does not hear them because she is "off in a world of dreams." Cinderella begs, she whimpers, and at last has to be rescued by—guess who—the mice!

There is also an easy-reading version published by Random House, *Walt Disney's Cinderella.*[28] This Cinderella commits the further heresy of cursing her luck. "How I did wish to go to the ball," she says. "But it is no use. Wishes never come true."

But in the fairy tales wishes have a habit of happening—*wishes accompanied by the proper action*, bad wishes as well as good. That is the beauty of the old stories and their wisdom as well.

Take away the proper course of action, take away Cinderella's ability to think for herself and act for herself, and you are left with a tale of wishes-come-true-regardless. But that is not the way of the fairy tale. As P.L. Travers so wisely puts it, "If that were so, wouldn't we all be married to princes?"[29]

The mass-market American "Cinderellas" have presented the majority of American children with the wrong dream. They offer the passive princess, the "insipid beauty waiting . . . for Prince Charming" that Rosemary Minard objects to, and thus acculturate millions of girls and boys. But it is the wrong Cinderella and the magic of the old tales has been falsified, the true meaning lost, perhaps forever.

NOTES

[1]Elizabeth Cook, *The Ordinary and the Fabulous.*

[2]Rosemary Minard, *Womenfolk and Fairy Tales.*

[3]There are a number of stories about Ash-boys. For this study, only tales with the heroine have been considered.

[4]Arthur Waley, "The Chinese Cinderella Story."

[5]Marian Roalfe Cox, *Cinderella: 349 Variants.*

[6]As quoted in Eileen H. Colwell, "Folk Literature: An Oral Tradition."

[7]"Cinderilla: or The Little Glass Slipper," in *The Classic Fairy Tales.*

[8]Frances Clarke Sayers, "Disney Accused." The word "lovableness" is Ms. Sayers' and terrifically accurate. The article is a classic.

[9]Marian Roalfe Cox, *op. cit.*

[10]Even boys and men share that dream. See Walter Scherf, "Family Conflicts and Emancipation in Fairy Tales."

[11]Richard Chase, *American Folk Tales and Songs.*

[12]There were already signs of change in the British mass-market Cinderella books. See *Aunt Louisa's Favorite Toy Book.*

[13]G.B. Bartlett, "The Giant Picture Book."

[14]"The Cinder-Maid."

[15]"The Dirty Shepherdess."

[16]Selma G. Lanes, *Down the Rabbit Hole.*

[17]Virginia Haviland, *Yankee Doodle's Literary Sampler of Prose, Poetry, and Pictures.*

[18]"Cap o' Rushes."

[19]"Cinderilla, or The Little Glass Slipper," *op. cit.*

[20]Selma Lanes, *op. cit.*

[21]"Rushen Coatie."

[22]"The Cinder-Maid."

[23]"Cinderella," from *The Complete Grimm's Fairy Tales.*

[24]Nola Langner, *Cinderella.* A fall from grace for Ms. Langner; the pictures in this are still charming.

[25]Eleanor Graham, *Bedtime Stories.*

[26]Richard Schickel, *The Disney Version.* The critical book on Disney. Witty and wise.

[27]Retta S. Worcester and Jane Werner, *Walt Disney's Cinderella.*

[28]*Walt Disney's Cinderella.*

[29]P.L. Travers, "Only Connect."

REFERENCES CITED

Perrault

"Cinderilla, or, The Little Glass Slipper" (1889) (Robert Samber version), in Andrew Lang, *The Blue Fairy Book* (1965).New York, Dover.

"Cinderella, or, The Little Glass Slipper" (1729), translated by Robert Samber (first published in *Histories or Tales of Past Times*), in Iona and Peter Opie (1974) *The Classic Fairy Tales*, London, Oxford University Press.

Cap o' Rushes

"Cap o' Rushes" (Joseph Jacobs version), in Rosemary Minard (1975), *Womenfolk and Fairytales*, Boston, Houghton Mifflin.

"The Dirty Shepherdess" (French version), in Andrew Lang (1892; reprinted 1965), *The Green Fairy Book*, New York: Longmans, Green; Dover.

"Katie Woodencloak" (Norwegian version), in Stith Thompson (1945, 1973), *One Hundred Favorite Folktales.* New York: Pantheon.

"Rush Cape" (Appalachian version), in Richard Chase, (1971) *American Folk Tales and Songs.* New York: Dover.

"Rushen Coatie" (English version), in Joseph Jacobs, (1894; reprinted 1968),*More English Fairy Tales.* New York: Schocken.

Peau d'Ane

"Donkey Skin," from *Cabinet des Fées*, in Andrew Lang (1900), *The Grey Fairy Book.* New York: Longmans, Green.

German (*Ashenputtel*)

"Cinderella," in Padraic Colum and Joseph Campbell (1944, 1972), *The Complete Grimm's Fairy Tales*. New York: Pantheon.

"The Cinder-Maid," in Joseph Jacobs (1916) *European Folk and Fairy Tales*, New York: Putnam.

Russian

"The Golden Slipper" (1945, 1973), in Afanasev, *Russian Fairy Tales*. New York: Pantheon.

Chinese

Waley, Arthur (1947), "The Chinese Cinderella Story," in *Folklore*, Vol. 58.

American Mass Market

Bartlett, G.B. (1881), "The Giant Picture Book," *St. Nicholas Magazine*, June 1881.

Cinderella (C. 1876), Aunt Kate's Series. New York: McLoughlin Bros..

Graham, Eleanor (1946), *Bedtime Stories*. New York: Wonder Books.

Langner, Nola (1972), *Cinderella*. New York: Scholastic.

The New Walt Disney Treasury (1971), New York: Golden Press.

Walt Disney's Cinderella (1974), New York: Random House.

Worcester, Retta S., and Werner, Jane (1950),*Walt Disney's Cinderella*. New York: Golden Press,.

Research and Critical Volumes

Arbuthnot, May Hill, and Sutherland, Zena (1972), *Children and Books*. 4th ed. Glenview, Ill., Scott, Foresman.

Aunt Louisa's Favorite Toy Book (c. 1876). London: Frederick Warne.

Chase, Richard (1971), *American Folk Tales and Songs*. New York: Dover.

Children's Literature: The Great Excluded. Vol. 3. Philadelphia, Temple University Press.

Colwell, Eileen H. (1973), "Folk Literature: An Oral Tradition and an Oral Art," in Virginia Haviland, *Children and Literature: Views and Reviews*. Glenview, Ill.: Scott, Foresman.

Cook, Elizabeth (1969), *The Ordinary and the Fabulous*, Cambridge: Cambridge University Press.

Cox, Marian Roalfe (1893), *Cinderella: 345 Variants*. London: David Nutt.

Egoff, Sheils; Stubbs, G.T., and Ashley, L.F., eds. (1969), *Only Connect: Readings on Children's Literature*. New York: Oxford University Press.

Haviland, Virginia (1973), *Children and Literature: Views and Reviews*. Glenview, Ill.: Scott, Foresman.

Haviland, Virginia (1974), *Yankee Doodle's Literary Sampler of Prose, Poetry, and Pictures*. New York: Crowell.

Hazard, Paul (1966), *Books, Children, and Men*. Boston: Horn.

Lanes, Selma G. (1971), *Down the Rabbit Hole*. New York: Atheneum.

Leach, Maria (1972), *Funk & Wagnalls Standard Dictionary of Folklore, Mythology, and Legend*. New York: Funk & Wagnalls.

Meigs, Cornelia, et al. (1953, 1964, 1969), *A Critical History of Children's Literature*. New York: Macmillan.

Minard, Rosemary (1975), *Womenfolk and Fairy Tales*. Boston: Houghton Mifflin.

Opie, Iona and Peter (1974), *The Classic Fairy Tales*. London: Oxford University Press.

Sayers, Frances Clarke (1973), "Disney Accused," in Virginia Haviland, *Children and Literature*. Glenview, Ill.: Scott, Foresman.

Scherf, Walter, "Family Conflicts and Emancipation in Fairy Tales," in *Children's Literature: The Great Excluded*. Vol. 3 (1974). Philadelphia: Temple University Press.

Schickel, Richard (1968), *The Disney Version*. New York: Simon & Schuster.

Travers, P.L. (1969), "Only Connect," in *Only Connect: Readings on Children's Literature*, Sheila Egoff, G.T. Stubbs, and L.F. Ashley, eds. New York: Oxford University Press.

Travers, P.L. (Fall 1975), "Grimm's Women," in "The Guest Word." *The New York Times Book Review*.

Suggestions for Further Reading
on Cinderella:
A Selected Bibliography

Bausinger, Hermann. "Aschenputtel: Zum Problem der Märchensymbolik." *Zeitschrift für Volkskunde*, 52. (1955), 144–158. A critique of symbolic and spiritual interpretations of fairytales in general, with some discussion of Cinderella.

Benet, Sula. "The Cultural Meaning of Folklore: The Cinderella Motif." In *VII Congres International des Sciences Anthropologiques et Ethnologiques, Moscou 3 août–10 août 1964* Vol. VI (Moscow, 1969), 1964, pp. 175–177. Cinderella used loosely as a metaphor for parent-child relations among American Indians.

Bettelheim, Bruno. *The Uses of Enchantment: The Meaning and Importance of Fairy Tales*. New York: Vintage Books, 1977. An extended Freudian analysis (pp. 236–277) of the significance of Cinderella as a symbolic vehicle for a young girl's maturation through sibling rivalry (evil sisters), and Oedipal/Electral anxieties (kindly father, wicked stepmother, etc.) to self-recognition of a readiness for courtship and marriage.

Blind, Karl. "A Fresh Scottish Ashpitel and Glass Shoe Tale." *The Archaeological Review*, 3 (1889), 24–38. A version from a Scottish informant in Australia is accompanied by a detailed solar mythological interpretation based largely upon a golden, shining shoe.

Boskovic-Stulli, Maja. "Grimms Aufzeichnung des 'Aschenputtels' (Pepeljuga) von Vuk Karadžić," *Deutsches Jahrbuch für Volkskunde*, 12 (1966), 79–83. A discussion of the Grimms' (especially Jacob's) reaction to the version of Cinderella sent to them circa 1823 by famed Serbian folklore collector Vuk Karadžić.

Christiansen, Reidar Th. "Cinderella in Ireland." *Bealoideas*, 20 (1952), 96–107. A sophisticated survey of the Irish version by one of Norway's leading comparativists.

Collier, Mary Jeffrey. "The Psychological Appeal in the Cinderella Theme." *American Imago*, 18 (1961), 399–406. A survey of the results of thirty-two college women answering questions about the appeal of Cinderella to them as children and as young adults.

Coote, Henry Charles. "Catskin: The English and Irish Peau D'Ane." *Folk-Lore Record*, 3, Pt. 1 (1880), 1–25. Discussion of European versions of AT 510B and its solar interpretations.

Cosquin, Emmanuel. "La Pantoufle de Cendrillon dans l'Inde." *Revue des Traditions Populaires*, 28 (1913), 241–269. A discussion of "shoes" (customs and beliefs) in India, taking as a point of departure Andrew Lang's remark that Cinderella could not have originated in a shoeless country. Cosquin, a comparativist committed to the idea that many European fairytales originated in India, demonstrates the existence of shoes in India but has difficulty in citing a complete Cinderella text (as opposed to individual motifs or traits) from that area.

—————. "Le 'Cendrillon' Masculin." *Revue des Traditions Populaires*, 33 (1918a), 193–202. A brief survey of European so-called 'male Cinderella' tales.

—————. "Cendrillon sur la Tombe de sa Mère." *Revue des Traditions Populaires*, 33 (1918b), 202–233. A discussion of the motif in which Cinderella's dead mother aids her daughter, with some consideration of how the Cinderella tale is often combined with the Frau Holle tale (AT 480, The Kind and the Unkind Girls).

—————. "Une Variante de 'Cendrillon' et un Episode de 'Dame Holle.'" *Revue des Traditions Populaires*, 33 (1918c), 245–253. A further discussion of the interrelationship of Cinderella and the Frau Holle tales.

Courtes, Joseph. "De la description à la spécificité du conte populaire merveilleux français." *Ethnologie française*, 2 (1972), 9–42. A semiotic consideration of linguistic variation found in French versions of Cinderella.

—————. "Une lecture semiotique de 'Cendrillon.'" in Joseph Courtes, *Introduction à la sémiotique narrative et discursive*: méthodologie et application. Paris: Hachette, 1976, pp. 109–138. An analysis of sixteen French versions of Cinderella demonstrating how oppositional patterning through mediation makes the tale a model of marriage relations.

Cox, Marian Roalfe. *Cinderella*. London: David Nutt, 1893. The first and still classic compilation of three hundred and forty-five variants, containing an introduction by Andrew Lang.

—————. "Cinderella." *Folk-Lore*, 18 (1907), 191–208. Synopses of some twenty additional versions, mostly from Scandinavia, plus bibliographical references to others appearing since the 1893 monograph.

Deulin, Charles. *Les Contes de ma Mère l'Oye avant Perrault*. Paris: E. Dentu, 1879. One of the earlier discussions (pp. 263–308) of Cinderella.

Dolle, Bernd. "Märchen und Erziehung: Versuch einer historischen Skizze zur didaktischen Verwengung Grimmscher Märchen (am Beispiel Aschenputtel)." In Helmut Brackert, ed., *Und wenn sie nicht gestorben sind . . . Perspektiven auf das Märchen*. Frankfurt: Suhrkamp Verlag, 1980, pp. 165–192. An attempt to consider the social-historical conditions and ideological premises which underlie fairytales, as well as the nature of the moral universe communicated by such fairytales as Cinderella.

Foley, Louis. "A Princess and Her Magic Footwear." *Modern Language Journal*, 38 (1954), 412–415. A brief discussion of Cinderella's name and an erroneous account of the verre-vair translation concluding that the English version is unique in having poor Cinderella wear slippers of glass.

Gardaz de Linden, Elisabeth. "Cendrillon: Mecomptes d'un Conte . . . Essai d'interprétation de quelques adaptations contemporaines françaises et étrangeres." *Cahiers de Littèrature Generale et Comparee*, 3–4 (1978), 77–89. A comparative consideration of translations, e.g., French and English of the Grimm version of Cinderella.

Gardner, Fletcher. "Filipino (Tagalog) Versions of Cinderella." *Journal of American Folklore*, 19 (1906), 265–280. Mostly texts, but accompanied by a discursive comparative note (pp. 272–280) written by W.W. Newell.

Gil, Avelina. "Mayyang and the Crab: A Cinderella Variant. *Philippine Quarterly of Culture & Society*, 1 (1973), 26–32. An analysis of five Filipino versions of the tale.

Glas, N[orbert]. *Cinderella: Meaning and Exact Rendering of Grimm's Fairy Tale.* Gloucester: Education and Science Publications, 1946. 33 pp. An anthroposophical commentary on the tale.

Glazer, Mark. "The Role of Wish Fulfillment in Märchen: an Adlerian Approach." *New York Folklore*, 5 (1979), 63–77. An application of Adlerian psychology with special reference to feelings of inadequacy or inferiority in French and Turkish versions of Cinderella.

Goswami, P. "The Cinderella Motif in Assamese Folk-Tales." *Indian Historical Quarterly*, 23 (1947), 311–319. Eight tales are summarized and compared to the European Cinderella.

Greimas, A.J., and J. Courtès. "Cendrillon va au bal . . . Les rôles et les figures dans la littérature orale française." In *Systèmes de Signes*: Textes reunis en hommage à Germaine Dieterlen. Paris: Hermann, 1978. Pp. 243–257. A complex analysis of structure and role in the French Cinderella utilizing the orthography of symbolic logic.

Hain, Mathilde. "Aschenputtel und die 'Geistliche Hausmagd." *Rheinisches Jahrbuch für Volkskunde*, 12 (1961), 9–15. A speculation on the possible relationship between an early Christian legend (in which the name Aschengruttel occurs) and Cinderella.

Hart, Donn V., and Harriett C. Hart. "Cinderella in the Eastern Bisayas (with a Summary of the Philippine Folktale)." *Journal of American Folklore*, 79 (1966), 307–337. Mostly a general discussion of taletelling in eastern Samar, with brief comparative remarks on versions of Cinderella in the Philippines.

Heuscher, Julius E. "Cinderella, Eros, and Psyche." *Diseases of the Nervous System,* 24 (1963), 286–292. A brief psychoanalytic treatment of Cinderella, followed by a spiritual interpretation.

Huckel, Helen. "One Day I'll Live in the Castle: Cinderella as a Case History." *American Imago*, 14 (1957), 303–314. A case history of a patient who had many characteristics of Cinderella.

Jacobs, Joseph. "Cinderella in Britain." *Folk-Lore*, 4 (1893), 269–284. In this one of a series of essays commenting on Miss Cox's *Cinderella*, the intent is to contrast English and Celtic variants of the tale, ending with an attack on Andrew Lang's alleged advocacy of independent invention (as opposed to borrowing via diffusion) to explain similar texts in different cultures.

Kleinmann, Dorothee. "Cendrillon et son Pied." *Cahiers de Littérature Orale*, 4 (1978), 56–88. A detailed account of foot and shoe symbolism as it pertains to Cinderella.

Krauss, Friedrich, S., and Th. Dragečiveč. "Aschenbrödel in Bosnien." *Am Ur-Quell*, 3 (1892), 129–135. A consideration of Cinderella in Yugoslavia.

Lang, Andrew. "Cinderella and the Diffusion of Tales." *Folk-Lore*, 4 (1893), 413–433. An attempt to reconcile the author's views on whether similarities in folktales in different cultures are to be explained by independent invention or by borrowing via diffusion. He admits that he no longer holds his earlier strict polygenetic views: "The more I have reflected on these matters, the more has borrowing seemed to me the general and prevalent cause of the likeness in the märchen of the world" (p. 420).

Leclère, Adhémard. "Le Conte de Cendrillon chez les Cham." *Revue des Traditions Populaires*, 13 (1898), 311-337. A lengthy Laotian version of Cinderella, followed by a commentary comparing it with versions from Cambodia and Vietnam.

Loucatos, D.S. "Cinderella [in Greek]." *Parnossos*. 1 (1959) 461-485. A survey of Greek versions of the tale.

Lüdeke, Hedwig. "Das 'Aschenbrodel' als griechische Volksballade." *Zeitschrift für Volkskunde*, 8 (1938), 87-91. The story of Cinderella as found in Greece in ballad form.

Maranda, Pierre. "Cendrillon et la Theorie des Ensembles. Essai de definition structurale." *Strutture e Generi delle Letterature Etniche, Atti des Simposio Internazionale Palermo 5-10 aprile 1970*. Uomo e Cultura—Testi 15. Palermo: S.F. Flaccovio, Editore, 1978. Pp. 101-114. [Also in Claude Chabrol, ed., *Semiotique Narrative et Textuelle*. Paris: Librairie Larousse, 1973. Pp. 122-136.] Diagrams and formulas facilitate a Lévi-Straussian reading of Cinderella in terms of kinship and marriage relations.

Marcus, Donald M. "The Cinderella Motif: Fairy Tale and Defense," *American Imago*, 20 (1963) 81-92. A psychoanalytic reading of the Perrault and Grimm versions, followed by case history of a woman who identified with Cinderella.

Mifsud-Chircop, George, "The Dress of Stars, of Sea and of Earth (AT 510B)—An Analysis of the Maltese Cinderella Märchen within the Mediterranean Tradition Area." *Journal of Maltese Studies*, 14 (1981), 48-55. A brief but technical discussion of the motifs contained in three Maltese texts within the framework found in Rooth's *The Cinderella Cycle*.

Mizusawa, Kenichi. *Echigo no Shinderera*. Sanjo-shi, Niigata: Nojima Shuppa, 1964. A collection of nearly one hundred versions of Cinderella from a single district.

Mulhern, Chieko Irie. "Cinderella and the Jesuits: An *Otogizōshi* Cycle as Christian Literature." *Monumenta Nipponica*, 34 (1979), 409-447. A survey of tales concerning stepdaughters in Japan, with a discussion of possible Jesuit influence.

Murray, Timothy C. "A Marvelous Guide to Anamorphosis: *Cendrillon ou la Petite Pantoufle de Verre*." *Modern Language Notes*, 91 (1976), 1276-1295. A close textual reading of Perrault's version in terms of kinship and marriage relations.

Nitschke, August. "Aschenputtel aus der Sicht der historischen Verhaltenforschung." In Helmut Brackert, ed., *Und wenn sie nicht gestorben sind . . . Perspecktiven auf das Märchen*. Frankfurt: Suhrkamp Verlag, 1980. Pp. 71-88. From clues such as social relations (daughters seeking help from dead mothers or animals) and clothing styles (wearing fur) as indicators of climatic conditions, literary archaeology would place Cinderella's origin in prehistory, possibly the Ice Age.

Noah, Jourdain-Innocent. "Beti Tales from Southern Cameroon: The Kaiser Cycle." *Diogenes*, No. 80 (1972), 80-101. A delightful re-working of the Grimm version of Cinderella followed by an insightful discussion of the various changes introduced which make the tale reflect the values of Beti culture.

Nutt, Alfred. "Cinderella and Britain." *Folk-Lore*, 4 (1893a), 133-141. In this first of a series of essays intended to discuss and criticize Miss Cox's *Cinderella*, the emphasis is on the "unnatural marriage incident" and its frequent occurrence in Britain.

————. "Some Recent Utterances of Mr. Newell and Mr. Jacobs." *Folk-Lore*, 4 (1893b), 434–450. A critique of W.W. Newell's and Joseph Jacobs' views of Cinderella, which were stimulated by Miss Cox's monograph.

Paulme, Denise. "Cendrillon en Afrique." *Critique*, 36 (1980), 288–302. A discussion of the possible influence of Cinderella on non-Cinderella tales in Africa.

Randall, Betty Uchitelle. "The Cinderella Theme in Northwest Coast Folklore." In Marian W. Smith, ed., *Indians of the Urban Northwest*. New York: Columbia University Press, 1949. Pp. 243–285. Cinderella as a metaphor for Northwest Coast tales in which initial poor or low status can be overcome. The tales are not versions of AT 510A.

Rapallo, Chiarella. "La Fiaba de Cenerentola in Sardegna." BRADS [Bollettino del Repertorio e dell'Atlante Demologico Sardo] 4 (1972–73), 74–86. A survey of the distribution of fifty-six Sardinian versions of Cinderella (including a map).

Rooth, Anna Birgitta. *The Cinderella Cycle*. Lund: C.W.K. Gleerup, 1951. The most comprehensive comparative study of the tale.

Rosenman, Stanley. "Cinderella: Family Pathology, Identity-Sculpting and Mate-Selection." *American Imago*, 35 (1978), 375–398. An analysis of the different attempts of family members (father, mother, stepmother) to mold Cinderella's character.

Saintyves, P. *Les Contes de Perrault et Les Récits Parallèles*: Leurs Origines (Coutumes Primitives et Liturgies Populaires). Paris: Librairie Critique Émile Nourry, 1923. Extended discussions of Cinderella (pp. 105–164) and "Peau d'Ane" (pp. 165–208) with ritual interpretations proposed, e.g., Cinderella represents the new season or the new year, with the wicked stepmother being the old year.

Sandford, Beryl. "Cinderella." *The Psychoanalytic Forum*, 2 (1967), 127–144. An English psychoanalyst analyzes a pantomime version of Cinderella, with solicited critiques by Robert J. Stoller, Virginia Leono Bicudo, Morton Levitt, Judith S. Kestenberg, and Alan Dundes, followed by Mrs. Sanford's rebuttal.

Singer, S. *Schweizer Märchen*. Bern: Verlag von A. Francke, 1906. The author's sophisticated comparative discussion of "Aschengrübel" (pp. 1–31) includes a useful summary of the various names of the heroine.

Smith, Barbara Herrnstein. "Narrative Versions, Narrative Theories." *Critical Inquiry*, 7 (1980), 213–236. A thoughtful consideration of the implications of the existence of multiple versions of a plot for narrative theory, with Cinderella used as an example (pp. 215–222).

Ting, Nai-Tung. *The Cinderella Cycle in China and Indo-China*. FF Communications 213. Helsinki: Academia Scientarium Fennica, 1974. A scholarly comparative account of Chinese and Indo-Chinese (including Vietnamese and Cambodian) versions of Cinderella.

Waley, Arthur. "The Chinese Cinderella Story." *Folk-Lore*, 58 (1947), 226–238. A new translation of the ninth-century Chinese version of Cinderella, with commentary on incidents in the tale.